THINKING
through
CREATIVITY
and CULTURE

THINKING
through
CREATIVITY
and CULTURE

Toward an Integrated Model

Vlad Petre Glăveanu
With a foreword by Jaan Valsiner

Routledge
Taylor & Francis Group

LONDON AND NEW YORK

First published 2014 by Transaction Publishers

2 Park Square, Milton Park, Abingdon, Oxfordshire OX14 4RN
711 Third Avenue, New York, NY 10017

Routledge is an imprint of the Taylor & Francis Group, an informa business

First issued in paperback 2017

Copyright © 2014 Taylor & Francis

Library of Congress Catalog Number: 2013042914

Library of Congress Cataloging-in-Publication Data

Glaveănu, Vlad Petre.
   Thinking through creativity and culture : toward an intergated model / Vlad Petre Glaveănu, Aalborg University, Denmark.
      pages cm
   Includes bibliographical references and index.
   ISBN 978-1-4128-5401-6 (cloth : alk. paper) 1. Creative ability. 2. Culture. 3. Folklore. I. Title.
   BF408.G53 2014
   153.3'5--dc23

                                                                2013042914

ISBN 13: 978-1-4128-5401-6 (hbk)
ISBN 13: 978-1-138-51729-5 (pbk)

Contents

List of Tables and Figures

Foreword

Creativity in the Practices of Living: Innovations within traditions

Creativity is a word. It could be claimed it is nothing more than that. Yet, as the reader of this book can experience, it is much more than that. As the young Romanian author of this book—a scientist and an artist fully blended together—demonstrates, creativity is everywhere. It is like a gentle wind that makes us wake up from the weary mundaneness of everyday life and see beauty in the eyes of children and animals and in the image of the sushi-master for whom each creation is unique—and each in its impeccable taste. Creativity is the core of our ordinary lives. Interestingly, it is only rarely that we notice it.

In psychology, the study of creativity is currently undergoing a major breakthrough—moving the focus from creative personalities to seeing creativity in everyday life. New young scholars have entered the arena of creativity research—among them, the author of the present book. Vlad Petre Glăveanu is a leader among the young generation of researchers who are setting the stage for this "new look" in creativity research. This new perspective locates acts of innovation in the contexts of everyday activities and insists upon the analysis of such activities in process terms (Tanggaard 2014). This change in focus—from the study of outcomes to that of processes (that lead to the outcomes)—is a crucial methodological turn in the social sciences of the twenty-first century. It is made possible by internationalization in our scholarly enterprise—researchers from any country in the world are now equal in bringing their ways of understanding into the public domain.

Glăveanu is deeply European in his innovation in the field of creativity research. He largely follows in the intellectual footsteps of his fellow Romanian, transplanted to Central Europe: Serge Moscovici. Moscovici has single-handedly and systematically changed the European mindscape of social psychology, turning it from mundane and mostly futile laboratory exercise practiced in North America into a creative idea complex of the social representation theory. Glăveanu in this book is doing something similar in creativity research: demonstrating, on the model of ordinary symbolic objects

(Romanian decorated eggs—objects that preserve cultural traditions), how innovation enters into tradition and makes it new, while not breaking with the old. The unity of the old and the new is what creativity research of the new kind looks at—using the framework of everyday activity contexts and analyzing the generative process of creativity in time. This perspective brings the axiomatic basis of developmental science into a field—creativity research—that has historically been nondevelopmental in its premises. This change is a major breakthrough. We are about to witness what concrete results in our understanding of creativity it will bring about.

Glăveanu works in a truly transdisciplinary way. His primary objects of interest—decorated eggs—represent Romanian cultural history and, as such, are unlikely to be found in the same form in other countries. Here the starting point is folklore, cultural anthropology—which becomes tied to cultural psychology by the author's focus on the generalized process of creative innovation *within* the context of maintaining cultural traditions. Here the centrality of generalization—the core of cultural psychology (Valsiner 2007, 2012)—has an advantage over its cousin, cross-cultural psychology. Comparing different social practices from different societies—the core of the latter subdiscipline— is put to use for finding general principles of human innovation. And that is universal. As human beings of any society, we cannot but innovate our ways of living. However, while doing that, we try to show, to ourselves and others, that we follow our historical traditions. Innovation is based on tradition and becomes a new tradition—that leads to further innovation.

Glăveanu's research has advanced the discipline of the *cultural psychology of creativity*. The chapters collected in this book include both theoretical elaborations and empirical findings that substantiate this field. Taken all together, they bring to the readers a consistent general theory of creativity based on five interrelated issues: *contextuality, generativity, meaningfulness, focus on development*, and *ecological embeddedness*.

All human conduct is context-bound, and that link with context is the universal characteristic of our human ways of living. The person creates the context together with the conduct—there is no form of conduct that has no context. To claim otherwise would amount to admitting that human beings could go on living if the air they breathe disappeared. Or—if one were to take seriously the idea of eliminating the weather—no matter how dreadful the weather on a particular day in Denmark or England might feel, one cannot eliminate it as such. One can, of course, change one's location—to move from the cold and snowy place to a hot and sunny one—but the weather as the context for one's relating with the environment remains.

Furthermore, weather is not a context only but also an example of a general meaning. It is our human way of thinking through our environment—a generalized symbolic sign that captures the totality of our being–on–the planet Earth. All animal species experience the actual conditions of rain, snow, and humidity, but only one—*Homo sapiens*—has developed means of reflecting upon these under one general term: "the weather." Human beings have created the cultural tools—signs—that allow us to complain about it, try to predict it using sophisticated instruments, and complain (again) when the weather forecast given by an authoritative source fails to come true. Having invented culture, human beings have opened to themselves infinite opportunities to complain about this or that. Talking becomes our new specialty, and complaining takes the place of acting.

Meaning-making creates both social borders and ways to transcend these. In some societies, talking about the weather has become the recurrent theme of starting up ordinary conversations. An English gentleman encountering a beautiful woman may start a conversation with her by referring to how beautiful is today's weather rather than to how beautiful he feels that *she* is. Politeness can be offensive, or—for establishing a new relationship—inevitable. When encountering people walking their dogs in a park, we happily compliment them on how beautiful we find the dogs to be while remaining silent about their owners. And the latter are pleased, rather than offended. Human meaning-making is a deeply paradoxical enterprise.

Statements about the weather, women and men, and dogs—or the ways in which eggs, clothes, or home interiors are decorated: Are these creative acts useful? Most relevantly, the author of this book leaves that question open—we do not (and cannot) know in which ways a newly created artifact is useful before it is put to use by somebody. And once it is, we are likely to be surprised. Not only creating the artifacts themselves but also the range of uses they assume in everyday practices follow Glăveanu's general theory of creativity. Utility is a dangerous criterion for evaluating human innovations, as it calls for preservation of the old and known and leads to caution about innovative adventures. It is the dynamic of the opposition between *useful* and *non-useful*—often taking the form of painful tensions—that keeps human beings creative in the practices of everyday life.

Creativity on Glăveanu's terms is *generative*. It makes use of the resources of the environment to change the very same environment into a new form, which provides resources for further acts of changing it. Generativity makes creativity open-ended and ecologically embedded. It also situates the "new look" at creativity clearly in the realm of general developmental perspectives; the heritage of James Mark Baldwin is one of the most notable contributions to this field of study (Baldwin 2010). Glăveanu offers a number of new solutions to the ways of studying the processes of *persistent imitation*—Baldwin's term for capturing the endless creative microgenesis of human living. The subcam techniques that Glăveanu outlines are a contemporary technological solution for looking at the act of creation from the visual perspective of the creator. To assess the creativity of the processes by looking at the outcomes of the creative act—a modification in the environment—Glăveanu offers a multiple feedback method that allows a researcher to avoid the tendency of taking a single perspective on a cultural product. The multivoiced nature of looking at everything in human life prevails—both within an evaluator and in a group of evaluators of a particular creative act.

All in all, there is much to discover in this book. The idea of bringing together in one place the author's various journal publications ensures that the work presented here will become publicly visible as a milestone in the advancement of creativity research. It represents a countertendency in our contemporary academic communication: instead of articles published in different places, we have one central location—a foundational book. As such, it stands out within the endless flow of journal articles, the publication of which earns academics local credits but does not facilitate communication within the field. Journal articles are like hamburgers in a fast-food eating place: quickly and standardly packed, edible only if one adds ketchup to them—with the memories of the encounter quickly fading away. In contrast, a book consisting of carefully selected and well-presented articles leaves the reader with the exquisite taste of intellectual gourmet—to be remembered and relived, thus leading to further creativity in our science as it unfolds within our lives.

Jaan Valsiner
October 2013
Aalborg

References

Baldwin, J. M. (2010). *Genetic theory of reality*. New Brunswick, NJ: Transaction (reprint of original from 1915).

Tanggaard, L. (2014). *Fooling around: Finding creative learning pathways*. Charlotte, NC: Information Age Publishers.

Valsiner, J. (2007). *Culture in minds and societies*. New Delhi, India: Sage.

Valsiner, J., Ed. (2012). *The Oxford handbook of culture and psychology*. New York, NY: Oxford University Press.

1

Introduction

I met Dănuţ Zimbru in September 2010 during my third field trip to the picturesque village of Ciocăneşti in northern Romania. I was then doing research on the craft of egg decoration and was eager to talk to the best-known male decorator in the community. Being a truck driver, Dănuţ didn't have much time for either decorating Easter eggs or talking to an insistent interviewer, but he kindly agreed to share his experience with me. At that time thirty-five years old, he had learned the craft as a young child, like many others in Ciocăneşti, from a relative nearby who knew how to "write" on eggs. After more than a decade of taking a break from this occupation, he returned to it following the rebirth of this tradition after the year 2007, when more and more people became involved with crafts and the village started organizing annual festivals dedicated to this folk art. Dănuţ talked modestly about his work and his role as an artisan: "[I am] a keeper of the tradition, I didn't create the motifs, I cannot say I created them. I take them forward, very little, the tradition." He uses the old technique of decorating eggs with wax and has mastered a series of motifs (principally geometric, specific to the region) that he employs again and again. "Well, you can add to that model something, make a little annex, add a little net, some dots, if you see it looks nice. . . . [But] you need to leave it as it was, the motif, as you had it, as you learned it. There are plenty of them that you cannot correct or make better." This is what he also tells his wife, whom he was then teaching to decorate. He taught his sister as well; she is now a known folk artist and creates "something else, more modern, more new." Dănuţ likes the motifs he knows, the ones he learned as a child; even when changing them a little, he intends to "make them as they were, and they will be beautiful."

In contrast, Marion Laval Jeantet is a celebrated French artist whose artistic vocation became known to her very early in life. In an interview with Ivan Toulouse (see Molina and Toulouse 2012), conducted as part the CREAPRO project between 2009 and 2012, Marion said that she, though born into a family of scientists, decided to be a child artist. Her taste for science, acquired early on, never faded, and her interests and art reflect her dual training—both scientific (in physics and chemistry, later anthropology and psychology) and artistic. From the age of four she saw an impressive number of exhibitions, mainly of cubist and interwar art. "Already, I had the conviction that I would love to be an artist, without knowing exactly what type of artist, because I wasn't feeling like a painter, and I saw only paintings. And in fact, towards seven or eight years of age, after Kandinsky's exhibitions, I told myself 'This is certainly what I want to do.'" And she began, from then on, to do "atypical things." Marion was age forty-two at the time of the interview. Her work—be it installation art, performance, video, or photography—is situated at the border between art and science (including biotechnology) and has been both fascinating and shocking for her audiences. "I work out a narrative. And the form needs to be adequate for this narrative. So, finally, it is not the multiplication of forms that generates different possibilities, it is my narrative desire that makes me experiment with all these different things." Working in close collaboration with her partner, Benoît Mangin, she develops shared "visions": "I have a vision of what the work will be, and I try to attain this vision." This is not always easy, and critics have not always been kind to the outcomes. But Marion is ready to confront such views because "I understood very early on that the type of art I make will not bring, cannot lead to a general consensus. Because in being consensual, one needs to compromise a lot." As an artist, Marion is not outside of the need to be recognized, but she tries to forge and follow her own path.

Finally, let us consider the story of a boy growing up in a placement center in Bucharest, Romania. I met Vasile (to use a pseudonym) in 2008 when I was conducting a study about how children represent and experience the world they live in (for details, see Jovchelovitch, Priego-Hernandez, and Glăveanu, 2013). He was one of the twenty-four children I talked to; I asked him to draw an image of his world and to build it using toys that represented people, cars, building blocks, animals, fences, trees, and so on. Vasile's drawing depicted a house, two trees, a car, a tulip, and his mother and father. Describing the car and house, he said, "It belongs to Mom and Dad." He was not in the drawing. His mother and father are "working," "they help people." I then asked him to tell me about the car. "[It is] nice, it takes people because it is a coach. Dad in front, Mom in the back." "Who usually goes with it?" "Me, you, my ten brothers." "And where are we going?" "To the mountains." Vasile said he had gone to the mountains before, but not with his family—with the "ladies from here." In an adaptation of Lowenfeld's (1939) world apparatus and Mucchielli's (1960) test of the imaginary village, I asked Vasile on another occasion to build for me his world as he sees it. In about three-quarters of an hour he managed to use almost all the toys available, including twenty persons, five toys, two dogs, six cars, eight fences, and eight trees. Asked what it all represents, he said, "A house for me and my children, my wife, my car, my yard with sheep"; the car "belongs to my brother Eric and his wife" (both near his family), and close by was "the house of my father and mother and their children." Eric is Vasile's older brother who lives with him at the center. "He is bigger than me [he used an adult figure] because he is fourteen and in the sixth grade. He has won a medal at football." "Why did you make houses for everyone?" "Because I like for each one of us to have a house, with his own room, to be nice and shiny." I was also curious to know why he used the two dog toys as sheep and placed them in an enclosure. "I wanted them to be sheep because I like cows and sheep, drinking milk from the cow, playing with the sheep." Moreover, it struck me that he depicted himself twice in the world construction, once as a little boy and then as an adult. Why was that? "There [on the side where he is an adult] is the last episode." "Would you add anything to the construction?" "Yes, all my brothers with houses for each."

What do the stories above tell us about creativity? At first sight we can think of Marion being a recognized creator with many accomplishments in her domain, of Dănuț as someone who does perhaps less creative work (at least by comparison), and of Vasile, a child who expresses his fantasy world through drawing and building activities. What makes Marion highly creative? Her motivation for artistic expression, her capacity to combine scientific and artistic means, her nonconformism and uncompromising attitude. The last two qualities are perhaps the clearest points of difference in relation to how Dănuț sees his own work. Instead of a rebellious attitude, he emphasizes tradition and continuity. He simply wishes to continue what he considers to have "received" and to create traditional and aesthetic objects (in his case, decorated Easter eggs). This may be an easy distinction to make, but what should we think about Vasile's "productions"? As any child, he draws and plays, so what is creative about this? Of course, he draws and builds a world that is different from the one he lives in, a world he aspires to while growing up in less-than-optimal conditions in a childcare center. But don't most children draw and play in ways that depart from what they actually experience? And at the same time, their drawings and games are very much rooted in current events, in what they know, in exercising the roles they see around them (doctor, mother and father, etc.). We can even ask ourselves if children can ever be creative in the same way we talk about the creativity of someone like Marion Laval Jeantet. But, on the other hand, why should we compare creativity in this manner? If products can more easily be evaluated against one another, what can we conclude about processes, about creativity as expression of the self in relation to the world?

If we reflect some more on the questions above, we will come to notice that our judgment about *creativity* relates very much to how we conceive *culture* and the *relation* between the two. To begin with, it is not by accident that I started with three examples that all come from the artistic domain: folk art, contemporary art, and the artistic and playful manifestations of a child. Western culture has long been shaped by a romanticist association between art and creativity (Weiner 2000; Runco 2007a). Those who use these cultural lenses, therefore, will be inclined perhaps to make an easy association between the two and evaluate most artistic things as potentially creative. But then another question arises: What is considered art? Certainly Marion has no difficulty, through her activity and studies, to identify herself as an artist. Her work is integrated into a cultural system that has a reserved place for artistic outcomes, even when people are, at first, shocked or enraged by them (in the end, this reaction conforms to the cultural norm of artists pushing existing boundaries). On the other hand, Dănuț and the field of folk art as a whole adopt other standards. His kind of craftwork, we are usually taught, is about tradition, about folklore and rurality, about keeping (even saving!) older ways of life in the face of rapid changes and the erosion of values. In a sense, we could say that the case of Dănuț is the most "cultural" one of all. Decorating eggs with wax is a custom—part of a material and symbolic (religious and artistic) cultural system specific to communities in the historical province of Bucovina, Romania, and, on a broader scale, to other countries in Eastern Europe of Orthodox Christian rite. And yet, isn't it striking that what seems to be most "cultural" appears also to be the least "creative"? Dănuț wants to both continue and respect his cultural heritage, whereas, as Marion's case shows, celebrated artists break norms rather than conform to them. And yet the opposite argument can be made, namely, that Marion has an even more important contribution to make toward her (French?) culture by shaking its conceptions and adding, in time, to its legacy. If we adopt this view, though, we can probably exclude Vasile, and any child of his age for that matter, from the realm of creativity, since in his case we cannot speak of any societal contribution being made. His outcomes express, at best, a personal form of creativity that has little, if anything, to add to the greater cultural environment he lives in.

If the above discussion aroused your interest and made you reflect on the questions raised (and formulate other questions or other answers), then this book is addressed to you. What you will find here is a collection of chapters on the topic of creativity from a cultural-psychological perspective. "Thinking through creativity and culture" means exactly this—a process, and not a definitive answer to any of the above. But it also means adopting and developing a certain theoretical position from which one can approach the three cases described above and the many questions they inspired. My own position is based on the belief that the three stories of Dănuț, Marion, and Vasile tell us something significant about creativity and culture because *they reflect both*. To determine which one of the three is more creative is not among the aims of this book. What I am trying to elaborate here is an account of *how and why* cultural manifestations such as egg decoration, installation art, and children's drawings are great examples of creativity, among many others. There is a clear difference between the "revolutionary" creation of an artist like Marion and the "evolutionary," pervasive creativity at the most minute level engaged in by people like Dănuț and his fellow artisans. But the fact remains that they all draw from a cultural system and contribute to it, in their own way and through their own means. There is also a clear difference between an Easter egg, an artistic photograph, and a drawing. However, the real interest for me is to relate these differences to the processes involved in creating each rather than to a predetermined definition of what is "more" or "less" creative. A second important point to make about the book is that any conceptualization of the relationship between culture and creativity is *extremely consequential* for how we define each, how we approach them, what kind of boundaries we set around them, what possibilities we give ourselves to act on and within them, and, essentially, how we see ourselves and others as agents in the extended field of cultural production.

1.1. Creativity, Culture, and Their Relationship

It is expected that a book with the words "creativity" and "culture" in the title will start with some definitions. I am not going to do this, and not because these terms designate phenomena that are so complex as to virtually defy (a singular and a final) definition. It is because both creativity and culture are *relational concepts* and, as I am trying to demonstrate here, relate essentially to each other. More specifically, defining creativity or defining culture cannot be achieved outside the context of their interrelation. And since there are multiple ways in which we can connect the two, there are also a myriad of potential definitions for each. The cultural-psychological approach I adopt here has, however, its own preferred view, and to build up to it, I propose below a logical exercise of thinking about how one can envision the link between creativity and culture. We can narrow down the possibilities to basically three main categories, as reflected schematically in Figure 1.1.

Perhaps the most common way of thinking about the relation between these key terms, at least in psychology, goes along the lines of the figure on the left, in which the "bubbles" of the two concepts *exclude* each other. This approach is apparent in the long tradition of mainstream creativity research: to argue for the individual basis of creative expression and to "locate" creativity as a phenomenon at the level of the individual person. Irrespective of whether this exact location has to do with personality traits, cognitive mechanisms, genes, or aspects of the brain and its functioning, one immediate consequence is the acontextual way in which we study and think about creativity. It comes as no surprise that such a serious attribution error (Kasof 1995, 1999) is pervasive and extends to common sense depictions of creativity. If we are to randomly

Figure 1.1. Conceptualizing the relation between creativity and culture: exclusion, overlap, identity.

ask people around us to give a few examples of what creativity is for them, they will very likely point to clearly identifiable persons (or products of these persons) celebrated as creative in their culture and society. The fascination with the individual creative self has deep historical roots, as we will see in this book, and, despite a growing number of social and cultural studies and postmodern "counterdiscourses" about creativity, it continues to hold strong. This is not to say that creativity has nothing to do with the individual, but, as argued here, the creative person is a sociocultural entity. Notice how in Figure 1.1 there are clearly drawn borders around both creativity and culture. The cultural-psychological approach to creativity doesn't deny that individuals are actors in the field of creation or that creativity involves the "mind" or, specifically, cognition; rather, it considers individuals' cognition to be social in origin and expression. In this sense, there is no dichotomy between creativity and culture, and depicting or theorizing them as two separate "bubbles" can only diminish our potential to see interconnections and place them in a broader context.

Granted, it is rare to find anyone who would support the view that creativity has nothing to do with culture. Even advocates of what I call here the "exclusion" perspective would most probably claim that creativity and culture influence each other. It is interesting to notice that, though historically (and this is certainly the case for philosophical and sociological accounts) creativity has been considered a main driver of cultural change or "progress," psychologists are much more interested in the feedback loop leading from culture (or, more broadly, the social environment) to creative action. The social psychology of creativity, at least in Amabile's (1996) formulation, is concerned mostly with the role that different social variables have in shaping creative expression. In this context, rewards, surveillance, peer evaluations, etc. have all been operationalized as factors that come into play and that can either increase or (more often) diminish the chances of someone being creative. The story of group creativity research (see Paulus and Nijstad 2003) is filled with illustrations of how collectives are not that good at acting creatively, at least when compared to individuals working separately to generate ideas. Once more, the "bubble" around creativity takes shape in an effort to protect it from social and cultural influences. Certainly there is also research showing that the social environment is not always harmful, and many try to focus today on designing this environment "better" and making it conducive to creativity.

What these studies and theoretical positions miss is the fact that society, culture, the group, etc. are not "outside" of creativity; rather, they are part and parcel of its process, outcome, and subjective experience. Culture is not only a set of variables that exist around individuals and condition their behavior—though this view (even when implicit) has been widely adopted by cross-cultural psychology (see Valsiner 2007). Equally, creativity doesn't "reside" in the individual, particularly the isolated and self-contained person, liberated from (or fighting against) culture and society. We need to think twice about the numerous past and present creativity models that include the environment as a component among many, a box linked to other (intra-psychological) variables by a series of arrows or lines. We need thus to move from a cross-cultural to a cultural understanding.

In light of what I just said, it might seem that the middle depiction in Figure 1.1, the situation of *overlap* between creativity and culture, represents a step forward. It clearly acknowledges that there is a strong connection between the two yet maintains spaces for individual creativity (outside of culture) and for cultural traditions (outside of creativity). If I discussed above, albeit briefly, the individualistic fallacy in the psychology of creativity (and this book will come back to this point in most of the chapters), something needs to be said about the misconception that tradition is the antithesis of creativity. The image of traditions and customs being "stuck" in time—unable to progress, encouraging repetition and conformity—is at best comical, at worst hazardous. Traditions constantly renew themselves through creative work, and this is what makes them adapt to ever-changing material and social contexts (Wilson 1984; Negus and Pickering 2004). At the same time, creativity is unthinkable outside the traditions that offer it resources and means of expression, regulate its manifestation, and integrate its outcomes. Even when they appear to be breaking with tradition, creators act on the basis of other emerging values that come to consolidate a neo-tradition. The case of Easter egg decoration as a traditional, creative type of craft will be presented at length in this book, and many more arguments and examples will be added to the above.

To return to the overlap perspective, we can understand it better by considering what is placed in its three spaces and, most importantly, why we need these areas of creativity, creativity/culture, and culture. To comprehend this type of segmentation, let's focus on the pressing issue of children and education. One age-old observation and question about child and adult creativity is succinctly captured by Anderson when he notes,

> This is to say, creativity was in each one of us as a small child. In children creativity is a universal. Among adults it is almost nonexistent. The great question is: What has happened to this enormous and universal human resource? (Anderson 1959, xii)

A great consensus nowadays, starting from Torrance's (1967) research on the fourth grade creativity slump, is that we need to look toward the culture of the educational system and, more generally, of the societies we live in, for a culprit. It is the culture of conformity (Sternberg and Lubart 1995a) that creates, through the means of a rigid educational system, little robots out of immensely creative children. In light of this, we can "read" the depiction in Figure 1.1 developmentally according to this conception: the child starts fully on the side of creativity, before acculturation; then he or she moves, in school, from first to fourth grade, into a sphere where creativity and culture (as inscribed in the school system) coexist; finally, the system wins out and diminishes creative expression. The end result: a fully socialized individual, educated but lacking the means to generate anything new. How much truth is there in such a simplified (or simplistic) vision? First, children are not born creative. They become capable of creative expression precisely at the time when they become actors of their culture and are capable of using symbolic means in their relation to other people (Winnicott 1971). Second, the apparent slump in creativity is more likely to be a change in the quality of its expression, a time when children go through a "literal" stage (Gardner 1982) that equips them for acquiring and mastering societal scripts. But this learning is not uncreative in either its path or its outcomes. It is again a matter of comparison; surely, we cannot and should not expect a child of ten to make the same drawings as one of four. The spontaneity of the former is not gone, but it is more disciplined and often channeled in other directions. Finally, there is no denying that teachers could do more to foster creativity in their pupils, especially when it comes to the current ethos of teaching "to the test," which excludes many other outcomes and student experiences. But even here we cannot make the simple and misleading statement that education as a whole (and, more generally, culture and its acquisition) is uncreative (see also Tanggaard 2011).

It is indeed encouraging to notice in the overlap model that creativity and culture can indeed occupy the same "territory." However, this happens only partially or temporarily. This is not the case, though, for the depiction at the right in Figure 1.1. There we have a view of *creativity as culture* and of *culture as creativity*. Certainly this kind of *identity* relation is intriguing. In the end, we don't say when people create something that they act in a cultural manner or produce culture, just as we don't consider all cultural forms to be based on and expressive of creativity. And yet we should. This is one of the key arguments put forward by this book through its analysis of creativity and culture in terms of representations, actions, evaluations, developmental trajectories, and so on. To say that creativity is culture and culture is creativity doesn't mean making one term redundant and replacing it with the other. Rather, this statement seeks to make us sensitive to the cultural nature of creativity and to the fact that creativity stands at the core of cultural production, continuity, and transformation. Let us take these claims in turn.

What does it mean to say that creativity has a cultural nature? To understand this assertion, we need to reflect on creativity developmentally. As briefly stated above, the birth of both culture and creativity is marked by the first generation and use of signs. This is what Winnicott (1971) metaphorically referred to as the "third" or "potential space" of existence—the realm of culture, first enacted in creative and playful games by children, between the "inner" and "outside" worlds we inhabit. Creative expression would be impossible in a cultural vacuum marked by the absence of semiotic means and socially organized practices. The "stuff" of creativity, its content, is invariably cultural, meaning it is generated, stabilized, and transformed in the relation between people, groups, and often entire communities or societies. If we think about the creative work of a poet or scientist, they both use cultural material, not least important language, and organize it in different ways. This new organization might be more or less novel or original or useful and thus evaluated as more or less creative by others, but nevertheless it is a reshaping of what exists in the cultural arena (Arieti 1976). What about the creative process? Isn't it unique, personal, outside any cultural normativity? It must be so, otherwise creative acts would become predictable and regular, and these qualities conflict with the heuristic essence of the phenomenon (Amabile 1996). This conception, as previously argued, establishes a false and unproductive dichotomy between the individual mind and culture. To think in this way leads to paradoxes, such as assuming that intrapsychological processes can be creative but their outcomes, once externalized (shared with others), lose this quality and can be used creatively only when they "reenter" the intrapsychological system of another person. A mechanistic model is thus set in place, a model that fails to account for the in-between, intersubjective space created in the relation that brings individuals together. Creativity as a process is cultural since cocreated and evolving cultural systems incorporate not only signs and tools but also algorithms, scripts, and prescriptions regarding the use of signs and tools. Cultural prescriptive norms are, however, not rigid but flexible (to different degrees), in order to ensure survival and, ultimately, growth. The creative process exploits this flexibility in ways that might initially contradict some cultural norms (while being convergent with others) and that, if successful, end up being accumulated and used in the future. And here is where we discover another dimension of creativity as culture: the existence of the "other" (person, group, institution, etc.) that observes, uses, confronts, appreciates, or censures our "creations." In this sense, creativity is not a personal but an interpersonal achievement. The creative act is an *encounter* between person, other, and world (see May 1959), the three elements that define, at all levels, any generative cultural system.

Culture is creativity. This other side of the coin regarding our argument is at first difficult to apprehend considering the long tradition of seeing creativity as an individual function. Moreover, creativity has a strong process dimension associated with it, while the word culture seems to indicate an accumulation of things, norms, values, ideas, and so on, something therefore more or less static or stable. How else would we be able, for instance, to make cross-cultural comparisons if cultures were constantly moving, changing, being created? And yet, this is precisely what cultural psychology teaches us. "The crucial tension in psychologists' discourse about culture is about treating it as an existing entity (for example, 'culture *is* X'), or a process of becoming ('cultur*ing* leads to X')" (Valsiner 2007, 20). This book, and the cultural-psychological approach advanced here, is less about culture (despite the title) and more about culturing, in essence, a creative process. To consider culture as an entity would assign creativity the role only of contributing to this entity from time to time. In contrast, culture as process points to constant micro- and macrotransitions and to the reshaping of culture through interaction and communication. Once again, the space of the creative encounter between self, other, and world comes to the forefront as the privileged arena of creating understood as culturing.

Two counterarguments will probably be raised here. One is that not all mundane creations, including the small changes Dănuţ makes to a decoration pattern or Vasile's imagining of a better future, can be raised to the level of "culture." To say this, however, makes culture synonymous with "high culture," meaning the world of technology, science, art, and societal innovation. The other assertion is that people, even through their interaction, don't have the power to fundamentally reshape their culture. Even if you and I are to talk about gender stereotypes and how harmful they can be, this doesn't mean that our conclusions will immediately shape the culture of our society. But is culture only the culture of a society, or can it be more broadly understood and defined at intergroup and even interpersonal levels? Does a reshaping of culture that has the right to be called "creative" necessarily have to be both revolutionary and durable?

The exclusion, overlap, and identity perspectives regarding the relationship between creativity and culture are simple and schematic models with powerful consequences. They influence the way we *define* the two terms as well as the way we approach them *methodologically and practically*. In essence, the exclusion view defines creativity as an individual process only remotely influenced, from the "outside," by social and cultural variables. Following this logic, we are compelled to ask: How can we manipulate the environment in order to increase the chances of creative expression? How does feature X of social interaction condition creativity? These questions may lead to neat designs and conclusions supported by statistical values, but, at a fundamental level, they are flawed because they ignore the interdependence between person and environment and their coevolution over time. The overlap view partially addresses this critique by allowing for a common space of creativity and culture. However, it also suggests that there are acultural ways of being creative and acreative ways of existing as cultural beings. The quest here becomes, at best, how to enlarge the space of creativity and culture and, at worst, how to eliminate or counter the "toxic" area of culture, which leads to the absence of creativity and to domination by mindless routines and conformity. The third view, proposing a relation of identity, resolves this dilemma at a conceptual level. It does so by acknowledging the fact that creativity works from within culture just as culture works from within creativity. According to this perspective, *creativity, expressed both at individual and social levels, is the process that ensures the continuity, renewal, and transformation of human culture (again, recognized at individual, interpersonal, intergroup, and societal levels).* This conception represents the basis for the cultural psychology of creativity proposed in this book.

1.2. "Principles for a Cultural Psychology of Creativity"

This is the title of an article (Glăveanu 2010a) I began writing in 2008, the first attempt to systematize my initial thoughts concerning the intricate relation between creativity and culture. It was also the time when I started my doctoral studies at the London School of Economics and Political Science, following an MSc in Social and Cultural Psychology at the same institution. I have had an interest in creativity for a long time, at least since my undergraduate studies in psychology at the University of Bucharest. In fact, this interest can be traced further back to my childhood years when, together with my mother (an art teacher) and my father, I was attending summer holiday camps for artists. My drawings from those years later became the topic of a book, in Romanian, that was essentially a reflection on the role of art in development and education (Glăveanu and Glăveanu 2004).

My conception of creativity was greatly enriched by my encounter with cultural psychology during my graduate studies. It seemed to me then that creativity theory was in need of cultural thinking, and I was frustrated to find little of it in what had been written on the topic in recent decades (except for the works of authors such as Keith Sawyer or Vera John-Steiner). On the other hand, I was surprised to see little concern for creativity on the part of social and cultural psychologists. It was disappointing to have work rejected by an established social psychology outlet for the reason that "creativity is not among the main topics of the discipline." Similarly, the recent and prestigious *Oxford Handbook of Cultural Psychology* (Valsiner 2012) lacks a chapter on creativity. Of course, this doesn't mean that cultural psychologists are not interested in creative phenomena, especially since they tend to adopt an "identity" view regarding creativity and culture (see Figure 1.1 and the previous section). What this absence indicates is a terminological void filled by terms such as imagination, emergence, construction, improvisation, novelty, and so on. To place creativity on the "agenda" of cultural psychology, we need to challenge the individualistic legacy of the word, a process currently underway (see Tanggaard 2013; Glăveanu, Gillespie, and Valsiner 2014).

Since 2008, my own research has tried to advance, through published work, the discipline of *the cultural psychology of creativity.* The chapters in this book include both theoretical elaborations and empirical findings that substantiate this field. Most of these findings emerged from my doctoral research, a four-year project that took me back to Romania—specifically, to the capital city of Bucharest and to a small village in the north of the country, the community of Ciocănești. I was, as a cultural psychologist, curious to explore a particular craft that I knew from my childhood and from many visits to the Museum of the Romanian Peasant in Bucharest. Egg decoration is a folk art with deep historical roots, a custom that reflects both a particular aesthetic and a religious symbolism (related to the Easter season) and that contributes to a vibrant folk life specific to this Eastern European country. Easter eggs were, therefore, the perfect case study for my creativity research considered from a cultural-psychological perspective. Within this domain, I "tested" for the first time my theoretical ideas and sociocultural models, and I learned about the creativity of everyday life, of social practices, of tradition. Unlike so many other studies of creativity that hurry to focus on celebrated creators and creations, I went against the grain and decided to look at creativity in the context of tradition, at the new in relation to the old, at change in its interplay with continuity. Within this project, which was published in several articles (many of which are included in this book) before I completed my doctorate, I considered three interrelated issues, all inspired by cultural-psychological scholarship: the representation of creativity and how people evaluate creativity within the craft; creativity as action and its unfolding in the relation between artisans and material objects and between artisans and their colleagues and customers; and the ontogenetic development of creative expression in craftwork. Throughout the research, a basic distinction was established between urban and rural environments based on clear differences in lifestyle among these communities and, more importantly here, in the way they approach the meaning and decoration of eggs. As such, the two cultural systems I considered in detail exist within the same country, though at two different "ends" of it, and I felt no need (at least at that time) to make cross-national comparisons.

The above observations correspond to the small set of "principles" I set for my project from the very beginning. In retrospect, this was a very ambitious attempt for a novice in the domain of creativity and culture. But, as it sometimes happens, it is the enthusiasm of the beginner that leads to ideas that might not have been formulated, at least in the same form, years later. Returning to my initial vision and these principles, published in *Culture & Psychology* in 2010, I am happy to find them as valid today as they were before I engaged in fieldwork. Now that I have completed a cycle of research, it is a perfect opportunity to return to these first theoretical formulations and revisit them in light of the studies I conducted since then, many of which are included in the chapters that follow. In essence, the cultural psychology of creativity proposes the following:

1. *A contextual understanding of creativity.* In the original article (Glăveanu 2010a), I made the point that current definitions of the phenomenon, emphasizing novelty and usefulness, are, in essence, acontextual. We don't exactly know how or to whom the creative artifact is useful, and we don't know how it is novel or what comparison is the basis of this novelty.

In essence, creativity has a "context" that is greater than any limited testing situation. In fact, creative outcomes have a history—a social history, to be more precise. Nowhere is this clearer than in the case of decorated eggs. The context of this creative craft extends beyond individual creations or creators to incorporate a tradition that has existed for centuries; a social network that includes fellow decorators, novices of the craft, and the public; and a long period of learning the craft and sometimes teaching it to others (as in the case of Dănuţ Zimbru). To understand this context and to study it means to focus on more than the features of particular Easter eggs and even to go beyond observing how these eggs are decorated. As such, during my first period of fieldwork, I was primarily interested in investigating the "life" of the craft in Romania and, more specifically, in exploring how the context of decoration (both in terms of action and representation) is shaped differently for people belonging to various groups relevant to this folk art: ethnographers, priests, art teachers, and the artisans themselves (see Chapter 6).

2. *A generative understanding of creativity.* This second principle builds on the basic assertion that creativity uses culture to produce culture (see also Chapter 3 for a more elaborate presentation of this argument). In this sense, creativity represents a generative capacity that individuals and groups have of transforming their environment using the means offered by this environment. It is not "out of nowhere" that we create, and the outcomes of this generativity are constantly used in the production of new artifacts (in the form primarily of objects but also of activities, performances, norms and values, and so on). To study Easter egg decoration as a generative process means to pay close attention to the "roots," both symbolic and material, of particular patterns and to explore the logic of their recombination and "translation" from one support to another. Chapter 7 offers a detailed description of decoration activities that strongly reinforces this principle; this is achieved through both accounts of the artisans and detailed observation of their practice, collected with the help of filmed observation (see Chapter 5). A generative understanding of craftwork reveals the role of combination and change, copying and translation, woven into the construction of a personal style.

3. *A meaning-oriented understanding of creativity.* Cultural psychology emphasizes the construction of meaning and the semiotic mediation and regulation of activity (see Valsiner 2007), including creative activity. If mainstream research strives to achieve an assumed "objective" perspective regarding creativity by excluding personal accounts of creative experience, cultural psychologists aim precisely to bring this experience and its associated meaning-making efforts to the fore. As argued in Chapter 9, creativity evaluations and implicit theories about what is (and is not) creative are necessarily integrated in broader social representations. These webs of meaning, constructed in the interaction between people,

don't always concern creativity alone. In fact, the everyday language of creativity and the criteria people use to assess it are much more diverse than strict conceptions of novelty and usefulness. In Chapter 8, other "local" meanings become apparent and creativity is associated with aesthetic aspects, with the time and effort spent to generate the outcome, and with one's personal involvement. In the end, we can conclude not only that creative artifacts acquire different meanings for different people but also that this meaning-making process itself bears the mark of creativity. In this sense, audiences become, through perception and dialogue, cocreators of the value and significance of a new object (see also Chapter 3 for a theoretical model).

4. *A genetic understanding of creativity.* To understand psychological phenomena, one needs to understand their development. This basic principle is equally applicable to the study of creativity. The present book includes examples of research investigating egg decoration at all levels of its genesis, from social and historical levels to ontogenetic and microgenetic ones. What is of utmost importance for a cultural psychologist, however, is not merely to distinguish between these trajectories but above all to unpack their interrelation. In the case of the craft, the sociogenetic emergence of new types of decoration (for example, the new technique of decorating with wax in relief or using wax of different colors) is connected to new forms of teaching the craft and shapes the exact ways in which work proceeds (for instance, the use of wax in relief changes the general stages of decoration). In turn, these microchanges of technique can—and often do—lead to new discoveries and further innovations (such as drawing people, landscapes, or other figurative elements on the shape of the egg). The specific question of how children learn the craft and become creative actors within it is addressed at length in Chapter 13.

5. *Ecological creativity research.* The last principle I proposed in the 2010 paper concerns methodology. It was argued therein that creativity research should move away from artificial study settings into the "field," that is, into those everyday contexts in which creative acts unfold. Both qualitative methods and process observation, mentioned in the paper, have been applied to the study of creativity in Easter egg making, from interviews and filmed observation of decoration to the analysis of children's drawings. This doesn't exclude quantitative methods, and research reported here about the representation of creativity includes, for instance, a survey of lay beliefs (Chapter 9). Cultural research tends to be initially descriptive and exploratory, and it is this exploration that can lead to novel theoretical developments. In the case of the craftwork project, these new developments concern the conceptualization of creativity as mastery (Chapter 10) and connecting creativity to material affordances (Chapter 11). Ecological research is well equipped to study creative action by situating it within a network of relations that reunite creators, their collaborators and audiences, and a wide array of existing artifacts.

1.3. The Present Book

This book consists of twelve chapters, not including this present introduction and a final discussion, grouped into six main parts: A. Theoretical Framework, B. Methodological Toolkit, C. Case Study: The Creativity of Craftwork, D. The Representation of Creativity, E. The Creativity of Action, and F. Creativity Development. These parts include chapters previously published as articles in different journals (*New Ideas in Psychology*; *Journal for the Theory of Social Behaviour*; *Journal of Constructivist Psychology*; *Creativity Research Journal*; *Psychological Studies*; *Psychology of Aesthetics, Creativity, and the Arts*; *Integrative Psychological and Behavioral Science*; *The International Journal of Creativity & Problem Solving*; *Review of General Psychology*; *Journal of Creative Behavior*; *Thinking Skills and Creativity*), and I am grateful for the permission to collect them into one volume. The text of the articles has not been modified except that minor editing has been performed, figures and tables have been renumbered, a unitary system of spelling has been adopted, and some of the references (placed at the end of the volume) have been updated.

Looking back and reviewing this work conducted in previous years, I cannot help but feel grateful for all the encouragement and support I received along the way. I will begin by expressing my gratitude to the London School of Economics and Institute of Social Psychology (LSE), whose generous funding allowed me to start my graduate studies and whose wonderful team of teachers and researchers guided my first explorations of social and cultural phenomena. My doctoral work was also supported by the Economic and Social Research Council (grant number ES/H/13199/1), and several field trips to Romania were financed by the Rațiu Family Foundation.

Regarding the LSE, I am particularly grateful first of all to my supervisor, Sandra Jovchelovitch, whose patient and stimulating guidance was invaluable for the present work. During my years spent in London, I was privileged to have studied in a thoroughly stimulating environment, and I would like to thank many people (too many for the limited space of a book!) for sharing with me their time and interest: Alex Gillespie, Saadi Lahlou, Caroline Howarth, Ivana Marková, Derek Hook, Claudine Provencher, Lucia Garcia, Martin Bauer, Helen Amelia Green, Fryni Mylona, Maria Brock, and Jap Dhesi.

I have been fortunate to move, following the completion of my PhD, to the psychology department at Aalborg University in Denmark, a thriving center for research on creativity and cultural psychology. Here I joined a group of dedicated and like-minded researchers who were tremendously welcoming and supportive. I am very grateful to my colleague Lene Tanggaard, with whom I am codirecting the International Centre for the Cultural Psychology of Creativity, as well as to Brady Wagoner, Svend Brinkmann, Thomas Szulevicz, Mogens Jensen, and Lena Lippke for their continual help and inspiring exchange of ideas. I am also particularly thankful to Jaan Valsiner for being always so kind and for encouraging all my projects, including this book.

There are many other colleagues from outside the United Kingdom and Denmark who made significant contributions to my thinking, including Todd Lubart, Maciej Karwowski, Ai-Girl Tan, Zayda Sierra, Tania Zittoun, Caroline Léchot, and Ana Moise. My gratitude extends also to several people in Romania who facilitated my research, in particular the egg decorators from the idyllic community of Ciocăneşti who generously shared with me their time, their values, and their art; the ethnographers from the Museum of the Romanian Peasant; and the school directors who welcomed me and my research. In the end, each and every participant in my studies made this volume possible; they all showed me the way forward and taught me something about their world and their love for decoration.

This book is dedicated to my parents, Ioana Corina and Petre—the ones who taught me the meaning and value of creativity.

Part A

Theoretical Framework

2

Paradigms in the Study of Creativity: Introducing the Perspective of Cultural Psychology[1]

We undoubtedly live in a world of change, a world in motion. It is change that takes place at all levels, that seems to get hold of every aspect of our life and our society. We feel it in the accelerated daily rhythm at work and at home; we perceive its consequences in the political and economical domain and its impact on the natural environment. This generalized sense of change often leads to anxiety (Negus and Pickering 2004), to the feeling that we are not "prepared," that what we normally know and do doesn't work anymore. It is under these circumstances that creativity becomes much more present and more important than before (Runco 2004), and it is claimed to help us achieve our goals as individuals, as organizations, as societies (Westwood and Low 2003). At the same time, the aura of panacea that creativity has gained pushes it more than ever into the scrutiny of psychologists and social scientists.

The number of ways in which creativity has been theorized and the variety of domains it has been applied to is impressive (for reviews see Runco 2004; Sternberg 2003): from behavioral approaches linking it to reinforcement and modeling (Epstein and Laptosky 1999) to the dominant cognitive approaches discussing it in terms of cognitive style (Martinsen and Kaufmann 1999) or problem solving (Weisberg 1988). Primary areas of application for creativity theories are educational settings (Cropley 1999; Hennessey 2003a) and organizations, especially theories related to studies of leadership (Mumford and Connelly 1999) and performance in heterogeneous teams (Puccio 1999).

In most of these areas, it is the individual set apart from his or her social context that constitutes the unit of analysis for creativity, an authentic bias in

[1] From New Ideas in Psychology, 28(1), Glăveanu, V. P., Paradigms in the study of creativity: *Introducing the perspective of cultural psychology*, 79–93. © 2009 by Elsevier, reprinted with permission.

the literature recognized only from the 1970s on (Hennessey 2003b). Be it the "lone genius" or the more "ordinary" person, he or she creates *outside* of social and group factors (Paulus and Nijstad 2003) and even *despite* them (Weiner 2000). Society and culture repeatedly act as the "villains" whom the creator fights against, and this generates a series of paradoxes that will be exposed further on in this chapter. One of them relates directly to the definition of creativity. "New" and "useful" as features of a creative product (Martindale 1994; Richards 1999; Stein 1953) are properties that easily describe the work of great creators and can be applied to certain products, particularly in the field of science, art, and technology, but they deny the creativity of children and the varied instances of "mundane creativity" (Cohen and Ambrose 1999).

This chapter seeks to unpack the social and cultural nature of creative acts. In doing so, I will start by distinguishing between three paradigms that led creativity theory and research: the He-, I-, and We-paradigm (see also Glăveanu 2010a). The first part will therefore focus on paradigmatic shifts from "positivistic research paradigms to more complex, constructivistic, systems-oriented research models" (Friedman and Rogers 1998, xviii). Nonetheless, it will be argued that even the models proposed within what is currently considered the social psychology of creativity, maybe "the least developed area in creativity research" (Amabile 1996, 264), can still be criticized for the individualism hidden behind their assumptions. To counteract such tendencies, an emerging multidisciplinary field is introduced: *the cultural psychology of creativity*, which conceives creativity as a fundamentally relational, intersubjective phenomenon.

2.1. Three Paradigms of Creativity Theory and Research

The study of creativity has known three paradigmatic stages: the genius stage, the creative person stage, and the "social" stage. By making reference to historical times long before the words "creativeness" or "creativity" entered our vocabulary (for the English language, this is the eighteenth and nineteenth century, respectively; see Mason 2003 and Weiner 2000) and before psychology became a science, the chapter will also consider centuries of prepsychological thought concerning humans' capacity to create. Though a historical progression is implied, it is likely that "instances" of these paradigms coexist at different times, and they are certainly intertwined in today's scientific landscape.

2.1.1. The He-Paradigm: The Lone Genius

The image of the genius is probably one of the most persistent representations in human history, with roots in Greek and Roman antiquity. The first links to be made were those between genius and divine inspiration (Friedman and Rogers 1998; Sternberg 2003). Yet, the Latin origin and meaning of genius as a guardian spirit changed in the following centuries (Negus and Pickering 2004). One turning point is considered by most to be the Renaissance (Montuori and Purser 1995), when the influence of God began to be replaced by that of genetic inheritance (Dacey 1999). This process of individualization of the genius continued on two different fronts: arts and the exaltation of imagination during Romanticism, and sciences and the exaltation of reason during the Enlightenment (Weiner 2000). Embracing such ideas about unique individuals, the He-paradigm, or the paradigm of the genius, has put considerable emphasis in describing creators on two main features: *exclusivity* and *disconnection*. Creativity is from this perspective "exclusivist" because only few are chosen for it (initially by God, later on by their biology), and the very few that are chosen must, as a prerequisite, stand apart from the masses because of their capacities. They create ex nihilo (Negus and Pickering 2004) and therefore need nothing to bind them to the world of others or existing knowledge. The He-paradigm ("He" since the creator is most often a *male other*) thus takes the strongest individualistic stance in the conceptualization of creativity.

Undoubtedly the father figure of the "modern" He-paradigm, Francis Galton offered the world, through his 1869 *Hereditary Genius*, the first scientific study of the creative genius (Simonton 2003b). His assumption was that, in the "competition between nature and nurture," when all conditions are equal, "nature certainly proves the stronger of the two" (Galton 1874, 16). By this Galton took genius out of the mists of the supernatural and gave it a solid basis: human biology. He also described it in terms of intellectual ability and eminence (Terman 1947/1970). While intellectual ability has to do with the creator's individual brain, there is a factor of social reputation in appreciating eminence. Nevertheless, the connection to the world of previous knowledge and the scientific (or artistic) communities is not understood here as interdependence but as the mere effect of the genius on existing social and cultural structures. Therefore, creativity in this paradigm refers strictly to the highest levels of creation, or what is known as historical creativity (Boden 1994; Fischer et al. 2005). The only things worthy of being called creative are those that introduce novelties, that generate new schools of thought, and that constitute landmarks in the history of a domain— sometimes even the history of humanity.

This represents the main limitation, but also the main attraction, of the He-paradigm. By glorifying creative breakthroughs, it makes creativity stand among the most desirable human capacities, but at the price of cutting off ordinary creativity (Bateson 1999) and common creative experiences (Stein 1953). Its focus has traditionally been on the study of "great men," especially eminent scientists, and this branch of investigation has grown in recent decades (though the emphasis on the biological basis of genius was not always maintained). Examples are found in the work of Roe (1952/1970), who examined eminent US scientists to build an "average" profile of their characteristics. The studies of Gardner (1994) on seven "creators of the modern era," each taken as an embodiment of a certain type of intelligence, have led to similar descriptions of the psychological profile and life path of exemplary creators. But research on scientific genius soon started to be questioned in relation to its implicit assumptions. In such a critical enterprise, Schaffer (1994) argued against the mythologies of the genius or what she calls the "culture hero" and the "fetishism" of discovery. Both scientific discoveries and their authors are "made up" or socially constructed by subsequent generations through processes of retrospection and celebration.

In conclusion, the He-paradigm—based on the individuality, insight, outstanding ability, and fertility of the genius (Mason 2003)—gives an *elitist* and *essentialist* account of creativity (Negus and Pickering 2004). The direct consequence of this is that it detaches the creator from community and, in so doing, ends up building a pathological image of him or her. As Montuori and Purser (1995, 76) argue, the fate of the genius is often represented as that of a person who is misunderstood, eccentric, and even antisocial. Such an account also excludes the role of cocreation or collaboration in the process of reaching "great discoveries" (Barron 1999). Its implications go beyond the scientific and even reach the ideological, since recognizing or not recognizing the "genius" is often a politically charged action (Negus and Pickering 2004). In the end, owing to the influence of institutional structures that reflect power relations between and within social groups, it is rarely creativity alone that decides who is a genius.

2.1.2. The I-Paradigm: The Creative Person

If the He-paradigm has deep roots in prepsychological thought, the I-paradigm largely emerged once psychologists started to focus on creativity. Put simply, the paradigmatic shift replaced the genius with the "normal" person while *keeping* the individual as a unit of analysis. It is what can be referred to as a "democratization" of creativity (Bilton 2007; Hulbeck 1945; Weiner 2000). Everyone is capable of being creative because it is no longer a capacity of the few chosen by God, biology, or unique psychological features. With this shift, the use of the term genius declined, leaving space for notions like gifted and creative (Friedman and Rogers 1998). The birth of the I-paradigm and its new terminology were affected by forces working from within the field of psychology and also from the outside—that is, the sociopolitical context in the United States after the Second World War.

> In the presence of the Russian threat, "creativity" could no longer be left to the chance occurrences of the genius; neither could it be left in the realm of the wholly mysterious and the untouchable. Men *had* to be able to do something about it; creativity *had* to be a property in many men; it *had* to be something identifiable; it *had* to be subject to the effects of efforts to gain more of it. (Razik 1967/1970, 156)

It was the background of an individualistic society that provided the perfect context for the emergence of the I-paradigm. As shown by Slater (1991), the "individual versus society" worldview is predominant in America. This myth is associated with the dream of escaping the influence of *outside* society and culture, seen as entities one can connect to and disconnect from (154).

In psychology, the voice behind the I-paradigm was that of Guilford (1950), remembered here for his historical American Psychological Association presidential address. He called the attention of psychologists to the topic of creativity and gave them a clear agenda: "The psychologist's problem is that of creative personality" (444) and "creative acts can therefore be expected, no matter how feeble or how infrequent, of almost all individuals" (446). And Guilford's message was heard, for during the following decades psychologists looked intensively to the personal attributes of individuals (personality, intelligence, etc.) and their link to creativity (Amabile 1996).

It is thus unsurprising that in 1981, when Barron and Harrington published a review of creativity studies, they offered it the title "Creativity, intelligence, and personality." More recent literature argues that *intelligence* is not a sufficient condition for creativity (Eysenck 1994), and therefore intelligent persons are not necessarily creative as well. Nevertheless, intelligence and creativity overlap in some respects but not in others (Sternberg 1999b). One hypothesis is that, instead of a single outstanding intelligence, the creative person possesses an unusual combination of intelligences (Gardner 1994). Studies of the *creative personality*, on the other hand, proved to be an even more fertile tradition. Among the most common traits encountered were the following: tolerance for ambiguity and orientation toward the future (Stein 1953), independence of judgment, preference for complexity, strong desire to create, deep motivation, many personal troubles, strong intuitive nature and patience (Barron 1999), relatively high intelligence, originality, articulateness and verbal fluency, and a good imagination (Tardif and Sternberg 1988). Finally, also within the I-paradigm, a special class of studies locates creativity not in the individual's personality but in his or her unconscious and acts of sublimation (see Freud 1908/1970; Noppe 1999) or even in pathology (see Eysenck 1994; Richards 1999; Storr 1972). Perhaps the most prominent manifestation of the I-paradigm, though, can be found in *cognitive* studies that look at processes of "creative cognition" (see, for example, Ward, Smith, and Finke 1999). What all these diverse approaches have in common is their attempt to relate creativity to something from *within* the psychology of the person.

The I-paradigm led to advances in theoretical models as well as to new research methodologies (see Mayer 1999). Psychometric approaches flourished, most creativity tests being developed to measure divergent thinking and problem-solving abilities (Barron and Harrington 1981; Sternberg 2003). In the spirit of the I-paradigm, these tests were validated on and applied to non-eminent persons (Runco 2004), but they remained open to criticism because they looked at the end product and not the creative process behind it (Barron and Harrington 1981). Overall, considering both theory and research methods, it can be said that the I-paradigm largely encouraged *methodological reductionism* (Montuori and Purser 1997) by focusing on intrapsychic processes to the exclusion of other levels. This generated partial theoretical models that explore individual cognition and personality in a social vacuum and conceptualize creativity as a quality of the lone individual. The critique of this decontextualized view led to the emergence of the We-paradigm.

2.1.3. The We-Paradigm: Toward a Social Psychology of Creativity

Driven by an attributional error commonly described in psychology, both laypeople and researchers generally attribute creativity to creators' internal dispositions, thus ignoring nondispositional influences (Kasof 1999, 156). In recent decades, several notable attempts have been made to correct this error by initiating research programs that investigate the role of social factors in the creative process (Amabile 1996). Along with these, a new vocabulary emerged, one bringing to the fore terms such as social creativity, that is, the creativity that results from human interaction and collaboration (Purser and Montuori 2000), and group creativity (Nemeth et al. 2003; Paulus, Brown, and Ortega 1999; Paulus and Nijstad 2003). In short, the We-paradigm ambitiously aims to "put the social back" (Hennessey 2003a, 184) into the theory of creativity and starts from the assumption that "creativity takes place within, is constituted and influenced by, and has consequences for, a social context" (Westwood and Low 2003, 236). Rejecting atomistic and positivistic standpoints and adopting *more holistic and systemic ways* of looking at creativity, the psychologists promoting the We-paradigm acknowledge the social nature of creativity (Purser and Montuori 2000), a process that develops out of transactions between self and others and between self and environment (Stein 1975).

However, though formally the social psychology of creativity has been proposed as such by Teresa Amabile since the beginning of the 1980s, much of the work done within it still endorses a vision of the social that corresponds more to individualistic paradigms than to a truly social perspective. In making this claim, I rely on Marková's (2003) discussion of external *ego–alter* relationships envisioning self and other, the individual and the social, as two distinct units. This kind of conceptualization, common in modern social psychology (Farr 1996), ends up portraying the social as an external environment, a set of stimulations that facilitate or constrain the creative act (the "press" factor; Rhodes 1961, cited in Runco 2004), and it therefore remains oblivious to the social roots, social dynamics, and social functions of creativity.

For example, Amabile's social psychology of creativity grants social factors a "crucial role in creative performance" (1996, 6). In her extensive work, she, along with collaborators, used a variety of methods to investigate the role of intrinsic motivation in creativity. Their conclusion, important for the psychology of creativity in general, is formalized as the Intrinsic Motivation Principle of Creativity, which states that intrinsic motivation, or doing something for its own sake, is generally associated with increased creativity, while extrinsic motivation, or doing something for an external goal, often leads to a decrease in creative performance (Amabile 1996; Hennessey 2003a). The role of motivation is reflected in Amabile's *componential model* of creativity comprising domain-relevant skills, creativity-relevant skills, and task motivation. Considering the above, a legitimate question arises: Where is the social in this model? Disappointingly, the answer offered is that "largely because they affect motivation, social factors can have a powerful impact on creativity" (Amabile 1996, 3). This is in tone with the declared aim of Amabile's social psychology of creativity, namely, "To identify particular social and environmental conditions that can positively or negatively influence the creativity of most individuals" (5). Consequently, the discussion of the social in her book is constantly framed in terms of choice, constraints, reward, competition, modeling, stimulation, evaluation, peer pressure, surveillance, etc., and therefore it does not abandon the understanding of creativity as an individual-level phenomenon "conditioned" by social factors.

Other accounts involving the social psychology of creativity depart from the study of the individual and focus on larger societal contexts. Using impressive collections of data on creative persons throughout history and quantifying aspects of the social world and the personal lives of the creators, D. K. Simonton (1975, 1976, 1999) reached several interesting conclusions about the way in which social, cultural, political, and economic factors influence creativity. His ample and fertile research, "the largest systematic program of research in the social psychology of creativity" (Amabile 1996, 213), used *historiometry* as a nomothetic approach to creativity. Though appealing for the rigor of its procedures, this specific methodology greatly influences the choice and selection of subjects as well as the nature of the conclusions. As is suitable to a historiometric analysis, Simonton (1988a) focused on scientific geniuses and, more generally, on "great" creative achievements to the exclusion of more common forms of creativity (something specific to the He-paradigm). Furthermore, the nomothetic orientation aims to unravel general patterns and correlations between factors at the cost of understanding the individual circumstances of the creators.

From the two accounts above, it becomes clear that what a social psychology of creativity needs is the ability to bring together both individuals and societal structures. Systemic models of creativity represent, from this perspective, perhaps the greatest achievements of the We-paradigm. A well-known example is offered by Csikszentmihalyi (1988, 1999), who proposed the connection in the creative production between a *person* (with his or her genetic pool and personal experiences), a *field* (social system), and a *domain* (system of symbols, related to the idea of culture). Though it mainly pays attention to historical creativity rather than more common instances of the phenomenon, this model is nonetheless essential for a We-paradigm, since, as an ecological and systemic approach, it "recognizes the interconnectedness between the self and the environment and attempts to discover relations between them" (Montuori and Purser 1995, 81–82). Furthermore, Csikszentmihalyi (1988) repeatedly stressed the contextual and generative nature of creativity. This means that creativity is explicitly considered as embedded within a social and historical milieu and that every act of creation must start from and build upon the existing knowledge within a "domain." It is because of these qualities that systems approaches in general have a great appeal for psychologists involved in the study of creativity, and we can now find a series of successful applications of these perspectives (e.g., the case of families of gifted children, Moon, Jurich, and Feldhusen 1998).

The systemic and ecological frameworks of the We-paradigm bring a series of advantages. First and foremost, they contextualize creative acts and give a more comprehensive account of how creativity takes place in all its complexity. Second, they are much better equipped to investigate *both* historical creativity (initially the He-paradigm) and everyday creativity (the I-paradigm). Third, on a practical note, they open a new world of opportunities for influencing creative behavior now conceptualized as less dependent on innate abilities and personality traits (Amabile 1996). Despite these benefits, reactions against the We approach didn't take long to materialize. Analyzing the social ethos in much of today's literature on creativity, Runco (1999a) worries that it is misleading and that, in comparing social with individual factors, "it is the social factors that are not necessary for creativity" (237). The author even proposes that we separate creativity from reputation and therefore cut the process from its context, since this would eliminate the "social noise" affecting the inner (and "real") dynamic of creativity. Needless to say, this chapter is intended to show that the social does not "perturb" creativity but *allows* it—for without the social context, there would be no creativity. In the words of Csikszentmihalyi (1988, 336), we must go beyond the Ptolemaic view that places the person in the center of creativity in favor of a more Copernican model. This is also the aim of the newest development within the We-paradigm: the cultural psychology of creativity.

2.2. The Emergence of a Cultural Psychology of Creativity

As argued above, the "social" of the We-paradigm often fails to go beyond an external-influence model and thus fails to see how creativity takes place within relations. In other words, the We-paradigm must rightfully acknowledge the *interdependence* between *ego* and *alter* (Marková 2003, xiii) in the creative act. This is the starting point for one of the newest perspectives in the field: the cultural psychology approach to creativity (see Glăveanu 2008, 2010a). It must be said that this discipline doesn't aim to replace the social psychology of creativity but to build on its conclusions and to reveal "another side" of the We-paradigm: the social and cultural working from *within* the creative person and process. This is the contemporary retake of an old theme in creativity theory, what Arieti (1976) called the "individual-psychological versus the sociocultural origin of creativity" (303). The cultural psychology position in this debate is that there is no versus between the two and, furthermore, that these two "segments" are not isolated but rather are elements that *co-constitute* each other.

Before introducing in more detail a cultural psychology framework of creativity, I will briefly discuss the characteristics of cultural psychology and focus on reviewing some theories or concepts within this discipline that address or could address the problem of creativity.

2.2.1. Creativity and Cultural Psychology

Not only are cultural psychology perspectives on creativity relatively recent, but cultural (or sociocultural) psychology itself has only (re)taken shape in the last few decades; it is now not a unified but an emergent field. Reacting to the search for inbuilt and universal processing mechanisms that took over general and cross-cultural psychology after the cognitive revolution, cultural psychology is, in the words of Shweder (1990), a study of how "cultural traditions and social practices regulate, express, transform, and permute the human psyche" (1). To understand these processes, cultural psychologists start from the basic premise of the interdependence between human beings and their sociocultural context. Therefore, the focus is not on the two as separate entities but on the *transactions* that define both of them and generate a symbolic world (Zittoun 2007b). This symbolic world grows out of processes of meaning-making and co-construction of knowledge (Valsiner and Rosa 2007), and this is why cultural psychology envisions human existence as essentially *mediated* through the system of symbols and norms that constitute culture. Consequently, the research focus in cultural psychology is on mediated action in context, on the sociocultural genesis of mental functions, and on the analysis of everyday life (Cole 1996, 104).

As a paradigm that examines systemic, interactive, and mediated phenomena (Zittoun et al. 2007, 208), cultural psychology developed a specific understanding of culture, described as a web of significance, an interworked system of construable signs, not external power but *context* (Geertz 1973). Furthermore, these meanings and symbols "stick" through time (Jovchelovitch 2007); they are preserved and transmitted to new generations, offering our symbolic universe a certain degree of stability. Simultaneously, they are open to change, elaboration, and transformation through collective processes of action and communication. Perspectives on culture that emphasize the construction and use of mediators are most easily integrated by cultural psychology, as, for example, in Michael Cole's (1996) understanding of culture as a system of accumulated artifacts of a group (110). The artifact, at once material and conceptual in nature (with illustrations ranging from language to pottery), mediates the relation between subject and object and is a result of communication between self and other (persons, groups, or societies).

In this context, creativity both relies on the accumulated artifacts and enriches culture through the generation of new artifacts. As such, creative processes should constitute a key point of interest for the discipline of cultural psychology. While there is so far no "formally" constructed cultural psychology of creativity, several sociocultural directions have recently inspired empirical research on collaborative creativity, resulting in books (see Littleton and Miell 2004) and journal special issues (see *Thinking Skills and Creativity*, March 2008). At a theoretical level, different traditions within cultural psychology can be built upon in constructing a cultural psychology of creativity; from them, the cultural-historical Russian school, and especially the writings of Lev Vygotsky, are particularly relevant. As one of the father figures of cultural psychology, Vygotsky (1960/1997) pointed to the importance of cultural mediation through tools and signs for the development of all higher mental functions. Vygotsky's early work on imagination and creativity in childhood (Vygotsky 1930/1998) laid the foundations for a cultural approach to creativity by asserting that 1) creativity exists in the everyday and not only in great historical works and 2) every creator is a product of his or her time and environment. What transpires from the cultural-historical perspective is that creators use culturally constructed symbols and tools to produce new cultural artifacts (see also Moran and John-Steiner 2003). Furthermore, Vygotsky was primarily interested in the ontogenesis and microgenesis of creativity and in creativity as a process occurring in real-life "collaborations" (like those between child and adult). It is because of these preoccupations that the Vygotskian perspective remains central to any cultural perspective on creativity, and this includes the proposed framework to be discussed later in the chapter. This framework also combines ideas from several lines of thought, three of which are briefly presented below: Winnicott and the notion of potential space, dialogicality and creativity as dialogue, and the everyday use of symbolic resources.

Similar to Vygotsky, "who proposed that creative imagination develops from children's symbolic play interactions with caregivers" (Smolucha 1992, 51), Winnicott (1971) developed an important thesis claiming that creativity and cultural experience are twinborn in the potential or transitional space through creative playing in early childhood. The notion of potential space, central to the conception of the Winnicott, is that of a relational space "between the individual and the environment" (100), a space of experiencing the world situated between inner self and external life; this notion came to be equated with the area of intersubjectivity. Creativity, therefore, has a strong social basis as it *emerges primarily in a relationship*, namely, that between the mother and the child. Besides establishing creativity as relational, Winnicott's account can be considered an excellent theoretization of everyday creativity in its most basic expression. For him, creativity is not embodied in products; rather, it is primarily a process, what he describes as "creative living," a healthy way of living that leaves room for personal expression and spontaneity.

If Winnicott's account can give us an idea of *where* creativity is located—in the space of interrelations—we further need to understand *how* exactly creativity emerges in relations. This is where notions of dialogue and dialogicality become instrumental.

> Dialogue is the meeting ground on which new questions are raised, the mating ground on which new combinations are found, and the testing ground in which novelties are critically evaluated and assimilated into the body of shared knowledge and thought. (Gruber 1998, 139)

Continuing his argument, Gruber asserts that all creativity requires, at least at certain points in the process, some form of communication or social exchange. This is not only applicable to explicit moments of social interaction because, for the cultural psychologist, the human mind is dialogical, meaning it can "conceive, create and communicate about social realities in terms of the '*Alter*'" (Marková 2003, xiii). The relevance of this perspective is supported by Barrett (1999), who recognized knowledge creation, therefore both thinking and creativity, as an *inherently* social-dialogical processes. This means that even when we are alone and apparently creating in complete solitude, we are still engaged in dialogue with internalized "parties" such as our mentors, our audience, and our critics. In the words of Negus and Pickering (2004, 23), creativity entails a communicative experience involving intersubjectivity and interactive dialogue. This dialogue is made possible by the use of cultural elements, and it is these elements that constitute the substance of our creative acts. A question remains, however, of *when* we are more likely to use cultural elements in a creative manner.

This leads us, finally, to the notion of *symbolic resources* as developed by Zittoun (2007a, 2007b). The main thesis of this conception is that whenever people find themselves facing a discontinuity—that is, a break or rupture of their taken-for-granted ordinary experience (of their inner self or of the relations with others or the environment)—they engage in processes specific to *transitions* and resort to symbolic resources to elaborate meaning and externalize the outcome (Zittoun et al. 2003; Zittoun 2007b). Needless to say, this outcome (not necessarily material) is most often creative, especially since it comes out of a situation where there is no learned or practiced solution (Torrance 1988). To qualify as a symbolic resource, the element must be used by someone for something, usually recontextualizing meaning into a newly resulting sociocultural formation (Zittoun et al. 2003, 418). Symbolic resources vary in nature, from concrete artifacts to conceptual and procedural elements. All symbolic resources emerge from social interaction (Zittoun 2007a) and require a symbolic labor—the work needed, in the terms of Willis (1990, 9), "to ensure the daily production and reproduction of human existence."

From the perspectives outlined above, some conclusions can be drawn regarding the cultural psychology conceptualization of creativity: (1) *it considers creative acts as sociocultural in nature and origin*; (2) *it stresses the role of intersubjectivity and dialogical interaction in the creative expression*; and (3) *it looks at how cultural symbolic elements come to form the texture of new and creative products.* All these basic premises are therefore at the core of the creativity framework discussed in the next section.

2.2.2. A Cultural Psychology Framework for Creativity and Its Implications

Definition and theoretical framework. As mentioned earlier, until now no "cultural psychology of creativity" has been formally constructed. Nonetheless, important theoretical leads, as previously reviewed, can support such a construction. A *cultural definition of creativity* would need to take into account the social embeddedness of creative acts as well as their relation to cultural resources. In the literature on creativity, some of these features tend to appear in a number of definitions:

> A creative individual solves problems, fashions products, or poses new questions within a domain in a way that is initially considered to be unusual but is eventually accepted within at least one cultural group. (Gardner 1994, 145)

> I define creativity as activity that produces something new through the recombination and transformation of existing cultural practices or forms. (Liep 2001, 2)

> Much human creativity is social, arising from activities that take place in a context in which interaction with other people and the artifacts that embody collective knowledge are essential contributors. (Fischer et al. 2005, 482)

Supported by these formulations, I will define creativity from a cultural perspective as *a complex sociocultural-psychological process that, by working with "culturally impregnated" materials within an intersubjective space, leads to the generation of artifacts that are evaluated as new and significant by one or more persons or communities at a given time.* As presented above, the sociocultural-psychological process is a dialogical one, the "culturally impregnated" materials are symbolic resources (signs and tools in a Vygotskian perspective) used in creative acts, and the intersubjective space is a potential space between creator and community. Adopting this definition opens up a new world of possibilities for studying creativity without individualizing it or looking exclusively at its cognitive aspects. In fact, the cultural psychology of creativity as proposed here "places" creativity inside the tetradic framework depicted in Figure 2.1.

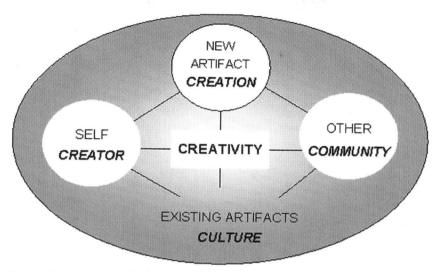

Figure 2.1. A proposed cultural framework of creativity.

In this framework, the *new artifact* (material or conceptual) is seen as emerging within the relation between *self* (creator) and *others* (broadly understood as a *community*), all three being immersed into and in dialogue with an existing body of *cultural artifacts, symbols,* and *established norms.* This model is not structural but dynamic because it is in the "tensions" between all four elements that creativity takes shape, with the "new artifact" becoming part of "existing culture" (for self and/or community) and constantly alimenting the creative cycle. As Zittoun et al. (2003, 441) suggest, "With the use of symbolic resources, there is always something produced, something externalized, which is attached to the producer primarily by the gaze of the other." This implies the strong links between the creative outcome and the identity of the creator (or creators), as well as the role of the other in constructing this identity. At the same time, creativity could not exist outside of our relation with other people within a cultural setting, since every new artifact needs constant meaning-making processes to make sense of it; this becomes possible only by using what Bruner (1990) calls interpretative procedures. Of key importance in the cultural psychology approach is that these interpretations are always context-dependent (Montuori and Purser 1995), and, therefore, there is no "real" or "objective" creativity but rather one that is constructed within communities, in relation to authors and creative products.

Another conclusion derived from this framework is that creativity is a generative process; it is connected to previous knowledge and cultural repertoires and is in a dialogical relationship with the "old" or the "already-there." Innovative ideas or objects never come ex nihilo, as in the romantic visions of the genius specific to the He-paradigm. This aspect was recognized early on in the literature: "Human creativity uses what is already existing and available and changes it in unpredictable ways" (Arieti 1976, 4; see also Hennessey 2003a; Liep 2001; Negus and Pickering 2004). Moreover, a history of misconception of what *tradition* is needs to be challenged. In the creativity framework above, tradition and previous knowledge are part and parcel of the creative process, since, as Feldman (1974, 68) notes, "All creative thought springs from a base of cultural knowledge and is therefore, by definition, part of a cultural tradition—even when it breaks with tradition." Furthermore, tradition itself is not a predetermined, singular, rigid, and abstract cultural entity (Negus and Pickering 2004); creativity and tradition are interpenetrated and, in all cases, the emergence and meaning of innovation is bound up with tradition (Wilson 1984).

Alongside these theoretical considerations, the cultural psychology framework presented above has a potentially strong influence on creativity research. The problems under the scrutiny of sociocultural psychologists correspond to the four composing elements of the tetradic framework and their interrelations. For example, when we look at the creative "self"—that is, the author or authors of the creative outcome—one central aspect to be investigated has to do with identity and especially "creative identities": how they are constructed, reconstructed, and manifested while performing the creative task and outside of the creative task. When focusing on "others"—the community or communities with which creators are in dialogue—it would be interesting to observe how members of different communities assess the creativity of one and the same artifact. Changing to "previous knowledge," three questions arise: How is it used in the creative act? What artifacts from our cultural repertoires become activated, turning into symbolic resources that sustain the creative activity? How do they combine in order to generate a novel output? This leads to the "new artifact" and the meaning-making processes taking place around the "new": how it is understood by both creator, community, and even society at large; how it is anchored and made familiar (to use a social representations theory terminology; Moscovici 2000a); and how it becomes part of the existing set of artifacts allowing further creative cycles to take place. Above all, what should come to the fore are the dialogical connections between self and other and between previous knowledge and new artifact; these are considered in any cultural research in their unity, as a dynamic and ecological whole.

What principally distinguishes cultural research on creativity is the *emic* perspective on the phenomenon (see Smith and Bond 1998). This ultimately means that researchers are advised to go to the field with the least amount of preconceptions about what creativity is or should be and to connect to the local ways of sense-making specific to the setting they are investigating. An emic-oriented researcher would be very careful about applying "scientific" Western notions of creativity to other parts of the world (for a discussion, see Westwood and Low 2003, 237–238). Consequently, social "constructions" of what a certain creative outcome is, how creative it is, and, above all, what creativity is, are all to be carefully collected from participants in order to capture how both the "image" and the "manifestation" of creativity are interrelated in any particular cultural setting.

Relevance and implications of the cultural psychology framework. The cultural psychology of creativity and, more specifically, the tetradic framework discussed above represent a proposition for a novel approach to creativity rather than a definite theory. It is a work in progress that, despite its general and abstract formulation at this stage, could greatly improve our understanding of creativity. The present chapter attempted to put forward a broad formulation of a cultural psychology of creativity that draws from both sociocultural theories (notions of artifacts and symbolic resources, the theory of dialogicality, etc.) and social, systemic models of creativity. What these two perspectives have in common are a rejection of an individualistic and reductionist view of creativity as a purely individual phenomenon and an emphasis on the role of self–other relations in creative acts.

In this regard, using a cultural psychology approach improves existing social-psychological accounts by going beyond the perspective of the social as an environment that constrains or facilitates creative acts. Creativity is not simply "conditioned" by social factors; rather, its very nature is relational because it could not exist outside of cultural resources and dialogical relations. The tetradic framework further elaborates current systemic models, such as that of Csikszentmihalyi, by using a *broader conceptualization* of the "field" (social structures) and the "domain" (cultural structures). While systemic models are useful for the analysis of socially valuable creations (cases of historical creativity), the cultural model aims to be relevant for the study of various forms of creativity, from "minor" creative expressions to revolutionary creations. In order to accomplish this, it conceives the field and domain in a more flexible and less "institutional" manner. The "field," seen as a group of experts allowing or not allowing the creation to enter a certain domain, is only a particular instance of the possible role that "others" play in the process of creativity. The notion of "other/community" used in the tetradic framework thus allows us to capture more facets of the "other": from persons in the vicinity of the creator to the members of different social groups that the creator is part of and, finally, to the institutions that validate a work as being creative or not. Similarly, the "domain" is more than a structured field of knowledge (such as a scientific branch or an artistic discipline) that will, in the end, incorporate or reject the creation. The notion of "existing artifacts/culture" I referred to in the cultural framework incorporates all forms of material and symbolic resources that inform the creative process, and these can be drawn from several "domains" as well as from commonsense knowledge. More fundamentally, the cultural psychology perspective advocates the *multiplicity* of "fields" and "domains" with which a person engages during any form of creative activity and the

33

necessity of studying as many levels of the "social and cultural" context of the phenomenon as possible, in order to gain a more comprehensive understanding of each particular situation. The theoretical position of cultural psychology sets two specific and interrelated goals for any sociocultural approach to creativity: (1) to unpack the microgenesis of creativity in community settings and (2) to operate with a contextual definition of creativity, dependent upon "local" or "folk" notions of creativity.

These two aims have a series of consequences for how we theorize and study creativity. The theoretical implication involves a reconceptualization of the levels of creativity by locating all of them at a community level. Thus, the practical implication refers to creativity assessment and the need for a more ecological and contextualized way of appreciating creative outcomes. Both of these are discussed as follows.

From a cultural psychology perspective, thinking in terms of *polarities*— such as P-creativity (creative for the person) and H-creativity (creative for society) (Boden 1994) or youthful creativity and mature creativity (Cohen and Ambrose 1999), or, respectively, "little c" and "Big C" (Paulus and Nijstad 2003)—is generally misleading. From the beginning these suggest a hierarchy in creativity that often trivializes the notion of everyday creativity (Bateson 1999). Also, though it is largely acknowledged nowadays that there is a continuum in creative expression (for steps in this continuum, see Cohen and Ambrose 1999), the habit of dichotomizing creativity can only disconnect the different modalities of being creative. Finally, this polarization also introduces the risk of unwillingly promoting the "dissolution" of creativity, either by considering every human act as creative or by setting standards for creativity so high that the vast majority of people could never reach it (Negus and Pickering 2004). What solution can be proposed?

A possible answer, reflective of the cultural psychology approach, is to acknowledge the social and cultural roots of *all types* of creative expression, from personal to historical. From this perspective, though there are numerous differences between the works of art of an established modernist painter and the drawings of a toddler, in the end they both emerge within a social context and through the use of cultural means. Creativity always takes place in a community, and the creative outcome is generally of interest for multiple communities. This helps us "relocate" creativity from the extremes (person or society) to the "middle" and, through this, to give it a more sensible position (Glăveanu 2010a; a similar assertion has been recently presented by Eteläpelto and Lahti 2008). As mentioned above, the notion of "field" from systemic models of creativity takes on a new meaning when social groups are theorized as *communities*. A community is not understood only in its topographical sense or as a local social system; it necessarily requires the existence of communion, of close ties and the feeling of belongingness between its members (see Urry 2007), and it can describe different social realities, from small groups to organizations and larger social structures. Communities exist where they are felt and experienced as such (Jovchelovitch 2007). Most importantly, communities support their own culture (Duveen 2007), and it is in communities that people find not only the resources they need to create but also the "parameters" for making sense of the world (Jovchelovitch 2007) and all its creative, new artifacts.

This last suggestion has direct implications for *assessing creativity*. As repeatedly argued, "The creativity of an idea depends not just on the content of the idea but the way in which that idea is developed, presented and inter- preted" (Bilton 2007, 6). This fact is stressed by most definitions of creativity (see Fischer et al. 2005; Gardner 1994; Stein 1962). The argument that "cre- ativity is socially defined" (Nijstad and Paulus 2003, 339) gives even more impetus to social and cultural psychologists by showing that there would be no creativity without others to appreciate it as such. In fact, what this approach affirms is that creativity is not inherent in artifacts or persons but is *socially attributed* to them. Furthermore, all judgments about creativity are histori- cally located—there is no "view from nowhere," that is, an absolute statement about what is or is not creative. Understanding how and why different social groups attribute creativity differently (or similarly) is one of the main tasks of a cultural psychology of creativity. And this is because being creative always means being creative *for someone* (person, group, society) in a particular time and place. Under these circumstances, the traditional practice of assessing creativity with the use of experts—that is, trained persons able to formulate "informed" opinions—offers only a partial picture. This practice further con- tributes to associating creativity only with certain types of "specialist" fields, such as art, technology, or science. It presupposes working with predetermined and universal definitions of creativity, and it therefore adopts an etic stand, as opposed to an emic one that is open to the local (personal and/or community) understandings of what is and is not creative.

But, as Amabile (1996) demonstrates through her Consensual Assessment Technique (also Hennessey 2003b), there is generally no need for already-made definitions. The basic assumption of this method is that appropriate observers (again, usually with some formal training in the field) implicitly work with similar notions about what is creative, despite the fact that they are not for- malized or given. Without getting into its details, this technique is based on the idea of consensus—of converging beliefs and perceptions about creativity.

From a cultural psychology perspective, creativity assessment should be as "ecological" as possible and should *rely on multiple feedback at the cost of getting diverging opinions* (and, to an extent, pursuing exactly that; see Chapter 4). More precisely, creative products and processes should be assessed by mem- bers of significant or relevant communities, which are those "affected" by or in contact with the creative work, as well as by the creators themselves. For example, a teenager's artwork should be subject not only to the judgments of experts (persons trained in art) but also to the judgment of peers, parents, teachers, and members of other groups and communities that see the creative productions or are generally interested in art (such as other artists and potential buyers). Since the creative outcome requires meaning-making processes and these, in turn, depend on the particular sociocultural circumstances of the persons attributing meaning, the "multiple feedback" is often less consensual but far more useful, including for the teenager in our example. The importance of this perspective resides in its simultaneous focus, in real-life contexts, on (a) the reasons behind attributions of creativity by several social actors, (b) the functions these attributions serve, and (c) the consequences they have for both creator and creative process. This technique certainly does not aim to promote the idea that higher consensus between different groups would validate something as being "in reality" creative, because the search for such "ultimate" and "objective" statements goes *against* the constructionist nature of the investigation. It also does not reject scientific or expert appreciations about the creativity of certain outcomes; rather, it considers them as one form of assessment among others, such as assessment provided by nonexpert but nevertheless relevant groups of persons connected in one way or another to the "creation." Since the meaning-making processes around creativity and their link to particular social milieus are paramount, there is no hierarchy of viewpoints to be established.

2.3. Concluding Remarks about the Future of the We-Paradigm

As argued in this chapter, there are three major paradigms that have shaped and continue to influence the trajectory of creativity in psychology. Historically, individualistic approaches constitute the norm, locating creativity either inside "unique" individuals (the He-paradigm) or inside each and every person taken separately (the I-paradigm). It is only in the last few decades that more emphasis has been placed on the role of social factors in the creative process. These are the first signs of a new paradigm, the We-paradigm, which aims to develop systemic approaches to creativity—that is, comprehensive views that incorporate multiple levels, from individuals and interpersonal interactions to groups and cultures (Simonton 2003b, 320). And yet, the whole project of the We-paradigm could be derailed by letting the theoretization go only halfway. This "incomplete" vision sees the social and cultural as coercive instances, as an environment that has the power to facilitate or inhibit creative expression. In the end, the person still sits "alone," self-contained and self-sufficient, ready to confront the "system" and, if "creative enough," to defeat it.

The cultural psychology of creativity advocated herein seeks to take a step forward in consolidating the We-paradigm. For those looking for universalistic claims and "fit-all" models of creativity, this approach will be disappointing. It has no "formulas" (Littleton and Miell 2004, 2) and promotes the *contextual and situated study* of creative acts, persons, and communities. What the cultural psychology of creativity will have to offer are, first and foremost, research examples of "good practice" and theoretical approaches that attempt to see creativity in all its complexity. This new direction also brings with it practical consequences outside of the scientific realm. One has already been formulated by Montuori and Purser (1995, 104): a shift from our cultural project of dominating the environment to nurturing and engendering creative relationships within it. It presents to us our responsibility as community members to build spaces for dialogue and creativity for both self and others; it reminds us that we live interconnected with other people, and thus our creative expression should be able to fertilize the common soil of creativity.

It is difficult to make predictions about the direction in which creativity theory will move. While the future of the We-paradigm is uncertain, the future of creativity in psychology is surely looking bright. As long as psychologists find creativity crucial to our adaptability, self-expression, and health (Runco 2004), it will continue to attract the interest of both theorists and researchers. But we should remember that creativity also exists beyond psychology. As Magyari-Beck (1999) argues when describing the new science of *creatology*, the nature of creativity research is increasingly cross-disciplinary, bringing together psychologists, sociologists, artists, educators, historians, managers, and economists in a common enterprise. Perhaps at this broader level, the We-paradigm will more rapidly become influential, and sociocultural psychologists could play a key role in this future development.

3

Creativity as Cultural Participation[1]

Mountain peaks do not float unsupported; they do not even just rest upon the earth. They are the earth in one of its manifest operations.

(Dewey 1934, 2)

Understanding creativity means understanding the various systems that contribute to its development and manifestation: from the biological to the cultural, from individual expression to social dynamics. This systemic view dominates today's literature on the topic, being explicitly adopted by Hennessey and Amabile (2010) in their most recent Annual Review presentation on creativity. The two authors, while supportive of this approach, also warned against fragmentation and lack of dialogue between specialists working at different "ends" of the creativity system. By definition, a system includes both components and interactions, and "the 'whole' of the creative process must be viewed as much more than a simple sum of its parts" (Hennessey and Amabile 2010, 571). And yet creativity in psychology has been very often "read" at only one level, the individual one, and only relatively recently have social and cultural perspectives been acknowledged as valuable for its study. This chapter aims to bring the two general levels of analysis together, arguing against segmentation and partial understandings that treat creativity as *either* individual *or* sociocultural. The main argument developed here is that creativity is *both* individual *and* sociocultural, mainly because individuals themselves are sociocultural beings. As a consequence, creative expression is also a form of cultural expression and, ultimately, one of the most illustrative forms of *cultural participation*: engaging with cultural artifacts to produce new cultural artifacts; employing culture to generate culture.

[1] Reprinted with permission from Journal for the Theory of Social Behaviour, 41(1), Glăveanu, V. P., Creativity as cultural participation, 48–67, © 2010 by the Author. Journal for the Theory of Social Behaviour © 2010 by The Executive Management Committee/Blackwell Publishing Ltd.

Creativity, or the capacity to bring about the new, has always fascinated mankind. This is reflected both in the numerous attempts to conceptualize creativity (in disciplines that range from philosophy and theology to neuroscience) and in the strong contemporary belief that creativity is "good for the economy, good for the individual, good for society and good for education" (Jeffrey and Craft 2001, 11). However, the complexity of the phenomenon presented to specialists several "difficulties of meaning" (Williams 1961, 3) and made E. P. Torrance (1988, 43), a towering figure in the psychology of creativity, state that "creativity defies precise definition." Owing to this complexity, creativity has been approached differently, as achievement and ability or as disposition and attitude (Barron and Harrington 1981, 441). Very fruitful for scientific investigation are those definitions that focus on the *creative product*, and in this regard there is quite a general consensus among specialists that something is creative when it is both new and useful, appropriate, or meaningful (see Stein 1953; Martindale 1994; Richards 1999). Other authors have added criteria to this traditional "pair": the heuristic task (Amabile 1996), purpose and duration (Gruber and Wallace 1999), and the conscious intention to create (Craft 2001).

In the end, to simplify the presentation, one can identify two basic perspectives on creativity that dominate today's theoretical landscape. In the words of Sefton-Green (2000, 220) these are the *romantic* and the *cultural* models of creativity. In essence, this distinction signals a deep and fundamental division between how scholars perceive—and consequently, study—creativity. Following a traditional "romantic" model means associating creativity with great creators and great creative achievements. Working within a cultural framework is reflected in greater concern for the social and cultural context of creativity and its everyday dynamics. The romantic view, heavily enforced by the eighteenth-century portrait of the genius (Banaji, Burn, and Buckingham 2006), defines creators as exceptional, fertile, superior, and often "pathological" (Montuori and Purser 1995; Mason 2003; Negus and Pickering 2004). This traditional position proposes a reading in which

> creativity is on the side not only of innovation against convention, but also of the exceptional individual against the collectivity, of the present moment against the weight of the past, and of mind or intelligence against inert matter. (Ingold and Hallam 2007, 3)

These dichotomies have critical consequences for the ways in which we characterize creativity—how we "discover" or "validate" it in the real world, including how we come to evaluate our own creative potential. Challenging "lone genius" and individualistic perspectives that dominated the first half of the twentieth century (see Barron 1995; Paulus and Nijstad 2003; Craft 2005; Glăveanu 2010b; Chapter 2), some researchers during the past three decades brought a general shift "from person-centered to social dynamic conceptions of creative cognition" (John-Steiner 1992, 99), "away from naturalism and individualism towards social understandings" (Jones 2009, 63). In this context, sociocultural theories of creativity and of learning were reaffirmed, and it became generally recognized that "culture clearly has a profound influence on the conceptualisation of creativity and on creative expression" (Rudowicz 2003, 285). It is precisely the nature of this "influence" that will be discussed in more detail throughout the present chapter, starting with understanding creativity as a cultural act and continuing with the analysis of this "act" in terms of its main actors and processes.

3.1. Creativity as a Cultural Act

The key assertion supported here is that creativity is a *sociocultural-psychological process*, and this means that creative expression is *at once* an individual, social, and cultural act. Creativity is individual because it relies on the individual's set of abilities and types of knowledge as expressed in the production of the creative outcome. Creativity is sociocultural because: (a) the set of skills and types of knowledge that individual actors possess are developed through social interaction; (b) creativity in itself is often the result of explicit moments of collaboration between individuals; (c) creativity is largely defined by social judgement or validation; and (d) creativity exists only in relation to an established ensemble of cultural norms and products that both aliment the creative process and integrate its "outcomes." This last point deserves particular attention because it postulates a very close connection between creativity and culture—an acknowledgement that led anthropologists like Wagner (1981, 35) to affirm that invention *is* culture. The "new" and the "old," in their never-ending interaction, characterize human culture and also define each other through this very process. To use a suggestive illustration for this kind of interdependence, one can think of the yin-yang symbol. The two "terms" exist only in their interaction and contain in themselves the seed of their opposite.

Figure 3.1 synthesizes a conception of creativity that brings together "self" and "others," the "new" and the "old," and captures the intricate relationships that tie them together in the form of creative activity. At the core of this diagram we find the fundamental relationship between creator, creation, and audience (what in art, for example, is the "core trinity of creator, work, and perceiver," R. Wilson 1986, 110; also Dewey 1934). Audience has been chosen here as a general term that signifies all "instances of the other" that are involved in the creative act. Stein (1953, 320), when using this term, referred for example to critics, patrons, followers, and "the population at large." At least three major instances of "audience" can be identified in this context: collaborators (persons who directly contribute to the creative work), users (persons who utilize the creation), and perceivers (persons who are simply in contact with the creation). All the elements of this creator-creation-audience triad are immersed in culture—that is, in a world of existing artifacts in the form of material objects, beliefs, norms, values, representations, conventions, and everything else that makes up the life of human communities (see Glăveanu 2010b; Chapter 2).

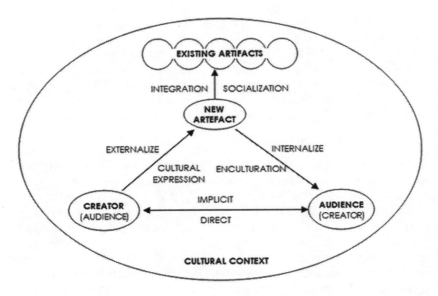

Figure 3.1. Creativity as a sociocultural-psychological process.

The framework discussed here relies on models and terms elaborated by several authors, including Ernest Boesch and, in particular, the cultural-historical Russian psychologist Lev Vygotsky. In one of his essays, "The sound of the violin," Boesch (1997, 183) described the invention of an object as a form of *objectivation*, the mastering of the object as *subjectivation*, and the integration of the object in "common frameworks of action and ideation" as *socialization*. Furthermore, the mastery of any object or subjectivation is in itself a form of *enculturation* of the user and the objectivation or production of the object can be considered as a form of *cultural expression*. In a similar vein, Lev Vygotsky discussed in his work the processes of *externalization*, resulting in "materialized meanings," and *internalization*, "the appropriation of cultural tools and social interaction" (Moran and John-Steiner 2003, 63). Creativity in his model, according to Moran and John-Steiner, is equated mostly with the act of externalization, while internalizations lead to development, allowing the creative cycle to continue. Figure 3.1 proposes a view founded on the same basic assumptions: (a) the creator is the "audience" for all the creations of others and "audience" members become creators by using new and existing artifacts and (b) creator, audience, and creation exist and function in a sociocultural setting described by social relations and accumulated cultural artifacts. Furthermore, several very important ideas come out of these distinctions, as presented in Figure 3.1:

1. Creative acts are simultaneously forms of externalization and cultural expression.

2. The "creation" is always socialized or integrated in preexisting cultural ensembles, and this requires social agreement and interaction.
3. Audience members internalize creations as part of enculturation.
4. Creators and audiences interact in multiple and dynamic ways in the creative act and in the reception of the creation.

In the following sections, each one of these points will be analyzed separately in order to gain a better understanding of the *microgenesis* of creative acts, from "great" creative achievements to the "minor" creations of everyday life. This is a difficult task because the processes described above are interconnected and concurrently contribute to the generation of the new. The final conclusions will refer to key implications of adopting this perspective on creativity.

3.1.1. *Externalization and Cultural Expression*

Creativity requires some form of externalization. Creative ideas can be put into words, into music, into drawings and schemes, into physical objects, etc. When it comes to artistic creativity, for example, it is obvious that most ideas take some kind of physical form, "*something* which can be seen, heard, held" (Becker 2008, 3). Artistic products serve therefore as "extensions of the individual projected into the world and materialized in visual and physical forms" (Zittoun et al. 2003, 429). They are expressive of the creator as well as the sociocultural context of the creator—something that is easily forgotten by strictly cognitive theories of creativity. The individualization of the creative process has led to the general opinion that creativity takes place "in the mind" as a kind of unseen, personal, and mysterious process unfolding more or less quietly in a social vacuum until expressed by the creator in some form of behavior. Of course, one can agree that creativity presents, alongside extrapsychic manifestations, intrapsychic dynamics and outcomes (see Barron 1995, 31), but at the same time it could be argued that there are no cases of absolute nonexternalization of creativity. Human beings think, feel, and act, and among these there is generally a unity and coordinated expression that is well reflected by creative processes. In the words of Negus and Pickering (2004, 22), "Creative experience requires a will to expression, and to communication with others."

In effect, since early beginnings, creativity, or the act of creating, has been associated with the generation of products through processes of externalization. Historical analyses of existing literature on the topic from the eighteenth and nineteenth centuries reveal, for example, that the three main metaphors used to describe creativity were expression, production, and revolution (Joas 1996). Creativity is meant to leave a "mark" on the world—on the lives of individuals, communities, and often entire societies—and this, to a certain extent, is its defining characteristic. Creative "externalizations" or "objectivations" have been so glorified by romantic views of creativity that, in the field of fine arts for example,

> When an art product once attains classic status, it somehow becomes isolated from the human conditions under which it was brought into being and from the human consequences it engenders in actual life-experience. (Dewey 1934, 1)

The "obsession" with creative products continued deep into the nineteenth century, and when psychologists started to increasingly focus on the issue of creativity, the *product approach* was readily adopted for purposes of definition and measurement. Among the most popular approaches to creativity today, Amabile's (1996) consensual definition and consensual assessment technique both revolve around the evaluation of creative products. How else would we be able to identify and study creativity in the absence of any form of externalization? Would creators themselves be able to identify something as creative in the absence of externalization and social interaction?

If traditional psychology speaks about creative products, using here the notion of *artifact* serves to underline the sociocultural nature of every creation, however "minor" it might be in terms of utility or value. An artifact, as described by Michael Cole (1996, 117), is simultaneously ideal (conceptual) and material ("objectivized" in a certain form). Artifacts are not made by individuals nor do they exist only for individuals; they require communication, attribution of meaning, and mediation between self and other—that is, between creator and members of the audience. Artifacts emerge and exist only in relation to other people and other artifacts, and only in a cultural system. This is the idea that Feldman (1988, 288) emphasized when arguing that "artifacts of creative work are available to the person who desires to make further changes in the world."

Once it is established that new artifacts emerge in a creative process of externalization or objectivation, it is necessary to understand what this process actually consists of. This is certainly one of the most difficult questions, and it stands at the core of creativity studies because it inquires about the nature of the creative process itself. This chapter is intended not to address this general and wide-ranging interrogation but rather to appreciate the cultural dimension intrinsic to creative externalizations. Hence, it should be noted that mainstream psychological theory associates creativity with certain kinds of *thinking processes*, especially divergent forms of thinking, and evaluates the properties of such thinking through tests that score certain qualities of creative products (see Runco 2004). The cognitive perspective, though excessively individualistic, is of course not to be altogether dismissed, and decades of research done under its auspices has produced interesting conclusions about the mental dynamics of creativity. Yet, the "connection" with the outside—that is, the social and cultural world—and the permanent exchange between creator and environment in the form of perpetual externalizations and internalizations constitutes the key to achieving a more comprehensive view of the creative process. In this regard, recuperating some old ideas, such as those of Piaget, may prove to be crucial to a better grasp of the phenomenon. Piaget is not acknowledged for writing on creativity, but his entire life's work dealt, in essence, with the issue of knowledge construction.

Ayman-Nolley's (1999) insightful discussion of Piaget's "theory of creativity" is very useful in this context. According to this perspective, creativity can be easily understood as the interplay between assimilation and accommodation processes. If we are to distinguish (as artificial as it may be) between creative thought and creative action (both essential for the whole process of externalization referred to here), then it becomes transparent that, in a Piagetian framework, assimilation is the primary process supporting creative thought, denoting a playful engagement with elements from reality, while accommodation dominates creative action as a stage of testing and adjusting the creative idea to external conditions. This is certainly a great simplification since, in effect, assimilation and accommodation are *dialectic* and *intertwined* in both creative thought and action (Ayman-Nolley 1999, 270). This perspective enriches our understanding of what is called here "externalization" and points to the fact that this process is less unitary than we may think. It also testifies to the dynamism of the framework depicted in Figure 3.1, where "externalization" and "internalization" are separated solely for analytical purposes.

Finally, even after a discussion about the mechanisms of the creative process, a question remains: Are creative externalizations also acts of cultural expression? If they are, is this the case for *all* of them or just for the rare "big" creative achievements? The perspective advocated here supports the view that all creative externalizations are simultaneously forms of cultural expression and that whenever we bring about the new, even in insignificant ways, we are dealing with cultural production. But this of course means operating with a broad definition of culture that encompasses both its "macro" and "micro" levels, both the art gallery or the inventors' fair and the everyday life of the streets, parks, and family homes. Nonetheless, as we will see, not all theorists endorse such a vision of culture and creativity.

3.1.2. Socialization of the Creative Artifact

The creative artifact is "socialized" through its integration in a cultural system of existing artifacts, a process that is dependent upon social interaction and validation. The idea of "integration" as used here designates several processes that can take place after the new artifact is "externalized": anchoring in existing systems of knowledge and practice, communication about and around the new artifact, social appreciation and use by the creator or other people, etc. In all these there is an almost implicit notion that others are involved in the socialization of the creation. This part of the creative process is by no means peripheral or redundant in comparison to the "externalization" or actual generation moment, and this is because no creative act is complete without being acknowledged, recognized, valued, and used. Such ideas are the cornerstone of one of the best-known systemic models of creativity: that proposed by Mihaly Csikszentmihalyi (1988, 1999). After decades of research, Csikszentmihalyi reached the conclusion that we cannot understand the creativity of individuals outside of their particular social and historical milieus. In fact, creativity takes place in the interaction between three systems:

> A set of social institutions, or *field*, that selects from the variations produced by individuals those that are worth preserving; a stable cultural *domain* that will preserve and transmit the selected new ideas or forms to the following generations; and finally the *individual*, who brings about some change in the domain, a change that the field will consider to be creative. (Csikszentmihalyi 1988, 326)

One logical consequence of this perspective is that creativity judgments are a fundamental part of creativity, and they are relative to the field of evaluators—the domain in which the evaluation takes place and the historical time of the evaluation. As Csikszentmihalyi (1999, 314) very clearly states, creativity "is constructed through an *interaction between producer and audience*," and hence it is not inherent in either creative person or creative product. This systemic approach, both contested and celebrated, managed to remain influential in the psychology of creativity over the last two decades and has been supported by several interesting pieces of empirical evidence (for a recent study, see McIntyre 2008).

When one analyzes the components of this approach, it becomes clear that all three constituents are also present, to a certain extent, in Figure 3.1: the person or the creator, the field or the audience, the domain or the world of existing artifacts. And yet Csikszentmihalyi's theory distinguishes itself by proposing an "institutional" understanding of both field and domain. The "social system" and the "cultural system" are both internally organized and acknowledged as such. They refer to structures that enjoy public recognition: for members of the field, recognition of their power to validate creativity; for domains, recognition as distinct and defined symbolic systems. As noted by Gardner (1994, 152), one important feature of the field is its hierarchical nature. There are "gatekeepers" who judge what should enter the domain as valuable and creative artifacts and what should not.

The consequences of adopting such an approach are radical. To answer the question set at the end of the last section: not all creative externalizations are also cultural expressions because they don't contribute to culture (or the domain) unless public agreement decides they do. This immediately *excludes* minor or everyday creativity, as well as children's creativity and any other manifestation that doesn't "benefit" from the existence of an organized and recognizable field and domain. Needless to say, this chapter supports an alternative perspective. While operating with a consensual definition of creativity as rooted in social agreement (see Amabile 1996), it considers "fields" and "domains" at *all levels* of their existence and functioning. To take the example of the field, or the "audience" in our model, it can be represented by an institutionalized authority (like a forum of art critics), but it could just as well be made up of persons who are close to the creator (such as family members). Creative acts and social judgment occur constantly in everyday life, and the fact that the vast majority of them are never spotted by the "radar" of highly formalized organizations doesn't affect their existence or their relevance.

This reality is exemplified by numerous pieces of research in the sociocultural psychology tradition. Gabriel Ivinson, for example, explored students' artwork in school and illustrated in great detail how, even outside the "official" field of high arts (and often with reference to it), social evaluations flourished. Who were the evaluators? Peers, teachers, family members, all "surrounding" the creation—members of the audience who managed very well to "anchor art objects within their own hierarchically structured systems of meaning" (Zittoun et al. 2003, 431). These creative expressions and creativity judgments were made in the classroom or the home, not at the academy or art gallery. Does this make them less pertinent or valuable? Does this take away from their quality as cultural acts? Is this microcultural level of expression less important than other "higher" levels? The firm answer given in this context to all the above questions is *no*.

The cultural model supported here goes both with and against that of Csikszentmihalyi. Though the main "actors" in both models are the same, their "roles" are different. It can be said that the cultural perspective extends the systemic perspective by incorporating multiple facets of creativity as they unfold in families, communities, and larger societies. Creativity is not confined to research laboratories or art studios; rather, it "happens in daily real problem-solving activities" (Fischer et al. 2005, 484). Furthermore, the fact that it happens at all these "micro" levels is by no means insignificant or inconsequential. On the contrary, this basic form of creativity is "an essential condition for existence" (Vygotsky 2004, 11) and, we might specify, for the existence of our cultures. In a very compelling presentation, Willis (1990) argued that symbolic work and symbolic creativity are instrumental for the (1) production and reproduction of individual identities; (2) placement of identities in larger wholes; and (3) development and affirmation of the powers and vital capacities of the self:

> We argue that symbolic creativity is not only part of everyday human activity, but also a necessary part. This is because it is an integral part of the *necessary work*—that which has to be done every day, that which is not extra but essential to ensure the daily production and reproduction of human existence. (Willis 1990, 9)

3.1.3. Internalization and Enculturation

If creativity emerges as a form of externalization or "objectivation," its dynamic relies on processes of internalization, or reception and engagement with existing cultural elements of an ideal/conceptual and material nature (from language to concrete artifacts). The importance of this connection between creator and culture, within a system of social relations, can hardly be overemphasized. The "domain," to use Csikszentmihalyi's terminology, is essential for creativity at the level of both creative expression and creativity evaluations. In effect, without this cultural basis, we would not be able to identify novelty since "without rules there cannot be exceptions" (Csikszentmihalyi 1999, 315): "Both creator and judges must know what is conventionally accepted in order to know whether something new is creative" (Craft 2005, 28).

This existence of cultural domains forces us, as Sawyer (2003a) affirms, to think about issues of internalization, appropriation, and mastery. And yet, the mere notion of internalization needs to be clarified in order to avoid certain misunderstandings about the nature of this complex process. To be clear on this aspect, sociocultural theory promotes a particular conception of internalization, one that rejects the idea of a passive actor "absorbing information from the environment without transformation or creative construction" (Sawyer 2003a, 46). To internalize doesn't mean to copy, to memorize, or to transfer something from the "outside" to the "inside." In fact, cultural approaches contest this traditional Cartesian image of a psychological world separated from the sociocultural world. Psychology and culture permeate each other (Shweder 1990), and therefore to "externalize" or "internalize" in this context means to *actively engage* with cultural artifacts and other social actors. The Vygotskian conception of internalization entails "a transformation or reorganization of incoming information and mental structures based on the individual's characteristics and existing knowledge" (Moran and John-Steiner 2003, 63). Internalization is thus an essential component of *enculturation*, supporting the process of learning one's culture and defining a position within it.

Internalization is also central to creativity, and no scholar today would doubt that "shaping new knowledge cannot occur without some understanding of what already exists" (Craft 2005, 33) or that "the human act of creation, basically, is a personal reshaping of given materials" (Barron 1995, 313). In the general literature on creativity, the issue of "existing materials" has been addressed under different names, most commonly as *knowledge, convention,* or *tradition*. Where knowledge and creativity are concerned, the common vision of the relationship between the two has been one of an inverse U curve: knowledge contributes to creativity until an optimal point at which too much knowledge becomes detrimental. Several authors have argued against this view (see Weisberg 1999), and it is now accepted that preexisting knowledge structures "of a rich and/or well-structured kind" (Boden 2001, 95) are integral to any creative act. Besides knowledge, there are also conventions pointing to "the right way of doing things." In creative acts, conventions are both violated and respected, and this is exactly what makes the new artifact creative and also understandable (see Becker 2008). Furthermore, from a sociocultural perspective, knowledge and conventions that make up what we can call "traditions" are never static realities but rather are deeply connected to creativity and innovation. The false dichotomy between creativity and tradition obscures the fact that, in essence, "one side of a dichotomy is incomplete without the other, even if each term appears to possess a clear meaning independent of the opposite" (Wilson 1984, vii; see also Negus and Pickering 2004).

Another misconception concerns the static quality of the "audience" when in the presence of cultural artifacts, especially novel and creative ones. Just as internalization is never a mere act of exposure, audience members don't simply watch the creation—they experience it, use it, and sometimes copy it as part of their own initiation of creative activities. All these instances are well discussed in relation to artistic creativity. To begin, let's take the situation of the beholder or perceiver of a creative artifact. His or her role is by no means passive, for the task of the perceiver, as part of the internalization process, is to "re-create" the object in ways similar to those the artist went through when creating it. As Dewey (1934, 56) suggests, having an aesthetic experience means that "there is work done on the part of the participant as there is on the part of the artist." Certainly, this work is not the same in a literal sense, but it does involve a similar process of organization—of abstraction, comprehension, ordering of elements, and attribution of meaning. True internalization (as opposed to simple "exposure") comes out of this work. As Dewey notes, those who are too lazy, idle, or stuck in rigid conventions will not "see or hear"—in other words, those members of the audience who don't engage with the creation (at a cognitive, emotional, and even physical level) will hardly benefit from it as a resource for their own creative processes.

This idea is extremely valuable in the context of the present chapter because it indicates that we are all *both* "consumers" *and* "performers" of novel works. Umberto Eco captured this dimension when arguing that "every 'reading', 'contemplation', or 'enjoyment' of a work of art represents a tacit or private form of 'performance'" (Eco 1989, 251). The vitality of creative artifacts, in his view, resides precisely in our capacity to constantly remodel and reinterpret them as part of ongoing creative cycles. The act of improvisation is a constant in our daily lives. In this context, even the notion of "copying" gains new meaning:

> Copying or imitation, we argue, is not the simple, mechanical process of replication that it is often taken to be, of running off duplicates from a template, but entails a complex and ongoing alignment of observation of the model with action in the world. In this alignment lies the work of improvisation. (Ingold and Hallam 2007, 5)

Internalization doesn't require less work, and indeed *less creative work*, than the act of externalization or creation itself. It puts persons in contact with culture and serves the purposes of enculturation, yet "by the individual variations in styles or ways of handling the object, [it entails] an *individualization* of culture" (Boesch 1997, 183).

3.1.4. Relation Between Creator and Audience

The processes of internalization, externalization, and socialization or integration of the creative artifact all require some kind of relation between creator and audience, between self and others. Creativity doesn't take place in a social vacuum (Lubart 1999); rather, it generally "involves some degree of social interaction" (Nijstad and Paulus 2003, 326). Creative acts depend upon social encounters and intersubjective and interactive dialogues, and they entail communicative experiences (Negus and Pickering 2004, 23). The intricate relationships between creator and audiences (collaborators, critics, general public, etc.) are not always overt or explicit—they often involve implicit or indirect forms of collaboration. In the end, though, the argument put forward here is similar to that advocated by Barron (1999): *all creativity is collaboration*. In support of this statement, let us first have a look at the moments of explicit social interaction in creative activities, then we will gradually reveal the inherently social aspects of creativity.

In everyday life, there are numerous occasions in which we work together with others to generate some new and creative artifacts. At school, at home, and often at the workplace, individuals are members of groups, and, as such, they engage with other group members in the development of creative ideas. Aware of this reality, many creativity researchers have focused their attention on *group creativity*, and this is today one of the growing bodies of literature in the field (see Nijstad and Paulus 2003; Nemeth and Nemeth-Brown 2003; Nijstad and Stroebe 2006). Results offered by this area of investigation are mixed, showing both positive and negative effects of group participation on creativity. Many researchers discuss possible gaps between the "promise" and "reality" of working in teams (see Mannix and Neale 2005). Nevertheless, there is also a strong consensus that we should try to understand and optimize group work, since this is an invariant aspect of human societies. The use of brainstorming and similar methods is a sign of this preoccupation, and numerous researchers now point to the necessity of testing group creativity enhancement techniques (see Paulus and Brown 2003, 2007; Paulus, Nakui, and Putman 2006). Simultaneously, an increased interest is shown by sociocultural psychologists toward issues of *collaborative creativity*. The difference between these two paradigms doesn't constitute the topic of the present chapter (for a discussion see Glăveanu 2011a), but it is sufficient to say that the notion of "creative collaborations" denotes realities that are different from "group creativity." "Long-term engagement, voluntary connection, trust, negotiation, and jointly chosen projects" (Moran and John-Steiner 2003, 82) are all features that define collaborations as different from "one-off" group meetings. In conclusion, the encounter between self and others in the context of everyday life takes many forms—some durable, some more sporadic, and all meaningful as collective forms of creative expression.

All the examples above address observable situations of explicit interaction between self and others in the context of a creativity activity. Social relations are not accidental or superfluous; rather, they lie at the very heart of creative achievements. This is perfectly illustrated by Becker's notion of the *art world*. In his use of the term, an art world is made up of

> the network of people whose cooperative activity, organized via their joint knowledge of conventional means of doing things, produces the kind of art works that the art world is noted for. (Becker 2008, xxiv)

This sociological approach is thoroughly relevant to our discussion. Its main assertion is that the production of new and creative artifacts (in this case, art products) is always the result of cooperation and division of labor, not only among a group of creators or a creator and his or her collaborators but also between all the people that make the production of the work possible (what Becker refers to as "support personnel"). This is valid for all kinds of creative acts, from the most explicitly social, such as participation in a theatre performance, to the most apparently solitary, such as writing poetry. The poet's work in this example relies on existing literary sources, continues certain literary traditions, and is supported by the use of materials (paper, pencil, computer, etc.) that are the result of social collaboration between a series of other people. Though this might sound like an extreme argument, it is often the case that we forget the *social nature and origin* of the world we live in and of all its artifacts. Creation never bursts forth from nowhere, with no roots and no help from others; rather, it "often requires as a minimum some dialogue and social exchange" (Gruber 1998, 142). To continue our example, after finishing the poem, our poet will find friends to read it, editors to publish it, critics to comment on it, and a general public to appreciate it. Returning to Csikszentmihalyi's model, creation can never be separated from social judgment and therefore, at least in this regard, from collaboration with other people.

And yet, whenever we think about human creativity, especially in the domain of the arts or sciences, it is not this image of collaboration that first comes to mind. On the contrary, centuries of scientific and artistic achievements are often summarized as the breakthroughs of a handful of great creators touched by the wings of genius. This image of the "culture hero," as referred to by Schaffer (1994, 19), is supported by mechanisms of retrospection and celebration and generates a true "fetishism of discovery." When one looks back on history, ideas appear as spontaneous creations of isolated minds "rather than way stations along the trails of living beings, moving through the world" (Ingold and Hallam 2007, 8). The myth of the "single creator" (Barron 1999, 49) is also a strong ideological category because recognition and legitimization of certain individuals as geniuses are dictated by specific social circumstances (Negus and Pickering 2004, 147). Concluding on this issue, it is useful to consider a suggestive analogy proposed by Collins (2007, 165):

> Though intellectual history is written in a discourse of individuals, they are only the façade, the glamorous images of the advertisements that surround the theatre; inside, it is truly the networks who are the actors on the stage.

All three social processes discussed above—collaboration, evaluation, and recognition—are to a great extent observable when we analyze the dynamics and products of creative work. But there is yet another reason why creativity is social and dependent upon the relation between creator and audience: the human mind is social. A set of arguments for this idea is offered by the theory of *dialogicality*, which basically states that "knowledge creation is an inherently social-dialogical process" (Barrett 1999, 133). This conclusion is by no means new; in effect, Dewey himself, in the first half of the twentieth century, mentioned that "the artist embodies in himself the attitude of the perceiver while he works" (Dewey 1934, 50). Every act of creation involves a continuous *internal dialogue* with others, and the reason for this is simple: creations are generally points of connection between self and other—they are shown to others, discussed with others, and, in the end, meant for others to see, use, and appreciate. As Dewey (1934, 111) so eloquently states,

> Even when the artist works in solitude all three terms are present [work, artist, and audience]. The work is there in progress, and the artist has to become vicariously the receiving audience. He can speak only as his work appeals to him as one spoken to through what he perceived. He observes and understands as a third person might note and interpret.

Creativity is never a solitary affair. The "audience" is always there, helping, in explicit or implicit ways, the externalization process, the socialization of the creative product, and the internalization of new creations. It is social interaction that turns the wheels of creativity, and, along with it, of cultural change and transformation.

3.2. A Final Note on Creativity, Culture, and Participation

The main argument put forward in this chapter is that creative acts are *simultaneously* individual and sociocultural. In support of this, it is important to advocate a particular understanding of both the human mind and culture.

The human mind has been considered fundamentally social, "a hotbed of tactical and relational improvisation" (Ingold and Hallam 2007, 9). Culture was defined here as an accumulation of artifacts (norms, ideas, beliefs, material objects, etc.) that is always changing through personal and collective acts of creativity, from the "smallest" and apparently most insignificant ones (that shape the microculture of families, groups, and small communities) to extremely important achievements (that leave their mark on the history of mankind). It is not common for these two understandings to be brought together—the prevailing viewpoint in psychological creativity literature is that creativity, defined as a process that leads to the generation of new and valuable products, takes place in the isolated mind and that culture is a rather institutionalized superstructure that only geniuses can influence. Of course, there have been exceptions. Authors like Vygotsky (2004, 30) started with a conception of creativity as "a historical, cumulative process," and their work continues to inspire sociocultural accounts.

Having read through the set of arguments presented in the sections above, we can now go back to the title, linking creativity and cultural participation and proposing creativity *as a form of cultural participation*. The notion of participation is surely a central one in social psychology, and participation in itself—in the existence of the family, an organization, or the community—is "an achievement of social and individual life" (Campbell and Jovchelovitch 2000, 264). Being an achievement, participation doesn't come "naturally"; it must involve some kind of work or effort on the part of the individual and society as a whole. This is also the case for creativity. To participate in culture means both to *engage* with existing cultural elements and to *contribute* to their transformation—both key processes of creative expression. This title then proposes that culture is vital for the existence of creativity and that creativity is vital for the existence of culture.

Why is culture important for creativity? Put simply, because the material used for the emergence of the "new" belongs to the common world rather than the self (Dewey 1934, 112). As a consequence, the "richer" a person's contact with cultural elements is, the more remarkable the creations. Using Vygotskian lenses, one can say that "the most eminent are those creators who best utilize the social and cultural tools and best fit with the social and cultural expectations of their time" (Moran and John-Steiner 2003, 80). Culture is not only a resource but also a directing force. Indeed, different cultures value different types of creative expression or the expression of creativity in certain domains and not others (Rudowicz 2003). Cultural influences greatly affect what is created, who is the creator, how the creation takes place, and what kind of functions or finality it serves (Ludwig 1992).

Why is creativity important for culture? Because it is the main engine behind cultural change and transformation. Whenever old solutions no longer apply or new problems emerge, creativity is called upon to add, change, enrich, simplify, or merely beautify the world. And it is not only the "few great creators" who play a role in this process—it is each and every one of us. If culture is "an open and complex system" (Liep 2001, 7) then even the smallest creative acts make a contribution to the system's dynamics; in this regard, it is precisely these "small acts of ordinary creativity [that] weave and reweave the fabric that makes social life possible" (Bateson 1999, 153). "Small" creations make up our lives as they made up the lives of our forebears. It has been suggested that existing tools and symbols are fossilized thoughts and ideas from our ancestors (Moran and John-Steiner 2003, 79). This is a valid metaphor, but culture itself is by no means fossilized; rather, it is very much *alive* and will remain so as long as we put to good use our potential to create.

The interdependence between creativity and culture proposed in the present chapter has several important theoretical, methodological, and practical implications. I will outline just one major contribution for each of these areas—a type of contribution, though, that can open the door to many new and innovative ways of theorizing, researching, and fostering human creative expression. At the theoretical level, the conception discussed here comes to challenge old dichotomies between "big-C" and "little-c" creativity (Paulus and Nijstad 2003), between historical creations and everyday life creations, between high culture and popular culture. All these different manifestations of creativity neither oppose each other nor exclude each other; rather, they share a very important similarity: they are all forms of cultural participation— examples of collaboration and social interaction, of active interpretation of cultural artifacts and successful construction of new cultural resources (see also Glăveanu 2010b, 89; Chapter 2). The aim here is not to obscure the differences between, for example, a sculpture by Rodin and a plastic model made by a home hobbyist; rather, the aim is to emphasize that both manifestations of creativity need to be set against a social and cultural background, outside of which they become incomprehensible.

This discussion connects to one significant methodological implication: studying the intrapersonal dynamics of creative processes *in the context of* the interpersonal relations that make it possible. Such an ambitious aim is met, of course, by a series of difficulties. It is because of the intricacy of analyzing both personal and social processes that creativity researchers often choose to look at half of the picture—that is, the individual level, for the study of which mainstream psychology has developed an impressive array of techniques. To clarify, the methodological discussion should focus not on methods per se but on their use, the assumptions they carry, and the necessity of triangulating methods to obtain a clearer image of a multifaceted reality. It is likely that more needs to be done in this area in relation to the analysis of complex, psycho-socio-cultural processes, and disciplines such as cultural psychology, social anthropology, and linguistics have important contributions to make in this regard.

Finally, at a practical level, today's societies (especially in the West) are ultimately preoccupied, sometimes excessively, with developing creativity. Why excessively? Because of the romantic reading of creativity (Sefton-Green 2000) that makes the cultivation and recognition of creativity depend on being original at all costs—breaking (at times violently) with tradition, with what already exists, and "fighting" the existing culture. A socioculturally informed approach to the education of creativity operates with a different set of assumptions and tools. It encourages active engagement with cultural resources and the exercise of joint activity in the production of new artifacts, and it values imitation with small but incremental changes as well as the modeling of creative activity through observation and communication. Many of these suggestions are of course part of the everyday practice of educators, but most often this is the case because they are considered fundamental for learning, adaptation, and enculturation. However, as the present chapter strived to demonstrate, enculturation is also the engine and the sine qua non of creative production as participation in human culture.

Part B

Methodological Toolkit

4

A Multiple Feedback Methodology for the Study of Creativity Evaluations[1]

This chapter is concerned with creativity evaluations and their fundamental role in the assessment of creativity. Creativity assessment, having a long tradition in psychometrics (Plucker and Renzulli 1999), is focused on evaluating the creativity level of certain products, persons, or processes. Today, one of the most widespread types of creativity assessment is based on expert judgments or evaluations regarding the creativity of products (Lubart 2003). Both the product and "expert" focus in the psychology of creativity came as solutions (partial as they may be) to the problems of what should be assessed and how. Products have the essential quality of being readily available for observation (and even measurement), and most authors consider products to be creative when they are both new or original and useful (Stein 1953; Martindale 1999). Because value and originality are, in the end, relative criteria (see Glăveanu 2011b; Chapter 8), creativity researchers have turned to agreement between experts (essentially between their creativity scores for different products) as an ultimate creativity measure. Social agreement as the basis for the evaluation of creativity has been both acclaimed and contested. Its supporters point to a gain in ecological validity and the capacity to reflect cultural and historical changes in the meaning of creativity (Amabile 1996). Its detractors claim that it makes creativity assessment too relative for scientific analysis (Runco 1999a).

The arguments presented in this chapter assert that social judgment is the most suitable criterion for the evaluation of creativity and criticize current forms of expert assessment on several accounts. From the perspective of cultural or sociocultural psychology, it is argued that the "social psychology of creativity" (Amabile 1996) stopped halfway in its theoretization and did

---

[1] Reprinted from *Journal of Constructivist Psychology*, 25(4), Glăveanu, V. P., A multiple feedback methodology for the study of creativity evaluations, 346–366, with permission from Taylor & Francis, Ltd.

not explore the final methodological consequences of its position. A threefold critique is developed here:

1. Expert judgments are perhaps more "ecological" than preset, standardized scoring systems, but in real-life situations evaluations are often formulated from positions other than that of "expert." If an expert is understood as a person with considerable expertise in the domain of the product (usually gained through formal training), it becomes clear that most ordinary situations and products do not benefit from the existence of recognized experts. An expert approach to creativity assessment confines the phenomenon to the realms of art and science and contributes to its separation from human experience in its broadest sense (Dewey 1934).
2. Expert creativity evaluations are often expressed in the simplest way possible, most of the time numerically, and thus their origins and particular logic tend to be obscured. Furthermore, creativity evaluations are usually unidimensional and concerned only with the creativity of the particular product under consideration, whereas such evaluations rest on a complex system of beliefs about the product, the creator, the domain of the creation, the assessment situation, and last but not least, creativity itself.
3. Expert assessment of creative products is fundamentally centered on ideas of agreement and consensus. The final creativity score is often the average or most frequent result of all evaluations, and great emphasis is often placed on the fact that expert judgment tends to be highly convergent (Amabile 1996; Kaufman, Baer, and Cole 2009). Homogeneity in terms of assessors and assessments again contradicts ecological, real-life situations in which the same product is appreciated by a diversity of persons with heterogeneous backgrounds who perhaps will reach different conclusions about its creativity.

To summarize, creativity evaluations as simple scores are only the visible part of the iceberg, lying on top of more or less explicit systems of beliefs and practices sharing both commonalities and differences between cultures, communities, and socioprofessional groups. These beliefs and practices are ultimately social in their nature, expression, and consequences (see Glăveanu 2011b; Chapter 8, on cultural reception), and as such they can be approached with the theoretical and methodological means offered by the theory of social representations (Moscovici 1984, 2008). Understanding creativity evaluations of a certain product as rooted in and expressive of social representations of that product held by members of different social groups would reconceptualize and transform our understanding of creativity. And yet, such a radical social-psychological perspective might be met by resistance from mainstream creativity researchers who, indebted to the psychometric tradition, refuse to abandon realist frameworks for more constructionist ones. At stake is the mere nature of creativity: *objective reality or social construction*?

The present chapter is based on an understanding of creativity as a social construction, and its primary aim is to contribute to the methodological discussion on how socially constructed creativity evaluations are to be studied. As such, it starts with a brief overview of creativity theories and their epistemological assumptions in order to locate the constructionist approach. It then focuses on social representations theory and its potential application to the study of creativity. In the end, a multiple feedback methodology is outlined, one that is better equipped to explore the multifaceted and heterogeneous nature of creativity evaluations. The methodology is presented in terms of its aims, possibilities for use (including a brief discussion of a case study), and strengths and limitations. It is ultimately argued that when one acknowledges the socially constructed nature of creativity and its assessment, the phenomenon is not dismissed but, instead, complexified.

4.1. Theories of Creativity and Their Epistemological Assumptions

In order to understand the current state of creativity studies and the methodologies used for the assessment of creativity, it is important to outline (albeit briefly for such an expansive topic; for more references, see Sternberg and Lubart 1999) the historical evolution of the field and its gradual transition from purely realist and individualist perspectives to more social and constructionist accounts (Friedman and Rogers 1998; John-Steiner 1992). In essence, a realist account is characterized by the assumption that creativity is real, objective, and measurable. In contrast, social constructionist perspectives point to the relativism and intersubjective nature of the phenomenon. As will be shown, realist assumptions have traditionally informed the psychology of creativity and cultivated a vision of creativity as existing either in the creative person or in the creative product. Constructionist perspectives adopt a "creativity in context" approach and are more specific to cultural or sociocultural theories. Teresa Amabile's (1996) influential work on the social psychology of creativity can be seen as an intermediate stage between the two conceptions.

What is specific about creativity is that it has conventionally been rooted in the individual mind. For centuries, this mind was the mind of the genius, though explanations of his (traditionally only the male gender qualified for the status of genius) exceptional abilities varied according to historical periods. Later, in psychology, creativity came to be acknowledged again as an individual attribute, but one that each and every individual possesses to a certain extent (Weiner 2000). Creativity assessment followed, in this context, mainstream theories of creativity and became preoccupied with the cognitive and even neurological mechanisms of the creative person (Galton 1874; Martindale 1999; Plucker and Renzulli 1999) and, in another vigorous strand of research, with the personality of the creator (Barron and Harrington 1981; Feist 1999; Stein 1953). Another major focus of conventional psychometric studies is represented by the creative product, that is, the outcome of creative activity. Products take many forms, from physical objects to abstractions or actions (Mason 2003), and it is believed, as MacKinnon argued, that "the starting point, indeed the bedrock of all studies of creativity, is an analysis of creative products, a determination of what it is that makes them different from more mundane products" (as cited in Plucker and Renzulli 1999, 44). This initial person and product focus in creativity assessment is depicted in Figure 4.1.

The "creativity in the person" and "creativity in the product" approaches have, without doubt, great historical value for the scientific study of creativity—and, in particular, for creativity assessment (Runco 2004)—and they are still greatly influential. However, a central limitation of these approaches is that they operate with a restrictive, decontextualized, and individualistic notion of creativity. On the whole, "The empirical study of this phenomenon has generally failed to include a consideration of anyone or anything beyond the individual doing the creating" (Hennessey 2003b, 254). It is mostly in the past three decades that several voices in the psychology of creativity (e.g., Csikszentmihalyi 1988; John-Steiner 1992) started to argue for a more social understanding of creative expression and assessment. This relatively new orientation generated *systemic models* of creativity, as opposed to strictly individual-based ones. The "other" as public or audience was therefore brought inside the equation of creativity (see Figure 4.2), and the social psychology of creativity proposed by Teresa Amabile (1996) outlined a consensual definition of the phenomenon (creativity as rooted in social agreement) and, with it, an important methodological tool: the consensual assessment technique (CAT). For Amabile—and this is reflective of a "creativity in expert judgment" approach—creativity assessment "must, ultimately, be culturally and historically bound" (Amabile 1996, 37). She designed CAT to take into account "real-world definitions of creativity" (Plucker and Renzulli 1999, 45) applied to

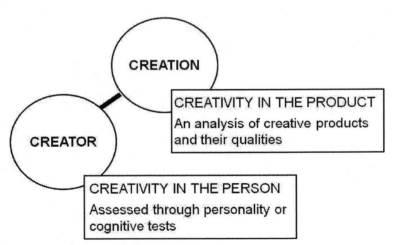

Figure 4.1. The traditional person-product focus in the psychology of creativity.

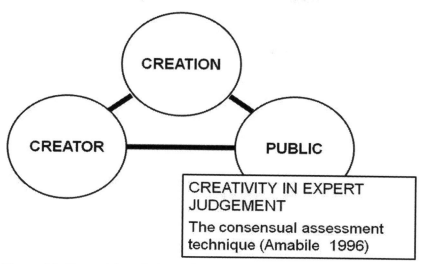

Figure 4.2. The social psychology of creativity and its focus on expert judgment.

more ecologically generated products. The conception behind this technique is summarized as follows: "The essence of the consensual definition [that CAT is based on] is that experts in a domain can recognize creativity when they see it, and that they can agree with one another in this assessment" (Amabile 1996, 42).

In applying CAT, one should first find an appropriate task—one that leads to a clearly observable outcome, is open-ended to allow for flexibility and novelty in responses, and does not depend greatly upon specialized skills. Then judges are needed, the "appropriate observers," who should be familiar with and even have some formal training in the domain of the product. "Novice judgments" are generally treated with caution (Kaufman et al. 2009). Finally, the procedure requires judges to make their assessment independently, to evaluate creativity and other relevant dimensions (e.g., technical, aesthetic), and to appreciate products relative to one another and see them in randomized order (see Amabile 1996, 41–42). With regard to CAT, it was concluded that "over 20 years of research have, in fact, clearly established that product creativity can be reliably and validly assessed based on the consensus of experts" (Hennessey 2003b, 257).

In spite of this, Amabile's social psychology of creativity achieved a limited "socialization" of creativity evaluations. The "other" in her model is a homogenous and rather institutionalized form of otherness (i.e., experts) and fails to reflect the complexity of social relations around both creative production and evaluation. Furthermore, the emphasis on agreement and consensus—a defining feature of CAT—ends up neglecting the basic observation that sociocultural contexts frame creativity evaluations and, as these contexts tend to

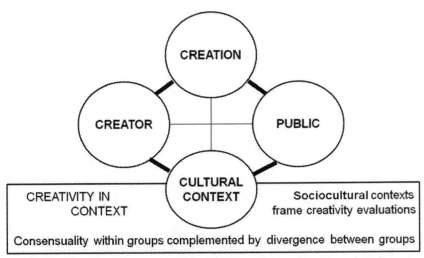

Figure 4.3. The cultural psychology of creativity and the role of the cultural context.

vary between groups and communities, that there is scope for heterogeneous types of evaluation, for debate within and between groups—in a word, for disagreement. This is the basis of the sociocultural understanding of creativity depicted in Figure 4.3. This approach can be considered to investigate creativity *in context*, and in so doing it does not ignore the creative person and product but positions them both in relation to society and culture.

Cultural psychology (for further references, see Bruner 1990; Cole 1996; Shweder 1990) understands creativity as a complex sociocultural-psychological phenomenon (Glăveanu 2011c; Chapter 3). This approach has several important implications, including in regard to how we theorize and study creativity evaluations. To begin with, and in line with its construction-ist epistemology, the mere idea of assessment (measurement expressed in a final, "objective" score) is a foreign notion for most cultural psychologists. Creativity evaluations, as with any form of belief, are highly contextual; they depend on the group of evaluators and their particular position in the social and cultural field. This ultimately means that, according to this approach, creativity is always in the making, attributed rather than intrinsic and relying on shared agreement and meaning-making between self and other. Further-more, cultural psychologists look for creativity "in the wild"—in the everyday contexts of its production—and from this perspective conduct research with high ecological validity. Finally, their focus is wide-ranging, including both celebrated creations and the minor creative expressions of daily life, and their interest is to uncover *emic* or local definitions of creativity (as opposed to etic, preestablished, and universal definitions). These characteristics are largely shared with researchers involved in the study of social representations.

4.1.1. Social Representations: A Source of Methodological Inspiration

Social representations theory is one of the major contributions of European social psychology; it took shape in the 1960s through the foundational work of Serge Moscovici. In essence, social representations theory (Jovchelovitch 2007; Marková 2003; Moscovici 1984) is a theory of social knowledge, of how systems of practice and belief emerge and transform in the communicative relation between persons, groups, and communities about an object (the object of representation). The role of the social representational process, according to Moscovici (1984), is to make something unfamiliar familiar. Here we find the first points of connection with the idea of creativity, the process claimed to generate new and original—and thus, at least initially, unfamiliar—objects and realities. Creative outcomes become appropriated, understood by persons and groups, and they find a place in the symbolic world through interaction and communication, leading to their social representation. Meaning-making processes around the "new" are constantly taking place, from the very creator who generated it to the communities that come into contact with it. Representation is a dynamic socio-psychological process, emerging in relation to particular sociocultural contexts and reflecting their transformation. Dialogue, debate, and contestation stand at the core of representation.

The original study of Moscovici on the reception of psychoanalysis in France in the 1950s captures such a controversy (Bauer and Gaskell 2008). The object of representation in this case was complex—the psychoanalytic approach to the human mind, a theory that argued for an unsettling (and creative?) vision of the human psyche and its relation to sexuality. As a knowledge system, psychoanalysis was both influential and important on account of its political nature: it constituted a potential alternative ideological system that competed with the other ideologies of the time (political, religious, etc.).

Moscovici's book, *Psychoanalysis, Its Image and Its Public* (original edition 1961; English translation 2008), looked closely at how psychoanalysis came to be represented, integrated, transformed, or rejected by members of the more or less institutionalized segments of French society: the Communist Party, the Liberals, and the Catholic Church. His methodological approach, of great interest to us here, was to collect data about the representational efforts of these three different communities in relation to psychoanalytic knowledge. Though belonging to the same society and historical period, members of these distinct groups reflected different sociocultural positions, organized around particular understandings of the world: the message of social and political revolution for the Communists, the message of spiritual salvation for the Catholics, and so on. For the members of these three groups, psychoanalysis was not only a new and foreign doctrine but a strong competitor that needed to be understood, positioned, and ultimately dealt with.

What can this teach us about the study of creativity and creativity evaluations? Though Moscovici's psychoanalysis study was not concerned with creativity per se, the methodology he established—collecting data from members of different groups or communities about the same social reality—has shaped research in the social representations tradition ever since. His concern was with how knowledge is constructed within particular groups and how it "travels," by means of interaction and communication, to members of other groups who problematize and transform it in ways that suit their projects and vision of the world. Ultimately, knowledge is bound to sociocultural contexts, and so are the evaluations about the object of representation. Creativity evaluations make no exception: it is through exploring the sociocultural contexts of different groups and communities that we can understand the convergence or divergence of their evaluative judgments.

4.2. The Multiple Feedback Methodology

Inspired by the social representations research model, a multiple feedback methodology is proposed here as reflecting the cultural approach to creativity assessment. Perhaps the consensual assessment technique is the closest to the method described in this section. Amabile's (1996) claim was that "a product or response is creative to the extent that appropriate observers independently agree it is creative" (33). As we have seen, the cultural approach also operates with a contextual definition of creativity. However, what is central to consensual assessment is, of course, the quest for consensus. This means that, presumably, appropriate judges sharing a similar background and forming a homogenous group will operate with comparable definitions of creativity. The cultural psychology method of assessment proposed as multiple feedback can be said to emphasize diversity instead of consensus, since it purposefully looks for several groups of appropriate judges having dissimilar backgrounds in order to understand how creativity evaluations are rooted in particular sociocultural contexts.

The multiple feedback method is by no means new to psychologists, and we can recall the 360-degree feedback considered by some "the most notable management innovation of the 1990s" (Waldman and Atwater 1998, ix). In essence, this type of evaluation in organizations provided an employee with feedback not only from upper management but also from subordinates, peers, customers, and so on (Payne 1998). The observation that led to this form of assessment was that different people from different groups have different perceptions of a common "reality" (Brogden and Sprecher 1964, 169)—in this case, the performance of an employee, and, by extension to our case, the creativity of a new artifact.

This is not merely an interesting empirical observation—it is of utmost importance if we want to understand everyday contexts and operate in them. Perceptions or conceptions are not inconsequential. On the contrary, as

Westwood and Low (2003) noted, "If creativity as a notion and construct is conceived of differently around the world, then it is likely that it will differ in form and practice" (238). The multiple feedback creativity assessment then brings together, as depicted in Figure 4.4, different groups characterized by distinctive sociocultural backgrounds (members of different communities, professional groups, groups sharing divergent interests, etc.) but nevertheless all relevant for the evaluation of a particular creation. Its graphic depiction is an adaptation of the wind rose model of social representation put forward by Bauer and Gaskell (2008). In Figure 4.4, the creation itself is perceived by members of different groups (becoming C1, C2, etc.) as a function of different representational systems constructed around it (REP-1, REP-2, etc.) in the interaction between group members (P1, P2, etc.). These constructions and their associated evaluations can be different (the case with Groups 1 and 2) or share spaces of similarity (Groups 3 and 4), accounted for in terms of the proximity of their sociocultural contexts, including overlapping group memberships (e.g., the case of P6). It is not to be forgotten that, in real-life group interactions, there are also important motivations at stake and relations of power set in place, and these are often crucial for determining how a reality ought to be represented, evaluated, and acted on. Moreover, in line with Bauer and Gaskell's initial conception, this model has a temporal element whereby representations are forged and changed in time through social interaction, thus acquiring an important historical dimension.

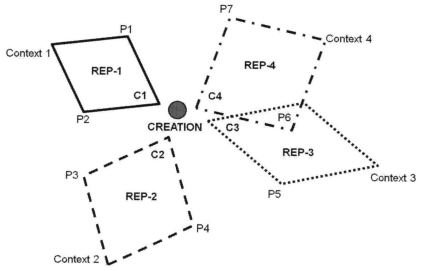

Figure 4.4. A schematic representation of the multiple feedback method.

4.2.1. Aims of the Method

Why should we use a multiple feedback approach to study creativity? One answer is that the multiple feedback method constitutes one of the most comprehensive and ecological forms of creativity evaluation. The three inter-related aims of this kind of assessment are

1. To study representations of creativity, how creativity is attributed by mem-bers of different groups, and why these attributions are made. Research on local or lay understandings is today one of the newest tendencies in the field, something referred to as *implicit theories of creativity* (Plucker and Renzulli 1999; Runco 1999b).
2. To appreciate how the attribution of creativity is rooted in and reflective of sociocultural environments. This goes a step further than implicit theories and looks at how different evaluations draw from a background of norms and beliefs that constitute a more or less distinct cultural reservoir for each group of assessors.
3. To explore how evaluations of creativity emerge out of and have conse-quences for creator–community relations, including the creator's own activity. Within this approach, there is more emphasis than ever on under-standing the creator's point of view and how it is developed in relation to a series of others: collaborators, competitors, critics, and so on.

By comparison with traditional psychometric measures, the multiple feed-back method does not offer a "result" in the sense of one final outcome. There are potentially more results, depending on the group of reference, and—what is fundamental to the cultural psychology approach—there is no hierarchy to be set between them. Some might argue that expert judgments certainly count more than other opinions (see the debate about science and common sense in Jovchelovitch 2007), but this is not an exercise of confirming or disproving lay judgments. Striving to reach objectivity by averaging ratings is what motivates the 360-degree feedback method as used in organizations (Payne 1998) or the application of the consensual assessment technique (Amabile 1996), but this is not the case for the multiple feedback method described here. This method aims to capture the *multiplicity* of viewpoints in relation to creativity and to understand their *origin* and their *consequences*.

4.2.2. Using the Method

The multiple feedback method can be used for the assessment of virtually every form of creativity, from the most mundane and private to the most publicly celebrated creative achievements. This is because, in the spirit of the cultural framework (Figure 4.3), there is room for flexibility and appreciation of multiple levels in what is meant by "creation/new artifact," "other/public," and "culture/existing artifacts." To use an example, when the creations are a child's stories, the others involved in their evaluation could be parents, teachers, friends, and peers, and the existing artifacts that support their appreciations may well differ (e.g., parents would compare them with stories from other children whereas teachers would use school-based definitions of achievement). In the case of a famous sculpture, of course, the appropriate others will change: fellow sculptors, members of the general public, the fine arts academy, and so on.

The key question here is this: How do we choose these "appropriate" judges? Which groups or communities should we consider? This has always been a difficult question, and the answers depend largely on the theorist and the purpose of the assessment. In CAT, the main criterion used is expertise in, or at least familiarity with, the domain of the product, and the validity of self-assessments is often questioned because they rarely match expert judgment (see Kaufman, Evans, and Baer 2010). In the case of 360-degree feedback, significant others are "knowledgeable about the individual and are people whose opinions are valued by the individual and the organization" (Tornow 1993, 211). The multiple feedback method follows similar ecological criteria for determining the participants. In principle, all persons who are in contact with the creator or creation can offer their evaluation. In practice, the following types of persons and groups should have priority:

- Those directly involved in the creation of the new artifact (the creator and collaborators)
- Those who necessarily experience the creation in their daily lives
- Those who use the creation or for whom the creation is important in several ways
- Those who are interested in the creation (from viewers to potential buyers)
- Those who have some form of power over the distribution of the creation
- Those who are considered experts in the domain of the creation

There is, of course, an argument to be made that some degree of knowledge is necessary in order to perform any evaluation. It would be hard to believe that persons who do not know much about a new artifact can express an opinion on it, especially if that artifact belongs to a highly specialized domain. However, it must be emphasized that evaluations obtained through a multiple feedback methodology are not judged on the basis of correctness or completeness. Even the most technical creative products, once they reach lay audiences, begin to constitute the object of representation, Moscovici's (1961/2008) example of psychoanalysis being eloquent in this case. These representations are important in their own right for how the creation is received, used, and finally understood, independent of its technical details or the initial intention of the creator.

Once the groups are established, a second important question concerns the exact ways in which data can be collected from participants. There are no prescribed methods for data collection, but typically this would include interviews or focus groups, observations, and analysis of creative products, along with more quantitative methods such as questionnaires and even experimental designs if some particular assumptions need to be tested. In essence, however, the researcher should be as unobtrusive as possible in terms of imposing his or her own conceptions about the creative artifact under evaluation or about the experience of the participants.

4.2.3. A Case Study Illustration

The first study explicitly using this methodology has been conducted for the evaluation of craftwork products. This research is reported later (see Chapter 6; Glăveanu 2010c); for the purpose of the present review, some reflections will be offered on the practical use of the method as well as its possible outcomes in terms of the three main aims of multiple feedback described above.

The study was concerned with the evaluation of Easter egg creativity, a common folk art in Romania, situated at the confluence of religion, art, and folklore. As such, the four groups of evaluators considered were priests, artists (art teachers), ethnographers, and the folk artists themselves. It should be noted that members of all these groups are in contact with the products of the craft and are in many ways interested in this type of creative expression: priests during religious service around Easter; art teachers in class activities during the same time of year; ethnographers more generally for activities at the Museum of the Romanian Peasant (in Bucharest); and folk artists throughout the year producing hundreds of eggs for growing national and international markets dealing with the distribution of craft objects. Giving voice to artisans themselves in relation to the products of their own work is a specific feature of this constructionist methodology, as more realist approaches to creativity usually consider authors' evaluations to be potentially biased.

The data collection method considered most appropriate for the task of uncovering representations of creativity in craft was the semistructured interview. In this particular case, the interview guide included three main sections: (a) personal relation to the craft, both in childhood and adulthood; (b) reflections on the craft and its place within local communities and at a national level; and (c) representations of creativity and evaluations of the creativity of Easter eggs. Though the first two sections were meant to introduce the topic, they were also useful for contextualizing the evaluations collected in the third part. This third part was fundamental to the purpose of the study and started by discussing the notion of creativity in general, unrelated to craftwork. It then asked the question, Can an Easter egg be considered a creative object? And if so, why? Finally, to anchor the discussion, four photos of different types of Easter eggs were shown to the participants, and comments about their creativity were invited. These evaluations were not quantified, and the emphasis was on explaining personal points of view. Importantly, the study was not concerned with the evaluation of specific artifacts (a certain Easter egg, for example) but with more general considerations about the craft itself and different types of Easter eggs. However, this does not make the multiple feedback method in any way unsuitable for more focused investigations of particular creative outcomes.

The data were analyzed afterward with the help of thematic networks analysis (see Attride-Stirling 2001), which is ideally equipped to reveal patterns of practice and evaluation within the interview material. The analysis was both data- and theory-driven, and the four main categories used as global themes were those of the cultural psychology framework presented in Figure 4.3: the experience of the creator; the contact with different social others; the cultural context (at local and national levels); and the new artifact, its types, and associated creativity evaluations. As such, it can be observed that evaluations of creativity per se constituted one point of interest in the larger context of personal, social, and cultural experiences with the craft. This was intended to highlight the ways in which evaluations are constructed by members of different professional groups—priests, artists, ethnographers, and folk artists—in relation to their interests, experiences, and general representation of creativity and the craft.

A brief summary of the main findings is offered here as an illustration of the potential outcomes of using the multiple feedback method. A general conclusion of the study was that, though "traditional" Easter eggs (decorated with wax and generally representing geometric motifs) were almost unanimously considered creative by members of the four groups, evaluations diverged in reference to other types of decorated eggs (eggs decorated with leaves, stickers, etc.). Moreover, the reasons underlying positive creativity evaluations of traditional decoration varied according to professional group: on the whole, they were appreciated for their artistic value, yet this reason was complemented by religious meaning in the case of priests, respect for tradition in the case of ethnographers, and aesthetic appeal in the case of artists. Folk artists themselves considered their artifact to be creative as long as it was made with "soul" and dedication (something that differentiates it from products made mechanically, in a series, only to be commercialized products). In the end, two broad patterns of practice and evaluation were abstracted from the data: one representing a "view from outside" Easter egg making, specific to priests and ethnographers not involved in any sophisticated form of decoration themselves, and the other representing a "view from inside" the craft, shared by folk artists and some of the art teachers. Whereas the former were more exigent in their evaluations and considered some Easter eggs to be more creative than others, the latter displayed a broader understanding of creativity as a potential that can be achieved by each and every egg. To conclude, this study offered (preliminary) information with regard to the three fundamental aims of multiple feedback: exploring attributions of creativity and appreciating their sociocultural embedded nature and the ways in which they reflect self–other relations in different social contexts (at church, in the market, in school, at the museum, etc.).

4.2.4. Strengths and Limitations of Multiple Feedback

What do we gain from using the multiple feedback method? When should we use it? Answering these two questions outlines the method's strong points and limits of applicability.

First, multiple feedback is used to contextualize creativity. The direct consequences of this are a much more comprehensive picture of how creativity happens in real-life contexts and, once this is achieved, a much more in-depth understanding of the situation and also the possibilities to intervene in it (should intervention—for creativity enhancement, for example—be the final purpose). The results of multiple feedback research are relevant for everyone involved in the generation and appreciation of a creative artifact. Furthermore, these results come out of a dialogical type of investigation (see Jovchelovitch 2007) in which the knowledge and experience of each participant and community are considered in their own right and recognized as valuable and motivated by particular social positions. Of course, this approach is not suitable for all investigations in all circumstances. To begin with, it requires a laborious process of participant selection and a lengthy period for data collection and analysis. Second, this type of research is likely to be more appreciated by social psychologists (or social scientists in general), as it places considerable emphasis on the social context of creativity. Researchers interested in the neurobiology of creativity or strictly the cognitive or personality dimensions of the phenomenon might be dissatisfied with this focus. Research purposes will dictate the choice of approach, and experimentalists who need to use creativity scores as one of their study variables would probably rely on psychometric measurement rather than multiple, socially constructed evaluations.

4.3. Conclusions about the "Reality" of Social Constructions

At present, the use of a multiple feedback methodology (or methodologies similar in aim) is scarce in mainstream creativity research. Yet the grounds for developing this methodology and enriching it with further examples can be found in both creativity and social representation studies. For the latter, a notable example is Gabrielle Ivinson's (as cited in Zittoun et al. 2003) investigation of what constitutes art in a classroom context, a space of dialogue between representations held by students, teachers, and parents. For the former, roots of the cultural approach can be found in different strands of research. To begin with, there are detailed case studies of creators and their productions (Gruber and Bödeker 2005; John-Steiner 1992) that shed light on how great creations were generated and appreciated by different audiences. Second, cross-cultural studies of creativity, now an expanding field (Lubart 1999; Westwood and Low 2003), point toward different understandings and evaluations of creativity existing in Western and Eastern cultures. At both macro- and microlevels, a complex image of diverse representations and judgments is taking shape in relation to creativity.

Regrettably, however, not all creativity researchers are interested in this kind of evidence. Constructionist claims frighten those who believe that they do away with the mere notion of creativity, which is left at the mercy of shifting social agreement (Runco 1999a). What these researchers forget is that a constructionist, sociocultural perspective on creativity makes the phenomenon not meaningless but, if anything, even more *meaning-full*. It does not reduce creativity to an invention outside the realm of reality but rather studies the reality that creative products and processes gain for different groups and communities. In the words of Moscovici (1984, 5), "Where reality is concerned . . . representations are all we have." Social constructions are not abstract or ephemeral; through processes of institutionalization, the symbolic environment often becomes more stable and concrete than the physical environment itself.

It is important to note in the end that the cultural approach does not seek to replace or disregard valuable conclusions about creativity coming out of decades of research in the realist tradition. It does not militate against creativity scores or expert judge evaluations. All it does is point to their one-sidedness as scores or judgments that reflect *one* possible reading of creative products—the reading of scientific psychology, for example. Many other commonsense readings are possible, and they flourish in a social world characterized by divergence and heterogeneity. Of course, not all evaluations—or not everything in an evaluation (or a representation, for that matter)—can be accounted for exclusively in social terms. This would generate a form of social determinism that is as counterproductive as the individualism and psychologism of traditional creativity theories. The individual, through his or her agency and personal experience, is shaped by but also shapes social contexts and experiences. In this interdependence, social constructions about the world become common reference points that help us navigate the world. Evaluations of creativity by experts and laypeople are the ones that, in the end, *constitute* creativity. Understanding the creative ways in which creators and audiences react to and transform such representational systems is a necessary step following the application of the multiple feedback methodology.

5

"Through the Creator's Eyes": Using the Subjective Camera to Study Craft Creativity[1]

The creative process has a dual inner and outer dynamic that is intrinsically difficult to capture using traditional methodologies. Piecemeal methods have been developed to explore it (e.g., think-aloud protocols for capturing creative thinking and online observation of creative activity), but the simultaneously psychological, social, and material character of creative processes is difficult to study in its entirety. The problem resides also in the fact that moment-by-moment descriptions of creative work are rare, and recording the microgenesis of creativity—its emergence in here-and-now contexts and creation processes that occur at the microscopic level (Valsiner 1997; see also Smith 2008)—requires methodological and technological innovations. This chapter demonstrates how new techniques using SEBE (subjective evidence-based ethnography; Lahlou 2011) enable us to go beyond the current state of the art in the study of creative activity, with illustrations from craft creativity.

To date, there have been few studies concerned with the topic of creativity in craft. When faced with easily detectible creative manifestations as embodied in great artistic or scientific products, why would anyone pay attention to almost invisible (and yet constant) forms of innovation in craft? However, despite the fact that folk art to some degree lacks the prestige of the higher arts, craftwork represents an excellent basis for studying creative processes in terms of both access and detailed possibilities for investigation. Indeed, folk art is defined by minute outbursts of creativity that are both easy to demonstrate through comparisons with a large sample of similar productions and clearly determined in time. Therefore, such creative episodes can be subjected to a fine-grained analysis of microgenetic processes in creation. Also, as craftwork is repetitive to

[1] Reprinted from *Creativity Research Journal*, 24(2–3), Glăveanu, V. P. and Lahlou, S., "Through the creator's eyes": Using the subjective camera to study craft creativity, 152–162, with permission from Taylor & Francis, Ltd. I would also like to thank my coauthor, Saadi Lahlou, for granting permission to republish.

a certain degree and widely practiced, it is feasible to conduct systematic scientific research to explore these forms of creative expression and their variations.

5.1. Studying Craft Creativity: Current Methods

One of the most notable studies of folk art, directly interested in how artists create their artwork, is Yokochi and Okada's (2005) investigation of the drawing processes of a Chinese ink painter. Their research revealed that the painter "gradually forms a global image as he draws each part one by one" (245), thus testifying to the importance of both planning and monitoring one's work throughout the entire drawing process. Again focused on Eastern artistic traditions is the study of Kozbelt and Durmysheva (2007), who, though not inquiring about creative processes per se, explored the patterns in lifespan creativity of Japanese *ukiyo-e* ("pictures of the floating world") printmakers. Moving to another cultural space, the ethnographic research by Cooper and Allen (1999) engaged with quilt makers in Texas and New Mexico. In this case, as in many others when it comes to folk art, the artisans were women and their work reflected personal, family, and community histories. Similarly, a female folk art is the Indian *kōlam*, a form of sandpainting on the thresholds and floors of houses and temples using rice powder; it is widespread across southern Asia. Careful investigations of this tradition exposed a "far greater degree of flexibility" in execution than observers are ready to perceive (Mall 2007, 70). This conclusion is echoed by Hughes-Freeland's (2007) study of traditional Indonesian dances. Though for an outsider the dance routine may seem completely scripted, "For individuals within the tradition, creativity, liberation and even immanent subversion were central to their understanding of the tradition in which they worked" (214). This commonly noted discrepancy between creators and observers, it will be argued, stems precisely from a lack of detailed and minute exploration of craft processes.

How can the microgenesis of creativity in folk art be studied? In most of the cases mentioned, and in others, a combination of methods is employed; among them, the central components are observation of craftwork, usually video recorded, and interview. This is valid for both anthropological work (see Cooper and Allen 1999; Mall 2007) and psychological research. Perhaps the best illustration of the latter is given by Yokochi and Okada's (2005) study. They recorded the ink painter while working with the help of two cameras (positioned on both sides of the *fusuma*, or sliding door, that he was decorating), followed by an interview about the drawing process (during which they viewed the videotape record). Yokochi and Okada were interested in several aspects of the drawing activity and coded them as behaviors in the video material: e.g., number of drawing-in-the-air movements and relation between pauses and hand movements. Recordings and field observations revealed interesting details about the creative process; for example, before applying the brush, the painter seemed to "rehearse his brush movement so that he can remember how to draw, and generate a mental image of what he plans to draw next" (Yokochi and Okada 2005, 253).

Though not yet used on a very large scale, video recording of the creative process has been more and more frequent in recent years in relation to a variety of domains beyond folk art, such as portraiture (Konecni 1991), design (Perez, Johnson, and Emery 1995), science (Dunbar 1997), improvised dance (Torrents et al. 2010), as well as the study of children's play (Baker-Sennett, Matusov, and Rogoff 1992; Russ and Schafer 2006) and music composition (Young 2003). Indeed, for the research of complex thought processes and their associated behaviors, observation alone is inadequate (Kay 1994), as is interview. For most researchers, "Videotape coding opens a window into actual task behaviors unfiltered through individuals' self-reports" (Ruscio, Whitney, and Amabile 1998, 245), which could suffer from many biases.

Using video recording facilities in research is commonly associated with a number of *opportunities*, such as (a) cheap and reliable technology enabling the filming of naturally occurring activities in detail, in their context, and as they happen and (b) having the recording available for thorough analysis (Goodwin 1994), with the possibility of it being repeatedly analyzed and shown to others, thus allowing intercoder agreement (see Heath, Hindmarsh, and Luff 2010). Still, videotaping creative activity has, of course, its own shortcomings. Beyond the preliminary difficulty of gaining permission for the research and the final impasse of analyzing a dataset of extraordinary complexity, there is also the fundamental question of how to set the cameras in order to capture creative processes. This challenge ranges from the more practical issue of how to record work done on very small objects often held close to the creator's (nontransparent) body, to the more theoretical reflection on the outsider perspective of the researcher positioned at the other end of the camera (see Paterson, Bottorff, and Hewat 2003). Unavoidably, it is the researcher who, by the mere placement of the camera and decision regarding what and how to film, actually shapes the reality under observation. This is further exacerbated when researchers interpret video data with no input from participants. A novel methodological approach constructed around the use of subjective cameras addresses these weaknesses.

5.2. Subjective Evidence-Based Ethnography (SEBE)

SEBE originated in workplace studies on intellectual workers, where, just as in art, it is essential to have both data describing the mental processes of the actor and a very detailed view of what he or she is actually doing (reflected in texts, graphics, computer screens, and the like). SEBE answers the old researcher's dream of knowing what the participant thinks as he or she performs, thanks to considerable progress in wearable capture technology and to some interesting characteristics of human memory. Every individual lives in his or her own *phenomenological tunnel* of chained perception-action loops, and only through this very personal perspective can situated action (Lave 1988; Suchman 1987) be understood. The major difficulty is how to access this phenomenological tunnel in ways that respect its subjective and situated nature.

In SEBE, first the participant records effortlessly the events with the subjective camera (or "subcam") from his or her own situated perspective, in real situations, without needing extra mental load or attention in this process. The use of wearable video cameras (Lahlou 1999, 2006; Omodei and McLennan 1994; Omodei, Wearing, and McLennan 1997), placed at eye level, provides a film from the exact perspective of the respondent ("subfilm"), which is crucial in the case of craft creation where there is a continuous adjustment of the artisan's action to the effect obtained by the previous act. The wearable microphone offers extra clues about the emotional state of the participant (e.g., breath, voice tone, exclamations, mumbles) along with the sounds of action, which are often critical feedback cues for the actor as he or she performs the activity.

Then the respondent is invited to analyze, ex post facto, the events with the researcher while reviewing the recordings in detail. These self-confrontation interviews are built on the experience of various verbal protocols (Newell and Simon 1972) developed in ergonomics and cognitive science and dedicated to understanding the rationale behind a person's actions. More specifically here, Russian activity theory (Engeström 1990; Leont'ev 1974; Nosulenko and Rabardel 2007) enables the researcher to peel away the various layers of goals and subgoals— part of the person's motivational orientation—behind each action; it can also guide the self-confrontation interview, as the respondent is asked to make explicit, step by step, his or her goals and thoughts during the process. Viewing the subfilm allows actors to be resituated in the exact context of action and to reexperience the journey through their own phenomenological tunnel; in doing so, the participant accesses his or her episodic memory (Tulving 1972), which, by its multimodal aspect, renders this reconstruction of mental states possible and accurate.

Finally, the respondent is invited to check the validity of the interpretations as reformulated by the researcher; this does not mean that the respondent's interpretation should always be accepted. Nevertheless, to understand fully a course of action, one needs to be aware of the way participants interpret their environment and how they account for it. The last stages are, therefore, a triangulation where two (or more) interpreters with different skills and knowledge compare their interpretations of the same material (the subfilm). In this way, SEBE can be said to provide a description that is acceptable both as emic and etic, in terms of both the actor and outside observers (Pike 1967).

In conclusion, SEBE uses the new affordances to capture, analyze, and share empirical data offered by information technology, especially video annotation techniques for annotating and collectively processing data (Cordelois 2010; Hollan and Hutchins 2009; Lahlou 2010). The reader who wishes to apply this technique can refer to a lengthy methodological paper describing the protocols in great detail (Lahlou 2011). The following sections will provide an illustration of the method that speaks for itself and demonstrates its relevance to the study of craft creativity.

Using the subcam: Easter egg decoration as a creative craft. Illustrations of the SEBE methodology come from the specific craft of decorating Easter eggs in Romania. Easter egg decoration is not restricted to this country or to Orthodox Christian communities, and egg decoration more generally has deep historical roots in many cultures across the globe (see Gorovei 2001; Marian 1992; Newall 1967, 1984). Though traditionally dyed in red (reminiscent of the sacrifice of Christ), decorated eggs in Romania often display a variety of geometric and figurative motifs and are nowadays at the center of a vital and creative custom situated at the crossing between art, religion, folklore, and a growing national and international market (Glăveanu 2010c; for more details see Chapter 6).

Decorated eggs (generally referred to as *ouă încondeiate*, where *condei* means also "writing tool") are produced in northern Romania by artisans (mostly women) throughout the year, but especially in the winter months preceding Easter. Different types of eggs are decorated, from chicken and duck to goose and even ostrich, and they are all prepared for decoration by removing their content (with a syringe) and thoroughly cleaning them on the inside and outside. Traditional decoration involves the use of natural wax, warmed until it liquefies and applied to the egg with the help of a special instrument known as a *chişiţă* or *condei* (a wooden stick with a metal pin at one end; see Figure 5.1). There are, at present, different styles of decoration, but the oldest one involves repeated stages of working with wax and immersing the egg in color (typically

Figure 5.1. Work tools: the tin can used to warm wax and the set of chişiţe.

yellow, red, and finally black). The traditional technique, therefore, requires much thinking ahead on the part of the artisan, since what is made on the egg in each phase is actually the negative image of what will be the final outcome after the wax is cleaned off. Finally, it is important to note that decoration colors and stages vary across different regions in Romania (and even among villages), and folk artists have at their disposal an impressive number of motifs that they combine and transform in producing each egg (Gorovei 2001; Zahacinschi and Zahacinschi 1992).

For this particular reason (namely, the innumerable possible combinations), the tradition of egg decoration has been chosen as a suitable example of craft creativity. As with any folk art, decoration has a set of rules, transmitted from generation to generation, that give it its distinctiveness and often make it a powerful identity marker (at a national and even a local level). Rules are, at the same time, a cultural repository of what works well capitalized through the work of many people; a way to demonstrate one's own mastery in their application and, therefore, one's social legitimacy; and a powerful generator for creativity, since they provide a stimulating framework for creation games. The famous Oulipo literary movement, which made formal constraints the framework for their creativity, is a paramount example. One of the most celebrated productions of this prolific group is Georges Perec's (1996) *La Disparition*, a three-hundred-page book written without using, a single time, the letter *e*, which is the most frequent letter in French. In the case of egg decoration, within the rules of the craft, artisans have an impressive degree of creative freedom in choosing what to represent, and how to represent it, on each egg, often innovating both in terms of work technique and content and personalizing their work (Irimie 1969). The question remains of how exactly this creativity is manifested in the micromoments of its production.

5.3. Method

The subcam was employed for the study of creativity in Easter egg decoration in the context of a larger research project conducted by the first author in Romania (see Chapter 7). For the purpose of this chapter, the research will be referred to here as an *illustration* of how the subcam can be used in fieldwork and its potential results in terms of capturing and understanding creative work.

Participants. The investigation was conducted in the village of Ciocăneşti (Suceava district), in the historical region of Bucovina. This location was selected for being the home of a large and vibrant community of decorators; it hosts a National Museum of Decorated Eggs and annual Easter festivals to celebrate the craft. The seven decorators whose work was recorded were all participants at a five-day summer school for egg decoration organized at the Museum and opened to both novice and expert decorators. They were all females, with ages ranging from eight to forty-one. For two of the participants, decoration was a major activity; the other participants decorated on occasion, and especially before the Easter season. The relatively small sample size is compensated for, as is shown next, by the richness of the data collected for each individual case.

Apparatus and materials. The study made use of the subcam, and the final dataset comprised about six and one-half hours of film. Preparation of the material aspect of the research included, therefore, pretesting the camera to see if it properly recorded activities performed on an object as small as an egg and held relatively close to the eyes. It was noticed that the usual procedure of applying the camera to the side of a pair of glasses didn't capture the decoration process well, so the researcher resorted to placing it below a sun visor, in a position close to the space between the eyes (see Figure 5.2). Two subjective cameras were used for the fieldwork, thus allowing two people to wear them simultaneously in each daily meeting at the Museum.

All material resources (eggs, chișițe, wax, color) were provided by the Museum and also by some of the participants, who occasionally brought their own work instruments. The researcher used his personal laptop to show the participants the resulting films, and confrontation interviews were also recorded with the help of a subcam and an audio recorder. Pretraining in using the camera and in conducting confrontation interviews in ways that reduce experimental bias was made available beforehand from more experienced researchers.

Figure 5.2. Researcher wearing the subcam and microphone under a sun visor.

81

Procedure. The study followed all the classical steps of SEBE, as discussed previously. SEBE is based on a combination of three techniques:

1. First person audiovisual recording with a miniature video camera worn at eye level, called the subcam (Lahlou 1999, 2006); this provides what the creator saw, heard, and did.
2. Confronting respondents with their first-person recordings to collect personal experience through evidence-based, controlled, analytic reconstruction; this enables the participants to explain what they thought at the moment of action.
3. Formulating the findings and discussing the final interpretation with the respondents; this ensures that the researcher correctly understands what happened.

In the preparation for the fieldwork, all participants were notified about the use of a camera during the summer school and were fully informed about the methodology and aims of the study. This ensured that the respondents understood the purpose of the research and provided maximum assistance; treating the actor as a partner in the research is a key aspect of SEBE. Their consent was recorded, and in the case of young children, parents gave their approval. All participants wanted to be identified by name in the research. The decorators found it easy to wear the camera and mentioned in the interviews that having the sun visor did not disturb their work and that seeing their resulting videos was a fascinating experience. The camera was not forgotten (as occurs in other contexts; Heath et al. 2010) because participants insisted on holding the monitor on the table so they could look at it from time to time and avoid situations in which their work would be "off" camera.

5.4. Illustration of Results

5.4.1. Filming the Craftwork

What needs to be emphasized from the start is that, in most cases, extremely clear footage of the decoration process resulted from artisans using the subcam. There were only rare situations in which, for a short period of time, the egg was not visible on film or was held too close to the camera, resulting in poorer image quality. Exemplifying the video material, Figure 5.3 depicts the process of making a particular spiral motif known as the "lost way." This motif involves drawing first three sets of parallel interrupted lines (that must necessarily include an even number of segments) and then reuniting them, initially first to second and second to third, and then back second to first and third to second. In this way, a structure of braided shapes is generated, enclosed on both sides by double lines (the motif continues with semicircles on the side of each external line).

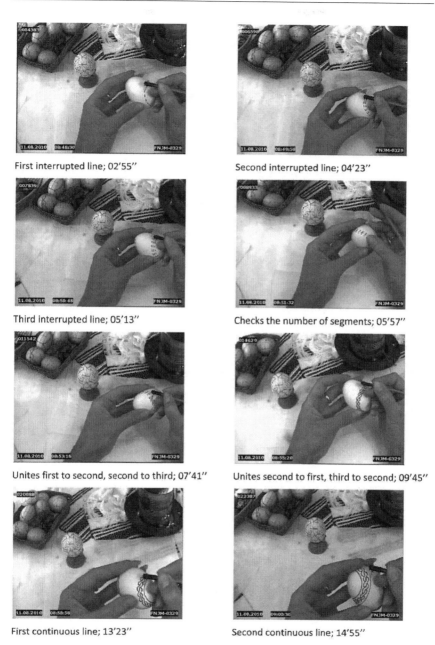

First interrupted line; 02'55"

Second interrupted line; 04'23"

Third interrupted line; 05'13"

Checks the number of segments; 05'57"

Unites first to second, second to third; 07'41"

Unites second to first, third to second; 09'45"

First continuous line; 13'23"

Second continuous line; 14'55"

Figure 5.3. Making the "lost way" spiral motif (Cristina Timu).

5.4.2. Discussing the craftwork

However insightful the recording of firsthand creative activities, seen from the perspective of the actor, might be, accurate interpretation of these recordings would be almost impossible without input from creators themselves. This is clearly demonstrated by the subcam material generated by folk artists, which must be complemented by confrontation interview data. During these interviews, decorators actualized the goals and personal experiences they had while working and revealed information that would not have been verbalized otherwise: namely, procedural and tacit types of knowledge (Nonaka 1994; Polanyi 1967). For example, one of the participants discussed, while watching the video, the way in which she covered the hole in the egg with wax and the reasons for this action. This particular reference was not made in previous interviews about her work, as acknowledged by both researcher and participant (she said it never occurred to her to say these things because she simply does them without paying attention).

The necessity of the confrontation interview is perhaps best illustrated, though, by those segments of activity that cannot properly be understood by the researcher alone. A first example of this is the process of choosing work materials, both egg and chişiţă. In the frequent cases in which participants didn't bring these from home, they had to start by obtaining them on the spot. Consequently, especially in the case of the chişiţă, there were numerous moments, recorded on camera, when folk artists picked up several work instruments and seemed to look for new ones. The question is, of course, Why? What made them change a chişiţă and, most importantly, eventually choose one? The interviews revealed a general sense that what was looked for was "a good chişiţă," and this was explained as a chişiţă one could work with continuously, without interruptions. But their needs were a bit more specific at different moments. For example, Laura Niculiţă wanted, at some point, a chişiţă that was "warm" and would therefore better apply wax to the egg. In contrast, Niculina Nigă looked at the beginning for the chişiţă she "worked best with," a "thinner" one since completing the first stage requires thinner lines. This was also mentioned by Marilena Niculiţă, who regularly "tested" each chişiţă on her fingernail before starting to write with it. Another recurrent question for the decorators was what exactly they were looking for when turning the egg around (frequent especially after finishing a segment). For an outside observer, these gestures would readily be interpreted in a general way, but it is again within specific situations that they acquire their true significance for the participants. For example, the egg was turned to "check if anything is missed," to "see what needs to be done next," to "get a general impression," or simply to determine if the decorator "likes" the outcome.

5.4.3. Discovering Instances of Creativity in Craftwork

The most important aspect to illustrate certainly has to do with how microlevel instances of creativity in craftwork can be documented through the use of subcam technology. After conducting SEBE, the researcher is left with a considerable amount of recorded material. Therefore, it is helpful, once one is familiarized with the material, to select fragments or episodes for further analysis (Lahlou 2006, 2011; also Heath et al. 2010). In the Easter egg decoration study, owing to the relatively short time interval in which decorators wore the cameras (on average forty-five minutes), it was possible to go through most of the recording with the participant without the need to preselect episodes. This helped to postpone the analytical stage of isolating creativity instances and actually allowed for identifying these moments in collaboration with the folk artists themselves. In the context of this chapter, for illustration purposes, three different examples of *creativity outbursts* are discussed, reflecting three different domains in which creativity tends to manifest itself in craftwork: (a) the technical or procedural aspect, (b) the completion of work, and (c) the content of decoration. Instances have been selected for each category in view of a basic definition of creativity as "the production of something new" (Torrance 1988, 43) or a novel type of behavior. In view of this working definition, it becomes even more clear how identifying creativity depends also on the creator's input, since behavioral novelty can be assessed by comparison with the existing set of data; this set, however, will always be limited.

Figure 5.4 illustrates an instance of technical creativity, when Laura was drawing the half-star motif in the opposing quadrants of the two main sides of her egg. The video recording shows how, initially, she started from making the angles and then continued with drawing the lines. When passing to the second of the opposing quadrants (at 25'34"), she suddenly changed her technique and abandoned the small starting point of the angles to depict first the lines. Interestingly, after this episode, she continued on the other side of the egg to complete the half-star motif in the opposing quadrants by drawing first the lines and then the angles. As a result of discussing this moment of the decoration process with Laura, she changed the depiction order because it was easier to start with the lines and because one gets a better chance at drawing the angles more precisely (lines offer "reference points" for the much shorter segments of the angles). This moment of spontaneous change did not modify the final outcome (the representation of the motif) but did improve the general technique; as such, it was a novelty to be remembered and used from that point onward. It should be noted that these little discoveries are specific to novices; more experienced decorators apply them almost automatically and pass them on to others as general rules of decoration (one of these being to always start with longer lines and finish with the details of the motif).

In Hutchins (1995), a similar example of learning in context how to realize a given task with less time or effort is described at length for navigators fixing their position. This form of technical creativity can be called a *procedural shortcut* (which, exercised further, can turn into a work tactic). Once a procedural shortcut is evidenced, the technique presented here makes it possible to document it in various ways. Systematic sampling of similar occurrences (in this case, all the half-star motifs in the videos) provides a retrospective sample (Lahlou, Nosulenko,

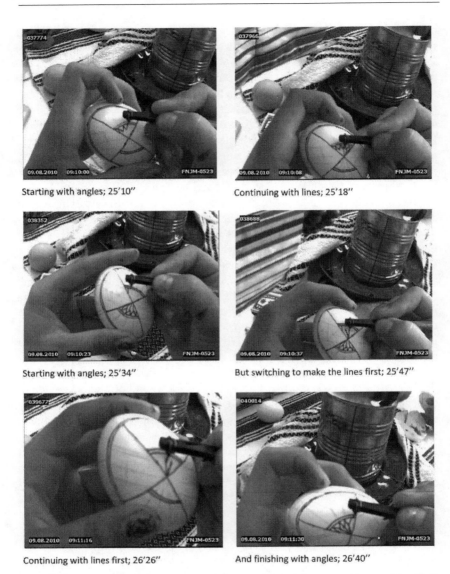

Starting with angles; 25'10"

Continuing with lines; 25'18"

Starting with angles; 25'34"

But switching to make the lines first; 25'47"

Continuing with lines first; 26'26"

And finishing with angles; 26'40"

Figure 5.4. Drawing the "half-star" motif—technical variations (Laura Niculiță).

and Samoylenko 2002) of type events as they take place in natural experiments (Lazursky 1911). The researcher can then compare variations statistically; see, for example, if they are linked with particular sociodemographics; ask participants who exhibit a specific creative variation how they came to learn it; and so on. This analysis can be done collectively with a group of experts to compare their perspectives (Cordelois 2010), leading to a more systematic analysis of craft creativity.

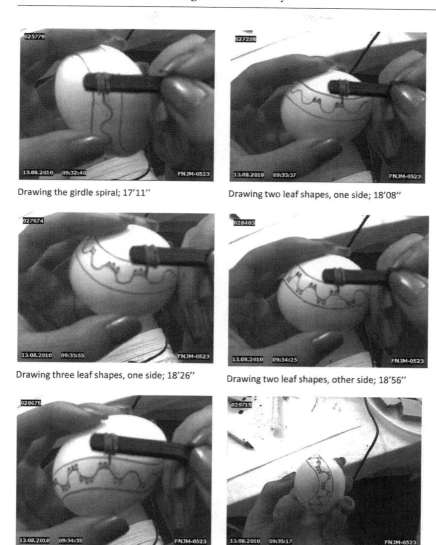

Drawing the girdle spiral; 17'11"

Drawing two leaf shapes, one side; 18'08"

Drawing three leaf shapes, one side; 18'26"

Drawing two leaf shapes, other side; 18'56"

Drawing three leaf shapes, other side; 19'07"

Checking the result; 19'48"

Figure 5.5. Making leaf motifs on a spiral girdle (Mihaela Timu).

One other general rule of decoration in the case of Easter eggs is the rule of symmetry. Usually, motifs are represented in symmetrical ways on the egg, and they themselves often have internal symmetry. As it happens, though, at times this regularity cannot be fully respected on account of space constraints related to how previous motifs were made. Figure 5.5 depicts a situation in which Mihaela, a more experienced decorator, made leaf-like forms on a spiral girdle going around the egg. It can be easily noticed here how she applied sometimes two and sometimes three such shapes, on each side of the girdle. In the dynamic of her work there was, therefore, an irregularity generated mostly by the fact that the spiral previously made had slightly unequal curves. What the interview added is an understanding of how irregularities in this case (and others) for Mihaela were not to be avoided but cultivated (recalling the notion of preference for complexity; see Ziv and Keydar 2009). She was conscious of not making the same number of leaves on each side and did not consider this to be a mistake, since "there is no rule" saying exactly how many shapes should be made. This is, therefore, an excellent example of the *situated nature* of creative work in craft—transcending and adapting broad norms to the circumstances of the here and now. The segments already made are not just completed pieces of the puzzle; they are active contributors to how decoration work is to be done in subsequent phases. As such, decoration is characterized by adaptability and flexibility as much as by routine.

These minute variations in classic motifs are based on a personal appreciation of what is good for a specific artist and are therefore a manifestation of *personal style*. Through a systematic study of these variations—e.g., measurement on the craft and comparison with what the artist says about it in the interview—the researcher is able to determine what are the relevant traits that the author considers in creation. Such systematic analysis has been developed for technical design based on verbal protocols and is known as *perceived quality* analysis (Nosulenko and Samoylenko 1997, 2001, 2009; Parizet and Nosulenko 1999). Transfer of these techniques would be an interesting avenue for creativity studies. In consequence, minute study enabled by SEBE could clarify the nature of style, as a personal way to pay attention to and execute specific characteristics of a classic feature, and of taste, determining what aspects are perceived as important for the final outcome.

Finally, the last example reflects creativity in the content of decoration. One of the common accusations when it comes to folk art is that, in contrast to fine art, it "shows a high occurrence of borrowing, repetition, use of conventional themes, plagiarism, and disregard for spontaneity and originality" (Cincura 1970, 170). This supports a vision of folk art motifs as static and manifested through meticulous processes of exact replication. Nothing could be further from the truth, as subjective camera recordings demonstrate. To argue this point, one need only look at the moment in Niculina's work when she deliberately attempted to copy a motif (see Figure 5.6). The model egg was positioned in front of her, and she used a pencil to make its main lines on her egg. As discussed in the interview, Niculina very much liked the motifs of this particular egg (two shepherd's hooks on one side and a grid with stars on the other) and had never seen them before. As is common in such circumstances, folk artists are very eager to "steal" the new models they encounter, since others don't often "give" or "share" their motifs willingly. The six screenshots reflect

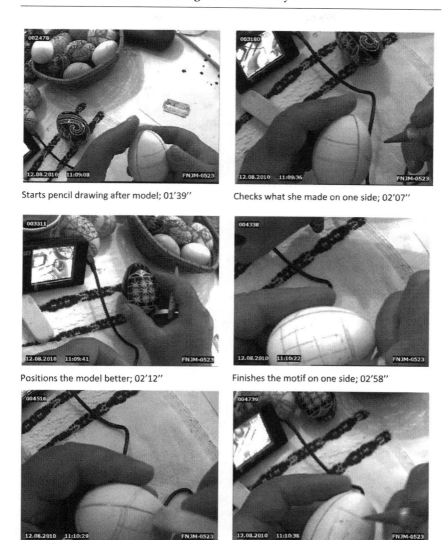

Starts pencil drawing after model; 01'39''

Checks what she made on one side; 02'07''

Positions the model better; 02'12''

Finishes the motif on one side; 02'58''

Erases what she did on the other side; 03'00''

Finishes the motif on the other side; 03'09''

Figure 5.6. Trying to copy a motif, drawing in pencil (Niculina Nigă).

the intrinsic difficulties of translating patterns from one surface to another, and it can be seen how an eraser was often used in the process.

What is most interesting here from the perspective of creativity is the intention Niculina had when working that particular segment: not to make the whole motif but to capture "the main idea," to *schematize* it because she will be able to change or add to it later ("from a single [model] I make several").

Furthermore, even outside of this goal, it would have been impossible to perfectly copy the motif (as she mentioned when she made it for one of the other participants), since no two eggs are absolutely the same: the one she worked on was smaller, and thus the model needed to be "crowded" on it. Russian activity theory, with its focus on the operator's goals (conscious representation of the desired state), uncovers how a specific artist will create a path from the current state to the goal. This is why the researcher should constantly ask the participants for their goals and subgoals during the confrontation interview. This enables one to know exactly what the artist tries to produce—in this case, it becomes obvious that it is not precise reproduction but rather a more general effect, in opposition to commonly held beliefs (Cincura 1970). A fundamental manifestation of content creativity in craftwork relates, therefore, to all the minor changes constantly made to old, established models, and this helps to define the real nature of a motif.

5.5. Discussion: Insights Afforded by the Subcam

The illustrations of creativity in folk art included in the previous section are meant to highlight the utility of using the subjective camera, in the context of SEBE, for the study of microgenetic creative processes. From the few examples given, one can already see the remarkable potential this methodology has for allowing one to pinpoint moments of creative production and to gain a better understanding of how creativity is intertwined with tradition in the craft of Easter egg decoration. The research uncovered signs of creativity in three particular domains: technical procedures (how things are done), completion of work (why things are done as they are), and content (what things are done). In applying this methodology, what is also gained is a more systematic and consistent grasp of complex phenomena such as style, taste, and motif. This procedure can shed light on the very process by which these phenomena occur in real situations, and it makes it possible to connect them to the representations and evaluations held by creators themselves.

Analysis of the current video dataset provides many more examples for each of these categories and thus enriches the classification. Parallels with previous studies of traditional art, such as Yokochi and Okada's (2005), using similar methodologies (videos, observation, and interviews), can easily be drawn. To begin with, both ink painting and egg decoration require hands-on activities, and, as such, they raise interesting questions about the relationship between creative cognition on the one hand and the movement of the body on the other. These investigations substantiate the conclusion that "artistic creation is a highly embodied process" (Yokochi and Okada 253) and that there is a *dynamic cycle* between creative idea or representation of the work and its realization in movement and action in the material world. The artisan's creativity unfolds as the work progresses and therefore resides neither in the mind of the creator nor in the materiality of the creation, but between the two.

The famous painter Jean Dubuffet, in his *L'Homme du Commun à l'Ouvrage* (1973), described how the artist builds on the surprises that the very execution provides, judging the effects as they emerge on the canvas. This supplies researchers with an insight of creation as a *path-dependent* process rather than a linear sequence in which the artist would reproduce on the medium a preexisting mental representation (links can be made with the idea of nonmonotonic exploration; see Simonton 2007; Weisberg and Hass 2007). Similar conclusions have been reached by other authors exploring creative action in different domains. Perez et al. (1995), for example, discussed the design process as an iterative type of activity and not a linearly deterministic progression from idea to outcome. For science, Dunbar (1997) concluded that novel ideas emerge not through revolutionary changes but rather through a series of minor mutations that accumulate and transform the content of one's knowledge. Serendipity (taking advantage of accidental discoveries) also plays a key role. A quick look at how Easter egg motifs and work techniques evolved during recent decades in Romania would undoubtedly support this perspective of incremental evolution.

Naturally, as in the case of any methodology, the use of the subcam has its downsides and limitations. An obvious one relates to the fact that the method cannot be successfully used at all times, with all people, and in all circumstances, owing to restrictions of access. Researchers don't have access to every creator and can't always be sure that they will record the most relevant segments of work. To take an extreme example, the study of creators from centuries past and their work continues to be approached through historical and biographical research alone. Moreover, in setting up a subcam study, some time is required to build the necessary bonds of trust between researcher and participants. The absence of this stage not only poses ethical problems but also can seriously affect the nature and quality of the data to be collected. Finally, as with any video recording, the material is never easy to analyze, and "developing inclusive, reliable coding schemes and training coders is very challenging and time consuming" (Ruscio et al. 1998, 259). However, this apparent disadvantage can be turned into an opportunity: namely, being able to analyze the same dataset from a multitude of angles and with a variety of research questions in mind. To give just one example for the Easter egg study briefly introduced here, the research could easily be expanded to explore differences between novices and experts in creative work or to build up activity charts for the decoration process (see Chapter 7).

In the end, there is a strong argument to be made for diversifying the application of the subcam to target other creative domains, such as art, science, and design, and other research problems, such as comparisons between beginners and experts, insight or the "Aha!" moment, stages of the creative process, and so on. Interest in some of these from a microgenetic perspective already exists (see Wallace 1991). It is also important to keep in mind the research questions one is aiming to answer and to not transform any methodology into an end in itself. This is particularly tempting when one is faced with the accessibility of recording devices, something rightfully noted by Loizos (2000, 105): "It is easy to get carried away by the idea of 'making a video,' and to end up letting the technology, or the excitement, dominate the research." An opposite danger is to not use subjective cameras or video recording technologies on account of rigid theoretical commitments. In this regard, it can be expected that researchers who are preoccupied with great creations and creators alone, or who consider that creativity takes place only in the mind, will have little use for subcams. On the contrary, those who want to understand the moment-by-moment dynamic of creativity in everyday life and the ways in which creativity presupposes a constant interaction between a creator and his or her world (material and social) will find this technique indispensable for their work.

Part C

Case Study: The Creativity of Craftwork

6

Creativity in Context: The Ecology of Creativity Evaluations and Practices in an Artistic Craft[1]

There are arguably two fundamental questions to be answered by the psychological study of creativity: Where is creativity located? and What is creative? The first is central to creativity theory and the second to creativity assessment; unsurprisingly, answers to one will greatly influence answers to the other. For example, in relation to the first question, a traditional answer has been that creativity exists at the level of the individual, and especially the individual "mind" (Amabile 1996; Montuori and Purser 1995). Consequently, the question about what is and is not creative (including the level of creativity) focused on the measurement of features of either the creative person or product. Again as a matter of tradition, the persons chosen for research were usually highly gifted individuals, recognized creators who enjoyed fame and the "status" of genius in society (see Galton 1869; Gardner 1994). The creative outcomes of these individuals were typically great achievements, revolutionary in the field of the arts, science and technology, politics, economics, etc. These are the origins of a "great divide" in the study of creativity, not only in psychology but also in connected disciplines—namely, the divide between famous creators and "lay" people, between exceptional creative achievements and modest "attempts," between art galleries, concert halls, and scientific laboratories on the one hand and the life of the streets, of the markets, of private homes on the other. In other words, the rupture between "true" creativity and everyday life.

[1] With kind permission from Springer Science+Business Media, *Psychological Studies*, Creativity in context: The ecology of creativity evaluations and practices in an artistic craft, 55(4), 2010, 339–350, Glăveanu, V. P.

This aspect has long been discussed, and the works of many theorists signaled the dangers of adopting such a view. Among them, the writings of Dewey on aesthetics and the theory of art are of great relevance here:

> When artistic objects are separated from both conditions of origin and operation in experience, a wall is built around them that renders almost opaque their general significance, with which aesthetic theory deals. Art is remitted to a separate realm, where it is cut off from that association with the materials and aims of every other form of human effort, undergoing, and achievement. A primary task is thus imposed ... to restore continuity between the refined and intensified forms of experience that are works of art and the everyday events, doings and sufferings that are universally recognized to constitute experience. (Dewey 1934, 2)

The task set by Dewey has been partially accepted by psychologists who, roughly by the 1950s, shifted their attention from great creators to the study of "ordinary" people, especially after the 1980s, when increased concern was shown for the social and cultural dynamics of creative acts, including in daily life (Craft 2005; Lubart 1999; John-Steiner 1992). The social psychology of creativity (see Amabile 1996) and, more recently, the cultural psychology of creativity (see Glăveanu 2010a, 2010b; Chapters 1 and 2) largely contributed to these changes and to a regained appreciation for the *creativity of everyday life*. The social approach influenced also the way in which we answer the second question: What is creative? A study of creative products made by individuals in the context of daily tasks became, in the last two decades, the standard for creativity assessment. Consensual forms of validation and culture-bound definitions of creativity (Amabile 1996; Hennessey 2003b) began to be used, and, along with them, a "new" conception of creativity was emphasized: the creative process that takes place in community contexts, embedded in a network of social relations and dependent upon social interactions and the use of existing cultural artifacts. It is precisely this conception, fundamental to the cultural or sociocultural psychology of creativity, that is supported by the present study.

The following research will illustrate an *ecological way of studying creativity evaluations*, one focused not on evaluations per se but on *evaluations in context*, on how evaluations are shaped by the particular positions and experiences of each group of evaluators. Aiming to reveal the social embedding of creative evaluations and their strong connection to creative practices, and being supportive of the notion of "creativity of everyday life," this research explores the Easter egg craft-world in Romania. As such, it continues a tradition of studies dedicated to creativity, arts, and crafts in different cultural contexts (Maduro 1976; Cooper and Allen 1999; Yokochi and Okada 2005; Mall 2007; Giuffre 2009).

6.1. Easter Eggs at the Confluence of Folklore, Religion, and Art

The egg has always been an object of tremendous symbolic value. Throughout history and in the modern world, eggs are associated with life itself, with birth, fertility, vitality, the forces of creation, and the act of resurrection. Unsurprisingly, a closer investigation reveals several *archetypal forms* structuring this symbolism: the cosmogonic egg (the beginning of the world), the cosmological egg (cosmos and all its elements), the magical egg (in therapeutic, magical practices), the mystic and eschatological egg (associated with regeneration), and the festive egg (evoking important events) (Marian 1992, 76). This great *polyphony of meaning* could only be accompanied by a *polyphony of practice*:

> Eggs are offered as gifts, paid as a due, and ornamented as a favourite decoration on festive occasions. They have been used in magic spells and in foretelling the future, in love potions and medicine, and have been thought effective in promoting healthy and fertile crops and animals. (Newall 1984, 21)

This system of beliefs and practices associated with decorated eggs is an integral part of Romanian culture, and it can be argued that Easter eggs today stand at the confluence of folklore, religion, and art. Eggs have been part of folklore and local mythologies since time immemorial. In ancient India, China, Tibet, Egypt, Phoenicia, Persia, and Greece (Gorovei 2001; Marian 1992; Newall 1967), they were often related to the origin of the world or the idea of totality. Traditions, especially in rural areas, still preserve some of the richness of egg decorating practices that date to pre-Christian times. However, in Romania and many other Orthodox Christian countries, folk practices related to egg decoration have largely been associated with Christianity, for which "the egg provided a fresh symbol of the Resurrection and the transformation of death into life" (Newall 1984, 22). Easter eggs, as religious artifacts, are an essential component of national identity, particularly in a country like Romania, which is characterized by "religious nationalism" and in which approximately 87 percent of the population is Orthodox Christian and 94 percent claim to believe in God (Barker 2009; also Müller 2008). Easter egg making is not reduced to merely coloring eggs but rather involves all sorts of decoration techniques that culminate in the highly elaborate designs used by "professional" folk artists. For them, Easter eggs acquire a new meaning as art objects appreciated both by the general public and by some experts who believe that "among all the folk arts Romanians have, decorating eggs is, in a way, the most 'artful' of all in the purest sense we attribute to this term" (Zahacinschi and Zahacinschi 1992, 15–16).

In conclusion, both the making and the use—or "reception"—of Easter eggs in the Romanian context are rooted in a diverse body of traditions and are open to a panoply of meanings and interpretations. This recalls Eco's notion of "open work," where the object is susceptible to "a virtually unlimited range of possible readings, each of which causes the work to acquire new vitality" (Eco 1989, 21). Understandably, then, the Romanian word for decoration in the case of eggs is *încondeiere*, related to the verb "to write" (*condei*, "writing tool"). The colors and motifs used in decoration are rightfully compared to a language (see Tzigara-Samurcaş 1909, specifically the reference to "the grammar of the ornament")—a system of symbols that seem to reunite old Romanian folkloric and religious traditions under the auspices of art.

6.1.1. Egg Decoration as a Craft-World

Describing the practice of Easter egg making in Romania essentially means revealing the actors, resources, and mechanisms of a craft-world (see Becker 2008; Fine 2004).

In relation to Easter eggs, there is a basic—and well-documented (Bodnarescu 1920; Gorovei 2001)—distinction between colored eggs (monochrome) and decorated eggs (usually polychrome). Colored eggs are often red but can be other colors. Decorated eggs have different names in different parts of Romania, and they all involve a traditional system of decoration (instruments, colors, motifs) that today is preserved almost exclusively in the rural parts of the country. "Urban eggs" are often the result of other types of decoration involving, for example, the application of leaves or stickers. The practice of coloring eggs—especially red, less elaborate, and highly evocative of religious significations—is widespread in both urban and rural settings.

The main "actors" of egg decoration are women and children, but there are also cases of male decorators. The making of Easter eggs requires collaboration within the family, less in the case of coloring and almost always in the case of decoration, by which tasks are distributed among family members, from children to elders (Zahacinschi and Zahacinschi 1992, 32). This occurs also because many folk artists have started in the last few decades to make a living (or to contribute to the family budget) by selling decorated eggs, and consequently they produce them in large numbers for what seems to be a growing market (Hutt 2005). This has made egg decoration an occupation that takes place throughout the year rather than an activity that is restricted to the days before Easter (usually Maundy Thursday). Furthermore, this has changed the types of eggs used in decoration—eggs are emptied and range from chicken and duck to goose and ostrich—and has generated an expansion in decoration techniques.

It is important to note that "traditional" egg decoration in Romania relies on a fairly common body of resources and conventions. Eggs are decorated with the help of a chişiţă or condei (see Figure 6.1), a stick with a metal pin at one end used to draw the motifs in wax. Eggs are successively covered with wax on certain portions according to the chosen design and immersed in color (traditionally yellow, followed by red and finally black) so that, in the end, after cleaning the wax off, the egg shows all the desired shapes and colors (Irimie 1969; Newall 1967; Zahacinschi and Zahacinschi 1992). There is an impressive

Figure 6.1. Decorating eggs with wax using a chişiţă.

number of motifs used in egg decoration (Gorovei alone listing 291), classified as geometrical, vegetal (phytomorphic), animal (zoomorphic), anthropomorphic, skeuomorphic (objects), and religious (Zahacinschi and Zahacinschi 1992, 35). However, the existence of traditional motifs doesn't reduce the possibilities for innovation; on the contrary, endless variations of established models are possible (see Figure 6.2), and professional decorators often create new motifs. In addition, decoration itself shows great local variability, and it is not reduced to the wax techniques above but includes many others possibilities, such as decorating eggs with leaves (fixing leaves on the egg before immersing in color) or with beads (applying small beads to a wooden egg previously covered in wax).

Finally, Easter eggs, whether full or emptied, simply colored or richly decorated, are used in a multitude of ways—most, but not all, of them connected to Easter celebrations. To begin with, colored eggs are present on the Easter table, and family and friends knock them against each other, saying "Christ has risen!" (*Hristos a înviat!*) and replying "Truly He has risen!" (*Adevărat a înviat!*). Eggs are also given as gifts, donated as charity, and used

Figure 6.2. Variations of the star motif. (white, yellow, and red shapes on a black background; Cristina Timu)

for reciprocal exchange. They have a strong social function (Bodnarescu 1920; Marian 1992), since both their decoration and use require the presence and participation of others.

6.2. Method

Theoretical underpinnings. The methodology of the present research is based on a cultural psychology approach to creativity and assessment (see Glăveanu 2010a, 2010b; Chapters 1 and 2). At a theoretical level, cultural psychology operates with a *tetradic framework* of self (creator) – other (community) – new artifact (creation) – existing artifacts (culture) for conceptualizing creativity, and it is therefore interested in how creative practices and evaluations are shaped by different sociocultural contexts. In terms of creativity evaluation, this approach favors a *multiple feedback methodology* (see Chapter 4) that involves the use of different groups of "appropriate assessors" to evaluate the creativity of a certain product or class of products. In this case, appropriate assessors are not necessarily experts but persons who are in contact with the creation, for whom the creation is relevant, or who have influence over the distribution of the creation. Furthermore, this methodology requires an in-depth understanding of the *context of creativity evaluations*, the social and cultural "circumstances" in which assessors find themselves—in other words, the communities they belong to, their experiences and interactions with others, and the norms and beliefs they draw from in making their judgments.

While the multiple feedback methodology continues in many ways the approach set by the consensual assessment technique (Amabile 1996), it also differs from it in terms of sample and purpose. It employs people from different groups rather than a relatively homogenous group of "experts" (or persons with at least some formal training in the domain of the creation), and it strives to capture and understand the *diversity* of creativity evaluations rather than the uniformity of participant rankings.

Participants. Easter eggs, as previously asserted, are at the confluence of folklore, religion, and art, and thus "appropriate" observers have been considered from the following communities: ethnographers, priests, and art teachers. Members of these distinct groups are in contact with the practice, have an interest in its products (especially ethnographers), and have a certain power over the "generation" and "distribution" of Easter eggs in specific social contexts—for example, fairs and exhibitions, church services, and school art classes. Also, as a requirement of a cultural psychology approach, folk artists themselves formed a group of evaluators. Nonetheless, it should be noted in regard to Easter eggs that *almost everyone* in Romania is involved in egg making or at least has close family members who make eggs for Easter, even if only colored. Thus, it becomes even more important to investigate not only how people evaluate Easter egg creativity but also how evaluations relate to their own engagement, in some form or another, with this practice. On the whole, the following set of questions guided the investigation:

1. How do ethnographers, priests, art teachers, and folk artists evaluate the creativity of Easter eggs?
2. How are their evaluations rooted in the particular set of norms and beliefs that constitute the "culture" of these four different professional communities?
3. What is the engagement of ethnographers, priests, art teachers, and folk artists with Easter egg making and what kind of self–other relations does it involve?

Procedure. In employing the multiple feedback methodology, a qualitative approach was considered to be the most suitable on account of its distinctive advantages: the possibility of taking account of contexts, an emphasis on describing the world as it is perceived by different observers, and a strong process orientation (Dey 1993). Data were collected with the help of individual semistructured interviews. The interview guide covered general topics such as: (a) personal experience with Easter eggs, (b) considerations regarding this practice in the Romanian context, and (c) creativity and Easter eggs. Interviews were generally opened by a free association task (first three words related to the Easter egg), and they incorporated, in the creativity segment, a discussion of four Easter egg images (colored eggs, eggs with leaves, eggs with traditional decoration, and eggs with stickers) used to prompt further considerations about creativity in Easter egg making. Notably, considering the qualitative nature of the investigation, respondents were not asked to "score" the creativity of the decorated eggs presented in the four images, since the purpose of this study was to explore creativity evaluations concerning a whole class of artistic craft products and not to assess the creativity of specific exemplars.

The study included a total of twenty-seven persons. Respondents were selected using convenience sampling but with attention paid to their typicality for the professional categories represented in the research. All seven ethnographers were employees of the Museum of the Romanian Peasant in Bucharest. The six priests served at churches in Bucharest, and the six art teachers, all graduates of the faculty of fine arts, taught children at different state schools in Bucharest. The eight folk artists mostly came from rural northern Romania (Suceava district), and all of them produced decorated eggs for selling, most being nationally recognized for their mastery of the craft. Data collection took place in March and April 2009 (Orthodox Easter was on April 19), and ethnographers, priests, and art teachers were interviewed at their workplace. Folk artists were interviewed during a national fair organized before Easter at the Museum of the Romanian Peasant. Interviews were audio recorded, and all respondents agreed to the conditions of the study.

Data analysis: The use of thematic networks. After data collection, all interviews were transcribed verbatim and coded using thematic analysis (Attride-Stirling 2001). This procedure, well established in the literature, involves "meaning condensation" (Kvale 1996) through revealing patterns in the information described as themes (Boyatzis 1998). The analytic process, facilitated by the use of ATLAS.ti 5.0, followed the classic steps of coding: (a) stating the research concerns and theoretical framework; (b) grouping together related passages and generating themes; (c) grounding the themes into abstract concepts consistent with the theoretical framework; and finally producing an overall narrative (Auerbach and Silverstein 2003, 43). In order to maintain the confidentiality of the data, the respondents received code names: ethnographers from E1 to E7, priests from P1 to P6, and art teachers from A1 to A6. The folk artists agreed to be named in the report. The coding process was *both data- and theory-driven*, and the four main elements of the tetradic framework served as global themes operationalized as follows:

1. *Self*: Included all codes that made reference to personal experiences with Easter eggs and Easter egg making, both in childhood and adulthood.
2. *Other*: Included all codes referring to people whom self interacts with directly or indirectly in the process of decoration (from family to larger community) or in the use or distribution of Easter eggs (professional contacts).
3. *New artifact*: Included all codes referring to particular Easter eggs made by self or family (their types, number, etc.) as well as beliefs about Easter eggs (issues of classification, value) and Easter egg creativity.

4. *Existing artifacts*: Included all codes referring to the system of norms, beliefs, and practices associated with Easter eggs (from Easter as a religious celebration to the resources involved in decoration) as well as with existing representations of creativity.

6.3. Results

6.3.1. Evaluating Creativity

Easter egg creativity: consensual views. One important result of this application of multiple feedback for the evaluation of Easter egg creativity is that across the four groups of "evaluators," *a high consensus was found in appreciating that there is creativity in Easter egg making.* When asked if they think of the Easter egg as a creative product, the vast majority of respondents stated that this is the case. Rarely was the Easter egg considered to be outside notions of creativity (P2) or "just" a minor form of creative expression (A3). Also, it became obvious that most respondents, when explaining why Easter eggs are creative, took into account "traditional" Easter eggs, meaning those decorated with wax and specific nowadays to rural northern Romania. These eggs, and not those colored or decorated with leaves, have come to embody creativity in the practice of Easter egg making:

> I: Have you ever thought about Easter eggs as creative products?
>
> R: Yes, but just if they are decorated [*incondeiate*; traditional decoration], are made. When it's just the red egg it is not necessarily something creative because it's too banal, if I could say so, anyone can do it. When [eggs] are decorated and made with soul and [are] beautiful yes [they are creative]. (P4)

High appreciation for traditional egg decoration was often articulated with enthusiasm, and some of the respondents expressed astonishment at how peasant women are capable of making such beautiful artifacts and at how they find time for this craft: "Because these women that made eggs and worked enormously for them, had children, had a husband, had work to do outside, work in the house" (E6). What is repeatedly stressed is the meticulousness involved in this kind of decoration, a complexity that made even art teachers recognize that they would not be able to reach "such rigor and such beauty" (A5). Similar opinions are also found in the literature, where authors like Zahacinschi and Zahacinschi (1992, 32) consider Easter egg decoration to be represented by its "preciseness, wealth and nobility of motifs, harmonic conjugation of colours, explosive imagination, spontaneity with which the craftswoman solves, 'as they happen', some of the most difficult artistic and technical problems."

Another common point in the discussion about Easter egg creativity is the frequency with which the *idea of art* came up, again across the four groups.

103

Decorated eggs are artistic creations that "lead you to the church" (P3) and entail "thoughtfulness, composition, line, color, everything involved in the domain of visual arts" (E1). Art teachers themselves were quick to describe Easter eggs as "very creative, very; surprisingly creative," a form of "pure art" (A6) and to locate them in the domain of folk arts (A2).

At the same time, there are differences—even within traditional decoration and between folk artists—that need to be acknowledged. As one of the ethnographers noted, "Indeed, there are some artists, but we can't include everyone in this category" (E7). At the same time, folk artists themselves, who were ready to appreciate both the creativity of colleagues whose work they knew and, with just one exception in the group of eight interviewed decorators, their own creative expression. Notably, that exception was also the only person to say that she took up egg decoration out of necessity (after losing a previous job).

What folk artists answered when asked about their work was that, while following some basic decoration rules, they "always invent something new" (Maria Zinici). If there is no specific order requiring the multiplication of a certain model, there "must" be something done differently for each egg (Ileana Hotopilă), and sometimes a completely new model is created. In the end, there are no perfect copies of an egg since "eggs don't have the same size, they couldn't, and colors are changed, it depends on the state of mind you are in at that moment" (Rodica Berechea). As Livia Balacian said laughing, "And even if I want to make a certain model, I still have to change something, it's like it is easier to change then to let everything be the same every time." This is the reason why most folk artists stated that they rarely know beforehand how the egg will turn out in the end—it all becomes clear in the process, and sometimes changes are "imposed" by the necessity of not juxtaposing certain colors (Veronica Iamnițchi) or by other stylistic requirements. Even artists like Dionis Spătaru—who respect in detail certain models (belonging to *Cucuteni* ceramics) and are keen to not change anything in terms of design and colors—appreciated that there is great creativity in "translating" an image from pot to egg and in all the adjustments that this work involves. This leads, for some folk artists, to the idea that Easter egg making entails *talent* (since some can do it and some cannot, even in the case of their children). It also means that artists develop a personal style that, as all agreed, can be recognized out of "thousands" of eggs (Maria Zinici).

Types of decoration and creativity: divergent views. As part of the interview, respondents commented on creativity in traditionally decorated eggs, eggs decorated with leaves, simply colored eggs, and eggs with stickers. Folk artists made reference to some of these forms spontaneously during the interviews. What emerged is a complex picture of divergent views, some within but mostly across groups, and four types of approaches to creativity in egg decoration became salient.

Ethnographers often described creativity in Easter egg making as a *continuum*, where traditional forms of decoration show the highest creativity, followed by eggs with leaves, then simply colored eggs, and finally, at the other end, eggs with stickers. If in traditional egg decoration combining motifs and choosing colors entails "maximal creativity" and "a lot of imagination" (E6), eggs with leaves are more "repetitive," a form of "small creativity" (E1) born out of the need to make something more beautiful (E3). What seems to underlie this distinction is the amount of *effort* and *skill* that people invest in making such eggs. If traditional eggs are carefully "thought through" (E5), eggs with leaves come second because they require "some cognitive effort" (E2), at least compared to simple coloring. But the category that was almost unanimously disliked by ethnographers was that of eggs with stickers. Often described as kitsch, eggs with stickers make no sense, "a synthesis made by people with no roots" (E6), and only respondents who had small children admitted to using them at times, though without necessarily appreciating this practice. In the kitsch category many ethnographers also included eggs decorated with Christmas motifs (E5).

The group of priests referred more to creativity and Easter eggs as *controversial*. Though they generally appreciated traditional decoration as a form of "art, culture" (P5), one stated that working on emptied eggs departs from the original purpose of these artifacts (P2). Another said that an Easter egg is creative

> for as long as the meaning of being an Easter egg is not lost. For as long as they are not dissociated from symbolism, for as long as the ones seeing the Easter egg don't forget the tight connection it has with the sacrifice of our Savior. (P6)

The same priest argued that this is why Orthodox Christians don't consider icons, for example, to be works of art. In this context, simple red eggs were regarded as most appropriate for Easter, followed by traditional decoration that draws from "the tradition of the church, then cultural traditions; from the artistic tradition of the church" (P4). The effort behind making eggs with leaves was often appreciated as well: if traditional decoration is a form of "art looking at eternity," eggs with leaves illustrate "art looking at the present" (P3). As with the ethnographers, eggs with stickers were seen as having "no religious significance" (P3), as being "a form of religious marketing" (P1), and as not representing Romanian traditions (P4) or spirituality (P6).

For the group of artists, the general admiration for traditional Easter eggs and the tendency to oppose them to eggs with stickers were again present, but they left room for a vision in which "all eggs are potentially creative." First, the egg in itself, as a shape, allows for multiple ways of decoration (A1). Traditional Easter eggs are creative for several reasons: they communicate deep meaning, they allow innovation, they stylize reality, and they are the product of hard work. Eggs with leaves were considered more "modest attempts" (A5), but they could be more expressive if different leaves were chosen and positioned on the egg in unique ways (A4); the leaf models could even be embellished with watercolors (A6). Even simply colored eggs could be made more creative by diversifying the range of colors (A5), and art teachers themselves often combine the colors they use for dyeing eggs. Finally, eggs with stickers were again considered kitsch: "distortions of meaning," "surrogates" (A3). Still, even in this case, there was an opinion that putting numerous stickers on the same egg is kitsch but a single sticker with the right kind of symbol could look beautiful in some ways (A6).

Folk artists mostly referred in their interviews to the use of traditional decoration in their own work and in the work of other artists. There was respect and recognition for the work of others ("This is my style, how I work. The woman across has another style, not like mine, her own"). In this sense, a general view that Easter egg making requires creativity working from within tradition was paramount. Furthermore, folk artists were less evaluative when it came to the creativity of particular forms of decoration. There was only one criterion that stood out as essential: the *quality* of the work. This relates to the dedication and skill each artist has and also to the motivation for making Easter eggs. Some make eggs only for money, putting no "soul" into their work (Maria Zinici). This is often the case of those who commercialize eggs with stickers, and these eggs are strongly disliked by folk artists because they "trick" buyers and destroy the value of real Easter egg making. In the end, what matters most is for the egg to be made "by the hands" of the artist.

It is important to note that this diversity of beliefs about which eggs are more or less creative is potentially underpinned by a diversity of conceptions about creativity itself. If ethnographers and priests discussed creativity in terms of an "improvement" of what already exists (i.e., traditional practices), artists and folk artists tended to emphasize the "naturalness" of creative expression and its connection to the *aesthetic* (that is, making something beautiful come into being). All these evaluations (both general and related to egg decoration practices) need to be further contextualized in terms of the social and cultural factors leading to their emergence.

6.3.2. Contextualizing Evaluations

Easter egg: traditions and conventions. It has been said about art objects that they "demand interpretation" (Zittoun et al. 2003, 429). This is certainly valid for Easter eggs, artifacts whose creativity and meaning are appreciated only with reference to a larger cultural background of existing artifacts, of norms and beliefs—in this particular case, the world of traditions concerning Easter and Easter egg decoration. Respondents from all four groups commented on this aspect, acknowledging that the value of Easter eggs resides in the synthesis they offer between constant innovation and a deep and meaningful Romanian tradition, where both terms—tradition and innovation—define and require each other.

Ethnographers were probably the ones who were in the best position to appreciate the richness of Easter egg decoration practices. This is how one finds in their set of interviews numerous remarks about the traditional making and use of Easter eggs. They referred to legends about Easter eggs, to the controversy around the proper day for coloring eggs, and to the customs of washing your face with water in which a red egg was placed, of keeping eggs or eggshells for protection, and of giving Easter eggs as charity or sending the shells to a legendary people called *Blajini*. Local differences in decoration were put in perspective as being reflective of the different living conditions in northern and southern Romania, in villages of the plains as compared to those of the mountains (E7). In the end, though, all customs and their variations constitute a unitary picture of Romanian folklore and confirm the fact that "Romanian folk culture is a culture of Resurrection" (E1). This is something with which priests were also in agreement: "The Easter egg encompasses the entire sequence of events from the crucifixion of Christ to His Resurrection and elevation to the heavens" (P6).

From the more practical perspective of art teachers and especially of folk artists, as persons involved in the actual decoration of eggs to different degrees, the practice of Easter egg making also includes a set of *conventions*, of basic rules that facilitate the decoration process and allow some forms of innovation over others. For art teachers, these were primarily artistic conventions guiding the use of traditional art elements (point, line, color) in ways that generate chromatic harmony and structural equilibrium. Many teachers prioritize specific shapes over others, for example rhombuses and curved lines (A6), and they promote the use of complementary colors to generate artistic contrasts (A5). Folk artists, on the other hand, have much more experience with working directly on the egg and using wax decoration. What they emphasized were basic rules of decoration, such as not making mistakes when working with wax, going from light to dark colors in decoration, starting with the segmentation of work fields on the egg, respecting distances in decoration and not juxtaposing similar colors, using clean wax, and, for eggs made with wax in relief, applying wax in consistent quantities. In the end, all creation must respect the "nature" of the craft, since

> you can't, no matter what you do, abandon tradition, because you would be making something else [not Easter eggs] and it would be worthless. Even if some things are added, a little flower, a square, anything, it is normal to create but you must always consider tradition. (Rodica Berechea)

The multiple faces of change. In agreement with the cultural psychology perspective on creativity, findings about Easter egg creativity reveal how important "existing artifacts" are for the generation of a "new artifact." In the words of Feldman (1988, 288), all "previous efforts, as represented in a culture's products, models, technologies, and so forth, are of enormous value to the creator." These assertions need further qualification in terms of a temporal dimension. Artifacts, norms, beliefs, and material objects don't just exist as a static reality. They constantly transform, grow, adapt. "Conventions represent the continuing adjustment of the cooperating parties to the changing conditions in which they practice; as conditions change, they change" (Becker 2008, 59). This dynamism is clearly illustrated by the custom of Easter egg making in Romania.

In all interviews, across the four groups, changes in Easter practices and egg decoration were noticed and commented on—changes related to differences both between past and present and between rural and urban. Common observations referred to Easter eggs being made throughout the year, to the use of emptied eggs and artificial color pigments, and to the expansion of commerce often associated with a diversification of types of decorated eggs (also in Zahacinschi and Zahacinschi 1992). This is what made some ethnographers notice that, today, what we call "traditional eggs" are no longer traditional in the strict sense of the word—they are the "neo-tradition" (E3), "a traditional model that adapts to a very modern market" (E5). In the end, there seems to be one constant in the process of change: eggs are and always have been central for Easter: "There is no Easter without the eggs" (A5).

Interviews also revealed important information about reactions to change and a rather common tendency of seeing this process as "bad." Across the groups, participants complained that things tend to be *lost*, especially in the city (A1), and even villages are turning into "small towns" threatened by globalization and uniformity (P1). Priests were especially sensitive to changes that "affect" not only egg decoration but also Easter celebration more generally; these changes point to the "secularization of Easter" and "commercialization of the festival" that authors such as Barnett (1949, 70) also referred to. Ethnographers noticed about Easter eggs that they (including folk artists) can no longer "read" traditional motifs: "We don't understand anymore what the women who drew the lost way, the plow, or the ram's horns, wanted to tell us" (E7). Losing meaning directly affects the value and importance of Easter eggs.

However, change was not perceived as bad in all cases. There were even ethnographers who were willing to accept that all the innovations contributed to keeping the craft alive and even caused it to expand (E2). Folk artists were the first to testify to the benefits of adopting many of the novelties that have transformed this craft-world in the past few decades. As the interviews show, there were distinguishable "narratives of change" that folk artists shared, and some included the appreciation of self as a *pioneer of change*. This is the case of Ileana Hotopilă who, along with her sister Maria Zinici, was proud to have introduced many innovations in egg decoration. Having collaborated with persons from the United States after the anticommunist revolution, both Maria and Ileana started to decorate eggs for different seasons and holidays during the year, including Christmas. The range of colors and motifs expanded and, very soon, other decorators adopted the "new trends" in ways that reflected their particular style.

In conclusion, there is always both stability and change in the practice of Easter egg making, and this qualifies it as a form of "great tradition"—that is, a tradition that incorporates activity and creativity (Eisenstadt 1973, 120). It is a *vital tradition* in the sense that it is constantly re-created, never finished or complete (Negus and Pickering 2004, 104), always in a movement toward the future, always "carrying on" (Ingold and Hallam 2007, 6). All these aspects are perfectly captured by an ethnographer's comment about creativity and tradition: "The world is made up of some customs that give you freedom, but this freedom is a freedom that keeps" and does not lead to a "rupture" or an "annihilation of old creation" (E1). This is why the multiple faces of change described in this section are all symbolically growing out of and continuing a "body" of tradition—the only one that can make their existence meaningful.

6.3.3. Expressing Evaluations

A polyphony of practices. When we turn to the *personal engagement* that respondents from all four groups have with the practice of Easter egg making, the resulting image is one of diversity. Some respondents (mainly priests and some of the ethnographers) don't color eggs themselves but "indirectly" participate by helping family members with Easter preparations. When eggs are just dyed, it is often only in red, or if more colors are used, red is sure to be one of them. Art teachers and ethnographers, especially those with small children, often make efforts to go *beyond* simple coloring of the eggs by combining primary colors (obtaining different tones of green, orange, and purple), decorating eggs with leaves, and even by adorning them with stickers—all for the enjoyment of their children. At the other extreme, folk artists decorate a large number of eggs and use different techniques (usually both traditional decoration with wax and wax in relief). Notably, though, the Easter eggs they make at home for their religious celebration are simple, generally colored in red and sometimes containing the symbol of the cross and various Easter messages.

This state of affairs is, to a great extent, expressive of the type of creativity evaluations made by members from each of the four groups. As many of the priests identify Easter eggs with red eggs and value their deep significance, they often encourage in their own homes the practice of coloring eggs red. Ethnographers and priests alike appreciated traditional egg decoration, but lack of skill and time makes these eggs an ideal that they felt unable to realize, and thus most tended to use in their homes the simplest coloring methods.

This is the case for some of the art teachers as well, but because most of them saw the potential for creativity and for the generation of beauty as being associated with Easter egg making, many experimented freely and came up with surprising results. For example, A6 has a collection of the eggs that she decorated in past years using a multitude of techniques, from painting to wax dripping and from decorating pigeon eggs to painting a coconut shell (resembling an ostrich egg). In the end, it is of course the folk artists included in the study who, as part of their "professional" activity, constantly develop and practice a vast range of decoration styles and techniques, using a variety of colors, motifs, and designs.

Regulation and resistance. Easter egg making is certainly a collective type of activity. It often depends on the help of others, and it is always directed toward others: people to share the eggs with, to show the eggs to, to sell them to, etc. Family members, neighbors, clients, members of the larger community—all participate in the life of this craft-world. The explicit and implicit presence of others is something that all respondents commented on. There were stories of collaboration and mutual agreement, referred to above, but also stories about the imposition of certain rules and reactions to them.

Some participants from the group of ethnographers took part, at times, in organizing Easter fairs and inviting folk artists to display and commercialize their creations. Efforts were made in these cases to discourage those who bring eggs with colors and motifs outside of "normal" conventions. Still, as noted by one ethnographer (E1), some folk artists regularly find ways to bypass the "censorship" and come with different types of eggs in different bags, some to be shown only when there are no museum personnel around. When discovered, they argue that "it is what the buyers want"; this, however, is not a valid argument for the many ethnographers who believe that folk artists should take more responsibility for their actions—"Now they like it because you [as producer] drug them with images and stories and then everyone becomes addicted but you drugged them, you made them addicted" (E1).

Animated by such views, some museum workers claimed that it is their *professional duty* to stop the proliferation of kitsch in Easter egg making (E7), and, in a more radical formulation, authors like Arthur Gorovei (2001, 110) came to argue that "the primitive art of peasant women from the depth of the mountains or the fields of the country is the only tradition that deserves to be researched." In contrast to this, other respondents disliked the idea of a selection process for fairs and exhibitions and argued that it is not aesthetics but "truth" and the objective analysis of current realities that should prevail in an ethnographer's work (E5).

A similar situation can be found in the case of priests, who in general considered that Easter eggs brought to the church (for Easter) should be red yet regularly found parishioners coming with eggs of all colors. This is where "the church has the role of educating people" (P4), and thus parishioners are directly or indirectly told to bring only red eggs. Nevertheless, there is also resistance to these ideas, and one of the priests mentioned that it is nowhere written that eggs should only be red (P5). Besides, if the wife at home makes eggs of other colors or if such eggs are received as gifts, "you can't say 'put these aside'" (P2).

Even more flexibility in terms of decoration was promoted by art teachers. Most of those who work with Easter eggs at school claimed that they allow children to make "a spontaneous, free creation, with no rules" (A2) and that they encourage all students, independent of their result (A4). But, as in any form of teaching, there are some basic notions regarding chromatic harmony and decorative art that teachers always want to convey. In the end, there is great appreciation for self-expression. Sometimes teachers also initiate larger interdisciplinary projects with students from several classes in order to explore a wide range of ideas.

6.4. Discussion: Views from "Outside" and "Inside" the Craft

In the previous sections, thematic networks were described in a compartmentalized way, guided by the three research questions. At this point, the analysis must leave space for an overall *synthesis*, one that can reveal final connections between the evaluation of and the practice associated with Easter egg decoration. This is imperative because the four elements of the tetradic framework of creativity (self, other, new artifact, existing artifacts) are conceptualized as *interdependent*. In the present discussion, therefore, emphasis will be placed on the *entirety* of the research framework and on the two main emerging patterns of creativity evaluation—one corresponding to the "view from outside" and the other to the "view from inside" the practice of egg decoration.

At this point, three observations are needed. First, the notion of "inside" in this context refers to direct participation in forms of egg decoration and is not meant to imply any kind of deeper of more valuable insight that "insiders" have over "outsiders." Second, generating patterns may have the benefit of bringing previously disparate pieces together, but this is done at the cost of losing much individual detail. Therefore, the patterns discussed next are reflective of the overall findings but may well be imperfect for describing individual cases. Third, patterns are based on the principle of correlation, not causality. They show how practices of the self, relations with others, and the use of cultural resources or beliefs about new artifacts "go together," and not how one aspect determines others. These are all issues to be unpacked through further research based on a different methodology.

The view from "outside." The starting point for generating overall patterns that can characterize the data from this multiple feedback exercise is *personal and direct involvement in elaborate egg decoration*. Using this perspective, the view from "outside" is constructed from responses of persons who, though closely connected to the practice of Easter egg making and its products, don't generally try egg decoration themselves, outside of coloring or other simple procedures (such as making eggs with leaves). From the data, it became clear that this group includes mainly ethnographers, priests, and some of the art teachers.

The key conclusion that can be drawn from this broad category of evaluators is that creativity *exists in some Easter eggs more than in others*, and there tends to be a clear separation between types of Easter eggs. Overall, traditional decoration is appreciated as highly creative, but, even in this regard, there seems to be a controversy about the value of certain "innovative" forms of decoration that radically depart from conventional ways. Respondents holding the view from "outside" are, by and large, strongly attached to the tradition—folkloric or religious—of Easter egg making. Basing their judgments on this consistent background of beliefs and customs, they *find it easy to appreciate certain Easter eggs more than others* (for example, they might value red eggs for their simplicity and deep symbolism). This is mostly why—being largely unable to decorate eggs traditionally owing to lack of time, skill, and practice—these respondents are inclined to not decorate at all and to keep eggs plain yet "authentic." Such appreciation also guides them in their contact with others, where they tend to "regulate" in some sense the production of Easter eggs to conform to an ideal set by tradition and therefore to teach others (folk artists, parishioners, children, etc.) the value of working toward this ideal.

These conclusions are of great importance for understanding how creativity evaluations are made by members of groups that are in contact with, and even have some kind of power over, the production and selection of creative artifacts. As Dewey (1934, 49) stated, "Perfection in execution cannot be measured or defined in terms of execution; it implies those who perceive and enjoy the product that is executed." Ethnographers, priests, and school teachers may seem on the "outside" of egg decoration as people who don't generally practice it in its most elaborate forms, but they are certainly very active "inside" the *validation* of Easter eggs' value and creativity.

The view from "inside." It is folk artists and a few of the art teachers who actually engage in elaborate forms of egg decoration, the first involved in selling Easter eggs and the second in making them at home or during art classes.

Respondents in this case formulate a different assessment of creativity, being inclined to see *most Easter eggs as creative in one way or another*, or at least as having the *potential to enhance Easter egg's level of creativity*. Working to decorate eggs and collaborating closely with others for this task (family members, school children, etc.) gives respondents an appreciation for the difficulties and also the opportunities inherent in Easter egg making, in terms of creative combinations and generation of "novelties." Furthermore, folk artists in particular are commonly open to diversifying their work techniques based on the requests of the "market." Respondents from this broad group also tend to be less evaluative about different types of Easter eggs and to appreciate each for its own virtues. When judgments are made, they are grounded more in aesthetics and concern beauty alongside the "quality" of the work. They acknowledge the existence of a solid tradition of Easter egg making and are more flexible in relation to it, perceiving its set of motifs, colors, designs, and conventions as resources ready to be used in creative ways.

To clarify further, this is not to say that tradition is in any way less important for folk artists than it is for ethnographers and priests. Folk artists are proud of working within a strong tradition and enriching it with their work. What differs to some extent is how tradition is approached in this case—more as a "resource" than as a "standard." If the relationship between tradition and innovation, constraints and possibilities, "can be viewed as a fight, a war, a revolution, or as an ongoing process of change and dialogue" (Montuori and Purser 1995, 74), it is certainly this last perspective that informs the practice of egg decorators and allows them to adapt to the ever-changing demands of the growing number of people, both from Romania and abroad, who are interested in Easter eggs.

6.5. Final Reflection on the Use of Multiple Feedback

The present research started from the general premise that "creativity takes place within, is constituted and influenced by, and has consequences for, a social context" (Westwood and Low 2003, 236). If cultural psychology contributes to psychology in general by emphasizing meaning, practice, and products (Markus and Hamedani 2007), an application of cultural psychology to the field of creativity—and, in particular, to creativity evaluation—was developed in order to obtain a more comprehensive view of creativity judgments as rooted in particular social and cultural contexts and bodies of established practices. Designing and using the multiple feedback method for the study of creativity in Easter egg making in Romania thus offered an ecological and situational understanding of how ethnographers, priests, art teachers, and folk artists formulate certain opinions about creativity and of how these opinions are embedded in larger complexes of cultural norms and self–other relations. As the final conclusions demonstrated, there are general patterns structuring people's conceptions about and engagement with Easter egg decoration, and these reveal important similarities, and also marked differences, among the four groups. Both the "generation" and "evaluation" of creativity can be fully understood only in the context of their production.

7

Creativity and Folk Art: A Study of Creative Action in Traditional Craft[1]

7.1. Why and How to Study a Traditional Artistic Craft

The present research chapter offers an exploration of creative situated action in a traditional artistic craft, namely, Romanian Easter egg decoration, focusing both on activity stages and their microgenetic characteristics. Folk art has generally received, with a few exceptions (Kozbelt and Durmysheva 2007; Ngara 2010; Yokochi and Okada 2005), limited attention from psychologists involved in creativity research, at least in comparison to fine art. Moreover, it seems to be a common belief that "folk art, when contrasted with fine arts, shows a high occurrence of borrowing, repetition, use of conventional themes, plagiarism, and disregard for spontaneity and originality" (Cincura 1970, 170). To understand this difference in the attribution of creativity, we need to consider what is specific to artistic activity on the one hand and to craft on the other and how their features correspond (or not) to the concerns of creativity researchers.

For instance, there is a long-standing fascination in the discipline with "great creators" and "great creations" (Glăveanu 2010b; Chapter 2; Montuori and Purser 1995), and celebrated artists and works of art embody for many the paradigm of the genius. In contrast, folk artists—especially those involved in traditional crafts such as pottery, quilting, wood carving, and so forth—are rarely known outside their communities, and the artifacts they create often bear the mark of anonymity. Furthermore, there is a proper, "institutionalized" domain of the arts (see Csikszentmihalyi 1988), including gatekeepers such as critics and museum curators and reward systems for excellence, whereas

[1] © 2012 by the American Psychological Association. Reproduced with permission. The official citation that should be used in referencing this material is as follows: Creativity and folk art: A study of creative action in traditional craft. Glăveanu, Vlad Petre. *Psychology of Aesthetics, Creativity, and the Arts*, Vol 7(2), May 2013, 140–154. doi: 10.1037/a0029318. The use of this information does not imply endorsement by the publisher.

craft is constituted more as a social practice rather than as an established domain (though signs of institutionalization do exist; see Becker 2008). Most importantly, there is also a sense in which folk art usually reflects traditional practices, and a widespread misconception portrays tradition or custom as the very opposite of creativity (see Negus and Pickering 2004; Wilson 1984). Indeed, in a classic separation between art and crafts, Collingwood (1938) claimed the latter to be, among other things, the result of "preconceived" ideas; in his words, "The craftsman knows what he wants to make before he makes it" (15–16).

No doubt, many differences can be found between folk and fine art in terms of the sources they draw from (traditional forms versus oftentimes a rejection of these forms), their audiences (the general public versus a cultivated public), and their uses (the practical aspects of life versus aesthetic enjoyment). However, a sharp (and in many ways artificial) dichotomy between the two, separating the "creative" from the "less creative" or "noncreative," can be contested on several accounts. For example, an increasing number of creativity papers have been dedicated in recent years to such notions as little-c (Craft 2001) or even mini-c creativity (Beghetto and Kaufman 2007) and, more generally, to everyday life creations (Montuori 2011; Sawyer 2000). This orientation turns away from Big-C kinds of expression and toward the much more mundane, numerous, yet in no way less significant types of everyday creativity. Craft certainly corresponds to this category and illustrates how ordinary and constant production is actually instrumental for the life of human communities, since it contributes to local identities and to the maintenance of social relations through processes of guided participation (see Rogoff 2003).

Other barriers faced by those interested in folk art are of a methodological nature. Little-c and mini-c creativity are notoriously difficult to capture and analyze, and this partially explains why creativity researchers often found refuge in the study of eminent creative products: they are much easier to detect and scrutinize. Dismissing folk art on the basis that it is "stuck" in tradition, convention, and repetition (thus disregarding the fact that creativity would not in fact be possible outside of conventions and constraints; Becker 2008; Csikszentmihalyi 1988) allows us to neglect the study of moment-to-moment creative emergence (see Beghetto and Kaufman 2007).

Furthermore, to incorporate this microgenetic aspect of craftwork, one would have to operate with a slightly different definition of creativity that, in the context of this chapter, can be summarized as follows: creativity is a type of situated action that leads to the generation of outcomes characterized, to different degrees, by novelty and utility as perceived by a person or community. This conceptualization resonates with Plucker, Beghetto, and Dow's (2004, 90) definition while considering the "interaction between aptitude, process and environment" to be what essentially describes human action (see Harré 1982) and acknowledging the fact that creative outcomes vary in their degree of originality and utility (a continuum that bridges Big-C and little-c views) and depend upon the evaluation of others, whether individuals (including creators themselves) or larger groups (in the case of craft, often rural communities).

In summary, what an action or activity approach to creativity outlines is the dynamic and situated nature of creative expression by placing great emphasis on both (a) the phases of action and (b) the context of acting in a simultaneously social and material world. It becomes clear, then, how such a perspective is very fruitful for the study of craft (and potentially beyond it), for craft is a form of activity that is deeply immersed in materiality and is organized around a series of practical steps. As a result, my main theoretical aim in this chapter is to advance an *action framework of creativity*, one that recuperates insights from early pragmatist writings. The current literature dedicated to the creative process is dominated by a cognitive approach (see Bink and Mash 2000; Finke, Ward, and Smith 1992) that emphasizes the "internal" dynamic of creativity but does little justice to the interaction between creator and his or her social and material environment. For a study of creativity in craft, the latter is a defining feature. To consider thinking processes in the case of artisans is not void of merit, but it falls short when it comes to capturing the practical ways in which craftwork progresses. In fact, and as demonstrated here, a major source of creativity in the practice of folk art (and art more generally) rests precisely in the continuous dialogue between creator and creation, between artist and his or her work (Mace and Ward 2002; Yokochi and Okada 2005). John Dewey (1934) expressed this state of affairs as follows in relation to the subject matter in art:

> It is a *developing process*. . . . The artist finds where he is going because of what he has previously done; that is, the original excitation and stir of some contact with the world undergo successive transformation. The state of the matter he has arrived at sets up demands to be fulfilled and it institutes a framework that limits further operations. (116, emphasis added)

It is this pragmatist orientation that guides here the analysis of interview and observation data concerning the activity of folk artists. Dewey (1934), for instance, pointed to the continuous cycle in artistic work between *doing* (acting on the world) and *undergoing* (taking in the reaction of the world to the doing), a type of dynamic that largely corresponds to action–perception loops (see Hutchins 1995). This process is alimented by different "impulsions" (motivations) on the part of the creator and often faces a series of "obstacles" or difficulties that require creative expression and that "save" the work from monotony. Finally, creative action is the acting of the "whole" person (involving cognition, affect, and volition) in the context of material constraints and social relations.

In light of this, the pragmatist approach is said to be concerned with *situated creativity* (Joas and Kilpinen 2006, 323), and as such it can be a very fruitful perspective for a study of craft creativity.

For this purpose, however, the framework needs to be operationalized in research, and this is one of the methodological contributions that the present chapter aims to offer to the field of creativity studies. This contribution is complemented by a methodological innovation, represented by the use of subjective cameras (subcams) for the study of creative action (see Chapter 5). These are wearable cameras, worn at eye level, that video and audio record the activity of participants *from their perspective*, offering the researcher a unique opportunity to see and hear what the participant saw and heard while performing his or her work (Lahlou 1999, 2011). The recordings can afterward be discussed with the respondent to gain further insight into the goals and thoughts of the person during the activity. There are numerous advantages to using subcams—instead of or in addition to external cameras—in creativity research, and they have been discussed elsewhere (see Glăveanu and Lahlou 2012; Chapter 5). The subcam is especially relevant to folk art, where the artisan tends to work on small objects held relatively close to the eyes and is more at ease with showing than with describing processes involved in the craft.

The above is very much valid for the type of folk art selected for this study, namely, Easter egg decoration in a rural Romanian community. This particular craft was chosen because of the strong traditional basis on which it builds, the general rules of decoration, an extensive symbolism associated with patterns and motifs, and the great diversity and highly aesthetic quality of its outcomes (Gorovei 2001; Zahacinschi and Zahacinschi 1992). Egg decoration is indeed a custom with ancient roots, probably pre-Christian, and is situated at the intersection of folklore, religion, art, and a growing market for the production and selling of eggs (see Glăveanu 2010c; Chapter 6). In Romania, the embellishment of eggs in general is practiced on a large scale in the days before Easter and the Ascension, usually based on dying eggs (typically red, recalling the sacrifice of Christ) but also incorporating other techniques such as applying leaves or stickers. Nonetheless, the oldest forms of decoration, the ones focused on in this chapter, involve the use of wax for drawing models and repeated immersion in color (drawing with colored wax has become increasingly popular as well in recent years). This practice is common in rural areas, particularly in the north of the country. It is here that Easter egg making has, in recent decades, seen a considerable expansion—it is now practiced throughout the year by entire families and communities, and in many cases decoration work is carried out by children as young as age seven. Yet despite this richness and popularity, egg decoration has not been thoroughly explored by ethnographers and has received even less attention from psychologists. As the present chapter strives to demonstrate, there is great value in focusing on the activity of Easter egg making for deepening our understanding of microlevel processes of creation, which are the subject of the following studies.

7.2. Methodology Outline

The overarching aim of the two exploratory studies reported here was to uncover the creativity of craftwork in two consecutive stages: first, a general description of decoration activity and its organization, obtained through the use of interview and observation, followed by a more detailed analysis of filmed recordings of the first work phase (for relatively similar designs in researching artistic crafts, see Yokochi and Okada 2005). Both studies were performed in the village of Ciocăneşti, Suceava district (Romania), which was chosen for its strong and vibrant community of decorators, the National Museum of Decorated Eggs, and its yearly festivals dedicated to the craft. Overall, this research follows a central or critical case strategy (Auerbach and Silverstein 2003), in which the topic and sample are selected considering their suitability for "testing" a newly proposed theoretical model.

7.2.1. Study 1: Interviews and Observation

A study of situated action necessarily considers both its general stages and microgenetic characteristics and their material and social context. For this purpose, and following a pragmatist-inspired framework, the first study distinguished between (a) the stages of doing (action), (b) their relation to forms of material and social undergoing (perception), (c) the role played by obstacles or difficulties in the dynamic between doing and undergoing, and (d) the types of knowledge and procedures that inform the doing of the artisans.

Participants. The study included sixteen decorators from Ciocăneşti. Data were collected in September 2009 and March 2010. The sample was generated through snowballing (see Streeton, Cooke, and Campbell 2004) and covered the most active and well-known decorators in the community, usually with seven to ten years of professional experience. The group included fifteen women and one man (the only known male decorator), with a mean age of 36.5 years (the range was thirty-one to forty-three, excluding a female decorator in her sixties).

Method and materials. As a first investigation, having the aim of "mapping out" creative activity, a combination of semistructured interviews (see Gaskell 2000) and, whenever possible, observation of the decoration process was considered most suitable. The interview started with a discussion of personal experience with Easter egg decoration and solicited a detailed description of activities and processes (what is done, when, how, with the help of what or whom, with what outcomes, etc.). Toward the end, participants were asked about the broader context of the practice (Easter and Easter traditions) and then about creativity and how it is reflected (or not) in their work. Whenever observations were possible, the first part of the interview consisted of describing and explaining actual decoration work.

Procedure. Interviews were audio recorded, and all respondents were informed about and agreed with the conditions of the study. All decorators from Ciocănești wanted to be identified in the research with the exception of two (one who started decoration more recently and another who was, at that moment, doing very little decoration work; participant names appear in parentheses following examples or quotes). Nine direct observations were performed within this group. During these, the author made notes and also took pictures of the process each time a new element was made on the egg or when a stage of decoration was initiated.

Data analysis: operationalizing a pragmatist conception. All interviews were transcribed verbatim and coded using thematic analysis with the help of ATLAS.ti. The coding frame was firmly, though not exclusively, guided by theory (from Dewey 1934, discussion of art and pragmatist accounts of craftwork; see Sennett 2008). The coding started from an initial set of categories: impulsion, obstacle, doing, undergoing social, undergoing material, undergoing before doing, and emotion. After the first five interviews were reviewed, some of the initial codes were segmented (e.g., descriptions of "stages of doing" became distinguished from "procedures" and "time" of activity) and new data-driven categories emerged (knowledge, prerequisites, undergoing final result, outcomes, setting). Definitions of main categories and examples are given in Table 7.1.

Table 7.1. Coding frame for interview analysis.

Code	Definition	Example
Impulsion	Motivations for action; why the action is done	To make beautiful objects, to create, to express, etc.
Obstacles	Difficulties or limitations that the decorator experiences	Fragility of eggs, poor quality of colors, mistakes made while working with wax, etc.
Prerequisites	Qualities needed for action to take place	Patience, drawing talent, ambition, etc.
Setting	Presentation of their community and local traditions	General notions about urban and rural decoration, the "style" in Ciocănești, etc.
Knowledge	The types of information required for decorating work	Knowledge of Easter traditions, motifs, material properties, etc.
Procedures	The different techniques used at different stages of activity	Procedures for making colors, working on the egg (repetition, symmetry, etc.)

Stages of doing	The different phases of creative work and how it advances	Preparing wax; decorating eggs on white, yellow, and red; immersing in color; etc.
Materials	All the materials needed for decoration work	Eggs, chișițe, wax, leaves, stickers, colors, etc.
Time of work	When decoration is performed	Before Easter, winter, day or night, etc.
Undergoing before doing	All the elements that prepared/enabled the creator to engage in creative work	Learning how to decorate, years of practice, observing/keeping decoration motifs, etc.
Material undergoing	The relation to the physical/material environment	Shape of eggs, properties of colors and wax, what has been done, etc.
Social undergoing	The relation to the social environment and social interactions	Orders from clients, tastes of customers, interaction with family members, etc.
Undergoing final result	Perceiving and judging the final outcome	What else is needed, what "worked," etc.
Emotion / fulfillment	Emotions experienced at any stage of the work process	Satisfaction, surprise, pride, anxiety, etc.
Outcomes	The results of work	Types of eggs, number of eggs, etc.

It should be noted that observation data were not analyzed per se but rather were used to contextualize interview accounts and for exemplification exclusively (photos of decoration). Owing to the interrelated nature of the elements above, double coding was not uncommon. For the purpose of testing the reliability of the coding, the researcher recoded the whole dataset six months after the initial coding; very few changes were made (less than 5 percent).

7.2.2. Study 2: The Use of Subjective Cameras

The aim of the second study was to explore in greater detail the intricacies of creative action in traditional egg decoration. The focus here was on (a) uncovering the "activity flow," the microstages of work, and their interconnections; (b) understanding the generalities and specificities of craftwork across decorators; and, in trying to account for them, (c) exploring differences between novices and experts in terms of process and output. The methodology of this research is discussed and illustrated in Glăveanu and Lahlou (2012); see also Chapter 5.

Participants. Data were collected during a third field trip to Ciocăneşti village in August 2010. The occasion was a five-day summer school for egg decoration held at the local museum, open to both beginners and expert artisans. Seven participants at the workshop took part in the research (three of which were also included in Study 1); all were females with ages ranging from eight to forty-one years. For two of the respondents, decoration was a major activity, whereas the other participants decorated eggs occasionally and especially before Easter.

Method and materials. This study made extensive use of the subcam as a tool for data collection and was designed in accordance with SEBE (Lahlou 2011). In summary, this involves (a) collecting first-person audiovisual recordings of egg decoration with the help of a miniature video camera worn at eye level, (b) confronting participants with the recordings to gather personal experiences of work in a process of analytic reconstruction, and (c) formulating findings and discussing final interpretations with the respondents (as well as other researchers). SEBE thus grants us access to the "phenomenological tunnel" of folk artists, enabling us to see and hear what they saw and heard at the moment of action. However, simply looking at the "outside" dynamic offers little information about "internal," psychological ingredients such as goals and representations. These are collected in follow-up interviews, through which the researcher can ensure that he or she understands correctly what happened from the "subjective" perspective of the creator, a perspective triggered by the "objective" nature of recorded material.

Procedure. Participants were notified in advance about the use of the subcam during the summer school and were fully informed about the methodology and aims of the study. They gave their written consent, and parents gave their approval for the participation of children. All respondents wanted to be identified by name in the research project. Preparation of the study included pretesting the subcams, which were eventually fixed below a sun visor, in a position close to the space between the eyes. Considering the relatively short time of wearing the camera (at one workshop session, it was forty-five minutes on average), it was possible to review the entire film with respondents during the follow-up interviews. This avoided the problem of selecting segments to be shown and discussed. A particular point of focus during these interviews was to understand the goals of the participant, her evaluations of work, and her comments concerning how things are done and when things are done "differently."

Data analysis: coding creative activity. The final dataset included about six and one-half hours of film as well as seven interviews. A pragmatist framework inspired again the coding frame for video materials, and data analysis started from three broad codes: doing (actions of the creator), material undergoing (relation with objects), and social undergoing (relation with other people).

Table 7.2. Coding frame for video analysis.

Maincode	Definition	Subcode
Doing	Actions involved in egg decoration	Choosing materials Drawing in pencil Drawing the belt Drawing the main motif Drawing the top/bottom Correction/completion Covering hole with wax Cleaning wax off fingers Drying color
Material undergoing	Perception of the results of action	Looking at other eggs Looking at result (turning the egg around) Looking at next motif (models in pencil) Looking at previous result Checking the model
Social undergoing	Relations and communication with other people	Looking at others Checking if help is needed Helping others (also with advice/information) Asking others Talking on the phone

In addition, accidental gestures were also coded. An analysis of the recordings progressively enriched these general codes with subcategories in a data-driven fashion; a summary of these codes is presented in Table 7.2.

It should be mentioned that not every action or reaction was coded (e.g., glancing at others or the environment, uttering one or two words as a sign of listening, etc.) because this would have made the presentation of findings and construction of activity flowcharts incomprehensible. Finally, the validity of the coding process was ensured through participant validation (in interviews and study follow-ups) and review of key moments in the video material with an experienced researcher.

7.3. Results

7.3.1. Traditional Easter Egg Decoration Activities

The main findings from Study 1 are presented as follows: Figure 7.1 depicts the activity stages and their associated characteristics. This figure includes information about premises of work (knowledge and procedures), doing (stages), and undergoing (social and material), as well as key obstacles or difficulties.

It should be noted that the phases of doing are linked by double arrows with the conditions of doing (knowledge of motifs, procedures, etc.) and forms of undergoing (relations with the world). This is in line with Dewey's (1934) premise of the interconnection between action, perception, and previous experience; this interconnection might, in its dynamic nature, be slightly less noticeable in the interview material.

For rural artisans, there were subjective, personal reasons to participate in professional decoration, and most related to the "joy" and "pleasure" said to accompany work (Cristina Timu) and the "passion" for this folk art (Marilena Niculiță). There was also an instrumental side to making eggs that was related to financial motives, gaining prestige in the community, and being able to exhibit one's productions (including at yearly festivals).

The work itself is not easy, and all participants acknowledged certain "prereq-uisites," such as patience, ambition, perseverance, and, most important, enjoying decoration. It is interesting that all participants claimed that drawing abilities were not necessary because they can be "formed" (Marilena). In any case, years of practice are essential to perfecting the craftwork, and the "undergoing before doing" began for most participants in childhood (though several respondents had taken up decoration five to seven years before, encouraged by the national festivals). "'After a thousand eggs!' a friend of mine used to say when I was ask-ing her, 'When, dear God, will I be able to draw straight lines like you?'" (Maria Ciocan). The learning process is continuous, and the craft is always "stolen" from others, from the motifs that decorators see on houses, clothes, carpets, postcards, and old eggs that are dutifully kept. The practicalities of work also need to be learned, and artisans usually prepare eggs in the summer and decorate them during winter. Hundreds of eggs are made by each for the Easter season (but not only for Easter); in addition to the eggs themselves (chicken, duck, goose, ostrich, etc.), plenty of other "materials" are involved: wax, syringes (for empty-ing eggs), colors, chișițe of different sizes, varnish, pencils, erasers, and so on.

The activity path in Figure 7.1 reflects what is specific to the main stages of preparation, work, and finish/use. The *preparation phase* can be divided into getting models or motifs, obtaining all the essential materials, preparing the eggs (wash, empty, dry), and organizing the work space (warming the wax, making the colors, etc.; see Figure 7.2). Every respondent considered properly washing and degreasing the eggs to be essential. All of the above-mentioned actions are necessarily informed by a strong knowledge base and a series of procedures. Decorators need to know where to get materials from (e.g., local chișiță makers, ostrich farms, etc.) and also must be familiar with their physical properties. For instance, it was common knowledge that duck eggs are better to work on than chicken eggs because they have a "whiter" shell and are more "resistant," "shiny," and "smooth" (Marcela Novac, Maria Ciocan, Maria Istrate). Procedures are required to make colors (e.g., adding vinegar and salt in the composition), to prepare the wax (e.g., "color" it by adding different types of oxide), and to

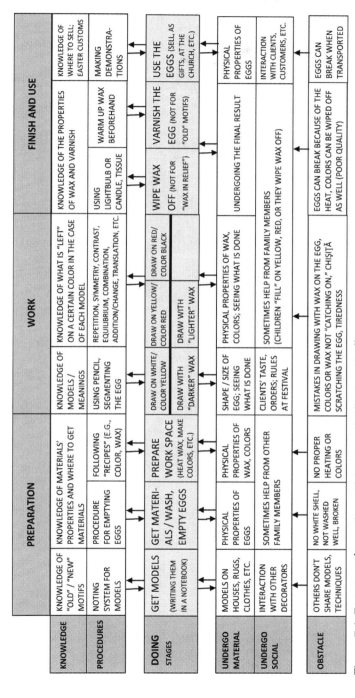

Figure 7.1. Easter egg decoration activity stages in Ciocăneşti village.

Figure 7.2. A typical work space (Marcela Coțovan).

maintain the wax (the wax needs to be kept at a constant temperature). It is interesting that certain forms of knowledge are admittedly lost—for example, the "recipes" for natural colors that used to be made by the elders of the village. All these physical and material properties also distinguish the undergoing processes taking place during preparation stages. Deeply embedded in the material world, the decoration practice was conceived of as a constant interaction with the egg, wax, and colors, as well as with social others, from family members to fellow artisans. The "obstacles" faced by decorators connect to these interactions when, for example, others do not share their knowledge or materials fail (eggs break, colors are not vivid enough, the heating is discontinuous, etc.).

The actual work stage can take many forms, but traditional techniques are defined by drawing motifs in wax. In all cases, the activity starts with segmenting the egg, normally in pencil. The traditional manner of decoration then involves making the model gradually with wax while immersing the egg successively in color (from lighter to darker colors; in Ciocănești, yellow, red, and finally black). Therefore, the activity is organized in three distinct stages known as "working on white," "working on yellow," and "working on red" (see Figure 7.3). At the end, after the egg is dyed black, all the wax is wiped off near a heat source. A more recent variation of the use of wax requires leaving it on the egg (in relief) and working only "on white," usually with two types of wax (lighter and darker brown). The innovation of coloring wax and applying it as such on the egg (something that came to the village in recent years from

Figure 7.3. The three stages of work and the final product (Maria Ciocan).

other regions such as Moldoviţa and Paltinu) is widely practiced, though it is not allowed at national competitions during the festival. Various forms of knowledge and procedures support decoration work. First and foremost, craftswomen displayed an extensive knowledge of patterns or motifs and of how they are made (e.g., what is left on each color).

Awareness of the exact meaning of every motif was rare, but most knew them by name and could describe the significance of basic shapes—for example, the net (separating good from evil), the cross (resurrection and hope), the star (femininity, perfection), and the color black (the "absolute," eternity, permanence). Procedures ranged from how the egg should be held to "rules" such as repetition, symmetry, combination, and contrast. For instance, if the main motif is complex, the belt needs to be simple, and if the main motif is simple, the belt needs to be complex (Larisa Ujică). The work was thus determined by material properties of the models and by the eggs' size and shape. More elongated eggs, for example, are better suited for motifs such as the "lost way," and rounder eggs are perfect for a bigger belt and the use of quadrants. Social forms of undergoing are also present, ranging from clients' demands and general taste (foreigners seem to have less appreciation for the black background) to help from family members, including children, who can "fill up" on yellow or red. At times, bigger orders are shared with other decorators. Among the most common difficulties mentioned was the fact that, once a mistake is made, it is virtually impossible to repair it and that eggs "in relief" require the uniform application of wax.

Last, the *finish and use* moments relate to finalizing the work (wiping wax off, as shown in Figure 7.4, and varnishing the eggs) and then selling them, offering them as gifts, or going to church with decorated eggs for the Easter service (these eggs are usually kept for the entire year following Easter). Selling is done from home (some artists have a basis of loyal customers), by going to different fairs across the country, and through the museum. Knowledge of where to go and what to do to distribute one's work is essential here. Social forms of undergoing are dominated at this stage by interactions with clients

Figure 7.4. "Cleaning" the wax off (Cristina Timu).

and organizers of fairs and exhibitions. A set of practical procedures also accompanied the final phase; these include how to "clean" the egg and polish it (e.g., the varnish needs to be kept warm before application). "Undergoing the final result" was also commented on, and what respondents looked for most of all in an egg was to be "liked" and "beautiful." This is why finishing the activity always stirs emotions, from being curious and worried to being thrilled and taking pride in one's products: "Indeed, we can hardly wait to see it at the end. We worked it, we made it, but we can't really tell [how it is] until the very end" (Marilena). This mild anxiety is justified considering that right before finishing there are still problems to face, the most common of which is breaking the egg, perhaps because the shell was too thin or because it was exposed to excessive heat (Niculina Nigă).

In conclusion, decorating eggs is never easy: the artisans work for hours during the day (or night), with eyes hurting and the whole body experiencing discomfort from standing still (Ionela Țăran); also, the smell of the wax causes headaches (Marcela). Despite the discomfort, folk artists said that they "need" to work almost every day; they are driven by an internal necessity—or "impulsion," as Dewey (1934) would call it—encouraged by the fact that decoration, with all its shortcomings, gives enormous satisfaction: for example, it "relaxes" (Maria Ciocan) and does away with any negative emotions and tensions (Larisa). Reaching a state similar to that of flow (see Csikszentmihalyi 1996) was specific to all those craft artists who felt "passionate" about their work and became absorbed into it. Hegarty (2009) referred to this experience in terms of creative leisure, which gives "a high sense of freedom, intrinsic motivation and reward" (11); in the words of one participant, "Seeing how [the egg] looks, and how you created it; that gives you a satisfaction and a pleasure for making it, producing a beautiful thing with your own hands" (Ionela).

7.3.2. Microgenetic Aspects of Traditional Decoration

Activity flow and variations. Study 1 helped to generate broad descriptions of activity in the case of Easter egg decoration. Primarily emerging from interview data, the resulting schema (see Figure 7.1) depicts rather linear paths of action (from preparation to work and then finish and use). However, another inquiry is needed to specify what exactly constitutes the "work" phase, especially for an intricate decoration process such as this traditional one. For this purpose, filming the activity, particularly from the perspective of the artisan, offers invaluable insight. It allows for the observation of microstages of decoration and the "ordering" of doings; in other words, it adds a dynamic element to an otherwise structural presentation. It has been said that "choosing one action always necessarily implies foregoing others" (Boesch 2007, 157), and this is certainly true of egg decoration, in which, besides a few basic steps, the creator is faced with a multitude of possibilities. In the end, there are no absolute rules of how the work is to proceed as long as it delivers the desired outcome. It should be noted that the data here reflect working on the white stage only (i.e., the initial decoration with wax on the white surface of the egg before immersion in any color). Video-recorded material covered mainly this first phase, which is the most complex and during which most of the motif is drawn.

Figure 7.5 offers a summary of work stages and the relations between them. The central ten-step succession is a "typical" one, averaging all observations available and not fully describing any one decorator in particular. This is because, as the side arrows suggest, decoration work is much more "messy" than any orderly beginning-to-end sequence. The left-side arrows in this case indicate where the pencil was used in subsequent phases, and the right-side arrows indicate transitions, forward or backward, from one stage to the next. This representation thus elaborates the doing part of the previous model (Figure 7.1) without considering, for the moment, forms of undergoing.

In a "typical" succession of events, activity starts with choosing materials, both eggs (in the workshop situation, either white or with motifs already made in pencil, especially for novice decorators) and a chișiță (either from the workshop or brought from home). Most decorators follow with drawing in pencil the main lines, and some even draw the details (primarily novices but not only). Then the application of wax begins, generally with drawing the main lines (the lines of the girdle or belt). They are doubled by virtually all decorators. Following this, the girdle is completed with details, and then artisans pass to the central motif, main lines, and details on one side and then the other ("sides" here are created by the girdle). Within any one side, further segmentations can be made, resulting in quadrants, and decoration can

129

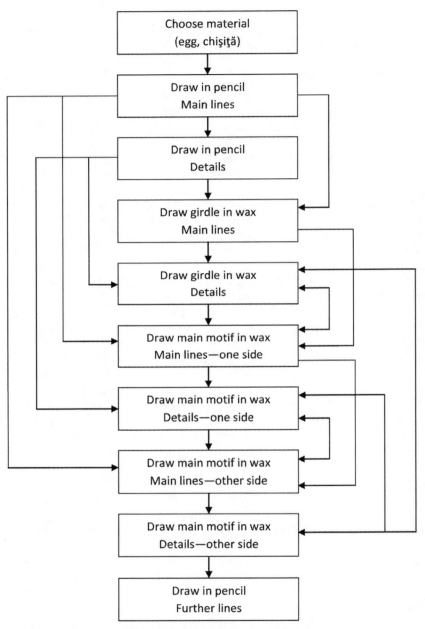

Figure 7.5. A typical activity chart and its observed variations.

progress by focusing on opposing quadrants (normally holding symmetrical motifs). Finally, after finishing work on the white stage, some artists may use the pencil again to draw the next lines, which serve as reminders of what is to be done subsequently on yellow and red.

There were many variations on this scheme, as the side arrows in Figure 7.5 suggest. To start with, the use of pencil was not always continued by drawing main lines in wax, and it was also not reserved exclusively for the beginning of the process. Main lines in pencil were sometimes made immediately afterward in wax (Laura Niculiță, Mihaela Timu), and then details continued in pencil before using wax again. Also, not all main lines or details were depicted in pencil at once; rather, they were completed or continued at different stages in the decoration process (Ancuța Nigă, Mihaela, Niculina Nigă). The order of actions themselves varied, and there was no one way for the decoration activity to proceed. For instance, in the case of working with wax, details were finished on one side, then the artist continued with the main motif on the other side before returning to the details on the first side (Ancuța, Mihaela, Laura, Marilena Niculiță); in another approach, main lines were drawn before any details on both sides (Mihaela). At times, the main motif was made before finalizing the girdle (Ancuța, Marilena), for example, drawing main lines on the belt followed by making the main lines of the central motif (Laura, Marilena), and details of the motif continued with the segmentation of the girdle (Laura). What all these instances reflect is a "back-and-forth" movement in which the typical sequence is disturbed by not finalizing one kind of action and alternating between actions. Interview material clarified in many cases why these "interruptions" occurred; often, explanations had to do with the fact that participants wanted to finish similar tasks first, to respect the principle of symmetry, or were simply trying to make the work less monotonous.

Generality and specificity in craftwork. After considering the course of activity as recorded and discussed by participants during interviews, it was important to further explore what was common across the sample and what the elements were that gave specificity to the work of particular individuals. To begin, a general note here is that most decorators at the workshop made eggs they knew from before and motifs they had practiced for a long time. However, the exact models became specified as the work progressed. For instance, in decorating a second egg with a "lost way" type of girdle, Mihaela decided on the spot what to put on the sides because "there were many options to choose from" (these options relate to the wealth of existing motifs combined with geometric possibilities of pattern association). In any case, because of accumulated decoration experience, most participants could tell what was to be "left" for the yellow and red subsequent phases, even when the actual model had not been done before in exactly the same way.

Artists were guided in such situations by a few basic principles of decoration (nets are white or yellow, the double-line filling is red, etc.) and also by personal preferences.

Another interesting aspect captured by the subcam was the relationship with work instruments, in particular the chișiță (a small wooden stick with a metal pin at the end, used to apply wax on the egg). It was noticed that all participants easily recognized their chișiță just by looking at it, and this happened in most cases before they began work on the egg. Selecting a chișiță to decorate with, however, was not an easy process, even when the artist had her own set, as Niculina did, and several changes of chișiță were possible during the activity (Marilena). What were decorators looking for in a chișiță? Interviews revealed the unanimous assertion that a good chișiță is one that "writes well" in a continuous manner. This quality is complemented by other aspects, for instance, the "thickness" of the writing (thinner instruments are used to draw on white, thicker ones for filling with other colors). During work, other particular gestures were observed, such as leaving the chișiță in the wax can between moments of drawing; this was strongly present in the case of Ancuța and her mother Niculina. In the words of Niculina, this is done because "wax catches on better." Also, before working on the egg with the chișiță, now full of wax, most artists first touched it to their fingernail, a habit prompted by the fact that larger quantities of wax can be accidentally deposited during the first application.

Another notable instrument is the pencil, and its use again demonstrated patterns of similarity and difference between decorators. Drawing the motifs in pencil before making them in wax was common, but what varied was the level of detail needed. Participants like Cristina made only the main lines in pencil, just to have essential reference points, whereas others drew more, including the main motifs. What is particularly interesting is that Ancuța depicted details in pencil for part of the segments of the belt but not all, saying afterward that they were not needed, that now she "knew." Ancuța also changed in wax some lines made before in pencil as she went on. This shows a relative independence from what was previously sketched and could suggest that drawing in pencil might be done not only to guide decoration in wax but also as a kind of "motor practice" anticipating action. Pencil work itself was not a necessity for all people in all stages of decoration (or even for the same person during different stages—Mihaela did not need helping lines for the first egg but used them for the second, more "complicated" model) and can be omitted. Finally, the use of pencil did not characterize only the preparation stages; it was also found later, when the work had finished, if decorators wanted to remember what to do in the next stages (Mihaela, Ancuța).

Perhaps the most eloquent example of how subcam recordings help to outline the individuality of work in the case of each decorator relates to drawing procedures. A central feature of traditional Easter egg making is the existence of motifs commonly used by folk artists. This gives continuity to the craft and substantiates a sense of national and local identity. Nevertheless, in addition to the fact that when the same ornament is made by different decorators it is never perfectly identical, the technical aspects of *how* the motif is made can vary. An illustration of this is given in Figure 7.6, in which two ways of depicting the same traditional pattern are juxtaposed. This particular belt model takes inspiration from the decoration of houses in Ciocăneşti, and the pyramid-like shape is quite specific to the region. In depicting it, Marilena (on the left) adopted an orderly approach by starting from one of the sides and progressively making the top, then the other side, and finally the bottom part. In contrast, Niculina employed a more strategic technique of first making the two sides, then the whole top and, after turning the egg, the bottom segments. The results, though generated differently, were quite similar in the two cases (the shapes are not identical, however, and it can also be noticed how, for Marilena, the belt displays half-motifs on the margin). This shows that, in the case of craftwork, combinations and small changes in content are complemented by different, personalized ways of representing that very content (see also Chapter 5). Procedural creativity is thus an integral part of the craft, and noticing it requires a shift in attention from "what" is made to "how" things are made.

Finally, some observations relating to generality and specificity point to forms of material and social undergoing. It was common across the sample for respondents to turn the egg around and look at it very quickly every time a segment of work (even minor lines or details) had ended or when the chişiţă was left in the wax can for a few moments (particularly Ancuţa). Why did decorators proceed like this? Follow-up interviews revealed the following: Younger artists wanted to see that they did not miss anything; others such as Mihaela looked to see whether she "liked it," because "first, I need to like it." More experienced decorators often looked back at their work to remind themselves of what was to be done next and to check "if everything is perfect," as Cristina put it. Other reasons included checking to see that the wax was still on the egg, because sometimes, depending on the temperature of the room, it can fall off (Marilena). This constant monitoring of one's work progress confirms von Cranach's (1982, 64) vision of goals as both action-preceding (because all decorators have a general idea of what the outcome should look like) and action-accompanying (because this envisioned outcome needs to be checked and, at times, changed in more or less significant ways). Changes can come about through talking with others, including asking for advice. It was noticed from the videos that whereas some of the participants tended to work in silence (indeed, Mihaela and Luminiţa Niculiţă said they prefer it), others were more talkative and open to social interaction (Laura). Some of these differences can be accounted for in terms of distinctions between expert and novice, considered as follows.

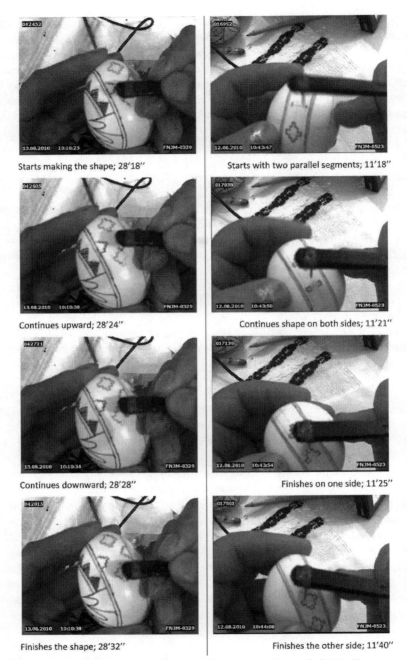

Figure 7.6. The same motif with two different procedures (left Marilena Niculiță, right Niculina Nigă).

Differences between expert and novice. A major source of variation in recorded material was the differences between experts and novices. Several of these were alluded to above, and in Study 1 respondents made comments related to this distinction (e.g., saying that beginners start by drawing a single line and gradually learn to make double lines). It must be mentioned that "expert" and "novice" are somewhat relative classifications, and there is more of a continuum between the two rather than a strict distinction. For the purposes of our discussion, the three child participants (Luminiţa, Ancuţa, and Laura—eight, twelve, and twelve years old, respectively) can be categorized as "novices" because of their age and amount of experience (an average of five years). Differences from (but also similarities with) more experienced decorators are highlighted next with regard to a number of criteria: timing of work, drawing technique, stages of decoration, forms of undergoing, knowledge base, and outcomes.

Arguably the most immediate dissimilarity between the two groups observed in video recordings had to do with the time of working continuously on the surface of the egg, something that demonstrates the importance of sensorimotor coordination and its gradual development. Drawing time was observably higher for experts (twenty to thirty seconds on average) than for beginners (ten to fifteen seconds). Of course, time varied according to circumstance (e.g., which chişiţă was being used), and more experienced craftswomen did not always work for longer intervals; however, it is safe to assume based on the observations that experts can decorate faster and in a more continuous manner. Niculina, for instance, was recorded working for thirty to sixty seconds without inserting the chişiţă in wax. Novice decorators appeared to take a small pause before actually applying the chişiţă to the egg, perhaps evaluating very quickly where they needed to start and get to with the line. On the whole, novices also talked more during decoration and were more easily distracted (Laura). There were, however, exceptions to this, and the youngest participant, Luminiţa, seemed to be quite focused on the task at hand.

Besides the time aspect, the work technique was not fully mastered by novices, something quite normal considering their young age. In fact, beginners in decoration of all ages gradually learn the craft and perfect their drawing abilities. Experts learn as well, but their learning has to do less with the "motor" aspects and more with new motifs and procedures of decoration. Returning to child novices, they tended to have their models made first in pencil, and often by someone else. This was the case with Luminiţa, who, at eight years of age, was one of the youngest students of the craft. One of the most problematic aspects for her was how to draw straight lines on the round surface of the egg. Figure 7.7 illustrates the effort of drawing continuous lines and the way in which Luminiţa proceeded by slightly rotating the egg and gradually lifting up her fingers, one by one, to make room for the advancing line. By repeatedly stopping to move the egg around, she interrupted the line, and this ended up contributing to a rather discontinuous aspect. This is certainly not one of

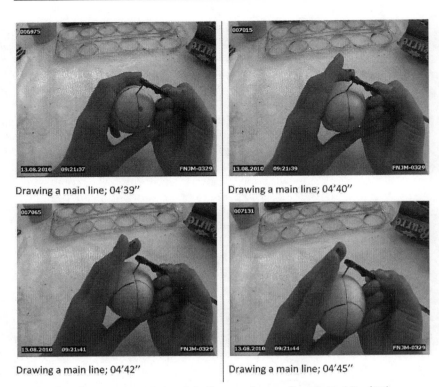

Drawing a main line; 04'39"

Drawing a main line; 04'40"

Drawing a main line; 04'42"

Drawing a main line; 04'45"

Figure 7.7. Drawing a main straight line on the egg (Luminiţa Niculiţă).

the most economical ways of drawing motifs, and more experienced artisans advise others to turn the egg around without lifting the chişiţă or their fingers. For them, drawing lines is an effortless job considering the "years and years of doing this" (Mihaela).

Moreover, novices were also less systematic in their work, and often they did not finish one set of elements completely before passing to the next (Ancuţa and Laura compared to Cristina and Mihaela). They more frequently departed from the "typical" activity flow described in Figure 7.5, and this increased the time of work (owing to the need to go back) and the probability that some segments would be forgotten. But even seasoned decorators such as Mihaela, who on the whole seemed to progress systematically with the drawing, did not repeat the same succession of moves for all models (she said that "it is not necessary, it is no rule"). Niculina is the best example of an expert with a less regular work process, oftentimes drawing in pencil, then in wax, then in pencil again, or revisiting what she had done before to complete the motif. These differences can be attributed to age and the years of experience that separate novices and experts and make them relate differently to the "rule" of decoration. If apprentices seem to be less organized, it is because they are making an effort to internalize the rule; thus, there is often a disorderly type of movement in search of skill. Expert folk artists, on the other hand, can follow a less regular process because they know and adapt the rule to their purpose and circumstances; changes are made deliberately in search of perfection rather than skill.

In terms of undergoing, beginners tended to look more at the result of their work, and they did so to see whether "anything was missed" or whether symmetry was respected. Ancuța, in particular, had the habit of turning the egg around at very short intervals, a routine gesture that allowed her to regularly perceive the work in its entirety. In contrast, decorators like Mihaela did not look much at the result (except at the end) because they "know how it should be" and are "sure" of what was done. Furthermore, though no major corrections were made on the egg by any participant, novices did use the eraser or razor slightly more frequently (Luminița also used her fingernail to remove wax). This happened in the case of Niculina as well when she tried to learn a new motif; this raises the interesting observation that experts turn into "beginners" when faced with a novel situation. The difference, however, might be that, in these cases, professional decorators do not necessarily require help from others, whereas beginners regularly ask others (including peers) for help and advice. Their knowledge of meanings and techniques is developing, and when they are young they do not usually know the name or meaning of the motifs they are making (though this is sometimes the case for experts as well). In terms of procedures, it was also less clear for some of the youngest participants what exactly needed to be made on yellow and red for a particular motif.

Another easily observed distinction relates to the quantity and quality of the final outcome. In the research group, beginners generally did not finish the whole egg on white during a work session (and when they did, some little elements were forgotten; this was not the case only for novices, however, and could have been attributable to previous moments of interruption). On the other hand, experts were more productive in a roughly equivalent period of time, Mihaela and Niculina each finishing two eggs on white and Cristina making one egg on white and yellow and two other eggs on yellow and red, respectively. As for evaluations, younger decorators were certainly more critical of their own work (Luminița, Laura) and even wondered whether they could "give it another try." This struggle for perfection represents an important motivation to learn and develop one's craft, which is a strong premise supporting the continuous accumulation of expertise (see the notion of deliberate practice in Ericsson 2006).

7.4. Integrating Findings: The Creativity of Craftwork

Two studies that looked at decoration activities have been presented. Both used a combination of interview and observation to capture action in its organization and situated nature. Having integrated key findings from both, we now turn to the final discussion and its central question: What makes a traditional craft activity creative?

First, one of the main "impulsions" for engaging in this type of work is connected directly to a desire for generating novelty and to curiosity regarding the final outcome. There is a certain intentionality of creation in the framework of a traditional practice. Craftswomen such as Maria Ciocan acknowledged this when saying that they are constantly thinking of "what to make new." Adding a personal note is often a preoccupation for artisans, perhaps more pronounced in the village of Ciocăneşti, where several transformations can be noticed in regard to how things were made and how they are now made. "Old" decoration, still very much appreciated and required at festivals, involves simpler motifs, no varnish, and working on chicken eggs. Today, however, most eggs are heavily ornamented, because people feel the need to "add something" (anonymous), to create eggs that are "more beautiful, embellished, catchy [*ochioase*], for others to have what to see on them" (Maria Istrate). A general drive to perfect "tradition" leads in this case to creative expression through "conscious attempts at improving habitual action" (Dalton 2004, 610). It also connects to previous definitions of mini-c creativity (Beghetto and Kaufman 2007) as new and personal interpretations of existing or established forms, experiences, and events.

Second, it is a common misconception about craft that everything is known in advance (Collingwood 1938). What these two studies have shown is that, indeed, the work virtually always starts from a certain pattern but the path from idea to realization is never linear. Dewey's (1934) cycle between doing and undergoing, between action and perception, points to this, and its utility for understanding craftwork has been repeatedly emphasized. The eggs "come out [while] working" (Elena Crăciunescu) and "when you work all sorts of ideas come to your mind" (Maria Timu). There is no routine or preset schema that can "determine" how an egg should be decorated from beginning to end. Consequently, one of the most frequent questions folk artists ask themselves while working is, "What could I make here?" (Marilena). The nature of craft is one not of mechanical repetition but rather of conscious engagement with the changing conditions of work in the here and now. This is why every egg is not progressively "made" but "discovered" (Maria Timu). And there is little surprise that this is the case, because "no schema can provide all the details of every situation, and no habit can anticipate the contours of each moment in which it may be invoked" (Dalton 2004, 615; also Ingold and Hallam 2007; Sennett 2008). In the end, we can safely talk about the unpredictability of craftwork: "I start a model but when I finish it, it is completely different, it is something else" (Elena).

Rural egg decoration creativity is thus defined by combination and change. These two processes shape the outcomes of work, considering that—with no exception—participants stated they do not normally even attempt to make the same model on more eggs (except perhaps when there is a special order), nor would they wish to. "I put one more line, I take a motif from there, one from there, I combine them" (Marcela). "Mixing, always mixing" (anonymous) motifs is associated with changing them in several ways. For example, colors (Maria Istrate) or the position of an ornament can be changed, obtaining a different effect (Maria Ciocan). Accidents have their value in this context (see also Meyers 2007 for an interesting discussion of accidental discoveries) and demonstrate that egg decoration constitutes an excellent example of what was described by Pye (1968) as the workmanship of risk. Making a mistake can "change the whole model" (Maria Ciocan), and very often for the better. This is acknowledged in the literature about egg decoration as well, in which authors such as Zahacinschi and Zahacinschi (1992, 32) considered how errors in decoration can be taken as starting points for new artistic developments. At times, these changes, intentional or unintentional, stand out; other times, they can hardly be perceived, and yet they are present: "You can think it is identical [to other eggs], but it is not" (Larisa). Figure 7.8 illustrates such "family resemblances" between three different versions of the same basic motif: the "lost way" or labyrinth.

However, even when these persistent variations are accepted, there is still a presumption that craft involves much "copying," that is, unchanged duplication; traditional decoration is often suspected of the "sin of plagiarism" (Cincura 1970) and of endlessly reproducing the same forms. Folk artists challenge such assumptions (see also arguments that copying enhances creativity in Kozlowski and Yakel 1980; Kentaro and Takeshi 2004). First, each and every egg is said to have "something special, set aside" (Marilena), and many decorators are ready to bet that no two identical outcomes can be found

Figure 7.8. Versions of the "lost way" motif (Cristina Timu).

in their work of hundreds of eggs (Valerica Jușcă). They could not be in any case, because no two eggs have the exact same size, shape, and color. Even if artisans would want to make identical eggs, it would be very difficult. Indeed, copying requires a degree of effort that is not seen as worthwhile; boredom sets in after the second (similar) egg, and a change is required (Maria Ciocan). There are perhaps two instances in which closer reproduction is sought: when learning the craft (based on exercising the same motifs) and when aiming to make "old" eggs with traditional models (because they need to be respected: "You can't add anything to a carpet on the wall, it is as your grandmother made it," Valerica). An example of trying to copy a "new" motif was offered by Niculina (see illustrations in Glăveanu and Lahlou 2012; Chapter 5). "Fitting" the model on a new egg proved to be a difficult task, and the use of an eraser became necessary at several points. Most importantly, the declared intention of the participant was not to make the whole motif but to capture "the main idea," to schematize it because "from a single [model] I make several."

The above example raises the issue of *translation* as a process through which new models are adopted and transformed instead of simply copied. Artisans from the village of Ciocănești live in a world of symbolic resources useful for their craft. These come from decorations on houses, clothes, carpets, table-cloths, and so forth. Motifs from these and more are "taken" and immediately tailored to suit current needs: "I saw a carpet, it seemed to me that it could be made on the egg, I instantly made a sketch, and after that I added from myself if I could, if not I've taken some things out" (Valerica). At any rate, models never remain the same—they are "adapted," and this depends on how they are "visualized" (Maria Ciocan). One clear source of inspiration is the work of others, typically encountered at festivals. Rivalries can then be born between decorators from different regions based on how some might have replicated the models of others. This idea is refuted by people like Elena who claim that motifs, even when taken, are translated into what is traditional in the region, and this involves changes in both form and color (see also Bartlett 1932). Even in the case of models collected in notebooks, they only serve as points of departure for current work (Ionela). Motifs are sometimes altered to such a degree that they are later kept as one's own creations (Elena). Of course, not all decorators were equally open to change, and they all rejected radical change. "I like to create, to come up with something new, but not modify much, eggs need to still be traditional for Ciocănești" (Cristina). One "interprets" tradition but does not depart from it, and, for many aspects, there might not be any correction to be made or any improvement to be added: "You took them as good and you have to keep them" (Dănuț Zimbru).

What changes amount to, however "minor" they may be, is a personal style. In the words of folk artists, "I have personalized my work" (Maria Ciocan), "brought a personal note" (Larisa). More than this, given the fact that deco-rators know how things are usually done or what motifs look like, they can and do distinguish novelty in their work and in the work of others. And they remember it, as Ionela did, being able to single out moments of innovation and personal, created models (see Figure 7.9). The sources of such creations are acknowledged, yet they also give reason to feel proud and express one's individuality. Indeed, there is much room for identity in craftwork, and identities are forged, recognized, and respected: "Each decorator has something specific, something distinguishable, each decorator from the village has her work and we know it" (Marilena). This work is identifiable, and participants demonstrated that they could tell which eggs were made by whom. Personal work especially is recognized, even after many years, "even from a thousand other eggs" (Cristina). This is also why sharing motifs with others is not perceived as giving them away—each artisan has his or her style, and the same motif will look different in each case (Larisa). A decorator may see a beautiful model made by a neighbor and deliberately want to replicate it, but "it will still be different" (Maria Ciocan). Thus, no one can say that "you've stolen this egg from me!" (Valerica).

Finally, we can discuss how egg decorators relate to their activity and how they evaluate it, including in terms of creativity. Is the creativity discovered in practice matched at the level of representation? The respondents had no doubt about the expressiveness of their craft, but not everyone was ready to acknowledge displaying a great deal of creativity. There is humility in self-appreciation, given that folk artists do not think that they can take credit for their art: "I can't say it belongs to me. There are eggs that I 'turned' from one side to the other, that I modified, that I can say 'yes, this is from me' but

Figure 7.9. A novel motif, created by Ionela Țăran.

no . . . everything came from somewhere else" (Maria Istrate). A particular view of creativity as absolute novelty emerging out of thin air seems to be at work here as well. And yet there is also pride, pride in belonging to a tradition and advancing it (Dănuț). In the end, "If we wouldn't create, the tradition would be lost. If we wouldn't take tradition forward, what would happen to it?" (Larisa). These are valid questions that come once more to emphasize the unbreakable links between creativity and tradition, between the effort to maintain and the impulse to generate, between the need to conserve communalities and the importance of being unique, different, and ultimately creative.

7.5. Final Reflections on Creative Activity

The present chapter has described and applied an action framework for understanding creative activity. This framework, inspired by a pragmatist approach, has the advantage of being more comprehensive than models focused exclusively on cognitive elements, and it contributes to a contextual or situated perspective on creative work (see also Hutchins 1995 for a discussion of distributed cognition). Through these lenses, the microgenetic emergence of creativity in craft is organized around notions of exploration, combination and change, copying and translation, personal style, and creative identity. All of these elements underline a fundamental characteristic of folk art, namely, generating novelty from within habitual forms of activity (Glăveanu 2012; Chapter 10). The creative achievements in the case of more "routinized genres" reside in "small deviations from artistic ideals or paradigmatic work" (Dalton 2004, 609). However small, these deviations are in fact continuous and are required by ever-changing circumstances. The creativity of folk art hence relies on the "spontaneous microadjustments of a highly prepared interpretation" (Chaffin, Lemieux, and Chen 2006, 200)—highly prepared and yet not rigid or fixed. "The unexpected turn," said Dewey (1934), "is a condition of the felicitous quality of a work of art; it saves it from being mechanical" (144). All of the examples in the two studies included here argue for this nonmechanical nature of craft. Final products are never "there" from the start; they are developing projects, and this development takes place in the moment-to-moment interaction between creator and work in the broader context of a social and material world.

It is hoped that the field of creativity studies would benefit in several ways from adopting an action approach and focusing on the minute details of human creative action. The findings presented above illustrate the value of extending our research interest to incorporate, for instance, the dynamic between creators and both material objects and social others. Taking the Geneplore model of creative cognition as an example (see Finke et al. 1992), it could be argued that there are parallels to be made between generative and exploratory processes on the one hand and the idea of a continuous cycle between doing and undergoing and action and perception in artistic work on the other. What this research further suggests in this regard is the following: first, the highly influential roles played by the physical properties of eggs, geometric motifs, and previous work in the generation of novel patterns and combinations, and second, the importance of tradition and convention for the exploration and selection of valuable outcomes. These insights can be grasped as long as we consider creative phenomena in context (and thus come to appreciate sociocultural and material constraints related to human activity) and in their unfolding—in other words, as long as we move from product alone to process. Easter eggs and other similar everyday artifacts, despite their aesthetic appeal, may not seem at first to be associated with groundbreaking novelty, and yet microgenetic analyses reveal the complexity and originality inherent in this type of decoration work.

The use of a subcam and a SEBE methodology has the potential, in this regard, to help document minute changes and discuss them with creators and others, capturing what otherwise might be lost: the microacts of adapting to and trying to transform and expand what is "given" in terms of both existing decoration patterns and techniques of craftwork. In the end, all creative action, independent of domain, is confronted with a series of constraints and involves a number of practical skills (see the componential model in Amabile 1996) as well as the gradual accumulation of expertise (very often years of practice; Gardner 1993). Under these circumstances, we could look at creativity less in terms of the "revolutionary" product and conceptualize it more as a form of situated and masterful activity, the type of activity abundantly illustrated here through exploration of a traditional craft.

Part D

The Representation of Creativity

8

Creating Creativity: Reflections from Fieldwork[1]

Despite what the title might initially suggest, this chapter is dedicated to the "reception" (by means of identification and assessment) and not the "production" of creativity. Its starting point is a fundamental question—When can we say something is creative?—and its main domain of focus is the creativity of everyday life. This has been chosen considering that "ordinary creativity" is both pervasive and oftentimes unremarked (Bateson 1999, 154). Acts of "historical creativity," like celebrated works of art or influential theories, tend to stand out as mountain peaks, and their creativity is frequently taken for granted. But creative expression exists also well beyond the world of research labs and art studios (Fischer et al. 2005, 484). In fact, as Ellis Paul Torrance (1988, 43), an illustrious figure in the psychology of creativity, stated, "Creativity is almost infinite. It involves every sense—sight, smell, hearing, feeling, taste, and even perhaps the extrasensory." For him, creativity is required whenever the person has no learned solution for an existing problem, and there are countless situations in our daily lives when this is the case. One should not disregard, of course, the power of "routines" in leading human behavior; yet, even when faced with habituated ways of doing things, novelty can characterize the details of our actions. Creativity and routine, the guiding principles of human behavior, illustrate a "reversible figures" situation where, depending on how we decide to look at things, one will stand as the main figure and the other as the perceptual background. In effect, whenever a creative solution is successful and moves beyond routines (Borofsky 2001, 66), it will undoubtedly become part of future routines, thus contributing to the never-ending cycle of our daily actions and interactions.

This state of affairs makes recognizing creativity difficult. If departing from what already exists is the defining feature of creativity, how can we determine when something is *sufficiently* different to be called creative? Furthermore,

---

[1] With kind permission from Springer Science+Business Media, *Integrative Psychological and Behavioral Science*, Creating creativity: Reflections from fieldwork, 45(1), 2011, 100–115, Glăveanu, V. P.

contemporary creativity theory, as we will see next, emphasizes that creative outcomes should also be of social or practical value. This twofold condition is typically difficult to appreciate or to satisfy. For example, is children's play creative? An overwhelming number of teachers and parents would be ready to affirm that it is. And yet, according to rigorous scientific definitions, children are unlikely to produce in their play anything of true value, and their "right" to creativity can be contested on this basis (Cohen and Ambrose 1999, 11). What about a musician playing in an orchestra? Again, who would deny creativity to an artist? However, strictly speaking, we could be the victims of an attributional bias in assigning creativity to musicians, dancers, comedians, and other "performers" instead of to the actual "authors"—composers, choreographers, and writers (Kasof 1995, 330). Of course, this argument can be challenged by pointing to the fact that every re-presentation is never simply a "duplication" but rather a new performance in itself (see the notion of "open work" in Eco 1989). But then what about copying and imitation? They must surely be uncreative types of activity. Well, pushing the previous argument further, one could come to see the important role of improvisation in aligning the observation of the model with acting in the world to produce the "copy" (Ingold and Hallam 2007, 5). Continuing from this last example, we start wondering if, in fact, *everything* is creative. Let's consider language as possibly the "best example of everyday creativity" (Runco 2007, x). We frequently "create" sentences that we have never heard before, and they all have an indisputable value (for communication, self-regulation, etc.).

This is probably a good time to think about the implications of considering that everything is (potentially) creative: simply put, this would do away with the notion of creativity. We must resist the temptation to collapse creativity into everyday life so as to make these two utterly indistinguishable (Negus and Pickering 2004, 45; also Hausman 1979). This is actually the stance of science, which, faced with the ubiquity of creative expression, searches for the limits of creativity (Rouquette 1973). A boundless phenomenon is also meaningless, and so is one whose specific qualities are not clearly distinguishable. In the case of creativity, this last remark raises the question of how we could separate the "creative" from the beautiful, the adaptive, the technically suitable, or the merely bizarre. Oftentimes, judging a creative outcome is intrinsically linked to considering its technical aspects or its importance for responding to society's needs (Lubart 2003). Furthermore, we are also confronted with the aspect of intentionality. Do "creators," when they "create," actually want to be creative? Or are they simply trying to make something beautiful, something interesting, something useful for their life or the lives of others?

And yet, despite all these difficulties, science perseveres in studying creativity, and the first step taken to differentiate the creative from the noncreative is to locate and "isolate" creativity. Traditionally, creativity has been associated in psychology with either the creative person or the creative product (Glăveanu

2010b; Chapter 2). From these two, the creative product approach seems to be the most commonly used and the most fertile for scientific investigations (Amabile 1996; Bailin 1988; Hausman 1979). Products have the obvious advantage of being available for measurement and evaluation. They also help us to make inferences about the "who" and "how" of creativity (person and process). Though this focus in the psychology of creativity has been questioned (see the notion of "product bias" in Runco 2007, 384), it is probably one of the best starting points in our quest to answer the question, When can we say that something is creative? There is great consensus in the literature that something is creative when it is both (a) novel or original and (b) useful or valuable (Stein 1962; Martindale 1994; Gruber and Wallace 1999; Mayer 1999; Mason 2003; Mumford 2003). These two criteria circumscribe the scientific vision of creativity—or, to be more precise, the Western scientific vision of creativity (Montuori and Purser 1995; Westwood and Low 2003). Is this also the basis for creativity judgments made by nonscientists? Is this what people take to be creative when they talk about creativity and "recognize" it? What does "common sense" say?

These questions have seldom been raised in the study of creativity, and when they are raised, it is mostly in the spirit of taking scientific definitions as the ultimate markers of what "true" creativity is. Indeed, science strives for objectivity, and creativity science uses its established definition to capture "creativity in itself." There is a clear underlying assumption that creativity exists as such—independent of social agreement and cultural conventions, above and beyond commonsensical ideas. However, even the act of defining creativity in terms of novelty and usefulness exposes its cultural relativity. In the words of Flaherty (2005, 147), "Using a lever to move a rock might be judged novel in a Cro-Magnon civilization, but not in a modern one." Usefulness also implies a relational standard of appreciation (useful to whom and for what?). Trying to achieve a "pure gaze" on creativity, researchers are often more preoccupied with great creations and great creators and forget the everyday dynamics of the phenomenon. In the end, any clear-cut distinctions between great creators and ordinary creators, between great creations and ordinary creations, do not hold. All creativity takes place in social and cultural contexts (Glăveanu 2010a, 2010b; see Chapters 1 and 2), and the study of how it is received and recognized in these contexts is of utmost importance. Scientific views are not to be disregarded, nor are they to be transformed into "ultimate answers." Science and common sense should not be mutual enemies, especially if we consider the multitude of ways in which they come to inform each other. The real question is, What does each do with the "inputs" received from the other?

The present chapter will therefore attempt to *integrate* scientific and "commonsensical" notions of creativity. In doing so, it will be structured around the scientific criteria for creativity (newness, originality, usefulness, expert judgments, etc.), and at the same time it will shed light on how these criteria are expressed in everyday settings. This will be facilitated by making reference to examples from an area often associated with "ordinary creativity," namely, folk art. In the end, based on both theoretical considerations and empirical illustration, the importance of "cultural frames" for the reception of creativity will become obvious. Conclusions will be drawn regarding a multilayered approach to creativity assessment, one intended to reunite the "objective" aspects of creativity with its critical, subjective, and social dimensions.

8.1. The Fieldwork

Empirical examples in this chapter come from a research project that explores creativity in Easter egg decoration in a Romanian context. Informed by a cultural psychology approach (see Cole 1996), the project uses primarily naturalistic observation and semistructured interviews to investigate the interdependence between creative expression and reception among adults and children from both urban and rural settings. The craft of egg decoration has been chosen for its richness of practices—which connect the realms of folklore, art, and religion—as well as for its relationship to the requirements of a growing market for the distribution of Easter eggs. The egg itself is an object of tremendous symbolic value in cultures around the world (see Newall 1984), and in Romania, egg decoration is a custom with ancient (probably even pre-Christian) roots (Gorovei 2001, 62) and is one of the oldest and most widespread folk arts in the country (Zahacinschi and Zahacinschi 1992, 22). Egg decoration before Easter is ubiquitous in Romanian cities and villages and is highly expressive of national and religious identities (for more details, see Chapters 6 and 7).

If in urban settings the decoration techniques are based mainly, though not exclusively, on dying eggs, principally in red (symbolic of the blood of Christ), it is in rural areas that traditional forms of wax decoration are practiced. Women are the main "artists" of the craft, often joined by children and sometimes by men, and they can produce, especially in villages in northern Romania, numerous decorated eggs by working throughout the year (Hutt 2005). Traditional decoration generates both monochrome and polychrome eggs (hen and duck most often, occasionally goose, ostrich, etc.), and it is based on applying wax in different stages on the emptied eggshell to draw the motifs while successively immersing the egg in color (usually yellow followed by red and finally black). There is an impressive number of motifs displayed on Easter eggs, representing geometric shapes, plants, animals, people, and familiar objects (typically in the form of schematized parts; Gorovei 2001). Decoration work involves combining these shapes and colors and oftentimes generating new ones, and this explains how the craft has changed over the last few decades—"getting further and further from the initial magical symbol . . . [and closer to being an] artistic jewellery that gives priority to beauty in itself" (Zahacinschi and Zahacinschi 1992, 50). Besides dying and decorating them with wax, there are many other ways of adorning eggs, including the use of leaves applied to the shell before coloring and the application of stickers—the latter in particular being a clear sign of modernity spreading rapidly from city to village.

In this context, the fieldwork for this research was very diverse and included such settings as private homes, schools, museums, fairs, and community celebrations. For the purpose of the present chapter, though, reference will be made exclusively to data obtained through interviewing seven ethnographers, six priests, six art teachers, and eight folk artists about the craft, about creativity, and, of course, about the creativity of Easter eggs (see also Glăveanu 2010c; Chapter 6).

8.2. New and Original

Novelty and originality can be said to represent the "essence" of creativity, and this is probably so for both scientific and lay understandings of the phenomenon. Creativity means, in the end, to bring something new into being, something that didn't exist before as such (Hausman 1979, 239). This feature is included, explicitly or implicitly, in virtually all definitions of creativity (Torrance 1988, 43; see also Barron 1995; Liep 2001). "New" is the necessary precondition but not the sufficient one. The creative product also needs to be original, meaning differing substantially from what already exists. Here things become more complicated, since something can be original for the person but not for the entire society. This led to established distinctions in the creativity literature between P-creative (new for the individual) and H-creative (new for society) (Boden 1994), or, more generally, between "mundane creativity" and "mature creativity" (Cohen and Ambrose 1999, 9). Reinforcing this division, modern Western societies are often characterized by their obsession with "high creativity" and originality at all costs (as clearly demonstrated by some forms of contemporary art). And yet, if we take into account the fact that all creativity is founded on the combination of old ideas (Liep 2001), the mere notion of "complete originality" becomes a logical impossibility.

The idea that one can be creative by following traditions and conventions— or further, that one *can only* be creative in the context of a tradition—is common knowledge among folk artists involved in egg decoration. Traditions and conventions give meaning to the creation. In the words of Rodica Berechea, "You can't, no matter what you do, abandon tradition, because you would be making something else [not Easter eggs] and it would be worthless." Novelty is recognized as part and parcel of the decoration work, especially since every Easter egg is different (after all, eggs never have exactly the same size and shape); "And, even if I want to make a certain model, I still have to change something, it's like it is easier to change than to let everything be the same every time" (Livia Balacian). This drive toward creating the new is frequently noted by folk artists; however, originality is never considered a break with tradition but rather a continuation of it. Even when highly innovative families of decorators contributed to diversifying the work techniques and the existing types of Easter eggs (e.g., working eggs with colored wax in relief; drawing pictures with colored wax; making Easter eggs for different seasons, which led to the now common "Christmas eggs"), everything done was believed to enrich the tradition and keep it alive. In the end, there is always a subtle dynamic between "new" and "old" that governs the craft of egg decoration, a dynamic beautifully captured in such appreciative comments as this: "We keep the tradition. But in every egg, in the colors, there is a little piece of us" (Rodica Berechea).

Assessing "objectively" and in absolute terms how creative an Easter egg is with regard to its originality would be a difficult task. It would require comparisons with each and every Easter egg ever made, and this is, of course, impossible. In fact, creativity test scoring systems themselves reflect this difficulty. Creative potential is usually measured using divergent thinking tests, which invite respondents to give as many answers as they can to an open-ended question and then score responses for fluency (total number of responses), originality (unusualness or uniqueness of responses), and flexibility (variety of responses) (see Runco 2004). This way, originality is evaluated based on comparisons between answers, and answers themselves are never capable of exhausting all possibilities. The fact is that when deciding what is new and original, we always rely on comparative judgments—that is, on the knowledge we and others have about the world of existing artifacts that makes up a cultural domain. This is why authors such as Montuori and Purser (1995, 71) emphasize the importance of studying the "'genealogy' of creativity and the contextual influences that lead us to consider works to be creative in our present period."

Looking into the genealogy of creativity in the case of Easter egg making reveals an interesting aspect for our understanding of creativity. Novelty and originality are certainly central criteria for "diagnosing" creative outcomes, but in everyday life the attribution of creativity is founded on much more than this, often involving *comparative judgments* between "classes of artifacts." An Easter egg, or a type of Easter eggs, is more or less creative compared to another egg or type of decoration. This is why there tends to be general agreement that traditional eggs are the most creative whereas eggs decorated with stickers are the least creative. Furthermore, when explaining creativity evaluations, people refer to a variety of aspects. Four associations are particularly salient. The first connects creativity and work, where higher creativity comes out of effort and skill, of "thinking through" and making "cognitive effort." The second one links creativity and beauty—creative eggs need to have aesthetic appeal. Third, creativity has to do with the "quality" of the work; this is a very important criterion for folk artists themselves, who believe that working with "soul" and dedication is paramount. Finally, creativity is intrinsically related to meaning. Eggs with stickers are often labeled uncreative and kitsch, especially because they are "outside" of the Easter tradition; they are, as one ethnographer put it, "a synthesis made by people with no roots." Of course, ideas of value and meaning are also important for the scientific definition of creativity, as we will discuss next.

8.3. Valuable and Useful

As mentioned above, psychology operates with the dual criteria of novelty and usefulness in distinguishing the creative from the noncreative. There is little ambiguity about what it means to be new and original, but the second dimension of creative products is presented under a variety of names. Authors use such words as tenable or useful or satisfying (Stein 1962), intelligible (Hausman 1979), appropriate or useful (Runco 2007; Martindale 1994), correct and valuable (Amabile 1996), significant (Mason 2003), fitting constraints (Lubart 2003), and compelling (Sternberg 2006). Moreover, it is slightly unclear what the reference term for this criterion is: the situation or task that generated the creative outcome or the group of people who use it, or both. This is quite an important aspect because it marks the difference between "objective" assessment (thinking about the nature of the task) and "subjective" assessment (thinking about how the creative product affects the existence of different persons and groups). Whatever the interpretation, though, the "value" dimension is meant to draw the line between a creative result and a merely bizarre one (Arieti 1976, 4).

Three observations derive from this. To start with, including usefulness in the definition of creativity raises some problems when it comes to evaluating all "original" expressions with no demonstrable social value. In this large category we can include dreams, unexpected thoughts, and the imaginative gestures resulting from children's curiosity (Barron and Harrington 1981, 441). It would certainly be appropriate in these cases to use a particular definition of "value" that is based less on tangible contributions and more on *adaptability and emotional impact*. Second, by adopting utility as a central aspect of creativity, we are confining this phenomenon to the bright side of human experience. This is a curious situation for scientific inquiry, which typically places phenomena on continuums and avoids assigning any moral dimension to them. Creativity, it seems, is always "good," and this is certainly well reflected in Western popular culture, where being creative is one of the most highly prized virtues. Finally, it should be noted that there is some *tension* between the two defining features of creativity, a kind of tension that is at the core of any type of creative expression: it is a tension between originality and appropriateness, between disrespecting rules and playing by the rules, between being "new" and yet fitting into the "old." As previously mentioned, folk artists are very much aware of this reality that shapes every aspect of their work.

What are the constraints that, once respected, make an Easter egg "valuable" and therefore contribute to its creativity? Unsurprisingly, there are different constraints for different people according to their professional background and engagement with decoration practices. Ethnographers and priests, for example, who are rarely involved in any complicated forms of decoration, emphasize traditional and religious constraints. For them, both red eggs (with clear symbolic value) and eggs decorated with wax are "appropriate" considering the nature and purpose of this custom as an integral part of the Easter celebration. In the words of one of the priests, Easter eggs are creative

> for as long as the meaning of being an Easter egg is not lost. For as long as they are not dissociated from symbolism, for as long as the ones seeing the Easter egg don't forget the tight connection it has with the sacrifice of our Savior.

Art teachers, who are sometimes involved in adorning eggs at home or with their students before Easter, focus more on the aesthetic constraints of the task. Without losing track of the traditional meaning of a decorated egg, they are preoccupied with chromatic harmony, with the choice of shapes and their distribution on the egg, with being able to apply colors on small surfaces and allowing them to dry before continuing work, etc. Such *practical constraints* are also essential for folk artists. When they talk about what makes a "good" Easter egg, they start explaining the rules of decoration, such as not making mistakes when working with wax (since even if the artist removes the wax, the surface will not preserve color properly), segmenting the egg before drawing the motifs, obeying the law of symmetry whenever possible, not juxtaposing similar colors, aiming for chromatic harmony, starting always from bright colors and ending with darker ones, and using clean wax and applying it in consistent quantities (for eggs with wax in relief). In the end, the final measure of "appropriateness" for folk artists is given by how much the eggs are appreciated and how readily they are purchased. These factors operate as selection criteria because, at the end of the day, it is the market that ultimately decides what is valuable and not valuable in terms of egg decoration.

8.4. Subjective Reception

At this point we can conclude that the evaluation of creativity depends on both "objective" and "subjective" criteria (see also Kasof 1995). We can also state that so-called "objective" measures (how different something is from what existed before, how well it conforms to the constraints of the task) are *relative* in themselves and often end up relying on *social agreement* (can we know everything that existed before? who sets the constraints of a task?). New artifacts, once they emerge, "demand interpretation" (Zittoun et al. 2003, 429), and interpretations require communication with other people and engagement with existing cultural artifacts. In fact, we can say that we never perceive creativity as such since it clearly lacks any physical reality; we *interpret* the outcome as creative, we infer that it came out of a creative process and even go as far as to attribute creativity to the "author." In all cases, creativity is based on subjective reception at the level of audience members: "Perfection in execution cannot be measured or defined in terms of execution; it implies those who perceive and enjoy the product that is executed" (Dewey 1934, 49). And, as Dewey goes on to argue, the creator, both while creating and once the work is finished, also acts as an audience as he or she attempts to interpret the work from the perspective of others.

This state of affairs brings a saying to mind: "Beauty is in the eye of the beholder." And if indeed creativity is so relative as to depend on the subjectivity of each and every individual, then surely science would not be able to say anything about the topic and would exclude it from its preoccupations. At the same time, it would be impossible to try to claim the absolute "objectivity" of creativity. So what are we to do? The answer that "solves" all these epistemological dilemmas is that one can try to *study creativity based on subjective reception or judgment* because subjective evaluations (especially in the case of experts) are extremely consensual. This is the basis for the consensual definition and assessment technique pioneered in the psychology of creativity by Teresa Amabile. Her approach to creativity is that "a product or response is creative to the extent that appropriate observers independently agree it is creative" (Amabile 1996, 33). Consequently, creativity is to be studied with the help of "appropriate" observers who ideally are familiar with the domain of the creation and who independently agree on whether something is or is not creative and on the level of creativity. Of course, the use of expert judges has deep roots in creativity studies; what makes Amabile's contribution unique is that she argued (and demonstrated in her research) that judges don't even need to start from an explicit definition of creativity. Subjective reception will do, and it will generally prove consensual. The consensual assessment technique is widely used today in the literature, and the consensual definition of creativity is accepted by most researchers (Lubart 2003). It is indeed comforting for creativity scholars to think—though "no person, act or product is creative or noncreative in itself" (Gardner 1994, 145)—that creativity "exists" at the level of subjective reception. In addition, we are on "firm ground" whenever experts, as compared to laypeople, evaluate creativity.

What would an exercise of using both expert and nonexpert opinions say about creativity? What would it mean to include the opinions of creators themselves? The study of Easter egg creativity with the use of multiple groups of evaluators, all belonging to different "communities of interest" for this artistic craft, shows how consensus in evaluations is always complemented by *divergence*. For example, there is great consensus among ethnographers, priests, art teachers, and folk artists that traditional forms of egg decoration require creativity of a higher level. At the same time, not all forms of wax decoration are considered equally valuable (to use the established terminology). Drawing on the egg with colored wax was described by some ethnographers as stepping outside of established canons. Moreover, eggs decorated with Christmas motifs were considered an expression of kitsch by several ethnographers, priests, and art teachers. Notably, folk artists are more open to "innovations" and show respect (or at least *claim* to show respect) toward all types of decoration. Red eggs, though largely considered to involve less creative ability, are nonetheless highly "valuable" for what they represent, especially for priests and ethnographers. Opinions diverge again in regard to eggs decorated with leaves. An illustration of "creativity in the small" for ethnographers and priests, they are potentially very creative for art teachers depending on what types of leaves are used, how the leaves are used, and whether the eggs are also painted with watercolors. In conclusion, evaluators from the four groups show that there are at least two different types of reception of Easter eggs, one supporting the idea of clear differences in creativity (found predominantly among ethnographers and priests) and the other advocating the creative potential of each decorated egg (more common among art teachers and folk artists). These different evaluations are rendered meaningful when we look at each group, its characteristic types of personal engagement with the practice, and its relations with others and with a shared sociocultural background (see Chapter 6 for details). Subjective reception of the new, as we will argue next, is rooted in the larger frames of "cultural reception" specific to every community and every society.

8.5. Cultural Reception

> Originality, freshness of perceptions, divergent-thinking ability are all well and good in their own right, as desirable personal traits. But without some form of public recognition they do not constitute creativity. In fact, one might argue that such traits are not even necessary for creative accomplishment.... Therefore it follows that what we call creativity is a phenomenon that is constructed through an *interaction between producer and audience*. Creativity is not the product of single individuals, but of social systems making judgements about individuals' products. (Csikszentmihalyi 1999, 314)

Positions such as that of Csikszentmihalyi might be considered extreme by mainstream creativity researchers, who would find unsettling the idea that all our criteria for recognizing creativity should be replaced by one and one only: social judgment. While one may justifiably dispute that novelty, originality, and utility are "not even necessary" for creativity to be attributed, it is certainly important to realize that *all* creativity evaluations are framed by sociocultural systems of beliefs, norms, and practices. The ultimate validation of creativity depends upon social agreement, which, in turn, is shaped by broader cultural structures. As Negus and Pickering (2004, 23) state, our actions and the products we create are never fully realized as creative acts until they are achieved within some form of *social encounter*. Our "subjective reception" of creativity is conditioned to a large extent by "cultural reception," that is, the set of principles and rules used in a particular culture (of a group, a community, or an entire society) to legitimize creativity. Since we all are subjected to processes of enculturation, we end up internalizing these "cultural lenses," which provide us with useful mental shortcuts or heuristics for deciding what is and what is not creative.

For example, there is a great tendency in many cultures to automatically consider everything labeled as art to be creative. The reverse is also true, and Runco (2007, 384) referred to this as the "art bias," by which creativity is reduced simply to artistic talent. This ends up making the terms "creative" and "artistic" interchangeable, a relationship that was evident in the study of Easter egg creativity. Asked whether or not Easter eggs, as a class of cultural artifacts, can be considered creative, many respondents from all four groups answered with arguments about their indisputable artistic value. The assumption is clear: Easter eggs are, in most cases, forms of art, and art involves creativity. Categories such as "decorative art" or "folk art" are frequently used in discussing the creativity of decorated eggs. Moreover, art teachers are ready to claim high artistic value for some Easter eggs as forms of "pure art." This naturally opposes them to more trivial, commonplace expressions and thus alludes to an implicit distinction between "high" art and "popular" or folk art, where the latter is always seen as less creative and valuable than the former (see Dewey 1934).

Culture doesn't only offer us lenses through which we can look at the world, and therefore also at creativity; it also, through social interaction and processes of education, gives us the ability to "decode," that is, to understand the objects and situations that we encounter. In this regard, Bourdieu (1993, 22) talked about *artistic competences* as forms of knowledge that allow us "to situate the work of art in relation to the universe of artistic possibilities of which it is part." Generalizing this, we might say that some people also come to acquire and be recognized for their "creativity competencies," meaning their ability to identify and evaluate creativity. We refer to these people as "experts," but it is important to keep in mind that a more accurate definition would be "persons who demonstrate superior ability in mastering the cultural codes that define creativity." In a way, they are the ones who "embody" the cultural reception of creativity, since their judgments not only are expressive of existing cultural norms but also constitute them. Cultural reception is therefore based on *culturally constructed codes* for distinguishing creativity. It consequently sets the boundaries of the creative domain and makes the question "Is this creative?" meaningful in certain situations and not others. To return to the example of Easter eggs, the question concerning their creativity was controversial for some of the priests. For this group in particular, Easter eggs belong to a different universe of significations, built around the notions of faith, religious practices, and the Resurrection, and thus evaluating these eggs based on their creativity is not the most appropriate or natural thing to do.

One conclusion emerging from the above discussion is that creativity evaluations are potentially consensual *within* the same professional group, community, or culture but are also potentially divergent *between* groups, communities, and cultures. The cross-cultural study of creativity testifies to the latter claim. Creativity in the West is very much product-centered, focusing on originality and the pragmatic aspects of problem solving, while Eastern cultures are more process-centered when it comes to creativity, emphasizing personal fulfilment, enlightenment, and inner growth (Lubart 1999; Raina 1999; Westwood and Low 2003). The scientific literature on creativity could not remain oblivious to these findings. The fact that lay conceptions are crucial for "discovering" the creativity of certain products or people inspired a growing body of literature on implicit theories of creativity. Though tempting as a theoretical perspective, the assumptions from which Runco (1999b, 27) starts when he defines implicit theories as belonging only to nonscientists (scientists always "explicate" their theories) and as being often "personal rather than shared" are surprising (for a critique, see Chapter 9). As the present chapter strives to demonstrate, personal constructs of creativity are always embedded in social constructs (see also Weiner 2000), just as subjective reception is framed by cultural reception. This does not mean that two persons from the same culture think the same about creativity and evaluate it in identical ways (in the end, culture is a plural phenomenon, and we cannot leave out personal life experiences); rather, it means that cultural values are powerful "guidelines" that we tend to follow in conscious or subconscious ways. The implicit theories of creativity held, for example, by ethnographers, priests, art teachers, and folk artists show both communalities and particularities, and these can be explained by the fact that, while all respondents belong to the same national culture, they are also members of different professional groups. For folk artists and ethnographers, creativity is a continuation of tradition; for priests, a form of improving what already exists; for art teachers, a natural ability alimented by our desire for the aesthetic. Thinking about creativity necessarily leads us to thinking about culture (see Chapter 1).

8.6. When Can We Say That Something Is Creative?

In the end, we have to return to our initial question and see what we have learned about identifying creativity in everyday life. As a starting point, we need to agree with Lubart's (2003, 11) assertion that "there are no absolute norms to judge the creativity of a product." And yet, both science and common sense make constant efforts to anchor the notion of creativity in products that are collectively recognized as creative. At the core of a potential definition of creativity seem to stand the features of newness and originality. Creativity means generating "difference," but not of any kind. When it comes to creative products, there is merit in being different (Hausman 1979, 240), and ideas of value and usefulness come to complement those of novelty and originality.

Within these grounds, specific to the psychology of creativity, there is an important argument to be settled: Is creativity evaluation an "objective" process? In other words, do we need subjective judgment to decide what is new, original, useful? This question is not inconsequential. In the efforts made to promote "objective" measures of creativity lies the assumption that creativity in itself has an "objective" nature, a supposition rightfully described by Csikszentmihalyi (1999, 321) as "too metaphysical to be considered part of a scientific approach." The arguments and examples given so far in this chapter indicate that, outside of "newness," appreciating originality and especially usefulness requires some degree of subjective judgment, and in any case these qualities are always relative (to what we know, to the reference points we take, etc.). This is how, in the past few decades, the emphasis on "subjective reception" increased, and today the use of the consensual assessment technique is widespread. Paradoxically, though, the grounds on which this methodology is employed can in fact take us back to the idea of an "objective" existence of creativity. If personal evaluations of creativity "naturally" converge then there must be something about creativity in itself that can be immediately recognized (at least by experts). But the real question is, Is it something about creativity, or does it have more to do with the *cultural lenses* we "wear" and "use"?

The first conclusion to be taken from this chapter is that *subjective reception is in fact conditioned, to a large extent, by cultural systems of beliefs and norms about creativity.* And these beliefs and norms are both similar and different across cultures. In the end, it might even be that ideas about originality and usefulness act as common cross-cultural "anchors" for creativity (though evidence suggests that they are more reflective of Western values). Of course, not everyone would happily accept this overall approach. Runco (1999a, 242–243), for example, advocated separating creativity from reputation and separating novelty and aesthetic appeal from social judgment and impact. This, in the author's vision, would make for "good science" and would also "increase the objectivity of creativity research." But is "good science" troubled by or unable to deal with the complexities of our existence as social beings? Is it upset by the idea of relativity and by the study of culture? For if this is the case, it is likely that creativity cannot be approached through scientific means. We could perhaps study "creation," understood as the mere generation of something different from what (we know) existed before, but not creativity. The richness, the complexity, and, in the end, the importance of creativity for our daily lives rest precisely in the fact that it is a *psycho-socio-cultural phenomenon* (Glăveanu 2011c; Chapter 3). When we lose sight of the social and cultural we "mutilate" the phenomenon we are aiming to study, and we end up studying something else.

The analysis of creativity in the context of Easter egg decoration in Romania points directly to the intricacies of both creative expression and evaluation. It shows that opinions tend to converge when it comes to the creativity of "traditionally" decorated eggs and also to the "uncreative" nature of Easter eggs decorated with stickers. The two ends of the creativity continuum, as it were, pose little difficulty. But what about the middle of the continuum? For example, participants found it difficult to appreciate the creativity of eggs decorated with leaves because the process is inferior to wax decoration, yet it does certainly involve more than the simple dying of eggs. It is also interesting to notice that though persons from different professional groups agree on the fact that creativity is involved in traditional decoration, the ways in which they reach this conclusion are slightly different. Ethnographers and priests emphasize the value of these products for perpetuating a deep and meaningful Romanian tradition. Art teachers and folk artists are more inclined to appreciate the beauty and artistic harmony of these products. Such discrepancies are important since, as this research demonstrated, members from all these groups engage in Easter egg decoration and relate to others who decorate in ways that are influenced by their conceptions of creativity, art, and tradition. Ethnographers decide what types of Easter eggs are to be displayed at museum fairs, priests tell their parishioners what types of eggs are to be appreciated, art teachers teach students how to make Easter eggs, and folk artists continue producing the kinds of eggs that correspond to what they like and what customers want. Thus, understanding creativity evaluations in this folk art context needs to take into account the *ecology of practices, social relations, and beliefs presupposed by the craft*. This is the case, we can assume, for all forms of creative expression, from the more modest to the most highly acclaimed.

In light of the above, one contribution to the literature on creativity assessment would be to define it as a *multilayered process*. Figure 8.1 is an attempt to depict the multilayered nature of our criteria for identifying and assessing creativity. This depiction suggests that while newness and originality are central to evaluating the creativity of products, they must always be qualified by reference to value and utility. Furthermore, all these aspects are often perceived and appreciated in "subjective" ways, and personal judgments about creativity are formulated in the broader context of cultural norms for the reception and recognition of creativity. This quality of being embedded in culture must be more seriously taken into account by current research on creativity, and especially by modern assessment techniques. In addition, the multilayered approach requires researchers to reflect upon and specify (a) the exact criteria used for assessment (novelty, usefulness, subjective judgment, etc.); (b) how these criteria relate to other microlevels or macrolevels of assessment (from more limited comparisons with a predetermined sample of responses to dialogue with larger cultural frames); and (c) who makes the assessment (the author, laypeople, experts, etc.) based on what theoretical assumptions (creativity as "subjective," as "objective," etc.) and with what practical implications.

How can we improve our research practice based on these conclusions? To begin with, we need to think about modalities of contextualizing creativity

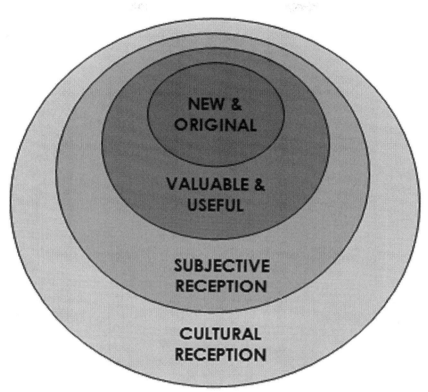

Figure 8.1. The multilayered approach to creativity assessment.

evaluations and of being more sensitive to the social and cultural dynamics behind their generation. We can always start our study of the cultural context by looking at what particular cultures (at a community or national level) celebrate as being creative and then considering how these "examples" infiltrate commonsense notions of creativity and become important points of reference for both acknowledged and anonymous creators. Besides, such criteria also "contaminate" the way in which we build and score creativity tests, and, in this area at least, serious efforts have recently been made to generate culture-specific norms for creativity assessment (despite resulting difficulties in comparing test results; see Lubart 1999; Westwood and Low 2003). Paying more attention to lay conceptions of creativity and incorporating these conceptual insights into our theories about the phenomenon and our assessment tools can only increase their ecological validity and will "help make our definitions more realistic and practical" (Runco and Bahleda 1986, 94).

Another significant question from a methodological perspective is, Who should judge creativity? Is it the author, the community, scientists?

If we do adopt a perspective in which creativity is to a large extent culturally constructed, then we come to realize that it is not important *who* evaluates creativity but *where* these evaluations come from and how they affect the creators and their larger communities. Anyone can evaluate creativity, and every one of us—in different circumstances (at home, at work, at school, in museums, at science fairs, etc.), explicitly or implicitly—does so. This doesn't mean that expert judges are to be dismissed; there is certainly value in the opinions of trained professionals. But again, perhaps more ecological value and more direct impact on the creation and the creator are carried by judgments made by people who are in a position to influence one or both of them (and who could be defined as belonging to "communities of interest"). If we are to understand creativity, we need to consider who the actors of creative acts are, and these actors are certainly more numerous than creators themselves (Glăveanu 2010b; Chapter 2). Finally, and related to the above, it would be also worthwhile to explore the following: mismatches in the evaluation of certain artifacts; instances of creativity being attributed to an object that was not intended by its author to be creative; and instances in which the status of "creative" is given after some time to certain creations (as in the classical case of Van Gogh) or, more interestingly, is taken away from them. These situations are most revealing of the "cultural frames" discussed in this chapter, and they point to their dynamic and co-constructed nature.

In conclusion, we return to the following question: How can we say that something is creative? We can now offer a tentative answer: *Something is creative when it is, to our knowledge, new and culturally validated as creative, which, in the West at least, often means being appreciated as original and useful.* Thus, nothing is creative because it just *is* creative. There is always a factor of subjective reception and social agreement involved. To say that creativity exists as such, independent of any context, is to be tricked by linguistic reification or to follow strictly positivistic criteria that struggle to eliminate subjectivity, relativity, and commonsense forms of knowledge. The psychological science of creativity should not fall into either of these traps. Operating with *emic*, locally informed criteria rather than *etic*, universal standards in the case of creativity (Glăveanu 2010a; see Chapter 1) leads by no means to the dissolution of creativity as a notion but rather to an integrative vision that does justice to the complexity of the phenomenon under study. Recognizing that we don't discover but *create* creativity takes nothing away from the importance of the concept or from the necessity of understanding its underlying processes. If anything, it opens a new and challenging path for researching the "creative" ways in which individuals and societies think about creativity.

9

Is the Lightbulb On? Social Representations of Creativity in a Western Context[1]

We live in a world where creativity is fashionable and desirable and embodies, at least in Western cultures, the necessity and universality of a true *social value* (see Mason 2003). And yet, what is creativity? What do psychologists mean when using the term? What about managers, teachers, art critics, etc.? Unfortunately, even after several decades of research, many would probably agree with Borofsky (2001, 69) that "grasping creativity is like trying to catch the wind." Despite the fundamental ambiguity and inherent complexity of the phenomenon, creativity is something that we comment on, that we "discover" in and around us, that we even make comparative judgments about. Since creativity basically deals with the emergence of the "new," of the "unfamiliar," its outcomes and processes are unavoidably accompanied by *collective meaning-making efforts*. The social representation of creativity, as will be argued in this chapter, has deep roots in social interactions among different actors in the public sphere—each and every one of us being, at some point or another, confronted with questions such as, What is and what is not creative?

The present chapter reports on a research project seeking to uncover the social representation of creativity. As such, it will start with a theoretical discussion concerning social representations and their points of connection with (or disconnection from) what are known as implicit theories of creativity. An argument will be made that looking at creativity *as a social representation* both enriches our understanding of the phenomenon and extends our practical means of studying it. The research discussed here uses several insights afforded by a social representations approach and explores creativity symbols and their relation with more general beliefs about creativity and with self-evaluations. It is hoped that through this approach a more contextual and more comprehensive view of what creativity is for "laypeople" and in everyday life (at least in a Western context) will emerge.

[1] Reprinted from *The International Journal of Creativity & Problem Solving* (published by The Korean Association for Thinking Development), *21*(1), Glăveanu, V. P., Is the lightbulb still on? Social representations of creativity in a Western context, 53–72, with permission from the editor.

9.1. Theoretical Lenses

The importance of studying laypeople's conceptions of creativity has been acknowledged relatively recently by researchers who focused primarily on the nature of the creative process and its enhancement (Spiel and von Korff 1998). In the past three decades, though, ideas about social agreement, the attribution of creativity, and its individual and collective representation became salient, and today we can find a fairly well-developed body of literature on "implicit theories of creativity." Nonetheless, folk conceptions of creativity have rarely been discussed from a more social and cultural perspective, as is found in the theory of social representations. Theoretical and empirical arguments will be offered for why this situation should be reconsidered.

9.1.1. From Implicit Theories . . .

The study of implicit theories is not restricted to creativity, not even to psychology in general, given that it represents a wide area of investigation involving most social sciences (Furnham 1988). Implicit theories are largely considered to be poorly articulated and to constitute core assumptions that construct reality and provide frameworks for thought and action (Dweck, Chiu, and Hong 1995). In a more recent formulation by Runco and Johnson (2002, 427), they are defined as "the constellations of thoughts and ideas about a particular construct that are held and applied by individuals." As such, implicit theories can and should be understood in their relation to "explicit theories," which are considered to be formal, logical, testable, and created by scientists. A great and somewhat artificial divide between laypeople and scientists is therefore set at the very core of an implicit theories approach.

Moreover, the mere distinction between "implicit" and "explicit" becomes *problematic* under further scrutiny. To take an example, Mark Runco (1999b), in his chapter on implicit theories, describes them in different ways: as belonging to laypeople, as personal, as often unshared, and as nonarticulated (in contrast to explicit theories). This understanding generally permeates his extensive work on the topic (see also Runco 2007a, 186). Many of these assumptions, however, contradict previous conceptualizations, such as that of Robert Sternberg who, in 1985, more generously defined implicit theories as constructions of people in general, useful in formulating "common-cultural views" (implicit theories are necessarily shared) and studied by looking at people's communications (hence, implicit theories need to be articulated in some form). The implicit–explicit opposition is therefore more blurred than current depictions would make us believe, and clear-cut distinctions—such as "science" versus "common sense"—often lead to oversimplification. As Furnham (1988, 7) readily admitted, "Lay theories *overlap* with scientific theories; they *function* in similar ways, indeed the one may be seen as an outgrowth of the other."

Despite theoretical debates, the actual research on implicit theories of creativity has seen a considerable expansion in recent years, and most studies use a social validation method to uncover the structure of lay beliefs. This procedure (see Runco 1989, 1999b) implies two stages: first, an open-ended exploration of what is considered "creative" by a certain group, and second, the construction of a checklist used to collect more quantitative data from an equivalent and often larger group. Research on implicit theories based on methodologies similar to the one described here has been conducted using various populations, from parents and teachers to managers and even scientists (Karwowski 2010; Runco 1989; Runco and Bahleda 1986; Runco and Johnson 2002; Sternberg 1985; Wickes and Ward 2006), sometimes from a cross-cultural perspective (Chan and Chan 1999; Lim and Plucker 2001).

The interest in implicit theories among creativity researchers is increasing, and it is alimented by both theoretical and practical considerations. At a theoretical level, it is hoped that an understanding of implicit theories will help to refine and develop our current scientific or "explicit" theories of creativity, to make them more realistic and to broaden their scope (Chan and Chan 1999; Runco and Bahleda 1986; Sternberg 1985). Perhaps even more important, implicit theories are studied for their *practical relevance*. Their value is twofold: in relation to evaluations and in relation to actual behavior. Implicit theories play an important role in how we assess creativity in ourselves and in others (Wickes and Ward 2006). This is by no means inconsequential, since holding an implicit theory involves a certain expectation, and expectations influence behaviors (Runco 2007a). Implicit theories are similar to standards we come to use, and from this perspective they have the power to either inhibit or facilitate creative expression (Runco and Johnson 2002). In sum, they "define how we think and behave with regard to creativity" (Wickes and Ward 2006, 138).

9.1.2. . . . to Social Representations

The same assumptions about the evaluative and behavioral consequences of lay beliefs are emphasized by social representation theorists. After the pioneering study of Serge Moscovici (1961) on psychoanalysis in French society, the theory of social representations took shape as a theory of social knowledge and moreover as a theory concerned with the transformation of knowledge as it "travels" through different communities and social milieus. Representation in this context is said to constitute the basis of all our knowledge systems (Jovchelovitch 2007, 2) and, as such, to make up our reality and the reality of the world around us (Duveen 2007; Moscovici 2000b). Representations are at once *symbolic and social* in their origin and expression. Once created, "They are autonomous" and "evolve beyond the reach of individuals" (Philogène and Deaux 2001, 6). Representations are bound to social contexts and, just as the latter are numerous in their diversity, so is our knowledge defined by plurality and heterogeneity. Last but not least, identities are also built on a foundation of social representations (Breakwell 2001), and it is argued that "social representations and social identities must be seen as two sides of the same coin" (Howarth 2007, 133).

Until the present moment, social representations have been studied in a variety of contexts and in relation to a diversity of social objects (for a review, see Jovchelovitch 2007), and yet there are still few studies that bring together creativity and social representations (Lancciano et al. 2010; Magioglou 2008). Perhaps the clearest attempts to reunite the two belong to the field of giftedness research. Tavani, Zenasni, and Pereira-Fradin (2009) investigated the social representations of gifted children. It has been suggested that the evaluation of creativity should also be based on an examination of social representations and experiences of creativity in different cultures (Häyrynen 2009). On the whole, the literature on social representations of creativity is underdeveloped, especially in comparison to that on implicit theories. A necessary question arises in this context: Are we not in fact studying the same realities under different names?

The answer to this is "yes and no." *Yes* to the extent that the results of implicit theories studies can be said to uncover social forms of representation, but *no* if we consider the different epistemological considerations that seem to underpin these two kinds of investigation. To elaborate on this second aspect, it became obvious from the above that implicit theories are often said to be "personal rather than shared" (Runco 1999b, 27), to "reside in the minds" of individuals, "in people's heads" (Sternberg 1985), though not in a complete social vacuum. In contrast to this view, the social representations approach would *emphasize* the fact that representations of creativity emerge out of *a space of intersubjectivity* and through different kinds of social interaction. In the words of Sandra Jovchelovitch (1996), social representations are never the solitary products of an individual mind, though they might find expression in individual minds. This distinction is paramount, since conceptualizing implicit theories as social representations opens up a whole new world of questions in which implicit theory researchers seem to have little interest: How do lay beliefs emerge in macrolevel and microlevel social interaction? How is it that individuals come to "acquire" certain representations? How does an individual engage with dominant forms of representation? How are identities "forged" in these representational fields? And so forth. In essence, if implicit theories are in the "individual mind," Where do they come from? What explains their variations and, more importantly, their transformation?

And yet, there are also many points of *connection* between implicit theories and social representations. In fact, authors such as Romo and Alfonso (2003) have defined implicit theories as "social knowledge schemas" (410). Even more, the very purpose of implicit theories seems to be similar to that of social representations: to make the world more stable, orderly, predictable, and understandable (Furnham 1988, 19). There are even many methodological similarities between implicit theories studies and traditional social representations research—for instance, the use of different groups of respondents (see Spiel and von Kroff 1988; Sternberg 1988), which allows for an appreciation of the context-dependent nature of creativity beliefs. This is why it is reasonable to state that much of the work on implicit theories is relevant for our understanding of the social representation of creativity. What, then, would be the contribution of social representations theory to the general literature?

9.2. The Social Representing of Creativity

To inquire about the social *representing* of creativity with the conceptual tools offered by the theory of social representations could help to clarify how representations of this kind take shape and function in society. It should be noted that what is referred to here is the representation of creativity per se and not of the creative person (something previously studied as well by Spiel and von Korff 1988).

One of the reasons why creativity should be studied as a representation is the function that social representations are said to have—namely, that of making something unfamiliar, *even unfamiliarity itself,* familiar (Moscovici 2000b, 37). And what can be more unfamiliar than creativity, the process by which unfamiliarity itself emerges? The seeming unpredictability of creativity can be unsettling for individuals, groups, and even societies and calls for constant representational efforts. The theory of social representations suggests what these efforts might consist of. Moscovici, in his seminal writing on "The Phenomenon of Social Representations" (2000b, 41–54; originally published in 1984), discusses the interrelated processes of *anchoring* and *objectification*. Anchoring, often reflected in naming and classifying, takes place when a strange reality is reduced to ordinary categories and images—when it is, in other words, set in a familiar context. Objectifying complements this by making the abstract (almost) concrete, by "saturating" the idea of unfamiliarity with reality, thus making it physical and accessible. As Moscovici (2000b, 49) describes it, "To objectify is to discover the iconic quality of an imprecise idea or being, to reduce a concept in an image." These processes can easily be illustrated by the case of creativity, where anchoring (in a certain domain, for example the arts) is supported by objectifications (e.g., the emblematic *Guernica* by Picasso, *The Persistence of Memory* by Dalí), which vary according to social groups and historical periods.

However, the logic of anchoring and objectification, and therefore of the production of representations, is not random. Its constraints have to do on the one hand with the inherent characteristics of the human mind and on the other with larger social, cultural, and historical contexts. Both these aspects are taken into account in more recent discussions about *themata and thematization*. Ivana Marková (2003) considers the fundamental characteristic of human thinking, language, and communication to be the quality of being based on oppositional dichotomies (e.g., individual/society, freedom/oppression, justice/injustice). It is such oppositions that, when thematized in public discourses, become the engine behind the construction of social representations. Science expresses themata in the form of scholarly debates between different orientations or schools of thought. In the creativity literature, for instance, we often find such polarities as child creativity versus adult creativity and creativity as domain-general or domain-specific (see the discussions by Sawyer et al. 2003). Naturally, commonsense functions follow similar principles, and it is repeatedly the case that scientific themata originate from lay thinking (Marková 2003, 184). However, as argued by Marková, themata in common sense are frequently dormant and become active only in the course of social or even historical events when established conceptions are challenged, either because new realities emerge or because existing constructions become obsolete. These kinds of situations are very common in everyday life, where the "creative" needs to be defended or separated from the "uncreative."

These ideas have many practical implications, several of which concern research methodologies. If representations are created in the course of communication and cooperation (Moscovici 2000b), then we would need to look for representations of creativity in everyday discussion, in the media, and in scientific discourses (Häyrynen 2009, 292). The link between science and common sense is in fact of maximal importance for the theory of social representations, as Moscovici's original project on psychoanalysis demonstrated. Similar to the notions of "unconscious" or "repression" in the case of psychoanalysis, psychological constructs such as "intelligence" or "creativity" "shuttle between the everyday talk and scholarly discussion, and bear traces of the former discussion when entering, for example, from everyday public treatment into scientific articulation" (Häyrynen 2009, 293). The guiding principle of social representations research is not to consider lay conceptions as "biases" and compare them to scientific—and therefore "truthful"—depictions (as sometimes occurs in implicit theories research) but rather to understand each and every construction in its own right.

9.3. Method

The research reported in this chapter was exploratory in nature and had the general aim of uncovering social representations of creativity among laypeople (non–creativity researchers) in Western countries.

Participants. The online survey designed for the research was answered by 118 respondents (by September 10, 2010). The major eligibility criterion was that a participant must be a national of a Western country (for greater cultural homogeneity) or must have lived in a Western country for at least five years. After excluding ineligible participants and incomplete responses, 106 participants were retained for the final data analysis. Over half of them (57.5 percent) were from the United States and a third (30.2 percent) were from the United Kingdom, so the results reflect largely an Anglo-Saxon cultural context. About three quarters of the respondents were females (76.4 percent), and the mean age for the sample was around twenty-eight (ages ranged from sixteen to sixty-three). Most respondents had completed higher education, at either a postgraduate (33 percent) or graduate (20.8 percent) level, and 34.9 percent were educated to a secondary or high school level. A third of the respondents (30.2 percent) were not studying at the time of the survey; those enrolled in education reflected a variety of disciplines, most notably psychology (25.5 percent of the entire sample). Finally, more than half of the participants (57.5 percent) were employed (with only five working in the arts or other creative sectors).

Materials and design. The research instrument was a questionnaire created by the researcher. The design of the questionnaire was guided by a social representations approach and combined closed questions (ratings on Likert scales) with open-ended questions (providing a better understanding of meaning-making processes). As previously argued, some important *premises* of social representations theory and research are the following:

1. Social representations are often "objectified" or "materialized" in concrete, even physical, forms in public discourses.
2. Social representations are "anchored" in bodies of previous knowledge that often exist antinomically, as part of larger themata.
3. Social representations are linked with identity processes and therefore with the positioning of the self in relation to the object of representation.

Considering the fact that a study of "objectified" depictions of creativity offers probably one of the best ways to start exploring broader patterns of representation, the present research centered on evaluations of "common" *creativity symbols*. Respondents were first asked to think of what the best symbol of creativity would be for them and to explain their choice. Then they were shown eight potential creativity symbols and were asked to rate them on how well they represent creativity and to comment on their link to the idea of creativity. A second part of the survey invited respondents to rate, separately, the importance of several factors for creativity: heredity, environment, originality, social value, perspiration, inspiration, domain-generality, and domain-specificity. These factors form dichotomies that underpin key debates in the literature and that help scientists (and potentially laypeople as well) to "anchor" the unfamiliar reality of the creative process in larger bodies of signification by means of definition and classification. Finally, self-positioning was also studied by asking respondents to estimate what percentage of people in the general population could be considered creative, rate their own overall creativity, explain this rating, and mention their most significant creative achievement to date. The survey ended with questions used to collect demographic information. It should be noted that all ratings mentioned above were made on seven-point Likert scales (where one was associated with low suitability or importance and seven with high suitability or importance) and that all explanations and comments were captured through open-ended questions.

169

One of the most important decisions to be made in designing the research instrument had to do with selecting creativity symbols. Since the process of objectification lends representations an almost material form, it was decided that pictorial depictions related to creativity in different kinds of public media needed to be explored. One of the most readily available "databases" for such depictions is, of course, the Internet, and thus a prestudy was conducted using the Google Images (UK) search engine on January 23, 2010. The first five hundred images resulting from typing the word "creativity" were selected, and forty-three of these were excluded on account of repetition.

The 457 remaining images were subjected to content analysis. There was not one code per image but potentially multiple codes, so double/multiple coding was not uncommon. The most frequent symbols (appearing at least more than once) were lightbulb (29), brain (15), paintbrush and colors (12), computer (10), toy (9), musical note (8), children's drawings (7), jigsaw puzzle (6), photo cameras (5), images of leaders or recognized creators (5), butterfly (5), lock and/or key (4), star (4), colored crayons (3), flower (3), birth/growth (3), images of flying (3), ship (2), Earth (2), bottle (2). A decision was made to select all elements with frequency above five, and thus *eight symbols*—a manageable number—were included in the questionnaire: lightbulb, brain, paintbrush and colors, computer, toy, musical note, children's drawings, and jigsaw puzzle. Respondents were prompted with verbal formulations and not with images, and the order of presentation was randomized in the survey.

Procedure. Participants were "invited to participate in a survey on creativity that focuses on creativity symbols, beliefs about creativity, and personal creative expression." They were informed about their rights and about the risks and benefits of participation, and their consent was recorded. The study was advertised on several online research websites (in the United Kingdom and the United States), and data collection started in February 2010. No material compensation was given for participation.

9.4. Results

The results of this research are presented in two sections. The current section looks at the main findings (generally quantitative) following the succession of questions asked in the survey. An important observation is that nonparametric statistics have been employed for data analysis considering the ordinal nature of Likert scales and the fact that ratings presented deviations from normality. The data discussed in the next section explore the "symbolic universe" of creativity more closely by focusing on participant interpretations (qualitative data) and by relating, whenever possible, laypeople's conceptions to the scientific literature on creativity. Depending mostly on the respondent's rating, associated qualitative answers were primarily grouped into favorable (for ratings of 5, 6, or 7), unfavorable (for ratings of 1, 2, or 3), and undecided (for a rating of 4). All answers in these preliminary categories were listed, and a synthesis of main points was made by the researcher for each and was illustrated with what were judged to be the most representative verbatim formulations. Many of them are included hereafter as direct quotations without a specified author.

The survey was opened by asking respondents to think of what would be the "best creativity symbol" for them and to explain their choice. Main categories are presented in Figure 9.1 (some responses were double coded). As can be noticed, most respondents mentioned symbols that have to do with *artistic expression* (paintbrush, color, and palette). Two other well-represented classes of response were "abstract" and "natural" symbols. Most abstract symbols chosen for creativity revolved around ideas of complexity, messiness, excitement, strangeness, and "infinite possibilities." Examples here are Möbius strip, Celtic knot, squiggle, infinity sign, question mark, yin-yang symbol, cross, Vitruvian Man, compass, prism, and empty chair. On the other hand, *natural symbols* were used to emphasize ideas of growth, mobility, change, and the ordinariness or simplicity of creation. Common symbols in this category were seed, flower, tree, rainbow, clouds, water, star, flame, hummingbird or butterfly, and blob of mercury. Not remote from the idea of "natural" symbols yet forming a clear category in itself was the concept of *brain* or *mind*, associated with creativity in twelve of the responses. In the fifth position in terms of frequency were *writing objects* (pen, pencil, crayon, even paper or quill), suggesting associations with literary forms of creativity but also chosen for their multifunctional nature—"Creative people doodle, draw, write and usually would use a pen to do so." This category was followed by the *lightbulb* symbol with nine responses, a choice often justified by its predominance in popular culture. *Manual work* symbols emphasized the role of hands and connected creativity to crafts and the activities of everyday life. Finally, *music note* and *computer* symbols were mentioned in two responses each. The "other" category included symbols

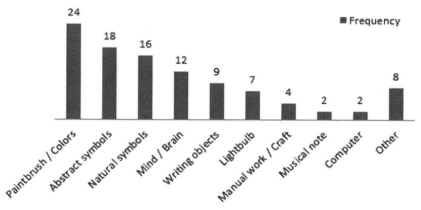

Figure 9.1. Categories of creativity symbols as proposed by the respondents.

that didn't fit in with the above; examples are dollar sign, autism, and dance. Standing out was the "no symbol" response and its justification: "I don't think you could give creativity a symbol because anything could be one." It is interesting to note that five out of the eight most common creativity symbols from Google Images were also spontaneously generated by the respondents; this supports the ecological validity of using Internet databases for research tasks of this nature.

When it came to rating the eight Google-generated creativity symbols on the 1 (poor creativity symbol) to 7 (great creativity symbol) scale, respondents generally appreciated "paintbrush and colors" the most (mode of 7) closely followed by "children's drawings" (mode of 6). The "lightbulb," "musical note," and "brain" symbols were slightly less appreciated (with modes of 5, 5, and 4, respectively), and "puzzle," "toy," and "computer" were least appreciated (with modes of 2, 2, and 1, respectively). Table 9.1 presents the descriptive results for each symbol. A Friedman test was conducted to determine whether participants had a differential rank ordered preference for the eight creativity symbols. Results indicated a significant difference, $\chi^2(7) = 214.25$, $p < .001$. The following section will return to these ratings and interpret them in light of the qualitative responses (participants were asked what they thought was the connection between symbol X and creativity). For the moment, it is important to keep in mind the apparent preference for art-related symbols (paintbrush and colors, children's drawings, musical note) and the apparent dislike for more "technical" associations (computer, puzzle) and for associations related exclusively to childhood (toy). The brain and lightbulb symbols generally obtained good ratings, but there were also reservations about their

Table 9.1. Descriptive results for proposed creativity symbols: frequencies for each Likert scale point,* median, and mode.

Creativity symbols	1	2	3	4	5	6	7	Median	Mode
Lightbulb	4	10	17	16	29	14	16	5	5
Brain	6	14	7	23	22	14	20	5	4
Paintbrush and colors	1	5	9	14	25	23	29	5	7
Computer	30	23	26	7	12	6	2	2.5	1
Toy	11	27	21	19	18	5	5	3	2
Musical note	4	16	17	14	23	18	14	5	5
Jigsaw puzzle	18	24	20	15	18	10	1	3	2
Children's drawings	1	4	12	19	22	26	22	5	6

* Where 1 is "very poor creativity symbol" and 7 is "excellent creativity symbol."

Note: Results based on the entire sample of 106 participants.

capacity to reflect the "true" nature of creativity. Even more interesting, if we look at Spearman correlation coefficients between the ratings of the eight symbols, we notice highly significant statistical correlations among the "triplet" of *paintbrush and colors, children's drawings,* and *musical note* (paintbrush and colors–children's drawings: rs(104) = .438, p < 0.001; paintbrush and colors–musical note: rs(104) = .344, p < 0.001; children's drawings–musical note: rs(104) = .378, p < 0.001) and also among the "quadruplet" of *lightbulb, brain, computer,* and *puzzle* (lightbulb–brain: rs(104) = .446, p < 0.001; light-bulb–computer: rs(104) = .263, p = 0.007; lightbulb–puzzle: rs(104) = .257, p = 0.008; brain–computer: rs(104) = .391, p < 0.001; brain–puzzle: rs(104) = .255, p = 0.008; computer–puzzle: rs(104) = .345, p < 0.001). Unsurprisingly, children's drawings also significantly correlated with toy, but the correlation was a bit less strong (rs(104) = .248, p = 0.01). This is already indicative of certain patterns of representation in relation to creativity and will be analyzed more carefully in the next section.

To help us clarify some of the general meanings associated with these symbols, we can consider a further piece of information that comes from the correlations that symbol ratings had with the ratings of the eight factors concerning the nature of creativity. Before considering these and in order to first summarize the results "within" pairs, let us note that the Wilcoxon test yielded significant differences between the medians of heredity and social environment, Z = −3.72, p < 0.001 (mean of ranks for heredity 33.13, for environment 46.52); of originality and social value, Z = −.611, p < 0.001 (mean of ranks for originality 45.88, for social value 34.21); and of inspiration and perspiration, Z = −4.65, p < 0.001 (mean of ranks for inspiration 40.73, for perspiration 37.32). No significant difference was discovered between creativity in a specific domain versus creativity in general (Z = −1.23, p = 0.219). Hence, to begin with, the respondents' representation of creativity emphasized *originality, inspiration,* and *the role of the social environment.* In regard to the ratings of creativity symbols, it is important to observe that the paintbrush and colors ratings correlated significantly and positively with scores on hered-ity (rs(104) = .295, p = 0.002) and negatively with scores on the importance of social environment for creativity (rs(104) = −.228, p = 0.19). This suggests that people who associate creativity mostly with artistic expression tend to consider it greatly influenced by heredity as well. Ratings for lightbulb cor-related with those for inspiration (rs(104) = .204, p = 0.036) and social value (rs(104) = .193, p = 0.047). The first correlation is not surprising since the lightbulb itself, as we will see, was appreciated as a symbol of inspiration, insight, and the "Aha!" moment. Incidentally, ratings for brain also correlated with those for inspiration (rs(104) = .298, p = 0.002). The second correlation in the case of the lightbulb symbol might be explained by an underlying con-nection with technology, and in fact, ratings for computer also correlated with social value (rs(104) = .289, p = 0.003).

The last part of the survey explored self-evaluations of creativity. The mean value for the general percentage of the population that respondents considered to be creative was 55.77, and their evaluation of their own creativity had a median of 6 and a mode of 7 (on a seven-point Likert scale). One can thus conclude that participants in the study tended to see themselves as *generally creative*. Furthermore, the two ratings were positively correlated (rs(104) = .234, p = 0.016), which means that persons who appreciated themselves as more creative also thought more people from the general population were creative. It should also be noted that one of the few correlations these two had with the other variables was with the ratings for creativity as domain-specific; particularly for self-rating of creativity, the correlation was significant (rs(104) = .270, p = 0.005). This perhaps suggests that people tended to see themselves as creative in particular domains rather than in each and every domain. There certainly are different ways of being creative, and when respondents were asked to comment on their self-creativity rating and to describe what they thought was their greatest creative achievement, responses followed three main categories (single coding). The best represented was the *artistic* one (50 percent of the cases), with participants identifying the following activities as creative achievement: painting or drawing, writing essays or poems, composing music, dancing, being skilled at photography or an artistic craft, and being interested in film or sculpture. The *scientific-professional* activities category (19.8 percent) was represented by creative activities such as being admitted to or completing a PhD program, writing an article or book, coming up with new methods of scientific investigation, and having innovative business initiatives. Finally, the *everyday life* creativity class, accounting for about a third of the responses (30.2 percent), included decorating a room or house, raising a family, solving problems and organizing daily activities, creating a personal style, improvising in cooking, creating unique gifts, having a sense of humor, and feeling creative as a person. What is salient here as well is yet another indication of how significant art is for the representation of creativity; indeed, it can be said to constitute the most potent "anchor" for understanding creativity (both in general and in regard to the creative expression of the self).

9.5. Interpreting the Results: The Symbolic Universe of Creativity

A classical social representations analysis would be incomplete without devoting attention to the actual reasons behind people's preferences, as expressed in their own words. Exploring the "symbolic universe" of creativity means exactly that: focusing not only on the *structure* but also on the *texture* of the responses, and this is accomplished by having a closer look at how participants create or comment on creativity symbols. The open task of choosing their own symbol suggested that creativity, as the ultimate "unfamiliar," is anchored in a variety of domains and is seen through a multitude of lenses. Most often these had to do with the arts, especially drawing and painting, but also with abstractions, nature, the human brain, manual work, etc. It can be concluded, just from this series of answers, that creativity is *multiply anchored and objectified* in laypeople's representations. This testifies to the richness and complexity of the phenomenon, something creativity researchers themselves are confronted with. The various connections between "lay" and "scientific" thinking, between "lay" and "scientific" concerns and dilemmas, will also become more clear as this chapter continues.

Paintbrush and colors and musical note. These two symbols are related to art, and though both were appreciated by respondents, it was clearly the paintbrush and colors that gained their preference. Behind the positive ratings of these symbols lies a strong association between *art* and *creativity*: "When someone is good with art, people will often label them as creative"; "Art is a field founded almost completely in creativity"; "When people think of creativity, art is usually one of the first things they associate it with"; etc. These kinds of associations seem to have deep cultural and historical roots, located by some authors as far back as ancient Greece (Friedman and Rogers 1998). The connection tends to be even stronger in the case of the paintbrush and colors symbol, as both ratings and comments have shown. This was considered the "typical symbol for creativity" since "painting is what many people think of as a major and important type of creativity." In comparison, comments for the musical note described it as creative because it is "one of the arts," but not necessarily the prototypical form of art.

Why is art creative? An analysis of the responses aids in understanding this. To begin with, art is a form of *self-expression*. Moreover, this expression is fundamentally *free* and open to "endless possibilities"—"A creative person can create anything with a paintbrush and colors"; "The possibilities are endless with musical notes"; etc. It also connects with *emotions and emotionality*, and this was seen as a requirement for creative production. "A note," it was said, "can mean anything, happiness, sadness, empathy, knowledge, even danger. It can be put anywhere on a measure line and mean something totally different." This is why artistic expression was also considered to reflect the *uniqueness* of the person. Finally, drawing and painting in particular are activities that many people considered to reflect "the actual making of something." Creativity is strongly related to *material outcomes* and processes of physical labor.

And yet, even these acclaimed symbols did not escape criticism, primarily for not representing the whole of creativity. The paintbrush and colors and the musical note were thought of as "context specific and limited," a "disciplined aspect of creativity" or "only one aspect of it," "a very narrow conception of creativity," "stereotypical and restrictive," etc. Summing up, two salient ideas emerged: "Creativity is much more than just having a talent" and "There is more to creativity than art." Further critiques were expressed in regard to the musical note symbol—it somehow contradicted the freedom that is specific to true creativity. Since music is written with notes, they are "the disciplining of music, the antithesis of creativity," a "plan of sound that has been followed," "a very rigid and controlled form of musical expression." But perhaps the strongest arguments raised against this particular symbol had to do with the fact that the mere interpretation of music is basically uncreative. In the words of one of the respondents, "I am not very musical, but at school I learned to read music and add chords using a method without any creativity." In contrast, "Musicians, especially composers, spontaneously create improvised melody. I'd say that's creative!" Distinctions such as these are also raised in the scientific literature, and authors like Umberto Eco would certainly argue for the creativity of each "interpretation," since every work of art "is effectively open to a virtually unlimited range of possible readings" (Eco 1989, 21).

In the end, there seems to be an acknowledged relation between the art of painting and the art of music (music notes were compared with blobs of color). Both notes and colors are "tools for creativity," and perhaps their most important virtue as creativity symbols is that they represent "something that all cultures and most individuals can relate to and readily understand."

Children's drawings and toy. These two symbols are, in essence, both related to children and childhood, and yet their ratings contrasted greatly. While children's drawings were generally appreciated as a very good symbol for creativity, this was not so much the case for the toy. It might be that the former was again associated with artistic expression, and in fact paintbrush and colors and children's drawings seem to be most preferred in comparison to the other symbols. A quick look at the qualitative answers supports such a supposition. Again, references were made to the arts ("anytime you draw you are creative") and also to imagination ("drawing images from one's imagination is a creative act"). But it should be noted that in the case of both Children's drawings and toy, most of the comments had to do with *children and their creativity*.

It might well be the case that children's creativity represents a themata in commonsense thinking because there are two opposing views on this matter, both supported by a series of arguments. On the one hand, and for most respondents, children were the actual *embodiment of creativity*—they "always have a creative mind" and "are some of the most creative beings." Why is that? Because children are "uninhibited," are "open to all possible ideas or solutions," "are less self-conscious," and "have the innocence and the imagination to create." They also "have a different perception on reality," have "various views of the world," and are "less constrained by what society wants." As such, they "are not afraid or discouraged to show what they want," "not yet restrained by convention." Their "open minds" and "wild imaginations" make drawing or playing unique, since "the same child will never produce two similar drawings, because their creativity explores different paths." In most of these accounts there was an explicit dichotomy at work between *children* and *adults*, the latter being more "logical," more "closed-minded," and much more connected to the real world ("adults feel much more constrained by the fact that their picture isn't a good representation of the real world"). Consequently, "The best creative minds, whatever the ideas they are working on, are those that can continue to be open, playful, experimental, questioning and flexible like a child's"—or, in other words, "The child within all of us is the part which longs to create and come up with answers to all things." Such statements are in fact mirrored in the scientific literature, and Freud himself made a parallel between children at play and creative writers (Freud 1970, 126–127, originally published in 1908).

Could anyone, faced with such compelling statements, doubt the creativity of children? Some of the respondents actually did, and they *problematized* this by proposing that creativity is actually developed "in older age" and that children's drawings stand for "less creative, more creation to come." As one of the participants put it, "Often children lack the technical ability to bring their creativity into fruition of a real product, so it is only a moderately good symbol for creativity." A strikingly similar argument was advanced in the creativity literature by Mihaly Csikszentmihalyi (in Sawyer et al. 2003, 223), who argued that creativity needs to have an effect on culture, and children can almost never achieve that. Other authors noticed the same contradictions arising when we operate with this kind of definition for creativity (Cohen and Ambrose 1999, 11). Furthermore, children are not always creative and can easily become uncreative, for example when "a drawing is something a teacher tells the child to make." One respondent said that "children draw creatively until we stifle their creativity," echoing larger debates about the "creativity slump" in school (see Lubart 2003). Finally, in regard to the toy symbol, questions were raised as to whether children's play is always creative. In this case, many considered it to depend on the toy, since "some toys encourage creativity more than others." This further connects to scientific concerns, since the traditional view in child's psychology was that play encourages an "autistic" mode of thought (see Harris 2000, 188), and "the question of whether play is necessarily creative (or, indeed, whether creativity is necessarily playful) is a persistent one" (Banaji, Burn, and Buckingham 2006, 35). For more discussions related to children and creativity, see Chapter 12.

Brain and computer. The brain and the computer are both highly complex systems, the former being the highest achievement of the natural world, the latter probably the greatest triumph of human thinking. This was well acknowledged in participants' comments, in which, for example, the computer was described as "an artificial brain." And yet these two were not the most popular symbols for creativity, and both were generally accused of being, in essence, "machines" associated with psychological functions other than creativity: "thoughts," "learning," "problem solving activities," "idea processing," "logic," "rationality," "science," "intelligence," "technological/scientific creativity"—in short, *cognitive processes and outcomes*. Considering, though, the difference in nature between a brain and a computer, both positive and negative views tended to be more specific, as follows.

The brain was seen as a relatively good creativity symbol (at least compared to computers), and among participants who supported this symbol there was a strong consensus that the brain is the one doing the creating: it is creativity's "place and motor," its "source," a "necessary" condition, it "allows creativity," it is "behind" it, it is "where creativity takes place," where it "comes," "originates," "stems" from. Summing up, the brain "controls creativity" and creativity "involves using brainpower," so "you need to be able to use your brain in order to be creative." Consequently, "Without brains, there wouldn't be any creativity." Such strong claims characterize lay thinking perhaps more than scientific thinking, in which, for example, neurological studies of creativity (see Martindale 1999) are a growing field but researchers do not (yet) claim the ability to explain away creativity as a purely cognitive process. In fact, though "the possibilities are promising, we are not anywhere near the point of being able to image the creative process as it unfolds in the human brain" (Hennesey and Amabile 2010, 574). Similar reservations were also expressed by some of the respondents, who considered the brain as the beginning of creativity but certainly "not the whole story." Moreover, we all have a brain but we are not all creative: "Creativity all comes from the brain . . . but so does everything else." The brain may well be "the powerhouse of all thought," but at the end of the day it is "merely tissue with potential (or sometimes, a lack thereof)."

Whereas the brain was considered to be an integral part of the story when it comes to creativity, computers were oftentimes completely excluded from it. The main reason: a computer "can only do things you tell it to do," it strictly follows "programmed instructions," it is "constrained to rules" and "can only manipulate facts." This is radically opposed to a vision of creativity as random generation, fluidity and flexibility, emotion and self-expression. In the end, "Electronics and creativity don't really mix—there is only one way to access the Internet, to use Excel or other programs." The natural reaction for some of the respondents when faced with this symbol was surprise or incredulous fascination: "How can a machine symbolize something as deeply human as creativity?" "Can creativity really be replicated in computers?" These kinds of questions are not uncommon in the scientific literature (see Runco 2007a). Directly interested in *computational systems*, authors like Margaret Boden (1994, 84) would answer that yes, they can certainly help us understand how human creativity is possible, and to a certain point they can appear to be creative and even appear to recognize creativity. These ideas are generally not widespread among laypeople, though occasionally some would say that "a computer in itself is a product of creativity as well as a major tool for creativity, especially today." Indeed, when one looks at the "bright" side of the associations between computers and creativity, there is a sense that computers are valuable *tools* for creative expression, especially in regard to graphics, design, multimedia, image creation, etc. They "open up opportunities" and also "limitless capabilities" for their users. Nonetheless, this point was counteracted by the belief that "you can do many creative things with a computer. But you can do many more non-creative things." Computers can promote "uniform thinking" and be "equally used to waste away time and energy as they are used to discover." All things considered, their connection to creativity seems to be bluntly rejected or at least carefully scrutinized.

Lightbulb and jigsaw puzzle. The lightbulb and the puzzle are also connected (as the quantitative analysis has shown) in some ways with the symbolism of the brain and the computer. Indeed, when one looks at the qualitative responses, associations with cognitive processes are predominant. The lightbulb, a classical symbol of *insight* (Runco 2007a, 21), was generally recognized by lay respondents as associated with ideas and idea generation in particular—the "Eureka" or "Aha!" moment, sudden thoughts, illumination, and inspiration. Intellectual kinds of association are also specific to the jigsaw puzzle, which was seen as connected to intelligence, problem-solving skills, "logical and practical thinking," and even to "mathematics" and the "brain." And yet, just as in the case of the brain or the computer, anchoring creativity in more technical or cognitive domains was not considered entirely "representative" for creative phenomena.

The lightbulb nevertheless was better received than the puzzle, though overall less appreciated compared to more artistic symbols (e.g., paintbrush and colors, children's drawings). So the title question of whether the lightbulb as a consecrated image of creativity is still "on" can be answered positively or negatively, depending on the comparison term. Partially to blame for its "moderate" popularity seems to be precisely its fame. The lightbulb appeared "conventional" and "over-used," and this made it "rather uncreative" for a creativity symbol. On the whole, though, the lightbulb's link to thinking and ideas worked in its favor because "a lightbulb, to me, means that you were able to think outside the box, pairing up the details, and coming up with a solution. It takes creativity to be able to come up with a bright new idea." And it is exactly the process of coming up with "bright" ideas that the lightbulb stands for. The experience of an insight and its connection to creativity have long been discussed in psychology, where inspiration attracted the interest of both psychoanalysts (see Slochower 1974) and Gestalt or cognitive psychologists (see Sternberg and Davidson 1999). Both approaches came to the conclusion that a considerable amount of *preparatory work* is needed before insights can take place. This is not so clear in the case of the lightbulb symbol, though, since "it suggests that creativity is an instant inspiration, that occurs as quickly as flipping a switch."

The lightbulb was also disliked for saying nothing about the *application* of an idea and the *intentionality* behind creative work ("it suits better the accidental discovery of an idea"). And even when it does seem connected to creativity, it was said to better represent the "academic," "practical," or "logical" aspect of it. In many ways, the puzzle symbol had the same "shortcoming" for the participants, one of whom thought that "it isn't really a symbol of creativity, more of a complex mind." Nonetheless, despite its rather low ratings, the jigsaw puzzle did have some recognized advantages as an image of creativity. "It involves critical thinking and looking at objects in multiple ways," and in the end, "creativity is about piecing together different ideas to make a whole one." Even the stages of the creative process were, for some, very well symbolized by the process of assembling a puzzle. First, in both creativity and puzzle assembly rests "an initial desire, wish or question," then "you have to think outside the box and put bits and pieces of information together"; this requires both time and patience, but "once you get a good start on that jigsaw puzzle, its quick to finish. And like creativity, once you warm up, thoughts start to fly out of your head." However, the primary justification for the low rating of the puzzle symbol is that most respondents focused on its "mechanical" side and its predictability. Puzzles were qualified as the opposite of creativity, since "there is no invention or new insight"—"a puzzle only goes together one way." Also, the process of making a puzzle requires more intelligence and problem-solving skills than creativity does. Creativity's connection to these cognitive mechanisms seems to preoccupy scientists (see Eysenck 1994; Lubart 2003; Runco 2007a; Sternberg 1999a) more than laypeople, who are more inclined to simply distinguish between creativity and cognition.

9.5. Discussion: Creativity as Representation

The present research explored current representations of creativity in a Western context, with a particular focus on creativity symbols as objectifications of creativity which are unmistakable signs leading us to the very core of representational systems. As Moscovici (2000b, 51) acknowledged, collectively constructed images of an object become objects in themselves; they no longer merely signify the object but "are what is significant." Creativity certainly is a significant object, and a study of its images among lay respondents emphasizes once more how *complex* and *multifaceted* the reality of creativity really is for each and every one of us. All eight proposed symbols were criticized—more than once—for not representing the whole of creativity, and there is a clear sense that perhaps *nothing* can represent the whole of it. Creativity will always have an essence that to some degree manages to *escape representation*. This is valid for both lay and scientific efforts to understand this phenomenon. And yet, paradoxically, this is exactly what gives *vitality* to the subject and keeps all possible and competing representations in (*creative*) *tension* with one another.

To begin with, there seems to be a deep-seated tension between at least two meanings of creativity: the artistic one and the scientific/technical one. Rooted in Romanticism and the Enlightenment, respectively (Weiner 2000), these thematized, dichotomous aspects continue to aliment both scientific and commonsense thinking. And yet, if there is anything this research demonstrates, it is the predominant tendency, at least among these respondents, to anchor creativity in the *artistic domain*: "Usually when we talk about creativity it is in the artistic domain so I think paintbrushes and colors symbolize artistic talent, which I find more strongly associated with creativity than the more practical/inventive creativity." Symbols like paintbrush and colors were not only the most popular when rated but also the most frequent in the case of spontaneous associations. Creativity researchers might consider this an *art bias*, "a *misunderstanding* of creativity that equates it with artistic talent" (Runco 2007a, 384; emphasis added). From a social representations perspective, this is an *understanding*—one that needs to be understood itself, in terms of both its roots and its implications.

And one of the most direct implications has to do with *self-categorization* in relation to creativity. In fact, when one looks through the justifications given for the ratings of personal creativity, many times they make explicit reference to art: "I am interested in the arts," "I am no artist but I do occasionally have good ideas," "I like making art but I don't have many original ideas so I don't consider myself creative," "I can generate original ideas so feel creative in that sense, but lack expertise in drawing or playing music so I rate myself as kind of average," etc. What becomes evident, especially in the last example, is the risk of sometimes being discouraged from developing an identity as a creative person by a lack of expertise in the arts. This can be even more problematic if we remember that ratings for the paintbrush and colors symbol were positively correlated with the heredity factor and negatively correlated with the social environment factor. What might emerge from this is a particular representation in which creativity is seen as more remote from actions of everyday life and everyday people and closer to the realm of great creators, especially artists (something also defined as the He-paradigm, Glăveanu 2010b; see Chapter 2). And yet, artistic expression is not always represented as "inaccessible." In fact, the children's drawings symbol, again very much preferred, effectively illustrates this because "it is the expression of creativity in a manner not reserved for artists but in a raw sense applicable to anyone." Furthermore, numerous comments on self-ratings explored this everyday life dimension, which portrays creativity as ordinary, natural, an integral part of people and actions: "My mind is constantly creating meaning as I interpret the world. In that sense, I am constantly creating a subjective experience. Like me, all individuals are inherently creative." As was found in previous research (Karwowski 2009), people tended to consider themselves capable of little-c creative acts rather than big-C creativity.

The present study is not without its limitations. To begin with, as in any convenience-based sampling, there might have been a self-selection of participants such that the survey was taken by those who were more interested in creativity and who considered themselves creative. Furthermore, the sample was not representative of the general population; rather, it was composed more of females, persons with higher levels of education, and students (many of whom were psychology students). While it was not the purpose of the study to make general claims (related to the Western context), it would be interesting in the future to develop comparisons between different groups using the same methodology: males and females, persons from different professional categories, persons from Eastern and Western cultures, etc. In fact, this design would be very much in tone with the social representations approach, which strives to connect systems of belief to the sociocultural context of the participants. Another possibility for future work would be to collect data using more methods, particularly from focus groups, which allow the researcher to capture social interaction and communication aspects that can only be inferred in survey research.

In conclusion, there is *no singular representation of creativity*, and this is noticeable at both an individual and a social level in both lay and scientific thinking. Controversies about what creativity is and is not dominate public as well as scientific discourses, and, as this research indicates, there are more points of connection between these than we might think. Similar types of questions preoccupy both lay respondents and creativity researchers, and among them we find the following: Is artistic creativity different from scientific creativity? Are children creative? Do toys and computers help or hinder the development of creativity? What is the relationship between creativity and the brain? Of course, there are differences in how these questions are answered and the context in which they are raised (a scientific reunion, a discussion at the local pub, an online survey, and so forth), and this puts certain constraints on the representational work and its outcomes. What is emphasized, though, by research on social representations or implicit theories of creativity— independent of whether they are studied as a personal or a social construct—is their *importance* for each and every one of us, and especially for scientists. Sternberg (1985, 621) once wrote that "the study of implicit theories has at least as much relevance as does the study of explicit theories, and perhaps even more relevance." This is especially true in the case of creativity, which all of us—implicitly and explicitly, individually and socially—are making constant efforts to *represent*.

Part E

The Creativity of Action

10

Habitual Creativity: Revising Habit, Reconceptualizing Creativity[1]

*We may borrow words from a context less technical than that of biol-
ogy, and convey the same idea by saying that habits are arts. They
involve skill of sensory and motor organs, cunning or craft, and objective materials. They assimilate objective energies, and eventuate in
command of environment. They require order, discipline, and manifest
technique. They have a beginning, middle and end. Each stage marks
progress in dealing with materials and tools, advance in converting
material to active use.*

(Dewey 1922, 15; emphasis added)

The present chapter aims to address the enduring dichotomy between creative
and habitual behavior. This dichotomy stands at the core of thinking not only
about creativity but about human action in general and human society; it articu-
lates greater philosophical concerns for understanding continuity and change
and the relationship between the "old" and the "new." What is attempted here is
the elaboration of an account that transcends such oppositional categories and
reveals the *co-constitutive* nature of creativity and habit, change and continuity,
the new and the old. The notion of "habitual creativity," developed in this context, argues simultaneously for the creativity of habitual action and the habitual
nature of creativity. This is a concept that can find applicability in theorizing
creativity as a whole, from more "minor" forms to "celebrated" creative achievements. However, the greatest contribution this notion makes is arguably toward

[1] © 2012 by the American Psychological Association. Reproduced with permission. The official
citation that should be used in referencing this material is the following: Habitual creativity:
Revising habit, reconceptualizing creativity. Glăveanu, Vlad Petre. *Review of General Psychology*,
Vol 16(1), Mar 2012, 78–92. doi: 10.1037/a0026611. The use of this information does not imply
endorsement by the publisher.

our understanding of everyday life creativity, with the help of which "we adapt flexibly, we improvise, and we try different options" (Richards 2007, 26) in our day-to-day existence. Many of the examples in this discussion, therefore, come from studies of folk art, but fruitful parallels are also made with other forms of artistic expression—for example, music, particularly jazz performances—and with any other everyday activities that require practice and mastery in execution. To achieve this broad aim, the chapter both reviews several strands of current empirical work and aims to recuperate theoretical insights from foundational scholarship in psychology and related disciplines in order to develop a more comprehensive, cross-disciplinary perspective on both habit and creativity.

10.1. An Apparent Paradox: Creativity as Mastery

This inquiry into the relationship between creativity and habit was prompted by a set of empirical investigations of craft activities, in particular Easter egg decoration in Romanian communities (Glăveanu 2010c, 2011b; Chapters 6 and 8). This folk art can be considered habitual at many levels, starting from identifying it as essentially a custom, a "social or community habit," to looking at its inner organization of action in which different techniques of decoration require different habits, and ending at a microlevel with the exercised and habitual depiction of motifs and patterns. At all these levels, one can see the expression of creativity. Decorators do not merely reproduce the tradition but "intelligently adapt customs to conditions, and thereby remake them" (Dewey 1934, 75). The repetition of a pattern is not essentially a routine or mechanical process and can "also be an opportunity for personal interpretation of that pattern" (Weiner 2000, 153). Finally, just as in music, where "spontaneity in performance is not an illusion" and "repeated performances generally differ in small but musically significant ways" (Chaffin, Lemieux, and Chen 2006, 200), each presentation of a motif is at the same time a re-presentation of it, a re-creation. Most important, higher levels of creativity in this craft (as appreciated by both artisans themselves and their customers) are associated with the continuous efforts to perfect the work, to achieve mastery over the technique. The "remarkable intuitive sensitivity" (Dobbins 1980, 38) that describes folk artists in any domain is the outcome of years of practice—of working at least the first "thousand eggs," as mentioned by one of the decorators. The nature and characteristics of this mastery need to be unpacked for a better understanding of both habit and creativity.

In light of the above, mastery can be defined as *the uppermost expression of habitual practice, at which action has been so well exercised and internalized that it often becomes associated with advanced forms of creative expression.* The fundamental question to be asked here is similar to that of Chaffin et al. (2006) concerning the activity of musicians: How can performance be both creative and highly automatic at the same time? Or, in other words, How can mastery involve both routinized habit and creativity of the highest degree? This relationship can be visually represented by an almost perfect circle, like the one depicted

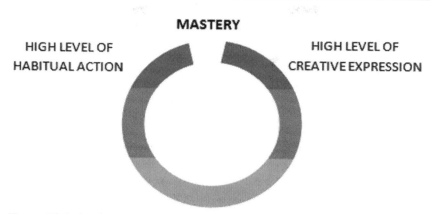

MASTERY

HIGH LEVEL OF
HABITUAL ACTION

HIGH LEVEL OF
CREATIVE EXPRESSION

Figure 10.1. A schematic representation of mastery.

in Figure 10.1. In this representation, habit and creativity are positioned on a continuum that, at all points, involves an integrated manifestation of both. Often, when the habit is still not fully formed, outcomes appear to be more novel in relation to conventional modes of actions. Conversely, a powerful habit might reduce variation at a surface level while encouraging microchanges and necessary adjustments of the technique. However, it would be incorrect to assume that as habit grows stronger the (perceived) creative quality diminishes, and this is reflected by the "extremities" of the continuum in Figure 10.1 not being opposed to each other but coming together in what is called mastery: the highest level of habitual action associated with the highest level of creative expression. In order to become more creative, one need not "break" with habit, as is commonly thought, but rather one should advance in mastering it.

In the psychological literature to date, this concern for how repetition and practice contribute to higher achievement and creativity has been considered in studies of *expertise*. Again, a central concern for this kind of investigation is to challenge the "widespread belief that all types of practice involve mere drill that is designed to attain rapid and effortless automaticity" (Ericsson 1998, 89). In other words, How can novices move to expertise in their practice without leveling off their performance after automatization? This question has been answered by Ericsson (1998, 1999, 2003) in a theory of expertise that centers around "deliberate practice." In summary, an improvement in performance is not an automatic consequence of additional practice (the mere repetition of the same activity day after day) but rather is the result of constantly raising the difficulty of the exercise and thus engaging in activities that require incremental development. The key element here, in Ericsson's view, is that such exercise needs to be deliberate and intentionally designed and carried out. In other words, the learner, sometimes assisted by a teacher or coach, needs to find suitable training tasks and master them sequentially (Ericsson 2006, 692). In his work, Ericsson (2003, 2006) presented numerous examples of successful deliberate practice activities (in sports, chess, typing, etc.) and thus built a picture of mastery and expertise acquisition that revolves around concentration and awareness rather than mindless repetition of the task. Expertise is not threatened by routines; rather, the path to mastery "involves problem solving, iterative refinement and, at higher levels of skill, the development of internal representations for planning, evaluating and monitoring mental representations" (Ericsson, Roring, and Nandagopal 2007, 21–22). This resonates with the usual practice of expert craftspeople, whose work necessarily requires concentration and rhythm, a coordination between hand and eye that balances "repetition and anticipation" (Sennett 2008, 176). Easter egg decorators, for instance, make regular changes in their work, commonly in the motifs they depict and sometimes even in the work techniques they employ. Learning the craft involves not reproducing the same motif endlessly but passing from simpler to more complex ornaments in an effort to create novel, more "beautiful" patterns (Glăveanu 2010c; Chapter 6). What Ericsson's theoretical framework shows—and these empirical examples argue for it as well—is that it is not only preferable but vitally important for novices and experts alike "to avoid mindless memorization and automatization of skilled performance in order to continue improving and increasing control over their performance" (Ericsson 1998, 94).

If we understand expertise as related to constant change and self-challenge, then we can legitimately ask whether creativity is the same as expertise or, to put it differently, whether creativity always requires expertise. There are many authors today who are ready to highlight the deep connections between the two; Sternberg (1998, 2001), for instance, famously endorsed a view of giftedness (and abilities more generally) as forms of developing expertise. However, alternative explanations of the creative process have also been put forward, most notably Simonton's (2007) perspective of creativity defined in terms of a Darwinian process of blind variation (though this "chance model" has thus far received limited empirical support; see Kozbelt 2008). Furthermore, a "tension" between creativity and expertise (see Weisberg 2006, 766) is often postulated based on several accounts, among them the pervasive association between expertise and an automatic way, anchored in the past, of responding to a situation; in creativity, in contrast, intentionally breaks with past experience. Considering several case studies of creative achievement, both Weisberg (2006) and Simonton (2003a) reached a similar conclusion, namely, that expertise may very well be a necessary but not sufficient condition for creativity. Indeed, mastery of a specific domain helps creative performance in that area but leaves unexplained all those instances in which people are creative without being experts (the classic example being when they answer general tasks on creativity tests). This reinforces componential models of creativity (see Amabile 1996) and highlights the interaction between both domain-general and domain-specific skills in creative action. Returning to the tension view, though, we can also find arguments for why "too much expertise" may be detrimental to creative activity (see Simonton 2003a, 229). This line of thought is supported by a frequent connection between expertise and increased inflexibility on the one hand and narrowness in thinking and action on the other. Exploring further the notion of "cognitive entrenchment," Dane (2010) came to the conclusion that there might be a trade-off between mastery and flexibility or even between mastery and creativity, but this is not always the case. In fact, Ericsson has offered a well-grounded rebuttal of the tension view and has presented evidence suggesting that experts "generate better actions than their less skilled peers even in situations they have never directly experienced" (Ericsson 1999, 331) and also are capable of adjusting their performance to changing contexts both *before* and *during* the competition (Ericsson 1998), thus disputing the idea that mastery is inflexible and fully automated.

What can be concluded from the above is that expertise is certainly an important condition for higher level creative achievement, but this does not imply that all experts are extremely creative or that beginners necessarily show little or no creativity. The question remains of how exactly mastery, acquired through deliberate practice, facilitates creative expression. As alluded to previously, for Ericsson the key to understanding expertise lies in the "refined mental representations" that expert performers develop, representations that are able to "maintain accessibility to relevant information and to support more extensive and flexible reasoning about an encountered task or situation" (Ericsson 1998, 91). Indeed, the automatization of action comes with a series of benefits, among them the way in which it frees mental resources and helps us focus on other aspects of the task while performing it. In the words of Sternberg, Kaufman, and Grigorenko (2008, 309), "In general, automatization lets people take in more of the world, and learn more"—and, we would continue, become more creative in engaging with the world. What is the mechanism behind this accomplishment? Perhaps one of the most interesting attempts to explain this process comes from Chaffin et al. (2006), who dealt specifically with musical performances. Their premise is simple: "If the musician is not paying attention to the music, then a performance can easily be automatic and lack the important qualities of vitality and spontaneity" (201). On the other hand, focusing too much on pitfalls and mistakes can make the outcome equally uncreative. What increases creativity is in fact thinking about *interpretative and expressive goals* while playing and detecting the cues that are associated with these particular qualities. Rehearsals of the composition ensure that performance cues "come to mind automatically and effortlessly as the piece unfolds, eliciting the highly practiced movements" (202). It is only through practice that such prompts can become an integral part of the recital, and only in this way can musicians free themselves from monitoring each and every movement and perfect those particular elements that give the whole performance its creative value. "Use of performance cues is," in fact, "an attention strategy that maintains conscious control of a highly automated performance" (215). The authors proposed a hierarchical classification of cues in the case of music: basic, interpretative, and expressive. Mastery is achieved after considerable practice, when basic and interpretative aspects of the performance have been fully integrated and the artist can focus entirely on expressive prompts. Examples from Easter egg decoration offer further support for the explanation above. In this craft, the performance cues to which most nonexpert decorators attend are related to how straight the lines are, if the model is symmetric, if colors have the proper shade, and so forth. In contrast, experienced artisans who have mastered the habit of drawing on the egg can "free" their attention from technical details and focus on aesthetic qualities, and they thus seize all opportunities for adding a personal element to the model being depicted (Glăveanu and Lahlou 2012; Chapter 5).

In conclusion, understanding the apparent mastery–creativity "paradox" requires us to think about the dynamic between *attachment to* or *immersion in* a domain of practice and *detachment*, meaning the capacity to creatively transgress its current state and envision its future dimensions. Unfortunately, this reality has rarely been theorized as such in mainstream psychology and mainstream creativity research. Moreover, as argued above, the concepts of habit, practice, exercise, repetition, and so forth have been treated with enduring suspicion in relation to performance and creativity on account of their assumed association with automated and mindless routines. Perhaps the work of Ericsson and others managed to "rescue" practice and exercise (in their deliberate versions) from this harmful conceptualization, but to date very little discussion has been devoted to habit, itself an outcome of and a powerful force behind exercised forms of practice. Several reasons for this are explored in this chapter.

10.1.1. Theoretical Difficulties: Creativity versus Habit in Psychology

It is a working assumption in psychology and beyond that human behavior has a "dual tendency," one leading toward innovation and creation, the other toward habituation (Crossley 2001, 129). This either/or type of relationship is widespread not only in scientific theory (where habit is considered "the most obvious barrier to creative thinking and innovation," Davis 1999, 166) but also in popular thought; in general, "Any discussion of creativity or innovation necessarily introduces a general opposed concept of habit" (Dalton 2004, 604). This dualistic view has important consequences, for it fundamentally segments human experience into "creative" and "uncreative" or "habitual." Given the old formulated view that habits cover a very large part of life (James 1890), such a distinction makes creativity a rare and unique moment in our existence—an exception rather than the rule of behavior. Our modern-day mythologies of genius and the gap between creativity and everyday life (see Glăveanu 2010b; Chapter 2) stem from this sort of distinction and contribute to the tendency to isolate and disconnect creative expression from lived experience. It is thus important to understand what the bases for the presumed dichotomy are, and in order to do this we need to consider the psychological interpretation of habit.

The term habit derives primarily from the Latin verb *habere* meaning "to have" or "to hold," and its meaning in psychology has been relatively constant throughout the last century. William James (1890, 107), for example, equated habit with "sequences of behaviors, usually simple . . . that have become virtually automatic." Automaticity as a central characteristic of habit makes it both a useful and desired process and a potential threat in our interactions with others. James himself encouraged the formation of habits out of "useful actions" and warned against turning unfavorable behaviors into habits; on the whole, he believed that "the more of the details of our daily life we can hand over to the effortless custody of automatism, the more our higher powers of mind will be set free for their own proper work" (122). Assertions of this kind, frequently found in the writings of prominent thinkers, helped psychologists to separate habitual from reflexive action and consciousness from habit (despite empirical examples that argue for a closer unity between thinking and doing; see Sutton 2007). Indeed, it became common knowledge that "the things we have learned to do best . . . require least thought, direction, feeling, consciousness" (Baldwin 1900, 168). The "breaking" of habit tends to take place when the relation between organism and environment is "ill-defined and subject to frequent and profound alterations" (MacDougall 1911, 327) because in these cases automatic responses become inadequate. Habit thus ends up being reflected upon and changed accordingly, and often these changes are themselves practiced and integrated in future behavioral routines. A circular picture of human development is therefore painted, going, in the words of MacDougall, "from preexisting habit through accommodation to later modified habit" (326).

Our contemporary understanding of habit, however, is largely shaped by an even narrower reading of the phenomenon imposed by behaviorism (see Wozniak 1994). While this school made habit the centerpiece of psychological research, it also reduced it to reflexes and grounded it in human biology, glossing over its psychological and cultural aspects. For John B. Watson (1914, 1919), habit is a system of acquired reflexes related to muscular and glandular changes that occur whenever the organism is exposed to a specific stimulus. Advocating an image of the human being as a "sum of instincts and habits," Watson managed not only to do away with consciousness as a psychological topic but also to lower habits to the level of simple repeated reactions. What followed was an impressive program of behavioral research into the laws and manifestation of habit. Hull (1943, 1951), for instance, concluded, based on his studies of humans and animals, that the automaticity of habit increases steadily with each repetition until it reaches a plateau, in a kind of asymptotic curve. Research like the above normally included physiological indicators, and the neurology of habit continues to attract attention to the present day (see Graybiel 2008). Indebted to the behaviorist legacy, recent scholarship takes habit to be an automatic gesture (Lally et al. 2010) based on the association between a cue and a response (Orbell and Verplanken 2010). Habits are said to be "learned through a process in which repetition incrementally tunes cognitive processors in procedural memory (i.e., the memory system that supports the minimally conscious control of skilled action)" (Neal, Wood, and Quinn 2006, 198). Considering the advantages of habits for human functioning, Wood, Quinn, and Kashy (2002, 1259) refer to aspects such as cognitive economy, performance efficiency, and greater feeling of control. However, on the negative side, the authors mention ineffective repetition and people's general view of habits as relatively uninformative about the self, a view that leads to habit being negatively evaluated. This can be partially explained also by the opposition between habit and creativity.

Unlike habit, creativity is largely appreciated as a social value (Mason 2003), and its importance is accentuated by the fact that creativity "involves going beyond the habituated. It moves beyond the standard, repeated routines of everyday life" (Borofsky 2001, 66). Consequently, creative products are more "esteemed" and expressive of self. Shattering "the rule of law and regularity of mind" is considered the core of creative processes (Barron 1990, 249), and deep and meaningful associations are often made between creativity and personal and societal progress. Indeed, in the Western world, it is not uncommon to perceive tradition as "backward" and repetition as "uncreative" (Weiner 2000, 153), and this pushes habit further away from creation and its "forward," progressive moments. Why is there a gap between creativity and habit? To answer this question, one need only look at basic definitions of creativity, which link creative action to situations in which "a person has no learned or practiced solution to a problem" (Torrance 1988, 57). The reverse of habit thus becomes a definition for creativity. Adding to the above, Amabile (1996, 35) included the heuristic nature of the task as part of the creative process. Unlike algorithms, heuristic paths might not have a clearly defined goal and do not unfold in a straightforward manner. This contrasts greatly with the routine ways of doing things associated with habit. Finally, Gruber and Wallace (1999), as well as Weisberg (1993), insisted on making purposeful behavior a condition for creativity. The postulate of intentionality not only safeguards creative expression from mere accidental discoveries but also distinguishes it from habitual, automatic responses. Such distinctions are paralleled by commonsense thinking on the topic—as noticed long ago by Baldwin (1906, 100), phrases like "divine creation" and "slavish imitation" convey a clear hierarchy of values.

The opposition between creativity and habit or tradition, however, is not only misplaced but also highly detrimental to our understanding of all these phenomena. With reference to this, Negus and Pickering (2004, 68) discussed the "beguiling but misleading view" that equates creativity with "freedom, agency and the unshackling of constraints." This assumption ignores the crucial role of conventions and repeated practices in creative expression while at the same time supporting the claim that "tradition stultifies innovation and stupefies creativity" (Wilson 1984, viii). Oppositions like these cannot be sustained in the face of theoretical and practical arguments. To support the split between creativity and habit or tradition would be as illogical as arguing that fantasy is the opposite of memory (Vygotsky 2004). Moreover, this dichotomy poses some conceptual dilemmas for performance arts such as music by imposing a forceful distinction between creativity and technical mastery (Graham 1998). It becomes thus important to acknowledge that all the above difficulties in conceptualization derive from a particular understanding of habit as mindless and uncreative routine. However, this is not the only understanding available, and there are vigorous strands of scholarship, in both psychology and sociology, that directly address this deep-seated dichotomy and seek to transcend it. It is to these critical approaches that I now turn.

10.1.2. Recovering the Meaning of Habitual Behavior

The concept of habit has a very long history (longer than that of the term "creativity"); it was used by Greek and medieval thinkers and by major figures of the Enlightenment, and it has a place in the philosophy of Kant, Mill, and Hegel. Reviewing the historical trajectory of the term, Charles Camic (1986) noted that, despite centuries of moderately similar usage, the notion was radically transformed in the nineteenth century by physiological literature that reduced it to acquired reflexes and a psychological approach that cemented this meaning. Kilpinen (2009) more recently distinguished between two different definitions: a "Humean" variant that considers habits to be routine-like behaviors outside of consciousness, rationality, and intentionality and a more "pragmatist" conception that understands habits as open to reflection during the course of action. It is this second conception that I am aiming to recuperate, a conception that emerges clearly from the important contributions of James Mark Baldwin, John Dewey, Hans Joas, and Pierre Bourdieu.

For Baldwin, habit, referred to more broadly as the principle of habit, "Expresses the tendency of the organism to secure and retain its vital stimulations" (Baldwin 1900, 216). This principle is complementary to that of accommodation, that is, the learning of new adjustments. Accommodation here leads to invention, and it would be easy to assume a dichotomy between habit and invention. However, Baldwin specifically rejects such a view when he states that "accommodation is in each case simply the result and fruit of the habit itself which is exercised" (217); in other words, "Accommodation is reached simply in the ordinary routine of habit, and is its outcome" (218). Baldwin's writings offer a very good example of how the notion of imitation can be placed at the center of a theory of human psychology and development. His thesis in this regard can be summarized as follows: "In the individual, invention is as natural as imitation. Indeed normal imitation is rarely free from invention!" (149–150). Baldwin's conception thus starts from the premise that imitation (especially what he calls "persistent imitation," an expression of will) requires invention, and this allowed him to regard imitation as the law of *progressive interaction* between the organism and the environment (Baldwin 1894, 1903). According to him,

> In all the processes of social absorption and imitation, therefore, we find that the individual thinks and imagines in his own way. He cannot give back unaltered what he gets, as the parrot does. He is not a repeating machine. His mental creations are much more vital and transforming. Try as he will he cannot exactly reproduce; and when he comes near to it his self-love protests and claims its right to do its own thinking. (Baldwin 1911, 151–152)

The above vision can be related to the American philosophical tradition of pragmatism, a system of thinking that intended to challenge many of the deep-seated dichotomies ingrained in much of Western philosophy. John Dewey, as one of the leading figures of this orientation, based his psychological and philosophical writings on a "principle of continuity" so as to counteract dualistic paradigms (see Alexander 2006, 189). One of the many oppositions Dewey was eager to transcend was that between habit, seen as necessarily conservative, and thought, understood as the origin of progress (and thus of creativity). For Dewey, "Thought which does not exist within ordinary habits of action lacks means of execution" and thus condemns our actions to becoming "clumsy, forced" (Dewey 1922, 67). Unfortunately, this insight was largely overlooked in the decades that followed, especially during the age of behaviorism.

Dewey's theoretical construction of habits begins with the fact that habits, like all other psychological and behavioral functions, require the cooperation between *organism* and *environment* (Dewey 1922, 14). These two concepts are not foreign elements of our psychological system but rather form an intimate part of ourselves, and this explains the power that some habits can have over us (24). We can think of habits in terms of a human activity that is influenced by prior activity (acquired), contains an ordering of elements of action, is projective and dynamic in quality, and remains operative even when not in explicit use. Most importantly, Dewey encouraged us to "protest against the tendency in psychological literature to limit [habit's] meaning to repetition," and he clearly stated that "repetition is in no sense the essence of habit" (41–42) and neither is "mechanization" (70); on the contrary, "Habit means special sensitiveness or accessibility to certain classes of stimuli, standing predilections and aversions, rather than bare recurrence of specific acts. It means will" (42). The assertions above are very much representative of the pragmatist position, for which "intentionality (or rationality) without habituality is empty, whereas habituality without intentionality and rationality of course is blind" (Kilpinen 2009, 105).

Moreover, this philosophical orientation has given us a clear description not only of the relationship between habit and thought but also of that between habit, action, and creativity. For instance, in a more recent elaboration, Hans Joas (1996) proposed creativity as an analytical dimension of all human action. In this view, creativity is not in itself a different type of action—alongside rational, normative, or impulsive behavior—but rather permeates all our manifestations and therefore deserves a central role in a discussion of human agency. We should also note here the two main tasks, according to a prag- matist philosophy, that the mind performs in relation to action: "It *monitors* or *supervises* the ongoing action process, and it *reconstructs* that process if it fails" (Joas and Kilpinen 2006, 325). The idea of action failure is in fact central for pragmatists and is one of the most important ways in which creativity is manifested in the course of activity—that is, reflecting on the outcome of a difficulty and the possible means to overcome it. This association between obstacles and creativity must be remembered, since, as we will see, it was scrutinized by later revisionist scholarship (Dalton 2004).

For the moment, we can also note that Joas's critique of rational or norma- tive action resonates with the tenets of Pierre Bourdieu's genetic sociology. In order to understand how "behavior [can] be regulated without being the product of obedience to rules," (Bourdieu 1990a, 65), Bourdieu proposed the notion of *habitus*. Often referred to as a "feel for the game" or a "practical sense," the habitus is a system of dispositions in the sense that individuals are disposed, not determined, to act in a certain way based on previous experience (Bourdieu 1990b). These dispositions are said to be durable (once formed, they last throughout life) and transportable (able to generate similar practices in different domains). It is important to note that they are structures of perception and appreciation structured by objective social conditions, and they in turn structure these conditions through the generation of flexible practices. The habitus is therefore marked by its historicical trajectory: "A product of history, [it] produces individual and collective practices—more history—in accordance with the schemes generated by history" (Bourdieu 1990b, 54). In contrast with the more psychological or physiological reflex-based definitions of habit, for Bourdieu, habitus is a thoroughly social construction—"the social embodied" (Bourdieu and Wacquant 1992, 128). It is acquired through socialization, especially in early childhood, and is related to particular and long-lasting experiences of a social position in society (Bourdieu 1990a). It can be easily seen how as a consequence habitus reflects the social hierarchy and is greatly shaped by the act of belonging to a certain social class (see Bourdieu 1984).

The above discussion reveals the sophisticated way in which Pierre Bourdieu managed to bridge the traditional gap between habit and creativity. Habitus is simultaneously firm and supple, "an *open system of dispositions* that is constantly subjected to experiences, and therefore constantly affected by them in a way that either reinforces or modifies its structures" (Bourdieu and

Wacquant 1992, 133). Habitus may be durable, but it is also "endlessly transformed" (Bourdieu 1990a, 116), an authentic "art of inventing" (Bourdieu 1990b, 55). There is no one-to-one link between a habitus and a single type of unchanging practice. Neither is habitus a social norm or a law that people must unwillingly obey. On the contrary, this "feel of the game . . . enables an infinite number of 'moves' to be made, adapted to the infinite number of possible situations which no rule, however complex, can foresee" (Bourdieu 1990a, 9). As such, "*The habitus goes hand in glove with vagueness and indeterminacy*" (77), obeying a "practical logic" defined by every new interaction with the world. However, there are also limits to the creativity of habitus, and these "limits are set by the historically and socially situated conditions of its production" (Bourdieu 1990b, 55). What the habitus produces, in fact, are "all the 'reasonable', 'common-sense' behaviours (and only these) which are possible within the limits of these regularities, and which are likely to be positively sanctioned" by society (55–56). Concrete circumstances have the capacity to change the expression of habitus, but even here Bourdieu reminds us that most experiences we have tend to confirm our habitus because people generally look for or encounter familiar situations (Bourdieu and Wacquant 1992).

In conclusion, Baldwin's acts of imitation, Dewey's and Joas's habitual action, and Bourdieu's habitus all acknowledge the relative stability of repeated behavior yet couple it with a significant potential for change, reflection, and even will (within personal, social, and historical limits). Their perspectives are therefore ultimately in agreement in regard to habits and their role for the individual and society. It is this unitary vision that will be taken in the present chapter as a starting point for a new elaboration of the notion of creativity.

10.2. Defining and Locating Habitual Creativity

In the previous section, foundational perspectives from psychology, philosophy, and sociology were applied to consideration of habit, habitual action, and creativity. For Baldwin, Dewey, Joas, and Bourdieu, conceptualizing habit is not possible outside of creativity and a comprehensive image of human action is unattainable without both. In the remainder of this chapter, a theory of creativity based on habit will be proposed, a theory that builds on all the accounts presented above. What brings together the four authors is precisely an understanding of habit as a *social, situated*, and *open* system. For all of these authors, without exception, habits are social in nature. Mainstream psychological literature affirms the acquired or learned nature of habit, but it largely fails to do justice to the social interaction behind it and to the societal dynamic intrinsic to the formation and expression of habits. Pierre Bourdieu's perspective is perhaps the most illuminating in this regard because for him, every habitus embodies a history of social relations. Furthermore, habits are very much situated in their manifestation and require, as stated by Dewey, the relation between organism and the environment. All three terms—the person, the environment, and their relationship—are equally dynamic, and thus habitual action can never be mechanical and deterministic. It needs to be open and generative in order to allow for processes of adaptation and growth. The acts of imitation mentioned by Baldwin, either "persistent" or not, never duplicate a model of behavior but rather reconstruct it according to changing circumstances. At the same time, habits do predispose persons toward particular processes and outcomes; however, they should not be mistaken for simple reflexes that link a narrow "stimulus" to a narrow "response." This reformulation of habit not only places it back on the agenda of social theorists but also could resolve long-standing arguments over the lack of consciousness, will, and creativity in habitual action. The degree of automatization of any one habit varies with its degree of specificity, but it never reaches an absolute level of mindless, uncreative routine—in such a case it would not qualify as a habit. In the words of Küpers (2011, 109), "Habits can also be *reflexive*," and, as such, a person can take on new habits and change existing ones—one can dehabitualize and rehabitualize behavior in a dynamic and creative way. What remains to be theorized here is precisely this relationship between creativity and habit and the implications of this relationship.

In essence, there are two broad options when it comes to conceptualizing this relation: either creativity and habit are kept as distinct processes, however interconnected they may be, or they are conceived of as a single type of action. If the first path is taken, then "moments" of creativity can be distinguished from "moments" of habit, and a theory of creativity can be built on how and when creative processes "intervene" in the course of habitual action. On the other hand, if creativity and habit *concurrently* describe action, then their separation, even for analytical purposes, becomes questionable. This is, in short, the critique raised by Dalton (2004) and others (Kilpinen 1998; Del Mar 2010) in relation to Joas's formulation of creative action and its pragmatist sources: it maintains creativity and habit as complementary phases and thus conserves the dualism between the two. The problem with pragmatism is that, despite its willingness to transcend dichotomic thinking, it nevertheless hypothesized an unbreakable link between problems or obstacles and conscious or "creative" thought (see Dewey 1903, 1910). For Mead (1964, 7), for instance, "Analytical thought commences with the presence of problems and the conflict between different lines of activity." Even Baldwin (1903), by referring to a "twofold factor" of organic activity, maintained the distinction between his principle of accommodation and his principle of habit. For Dalton, this makes creativity "episodically" involved in habit, especially when difficulties occur that need creative solutions and adaptations. Bourdieu achieved with the notion of habitus a much better conceptual integration, though he gave a relatively secondary role to creative achievements and restricted them greatly in relation to social constraints. Aiming to reconcile and retain the best from both theories, Dalton (2004, 604) asserted the "simultaneous presence of habitual and creative elements in all moments of action," where actors, in the course of habitual acts, "implement contingent techniques suited to the moment" and where "the perfection of habit can lead to creative action" (609).

Building on this preliminary insight, I can now introduce and define the notion of *habitual creativity* as a further attempt, from a psychological perspective, to overcome the dichotomy between habit on the one hand and creativity on the other. In a tentative formulation, *habitual creativity defines the ways in which novelties form an intrinsic part of habitual action by constantly adjusting it to dynamic contexts, by allowing for transitions between and combinations of different "routines," and by eventually perfecting practices, thus resulting in mastery.* Habitual creativity is, in this regard, the conceptual complement of habitus, describing the same phenomenon but from its "creative end"; the focus on "novelties" in behavior does not override its behavior but rather addresses Dalton's critique of overemphasizing structural elements. Habitual creativity is a microgenetic phenomenon (with potential sociogenetic effects), and the definition above stresses, without exhausting, the many ways in which its dynamic takes place.

By far the most agreed upon form of novelty emergence in habitual action has to do with the "adjustment to dynamic contexts" mentioned above, a feature that was acknowledged by Baldwin, Dewey, Joas, and Bourdieu as well as by many other authors. At a macrolevel, Weiner (2000, 158) asserts that "the process of adapting tradition to changed circumstances will always involve some degrees of problem-solving, inventiveness, and/or imaginative expression." Considering the more concrete example of music performance, Chaffin et al. (2006, 200) state, "Performers adjust to the idiosyncratic demands and opportunities of each occasion. . . . The creativity involved in this kind of spontaneous microadjustment of a highly prepared interpretation makes each performance a creative activity." More examples could be provided. The other two possibilities of combining (interpolating "stretches of previously rehearsed behavior," Bateson 1999, 157) and perfecting habits are most clearly illustrated by craft activities such as Easter egg decoration, and the idea of mastery was introduced at the beginning of this chapter. The following sections will elaborate on the implications of this notion of habitual creativity, principally the grand claim that "all creativity is habitual." Some distinctions will be made afterward between habit, improvisation, and innovation without introducing any further dichotomies and oppositions. An interesting appendix to this discussion is represented by a brief overview of why psychology tended to neglect habit and improvisation while focusing on innovative behavior.

10.2.1. Creativity as Habitual

Previously, the argument was made that all habit is, by definition, creative. The notion of habitual creativity is concerned with the converse statement that all creativity is, itself, habitual. What this means is that creativity in all instances relies on the existence of habits, of known and exercised ways of interacting with the world. Since proposing the creativity of habit implies the habitual nature of creativity, it is not surprising to find supporting statements in this regard within the writings of Baldwin and Dewey. In addressing the issue, Baldwin summarized his view as follows: "Let us say, once and for all, that every new thing is an adaptation, and every adaptation arises right out of the bosom of old processes and is filled with old matter" (Baldwin 1903, 218). Dewey (1934), starting from the premise that each great cultural tradition is "an organized *habit* of vision and of methods of ordering and conveying material" (276, emphasis added), concluded as follows: "[Just like the artist,] the scientific inquirer, the philosopher, the technologist, also derive their substance from the stream of culture. This dependence is an essential factor in original vision and creative expression" (276–277). For both authors, then, the habits formed by taking part in the culture and traditions of a society and its different communities are a sine qua non of creative achievement, and this is equally valid for all creative domains. Creativity is never "free" from tradition and habit, and its central characteristic is not to contradict them but to work from within them and perpetuate them in new and significant ways. In the words of Feldman (1974, 68), "All creative thought springs from a base of cultural knowledge and is therefore, by definition, part of a cultural tradition—even when it breaks with tradition."

If these assertions are correct, two implications can be derived: first, creators need some time to incorporate the "habits of vision and action" of their cultures and master them, and second, as cultures and traditions are so diverse, creative expression will be channeled and will manifest itself differently around the world. Both ideas are supported by the psychological literature, in which it has long been established that "the human act of creation, basically, is a personal reshaping of given materials, whether physical or mental" (Barron 1995, 313). There is not a hiatus but a continuation between the "new" and the "old," and this makes the generation of novelty dependent upon processes of socialization and acculturation. Csikszentmihalyi's (1999, 332) systemic model of creativity emphasized this by relating the creator and creation to an existing field and domain: "In order to function well within the creative system, one must internalize the rules of the domain and the opinions of the field." This premise is corroborated by research findings suggesting that major creative breakthroughs usually happen within a decade after mastering the rules of the domain (see Gardner 1994). What is known as the "ten-year rule" originates from the work of Chase and Simon (1973) on expert performance in chess; they discovered that players need approximately a decade of practice before great achievement. This rule was later confirmed in terms of creative activity in several domains (see Hayes 1989), and, more recently, authors have proposed that another ten years after achieving expertise might very well be needed in order to reach the level of "creative greatness" (Kaufman and Kaufman 2007).

Regarding the second implication, cultural traditions not only shape the mechanisms of recognition in cases of notable breakthroughs but also orient the creative energies of individuals and groups. Different talents tend to be fostered in different cultural contexts (Runco 2007a, 273; also Westwood and Low 2003) and thus help to define the ortgeist and zeitgeist of different cultural-historical positions in the world (see Simonton 2003b). As an example, Indian culture has long favored innovations in the field of spirituality compared to other domains (for a review of this, see Bhawuk 2003).

The claim that creativity is habitual, however, goes beyond illustrations of celebrated creations and reflects a much deeper, *existential* dimension. A "habit of being creative" (conceptually close to the notion of reflexive habituality in Kilpinen 2009) can be hypothesized in relation to each and every individual, something akin to what Baldwin (1903, 220) suggested when he stated that "the very fact of accommodation itself [is] the great deep-seated *habit* of organic life." Outside of these biological roots, there are also strong cultural imperatives to create, and Wilson (1984, 101) refers in this case to innovation becoming "a tradition" in contemporary societies. In her empirical research, for instance, Stokes (2001, 356) mentions "Monet's high habitual variability level," thus implying that artists may very well habitually impose on themselves the constraint of varying their styles, work techniques, and themes. The premise that human life is inherently creative resonates also with the psychology of Donald Winnicott (1971, 67), who was primarily interested in a universal type of creativity, one that "belongs to being alive." For him, being creative means being able to use one's whole personality in acts of self-expression and is associated with healthy living and functioning. Creativity reveals itself as the rule rather than the exception of human existence if we come to think about the continuous, moment-to-moment meaning and linguistic production of the self and world. As Josephs and Valsiner (2007, 55) remind us, "Semiotic construction is constant and overabundant: the creativity of human *psyche* is generating new meanings while living one's life is hyper-productive" (see also Barrett 1999). This basic capacity for creativity that we all possess has more recently been conceptualized by Beghetto and Kaufman (2007, 73) under the term "mini c," or the "novel and personally meaningful interpretation of experiences, actions, and events." It doesn't matter from this perspective if the creative constructions are ephemeral and do not leave a lasting mark on human society; as a form of ordinary creativity, they become indispensable and "weave new meaning in [individuals'] lives and relationships" (Bateson 1999, 170).

As appealing as this approach to creativity is, there are also several authors who voice their concerns over equating creative action with all human (habitual) action. Negus and Pickering (2004, 45), for instance, warn that "we cannot collapse creativity into everyday life, as if they are indistinguishable." In a similar vein, Hausman (1979, 240) worries that universalizing creativity makes the meaning of the concept "too broad" and leaves us incapable of discriminating between creations. However, the notion of habitual creativity does not aim to cover all forms of ordinary human action, since not all action is in fact habitual, and it does allow for differentiations in creative expression. Let us take these in turn. Human action is habitual, but it can also be normative, impulsive, and so forth. The habitual mode of action is certainly pervasive, but it doesn't exclude other forms of manifestation. Bourdieu (1990a, 108) acknowledged this when he mentioned that "habitus is one principle of production of practices among others and although it is undoubtedly more frequent in play than any other . . . one cannot rule out that it may be superseded under certain circumstances . . . by other principles, such as rational and conscious computation." It is for this reason that habitus can be "controlled" and, at times, consciously analyzed and modified (116). Furthermore, habitual creativity is "persistent" but also differentiated. To understand this, we need to consider habits in their relation to improvisation and innovation.

10.2.2. Habit, Improvisation, Innovation

The psychological theorizing of creativity has a long tradition of establishing "types" and making distinctions between different "forms" of creative work. Often these come in a hierarchy—for example, the classical typology by Irvine Taylor (1959), which ranges from the expressive creativity displayed in spontaneous self-expression to emergenative creativity that constitutes the basis for the formation of new schools of thought. More recent approaches refer to a "continuum" of creativity, and Cohen and Ambrose (1999, 18–21), for instance, segmented this range into seven levels: learning something new (universal novelty), making connections that are rare among peers, developing talents, developing heuristics, producing information, creating by extending a field, and creating by transforming a field. What can be noted from the above is that classifications of creativity tend to be formulated around outcome criteria, especially the "value" and "novelty" of the outcome. To simplify things, many authors employ a straightforward dichotomy between Big-C, mature creativity or H-creativity (historical creativity) on the one hand and little-c, mundane creativity or P-creativity (personal creativity) on the other (see Craft 2001; Cohen and Ambrose 1999; Boden 1994). The common view behind such distinctions was metaphorically summarized by John Liep (2001, 12) when he stated, "If 'conventional creativity' spreads like an ocean on the surface of the world, 'true creativity' rises like islands here and there." There are many assumptions packed into formulations such as these, the most obvious being the existence of a "true" creativity that is both noticeable and very rare. However, the separation between true or exceptional creativity and conventional or everyday creativity soon encounters conceptual problems because "one confers on the term a rarefied and occasionally mystical air, the other can make the word seem commonplace and even banal. Rarely have the links between both these senses of the term creativity been retained and explored" (Negus and Pickering 2004, 1). It is precisely this exploration of links between different manifestations of creativity that is attempted here. Moreover, in light of our previous discussion, the different types of creative expression mentioned next will not be considered as separate, which would result in "distinct forms" of creativity, or hierarchical, which would reflect an organization based on value of outcome.

The three types proposed are *habitual, improvisational,* and *innovative* creativity. Of these, habitual creative processes have been addressed already, and the preceding section supported a strong claim that perceived all creativity as ultimately based on the expression of habit. This raises a question: How is it then possible to postulate other types of creativity without contradicting this premise? To begin with, there surely are some differences between the emergence of novelty resulting from the practice of habitual action and the emergence of novelty resulting from dealing with obstacles (sometimes) faced during this action. The latter is specifically what Joas (1996) and the pragmatists consider to be creativity in the strict sense of the word. This dilemma can be resolved if we envision habit, improvisation, and innovation not as separate entities ordered in any kind of continuum but as embedded within each other. As a result, the difference between the three is not that improvisation and innovation break with habit—they are still grounded in forms of habitual action (see the preceding section)—but that the processes they denote show particularities due equally to the external and internal-psychological circumstances of the creator. To be more explicit, it is argued that we can talk about improvisational creativity when there is an *obstacle* or *difficulty* in the course of habitual action that requires some form of interruption and deliberation. Further, we can call innovative creativity the process of dealing with such an obstacle or difficulty when there is a clear *intention* on the part of the actor to generate novel solutions (in the purest form, the intention to "create"). These features are summarized in Figure 10.2. Before further analyzing this classification, it should be mentioned that the meaning of improvisation and especially of innovation, as used below, may differ from standard definitions. Second, and this is extremely important, the three forms of creativity deal in a sense with "ideal types," and in practice they often blend into one another and thus can be difficult to analytically distinguish for several reasons, some of which are discussed below.

The notion of *improvisation* commonly designates "something that was done to face some unforeseen circumstances" (Montuori 2003, 245). It is this basic meaning that I employ here as well, and from this perspective a person improvises when his or her (habitual) action is faced with an obstacle or difficulty. In the words of Bateson (1999, 154), improvisation is "a way for individuals to bridge discontinuity." Problems disrupt the "regular" ways we have of doing things and thus call for creative or novel forms of behavior. This relationship between problems and creativity has deep historical roots

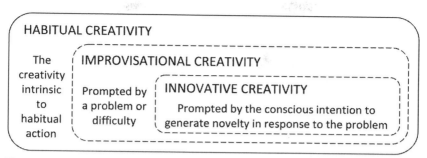

Figure 10.2. The "nested" depiction of creative expression.

and is reflected in current cognitive approaches that define creativity in problem-solving terms (for a discussion, see Runco 1994). However, despite this association, improvisational creativity as such has rarely constituted the focus of mainstream research. This is explained by authors like Sawyer (2000) as a consequence of the nature of improvisation, which, unlike product-based forms of creativity, is usually manifested in "performances." In the case of improvisational creativity, on many occasions "the process is the product" (Sawyer 2000, 150), and improvised performances are characterized by contingency, emergence, and participatory learning (Sawyer 1997, 4). For Ingold and Hallam (2007, 3), improvisation is generative, relational, and temporal and expresses "the way we work." This last feature raises an interesting point of connection between habitual and improvisational creativity and comes to argue for continuity between the two. In the words of Liep (2001, 2), "Improvisation indicates a more conventional exploration of possibilities within a certain framework of rules" (also a framework of *habits*, to use our terminology).

Improvised jazz sessions constitute a prototypical example of improvisational activity, one that is very much able to shed light not only on the processes of improvisation itself but also on their connection to habitual forms of behavior. To begin with, it is important to note that jazz sessions, spontaneous as they may be, always occur "in a context, and [are] performed by someone with a history, with cultural, economic, political, and philosophical contexts, with perspectives, habits, and eccentricities, with the ability to make *choices* in context, which choices in turn affect the context" (Montuori 2003, 246). Inherently occurring as part of a collaboration, jazz improvisation relies on two kinds of processes, as distinguished by Seddon (2005): a sympathetic type of attunement, based on collectively sharing a stock of musical knowledge and experience, and more importantly, an empathetic kind of attunement that relies on decentration and introspection in order to generate an atmosphere of trust, conducive to creative risk-taking and spontaneous expression. This does not mean that the repertoire of shared cultural knowledge is less significant; on the contrary, Sawyer (2003b, 114) makes the clear point that "improvisation always occurs within a structure, and all improvisers draw on ready-mades, short motifs or clichés—as they create their novel performance." Moreover, stressing even further the link between habitually acquired motifs and practices and the generation of novel performances, Sawyer continues by saying that jazz musicians "practice and perform the same songs repeatedly, and can often express themselves more effectively when they have a predeveloped set of musical ideas available." Repetition and exercise may introduce a certain regularity and predictability in any performance, but at the same time there would be no performance in their absence. What to an outsider could seem thoroughly improvised is often the result of hours and hours of practice, an outcome resulting from "snippets the players had played hundreds of times before" (Becker 2000, 171). The notions of "rehearsed spontaneity" and "planned serendipity" (Mirvis 1998; see also Vera and Crossan 2005) might sound oxymoronic but very much fit with the vision of mastery presented at the beginning of this chapter (see Figure 10.1).

Improvisation thus draws from habit and succeeds in shaping it, "compelled" by the fact that "no system of codes, rules and norms can anticipate every possible circumstance" (Ingold and Hallam 2007, 2). One can never create or improvise something from nothing (Lemons 2005; Kamoche and Cunha 2001; Mirvis 1998) and "improvisational freedom is only possible against a well defined (and often simple) backdrop of rules and roles" (Eisenberg 1990, 154). This is how we can conclude, together with Küpers (2011, 115), that "spontaneity and improvisation must be anchored in habitual patterns of behaviour." This is necessarily so because habits play a multitude of roles in relation to improvised expression: they are the generator and organizer of such practices, offer them structure and consistency over time, and remove the possibility of totally chaotic creation (Slutskaya 2006, 154). On the other hand, "During improvisation the in-habited 'world' and its habitual realities or practices are *reconfigured*, and the order and meaning established by given conventional procedures are disrupted" (Küpers 2011, 117). For these reasons, the distinction between habitual and improvisational creativity can become blurred, and this exposes their fundamental intertwining: habitual action generally presupposes microimprovisational acts—as Dalton (2004, 615) rightfully remarked, "[Any] problem is a general difficulty in all moments of action." There is an important overlap between habit and improvisation, and, based on our definition of "problem" (see Dewey 1910, 9), we can more or less easily observe the differences between the two. It is argued in this chapter, however, that improvisational forms of creativity, working from within habitual action, can be distinguished for both analytical and practical purposes; a valuable indicator in this regard is, for instance, when activity stops because of encountered difficulties or when, just as in the case of improvised jazz or theater performances, responses are contingent on moment-to-moment inputs received from the actions of others. Improvised "solutions" in these circumstances reuse, alter, or combine habitual forms and, when successful, become a constitutive part of future habitual action.

Unlike habitual and improvisational creativity, *innovative expressions* of the phenomenon have for decades constituted the central theme of creativity research in psychology. Our definition of the term here is in line with the conception of several other authors; for example Weisberg (2006, 761), who claimed that an innovation "emerges when an individual intentionally produces something new in attempting to meet some goal," and Kaufman and Kaufman (2004, 148), for whom the ability to innovate means creating something that is new and different "with the specific understanding that it is new and different." While sometimes the process of innovation is conceptualized as "the practical application of creative ideas" (Westwood and Low 2003, 236), the notion is not used now with such applied connotations. Innovative creativity is considered in our context simply the act of addressing a difficulty or problem with the intention not only of "solving" it but of solving it in a creative or novel way. As an "intentionally creative" type of action, innovative creativity normally leads to physical products that can be more easily observed and evaluated. Great works of art, inventions, and scientific theories are, to a large extent, the outcome of this particular form of expression. The mere presence of a creative intention, it seems, can make a significant difference in how people respond to a task and can, in most circumstances, increase the level of creativity. This observation is supported by a series of studies that gave respondents explicit instructions to "be creative" when completing different creativity tests (Harrington 1975; Runco and Okuda 1991); this approach was tested on several populations, including children (Lee, Bain, and McCallum 2007) and groups composed of people from different cultures (Chen et al. 2005).

However, "truly" innovative acts performed outside of the laboratory or the testing room and studied by creativity researchers are normally Big-C achievements. From this perspective, one can conclude that traditional models of the creative process in psychology are meant to explain first and foremost innovative behaviors: for example, Wallas's (1926) succession of preparation, incubation, illumination, and verification applies very well to deliberate, medium-term, or long-term creative work. Even typologies of the creative outcome favor innovation, and we can take here the example of the propulsion model (see Sternberg 1999b; Sternberg, Kaufman, and Pretz 2002), which discriminates eight different ways of being creative, all requiring an awareness of the field one is working in as well as a more or less conscious decision to position and express oneself in a particular way in relation to existing paradigms (either accepting, rejecting, or trying to integrate them). Conceptually close to this typology is the investment theory of creativity (Sternberg and Lubart 1995a, 1995b), which starts from the clear premise that creativity is basically a decision (see also Sternberg et al. 2008). According to this account, creative persons "buy low" when they present a unique idea and try to convince others of its value. After gaining recognition for their innovation, they "sell high" by leaving the idea to others and moving on to another neglected area that they can invest in. This hypothesized trajectory seems to apply well in the case of established creators (such as Matisse, Monet, Beckmann, and Guston), who remained creative over the course of their entire career because of their capacity to deliberately "select novel goal constraints and, second, to strategically select source, task, and subject constraints to help realize them" (Stokes and Fisher 2005, 291). Innovative creativity is not by any means portrayed in this context as an inherently superior type of creativity (this is a common bias in both scientific theory and lay thinking on the topic), since, as argued previously, extremely valuable creations can come out of habitual or improvisational processes. The intention to create doesn't guarantee the quality of the work, and its absence doesn't make the outcome any less creative (especially since creativity itself is a matter of social agreement; Glăveanu 2011b; Chapter 8).

At the same time, we should keep in mind that innovative creativity is here considered to be a particular case embedded within improvisational and habitual fields of action. Habit and invention are continuous since, as mentioned by Baldwin (1906, 180), "effective invention is always rooted in the knowledge already possessed by society"; "no effective invention ever makes an absolute break with the culture, tradition, fund of knowledge treasured up from the past." On the whole, though, it is acknowledged that some habits can lead to innovation while others can hinder it (Cavagnoli 2008), particularly in organizational settings. One way in which managers can capitalize on existing habits and stimulate breakthrough innovation is by harnessing the pool of tacit knowledge possessed by individuals and entire teams (Mascitelli 2000). In a similar vein, to understand the connection between improvisation and innovation one can think about concrete examples from industry in which teams innovate successfully using an improvisational approach (see Sawyer 2006; though past research has shown that engaging in improvisation does not necessarily or immediately lead to innovation, Vera and Crossan 2005).

As for the important differences between the two, they have been captured quite well by Lévi-Strauss's (1966) distinction between the *bricoleur* and the engineer. Improvisational processes are very often a form of *bricolage*, of making the best with what is at hand while generally remaining within a set of existing rules; in contrast, "The engineer is always trying to make his way out of and go beyond the constraints imposed by a particular state of civilization" (Lévi-Strauss 1966, 19; see also Louridas 1999). Hence, if both improvisation and innovation can be associated with problem-solving activities, then the latter usually reveals a more proactive type of creativity, in which problems are not simply encountered but often looked for, anticipated, and intentionally formulated (see Runco 2007b). However, the boundaries between these two phenomena are often blurred by the fact that creative intentions (specific to innovation) tend to exist among other motivating factors (doing a good job, making others happy, enjoying the activity, etc.). This recalls the example of jazz performances, in which "a commonly shared goal is *to create* within a musical and social context, requiring both control and spontaneity, constraints and possibilities, innovation and tradition, leading and supporting" (Montuori 2003, 239; emphasis added). Furthermore, musicians who improvise retain certain works in their repertoire and perfect them over many years (Dobbins 1980), thus demonstrating how an act of improvisation can become, in time, one of innovation.

In conclusion, habit, improvisation, and innovation are not three separate forms of creative expression but rather refer to three instances of the same basic phenomenon. As such, they are sometimes difficult to differentiate, especially through microlevel analysis, and there are many "gray zones" among them to be considered. However, this classification is necessary as it allows us to appreciate the simultaneous diversity and internal unity of creative manifestations. As an example from a case of craft, in traditional Easter egg decoration one can identify all three types—habit, improvisation, and innovation - while looking at the work of different decorators or of one decorator over time. On the whole, this practice can be said to illustrate best the mechanisms of habitual creativity. This is because decoration activities rely on a strong knowledge base and require the exercise of technique through reproducing and combining, as well as perfecting, a number of traditional motifs. The stages, properties of materials, and work procedures are all learned early on, and this considerably reduces the number of difficulties encountered. But obstacles are certainly not absent, and thus artisans become improvisers when confronted with "accidents" in drawing or coloring or when they experience "inspiration blocks." Inventing (e.g., coming up with a new motif or work technique) is also constant in this folk art, but mostly as part of habitual-improvisational forms of expression. Decorators want to express themselves through their work and continue a tradition they value; they do not necessarily wish to "create" or "change" things for the sake of change (Glăveanu 2010c; Chapter 6). Innovation in Easter egg making is mostly led by necessity rather than innovative creativity in the sense of the term offered here. Still, there are cases of recognized innovators who deliberately search for novelties, mostly in order to respond to the changing needs of customers and to expand the market. This is how Christmas eggs or the wax-in-relief procedure of decoration were "invented"; rapidly spreading to other decorators in the region and the country, they then became part of existing habitual practices and thus subject to continuous reinterpretation and improvisation. In the words of Sennett (2008, 9), "Every good craftsman conducts a dialogue between concrete practices and thinking; this dialogue evolves into sustaining habits, and these habits establish a rhythm between problem solving and problem finding."

10.2.3. On the Neglect of Habit and Improvisation

At this point, it is important to make a few observations about the relative neglect of habitual and improvisational creativity in psychology and about the unintended consequences of this neglect. On the whole, we can consider these expressions to represent the core of "everyday life creativity," that is, the creativity that permeates all dimensions of our existence (Montuori 2011). However, this is not to say that everyday life creativity is opposed to innovative forms of creativity or that the latter are associated exclusively with achievements in art and science. As the previous sections argue, "ordinary" creativity can lead to innovation, and innovations themselves grow out of a habitual and improvisational basis. And yet, scholars have often focused "on eminent or unambiguous rather than everyday creativity" (Runco 2007a, x), which, though a clear sign of our "vibrant symbolic life," unfortunately is "sometimes invisible, looked down on or spurned" (Willis 1990, 1). In agreement with Richards (2007, 26), we can assert that "our [everyday] creativity is often underrecognized, underdeveloped, and underrewarded, in schools, at work, and at home." The reasons for this are both theoretical and methodological.

To begin with, contemporary (Western or Westernized) societies are based on a glorification of Big-C creativity, that is, great creations and extraordinary creators. This stems, to a large extent, from a general vision of the opposition between individuals on the one hand and society and culture on the other (Slater 1991). The implications of this are extensive; for example, focusing on eminent creative achievement alone "precludes the study and understanding of more common forms of creativity" and can "fuel problematic beliefs and stereotypes about the nature of creativity" (Beghetto and Kaufman 2007, 74). This is especially the case for aspiring creators who, in order to achieve social recognition, frequently feel the pressure of departing from what already exists in radical ways, of "fighting" against convention. Indeed, in the arts, "Totally conventional pieces bore everyone and bring the artist few rewards. So artists, to be successful in producing art, must violate standards more or less deeply internalized" (Becker 2008, 204). Habitual creativity is, therefore, completely excluded by this logic. Improvisation may be appreciated in art, but it can also carry undesirable associations with "makeshift" and "the next best thing." In the words of Montuori (2003, 245), "Improvisation is thought of as making the best of things, while awaiting a return to the way things should be done." The oftentimes "ephemeral" nature of its products (Sawyer 1997) further decreases its value and makes it "resistant to operationalization and analysis" (Sawyer 1995, 173). In addition, a series of methodological difficulties need to be confronted by those interested in habitual and improvisational creativity, principally the fact that they require *a microgenetic and situated approach*. To understand the nature of habit and improvisation, one must see them in the broader social and material context of their emergence, as well as in their moment-to-moment dynamics (for a proposal in this regard, see Glăveanu and Lahlou 2012; Chapter 5).

The neglect of everyday life forms of creativity not only "deprives us of a range of models for the creative process" (Bateson 1999, 153) but also, according to the perspective adopted here, deprives us of some of the most important and basic models of creative processes, namely, those for habitual expression. This is all the more surprising since it has been argued for a while in the psychology of creativity, especially by authors like Weisberg (1993), that "novelty is the norm of all behavior" and that "ordinary thinking processes" produce novel works of value and "must underlie even the most exalted examples of creative thinking" (11). For Weisberg, "A cornerstone of the concept of ordinary thinking is that it is based on continuity with the past" (21), a definition that is very much in line with the notion of habitual creativity. By reviewing laboratory studies and historical examples, he offered compelling evidence that the processes—e.g., continuity based on near analogies, discontinuities based on reasoning and sensitivity to external events (255)—that lead to extraordinary creative achievements are not qualitatively different from the ones we use in our daily activities. In a formulation by Bink and Mash (2000, 60), "These processes do not functionally differ between the genius and those who appear (prima facie) less gifted." In fact, the dominant creative cognition approach (see Ward, Smith, and Finke 1999, 189) is founded on the assumption that "creative accomplishments, from the most mundane to the most extraordinary, are based on . . . ordinary mental processes that, at least in principle, are observable." And yet, despite this similarity of perspective, cognitive studies for the most part did not inquire into the nature of habit itself and employed a series of laboratory experiments generally remote from the nature and complexities of everyday life action.

The theoretical perspective put forward in this chapter makes some simple and yet consequential distinctions between different types of creative expression while emphasizing their intrinsic unity as ultimately grounded in habitual forms of activity. In this context, habit is understood in ways that are more open, flexible, and reflective than those found in mainstream psychological literature. The vision of the embeddedness of "higher" manifestations of creativity in basic action and thought processes is not a novel proposal in itself. Runco (2007b, 103), for instance, argued recently that both people who are not usually creative and creative luminaries equally "rely on the same processes and mechanisms for their creativity"—essentially a personal creativity expressed in the generation of original interpretations and understandings of one's daily experience. This can easily be connected back to the existential meaning of habitual creativity previously referred to—that is, the idea of mini-c creations. In fact, Beghetto and Kaufman (2007) have already claimed that little-c and Big-C expressions necessarily have their *genesis* in mini-c interpretations: "In most cases, mini c can become little c; in extraordinary cases, little c may then turn into Big C" (Beghetto and Kaufman 2007, 76). Parallels can be drawn here to our discussion of habit, improvisation, and innovation (without assuming a one-to-one correspondence between these typologies).

As for our conception, empirical evidence concerning the relationships between habitual, improvisational, and innovative creativity is gradually accumulating. For instance, Chua and Iyengar (2008) examined the effect of prior experience (habitual action in our model) and explicit instruction (initiating the innovative drive to "be creative") on creative performance when respondents have a high degree of choice in how they approach the task (a basic condition for improvisational behavior). It was found, in two experiments, that superior creative achievement is obtained only in situations in which participants both have experience in the task domain and are prompted to make an effort to innovate. As concluded by the authors, creativity seems to require "a 'perfect storm' of high choice, high prior experience, and explicit creativity instructions" (Chua and Iyengar 2008, 169).

10.3. Some Concluding Remarks

The present chapter argued against a dichotomic understanding of creativity and habit—an understanding that is rooted in the psychophysiological vision of habitual action as automatic, almost mindless activity. It was shown here how an alternative conception of habit not only is possible but actually was preferred by several important psychologists from the beginning of the twentieth century; in addition, this alternative conception has been developed in related fields of study. Considering the substantial literature on creativity as action developed in sociology, it is bewildering when one confronts the limited extent to which this debate has gained the attention of psychologists and creativity researchers. There are various reasons for this, from the general scarcity of interdisciplinary endeavors to the highly experimental and sometimes atheoretical approach to the psychology of creativity that is cultivated today by many books and journals. Recent studies have looked at parts of the issue—for instance, the importance of the knowledge base (Weisberg 1999) or the role of self-imposed constraints (Stokes 2001)—but they often miss the whole, that is, the integrated expression of creativity in human action. It was argued above that as a result of this tendency, great opportunities are lost, both in terms of theory and practice. The former is exemplified by a strong trend of confining creativity to the mind, almost exclusively to cognition, and thereby losing sight of the coordination between thought and action, between the simultaneously "internal" and "external" dynamic of creativity. Creative cognition deals more with regularities of thinking and less with regularities of action, and as such it alone cannot address the complexities of habit, which is grounded in the interaction between person and a social and material environment.

This has important consequences, particularly for how we recognize creativity and legitimize who and what is "creative," and hence valuable. Reevaluating and revaluing habit as an intrinsically creative manifestation would not only open up a whole new field of inquiry but also direct our attention toward the creativity that each of us displays in our everyday contacts with others and with the world. In this regard, making the phenomenon "ordinary" rather than "extraordinary" takes nothing away from our appreciation of it in its highest forms; on the contrary, it can inspire our efforts to reach them.

11

What Can Be Done with an Egg? Creativity, Material Objects, and the Theory of Affordances[1]

A chapter addressing the topic of material objects, and the physical environment more generally, may seem relatively unusual considering past and present literature on creativity and psychological literature as a whole (with a few notable exceptions, see Csikszentmihaly and Rochberg-Halton 1981). While psychologists concern themselves with persons and particularly the mental processes of individuals, they tend to disregard a fundamental reality: namely, *people necessarily live in a material world.* This undeniable fact has received extensive attention in related disciplines such as anthropology and even sociology, and today the study of "material culture" is flourishing (see Dant 1999; Gell 1998). However, psychology is lagging behind, and, while still struggling to incorporate the materiality of the human body into its theories, it largely considers what is outside the mind as also exterior to its interests. The old Cartesian split remains very much situated at the core of the discipline, despite repeated challenges in recent decades (see Jovchelovitch 2007). This dichotomy between mind and body, psychological and material, inner and outer, is all the more problematic for the study of creative phenomena, which necessarily involve a creator working in a simultaneously social and material environment to produce oftentimes tangible, physical outputs (Getzels and Csikszentmihaly 1976). Traditional approaches to the study of the creative person (Barron and Harrington 1981) or process (Ward, Smith, and Finke 1999) do little to conceptualize the determinant role that objects and their properties play in creative production.

---

[1] Reprinted with permission from *The Journal of Creative Behavior* (published by John Wiley & Sons, Inc.), *46*(3), Glăveanu, V. P., What can be done with an egg? Creativity, material objects and the theory of affordances, 192–208. ©2012 by the Creative Education Foundation, Inc.

There are, however, certain developments within philosophy and cognitive science that are trying to correct this state of affairs and to introduce the physicality of the world into theories of psychological functioning. Examples of these are found, for instance, in current discussions of the embodied (Lakoff and Johnson 1999) and distributed mind (Hutchins 1995). What these perspectives are arguing for is a relocation of mental processes from "inside" the brain to "in between" mind and body, "in between" person and the surrounding environment. Creativity studies have not been totally indifferent to such ideas, though the notion of "distributed creativity" (see Miettinen 2006; Sawyer and DeZutter 2009) is far from a clear theoretical formulation; it is used to consider primarily collaborative creation rather than "physical" aspects. This is also the case for the growing sociocultural literature on creativity (Glăveanu 2010a; John-Steiner 1997; Sawyer 1997), which, despite presenting a Vygotskian understanding of creative work in relation to a series of mediating artifacts, generally focuses more on social interaction and less on the interaction between creator and material tools. To properly unpack the material nature of creative production, these approaches need a theory of what the environment has to "offer" in relation to the creator and of how it guides, facilitates, and also constrains human activity. This is precisely what Gibson's (1986) notion of affordances was designed to capture, and it will be argued here that a sociocultural understanding of affordance theory can revitalize the study of creativity as a *situated, materially grounded, and distributed process.*

In this context, the aim of this chapter is twofold: first, to propose a model of creativity based on different types of affordances that can be exploited by creative action, and second, to apply this model to an analysis of creativity in Easter egg decoration in rural Romanian communities. Folk art is a particularly good example of an activity that is deeply engaged with the materiality of objects while at the same time immersed in a world of customs and repeated practices (Cooper and Allen 1999; Giuffre 2009); the specific craft of egg decoration captures very well this dual—that is, material and cultural—determination of creative expression. In the end, and in light of this example, potential benefits of adopting an affordance perspective of creativity will be outlined for both theory and research.

11.1. The Theory of Affordances: A Sociocultural Perspective

However, before we outline an affordance model of creativity, it is important to consider briefly the theoretical grounds for this proposal and to clarify the present use of the notion. The term affordance and its initial development took place in the 1960s with the work of James Jerome Gibson. His well-known theory of visual perception (see Gibson 1950, 1966) needs to be acknowledged here not only for making one of the most significant contributions to ecological psychology but also for reopening and attempting to "resolve" the long-standing debate over the mental and the material in psychological studies. Drawing inspiration primarily from gestaltism (Heft 2003), Gibson invented the notion of affordance to be able to make reference simultaneously to the "animal" and the "environment." In an oft-cited definition, "The *affordances* of the environment are what it *offers* the animal, what it *provides* or *furnishes*, either for good or ill" (Gibson 1986, 127; see also Gibson 1966, 285). For instance, surfaces afford posture, locomotion, and manipulation and fire affords warming and burning. His basic proposal was that we should stop conceptualizing objects in our perception theories as a sum of static "qualities"; rather, we should see them as dynamic affordances, since this is what the person actually pays attention to in the environment. The ontological assumption that "meaning" exists in the world and is not solely a construction of the isolated human mind resonates strongly both with contemporary distributed cognition views (Hollan, Hutchins, and Kirsh 2000; Hutchins 2000) and with old scholarly sources, from Russian cultural-historical theory to American pragmatism.

However, Gibson's original formulation was often contradictory regarding the features of perceiving affordances. His central claim seems to be that affordances are perceived and guide behavior *directly* (see Heft 2003), and this means that a person does not need to learn or to reflect upon what the affordance of an object might be—it just reveals itself "in ambient light" (Gibson 1986, 140). Gibson also affirmed the "independence" of affordances relative to observers and the invariant nature of the former. In any case, he did acknowledge the dynamic and action-oriented aspects of our perception. Affordances make themselves "apparent" only to an actor who is engaged with the environment and tries to navigate it effectively. What the above suggests is that Gibson's thoughts on the topic of affordances were evolving and were somehow left unfinished, and this explains why the theory has known several refinements and reformulations in recent years (Jones 2003). Perhaps one of the most systematic accounts to date was offered by Chemero (2003), who defined affordances as relations between the *abilities* of the subject and the *features* of the environment. In his formalization, the logical structure is "Affords φ (environment, organism)," where φ is a behavior; this is somewhat loosely translated as "the environment affords behavior φ to the organism" (Chemero 2003, 187). In other words, the function defined by affordances needs *both* the environment term, represented by the environment's features or properties, and the organism term, represented by the organism's abilities (see also Greeno 1994).

Starting from this relation between features of the environment and the organism, we can offer a novel conception of affordances in light of sociocultural psychology sources and along the lines of Costall's (1995, 2006) critique of Gibson's theory. Cultural or sociocultural psychology (see Cole 1996; Valsiner and Rosa 2007) is a theoretical orientation that, not unlike ecological psychology, considers how objects mediate psychological functioning and the action and development of the person. It assumes that we live in an "intentional world" made up of "intentional (made, bred, fashioned, fabricated, invented, designed, constituted) things" (Shweder 1990, 2; see also Boesch 2007). This "intentionality of objects" converges in what is commonly meant by affordances while stressing the basic fact that objects bear the mark not only of their physical properties but also of the intentions of their designers and users. Objects made by human beings are considered to be concomitantly "natural" and "cultural," "material" and "symbolic" (i.e., meaningful), and thus they are usually classified by cultural psychologists under the notion of *artifacts*. According to Cole (1996, 117), "An artifact is an aspect of the material world that has been modified over the history of its incorporation into goal-directed human action." This reflects a Vygotskian (1978) line of thought—artifacts, from chairs and pottery to language, mediate our relation to the world and our relation to other people.

Considering the above, we can conclude that "the affordances of artifacts are themselves, therefore, a focus of enduring, and cumulative, social influence" (Costall 1995, 471). As previously mentioned, the mere assertion of "direct" or "unmediated" perception (combined with granting affordances "reality" independent of the human organism) is highly problematic. This is because we, as members of certain communities, engage with the environment in cultured ways—we "learn the affordances of things *through* other people" (Costall 1995, 472), with or without explicit instruction. The infant might arrive into a world that seems external and strange, but it is in fact the result of centuries of human activity; from the first months of life, this unfamiliar environment starts to be "tamed" through constant interaction with caregivers (Cole 1996; John-Steiner 1997). Material potentialities are commonly "matched" with a set of cultural rules and restrictions; this facilitates our encounter with the world and allows us to continue transforming it in specific ways, according to our needs. Objects can never be perceived with a "naked eye" by a socialized individual, and this is how culture becomes not a second nature but the *one and only nature* we know (see also Costall 1989). It is indeed true that culture ultimately "determines how we make use of and live with things" (Dant 1999, 14; also Csikszentmihaly and Rochberg-Halton 1981, 50). In fairness to Gibson, this particular insight concerning the sociocultural-physical nature of affordances did not completely escape him. By claiming that we must "learn to see" what things really are (Gibson 1986, 142), and through his well-known mailbox example (one must know about the postal system to use the affordance of sending and receiving letters), he also hinted at the culturally mediated aspects of perception and action.

In summary, we need the notion of affordances to theorize our relationship with material objects because it eloquently captures the mutual dependence between our goals and actions on the one hand and what the environment can offer us to attain goals and facilitate action on the other. It is also important for perceiving affordances as *equally* dependent on the physical properties of objects and the psychological and physical abilities of users. What the sociocultural approach contributes to is a consideration of such properties and abilities as codeveloping in a cultural and historical context and thus as largely constructed rather than simply "predetermined"—often "potential" rather than merely "given." It is this aspect of potentiality that creates a direct and necessary link between affordances and a discussion of creativity. Indeed, the sociocultural theory of affordances is concerned with the dynamic and supple relationship between creators and the world. Affordances, just like objects and persons, are subjected to constant transformation and sociocultural change, which ensure that "new entities with novel affordances are introduced into the culture, new affordances of familiar objects are realized, familiar affordances are sustained over time through continued use, and affordances fade from the scene through disuse" (Heft 2003, 175–176). As such, we can conclude that what we mean by creativity and what we mean by affordances often overlaps and that creativity can be defined as *the process of perceiving, exploiting, and "generating" novel affordances during socially and materially situated activities*. This tentative formulation will be refined with the help of an empirical example, but first we need to outline the exact components of the model proposed in the present chapter.

11.2. An Affordance Framework for Creativity Theory and Research

One basic conclusion from the previous section is that "any object or situation we encounter has a *limitless* number of affordances (although this does not mean that we can do *anything* with *anything*)" (Costall 2006, 24). The last remark leads to an interesting question for any creativity researcher: What constrains our possibilities of acting and, specifically, of creating new artifacts? It is argued here that to understand this aspect we need to consider what *the environment affords* in relation to two other crucial factors: the *intentionality of the actor* and the *normativity of a given cultural context*. Figure 11.1 graphically depicts the three factors above and outlines the significance of using this tripartite model for theorizing creative acts (see also the world installation theory; Lahlou 2008). In this figure, the first thing to be noticed is a large central area in which intentionality (what a person would do), affordances (what a person could do), and normativity (what a person should do) overlap. This is the space of everyday action, of "what is usually done" considering physical, personal, and sociocultural constraints (something associated also with "canonical" affordances of objects; Costall 1995). However, of special interest for a theory of creativity are the marginal segments of the figure, the ones that contain "unperceived," "uninvented," and "unexploited" affordances. Let us explore these in turn.

The sector of *unperceived affordances* holds all those possibilities of action that are materially achievable and do not violate any particular cultural norms

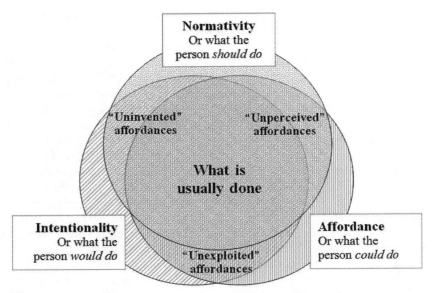

Figure 11.1. A sociocultural model for an affordance theory of creativity.

but that do not represent, for various reasons, what the person "would do" in the situation. The individual (or group) has no explicit intention of making "use" of these affordances because typically he or she (or they) is not *aware* of their existence. Gibson referred to this problem with the following concise formulation: "The central question for the theory of affordances is not whether they exist and are real, but whether information is available in ambient light for perceiving them" (Gibson 1986, 140). Being able to actually recognize existing affordances (a question that moves us further away from the strict hypothesis of "direct perception") has preoccupied researchers for some time; see, for instance, the work of Norman (1988, 1999) on the activity of designers. When designing objects, it is not so much an issue of them affording action X but of their being able to signal effectively the fact that action X is afforded; indeed, "Affordances are of little use if they are not visible to the users" (Norman 1999, 41). Perhaps the most straightforward link to creativity in this context can be made through the notion of creative insight (see also Sternberg and Davidson 1999). Duncker's well-known candle box problem is paradigmatic in this regard. In his classic experiment, participants were asked to attach a candle to the wall in a way that would prevent wax from dripping on the table below; they had at their disposal a box of tacks, candles, and matches. Failure by many to use the box as a candle holder was explained in terms of functional fixedness—a mental block that prevents the use of an object in a new way that is required to solve a problem (Duncker 1945). The fact that the box can support the candle is entirely "affordable" and does not contravene cultural norms. Yet, to enable the creative solution, this affordance had to be properly perceived or discovered in the situation.

Another form of "missed possibilities" lies with all affordances that, though wanted by the person and granted by society, are not yet "invented" or available. The word "invented" needs to be used here with great care because it can easily be argued that affordances, as relations between features of the material world and an agent's abilities (Chemero 2003), either exist or not—they cannot be generated in any literal sense of the word. For instance, water (and liquids more generally) "affords" getting wet through contact, and there is nothing we can do to fundamentally change its nature (this excludes altering condensation states). However, there is something we can do to protect ourselves from getting wet on a rainy day, should this be our intention, and for this purpose we have "invented" umbrellas and raincoats. In this case as well the logic applies: impermeability as a feature was not created, though objects that make excellent use of it were. It is in this sense that we consider here "uninvented affordances" as new collections of affordances generated by the combination or transformation of basic (existing) potentials. Complex or compound affordances describe in fact most of the artifacts produced and re-produced by human societies and cultures, since we live in a world of objects that have more than one property and that can "obtain" additional capabilities through processes of invention. For example, Will Gibson (2006, 184), when referring to the sound of musical instruments, noted that they afford "the production of some sounds and not others," while at the same time, "through alterations in technique or indeed the objects themselves, new sets of action possibilities are realized and the boundaries of possible musical action shift." An illustration coming again from the area of creative problem solving is Köhler's (1925) famous chimpanzee studies, which reflect the "invention" of affordances (or, more accurately, of objects holding new affordances). In reaching the remote bananas, chimpanzees were able to assemble sticks together and/or pile up boxes to stand on, in both cases "shrinking" the unaffordable and expanding their possibilities for action.

Finally, another class of affordances includes what a person would and could do yet remains *unexploited* for cultural reasons. As argued above, there is a certain normativity guiding the use of objects, and this is embodied in the "canonical" and socially accepted ways of thinking about or interacting with the material world. Arbitrary conventions (Norman 1999) play a great role in determining what affordances we exploit and, indeed, what affordances we perceive (see the discussion about unperceived affordances above). Falling outside current norms of action can have potentially negative consequences. As Costall (1995, 472) reminds us, objects "can be used in other ways, but even when these alternative uses occur to us, there may be sanctions against such deviation"—sanctions that would result in embarrassment for our acts. Costall continues and points to the fact that norms tell us not only what objects "should" do but also who is entitled to use them in a certain way (raising issues, for example, of ownership). To illustrate unexploited affordances with the help of another problem-solving exercise, we can think about Bulbrook's (1932) beads experiment. She gave participants a string of beads consisting of alternating small white beads and bigger yellow beads, except for the middle portion where there were five white pearl-like beads. The task was to make a single regularly repeating pattern without unstringing or restringing the beads and without knotting or breaking the thread; the solution was to use available tools (placed on a nearby table) to break the white beads. Despite the simplicity of the answer, not many respondents found it (or even thought of it), and this can perhaps be accounted for in terms of a cultural norm: the integrity of objects must be respected, especially in the case of precious things such as pearls (see Zlate 2006). "Overcoming" this principle offers here the appropriate response.

In summary, creative expression is associated in our model with an exploration of environmental affordances previously unavailable to the person because of their unperceived, uninvented, or unexploited nature. Before I continue with a case study that illustrates such creative explorations, it is important to make some final observations regarding the proposed schema. To start with, in every concrete situation there will always be a "mixture" of all three elements postulated here (intentions, affordances, and norms), and thus confusion may result from the fact that the three particular areas holding potential for creativity in Figure 11.1 seem to "lack" one of the three. To be clear, actions that uncover previously unperceived affordances lack not all intentionality but only the intention to exploit the affordance in question; actions meant to "invent" new affordances are not possible outside of any existing affordances but lack precisely the affordance being "generated"; and actions that explore affordances previously disregarded on account of normative aspects are not outside all cultural norms but rather contradict only a specific norm related to that particular object use. This makes us think also about "degrees" of creativity (e.g., the continuum from personal to historical novelty; Boden 1994) and about how these degrees can be conceptualized within the present framework. Here we can certainly distinguish between affordances being perceived, invented, or exploited *with reference to* individual action (where others may have "discovered" them already and where there might even be a societal use that the individual is not aware of) and those being perceived, invented, or exploited *with reference to* entire groups or societies. For example, children, as they grow up, often learn the affordances of their environment through trial and error. A child's "micro" acts of creativity should not be discounted in light of the above but rather should be considered in relation to the intentions, norms, and affordance uses specific to that child (or to children of that age). Finally, a temporal dimension must always be present in applying the model because it is intended to be a dynamic vision of human action in relation to environmental potentials. As such, creativity is not "in" the newly perceived, invented, or exploited affordances themselves but rather is "in" the very acts of perception, invention, and utilization. This is important because the framework aims to unpack how areas situated outside canonical uses of objects are gradually discovered by people in their daily interactions and are—once discovered, and if they are of value—often built into "what is usually done," allowing new "areas of possibility" to emerge at the margins of routinized action in an ever-advancing cycle. Empirical examples of this dynamic are presented in the following sections.

11.3. So, What Can Be Done with an Egg?

To exemplify the use of this framework (Figure 11.1), let us now focus on the title question and take the case of a very common object: the egg. Bird eggs have a series of affordances we are familiar with; for instance, they can break, they can usually be cooked and eaten, and they are occasionally used as projectiles helping to express a state of discontent (something that unlucky politicians or performers know all too well). These rather "conventional" uses, however, are exceeded in number by a variety of highly creative possibilities: an egg can make an interesting paperweight, empty shells can be used to store little items or turned into candleholders or even percussion instruments, egg whites make good glue, yolks can serve as skin moisturizers, and so on. All the above afforded uses are based on a number of basic physical features— eggshells are solid, egg whites are naturally sticky, yolks are rich in vitamin A, etc. In this section, we will concentrate on a particular creative practice known as *egg decoration*. Being able to decorate eggs is itself an action facilitated by a series of material properties that allow different elements to be applied on or to color the outer surface of the shell. This is how eggs and eggshells came to be dyed; painted; decorated with leaves, wax, beads, and miniature horseshoes; or even artistically sculpted. Then again, the act of decoration is also impeded by other features of eggs, in particular their fragility, relatively small size, and distinctive shape, all of which make drawing patterns on the egg quite challenging, especially for beginners.

The practice of Easter egg decoration is widespread in the Christian world, particularly among people from Orthodox Christian communities, and this supports previous observations concerning the cultural aspects of object design and use. The embellishment of eggs ceases in these cases to be a simple affordance or potentiality that is or is not actualized and acquires all the characteristics and normativity of a *tradition* (informed by religion and folk beliefs) dictating what is to be made as well as by whom, in what number, when, and with what means. Nevertheless, it is important to notice that eggs have been decorated for millennia, as indicated by evidence found around the globe, and carry with them a deep symbolism marked by ideas of life, fertility, and rebirth (see Gorovei 2001; Marian 1992; Newall 1967). As such, the egg,

221

Eggs decorated with wax (Ileana Hotopilă)   Eggs with wax in relief (Niculina Nigă)

Eggs with beads (Rodica Berechea)   Eggs with leaves (Luminiţa Cană)

Figure 11.2. Different styles of Romanian Easter egg decoration.

in past and present human societies, is not simply a "natural" object but is a proper "artifact," being defined, integrated, and utilized in culture-specific ways. The decoration of eggs certainly reflects the wealth of practices and meanings associated with the craft in different parts of the world (Marian 1992). For example, Figure 11.2 illustrates several types of ornamented eggs from urban and rural Romania, showing the variety not only of motifs but also of work techniques and material resources involved in Easter egg making. Indeed, as with many other folk arts, egg adornment is *embedded in a material universe* that in the case of traditional Romanian decoration includes, in addition to various types of eggs (quail, chicken, duck, goose, and ostrich), beeswax (melted to afford application to the egg surface), chişiţe (traditional instruments for "writing" on eggs made of a wooden stick with a metal pin at the end), and color pigments (red, yellow, black, etc.).

Considering this diversity of outcomes and resources, as well as the intricate nature of craftwork itself, Easter egg decoration constitutes an excellent case study for creativity researchers, and its underlying processes have been described in detail elsewhere (Glăveanu 2013a; Chapter 7). For the purposes

Figure 11.3. Drawing motifs with wax in the "white stage" of decoration (Valerica Juşcă).

of this chapter, I will make use of several empirical examples collected through interviews and observation (including filmed observation) sessions with artisans from the village of Ciocăneşti in northern Romania. During these sessions, folk artists repeatedly commented on the importance of the egg's size, color, and actual shape. For instance, wider and more elaborate models can be depicted on a larger surface; eggshells need to be perfectly white, otherwise the overall color contrasts will be less noticeable; "elongated" egg shapes invite the artisan to depict specific motifs such as the "lost way," while "rounder" ones are perfect for making "belts" that go around the egg; etc. Craftspeople normally prefer duck eggs to chicken eggs because they have a more "shiny" and "smooth" surface that is easier to decorate. Also, chişiţe, the instruments used to apply wax, must have certain properties; for example, they vary in the "thickness" of writing according to the size of the metal pin. The work process of traditional wax decoration, corresponding to the central area of Figure 11.1—the "usual" of Easter egg making, at least for rural artisans—involves repeated stages of drawing models with wax on the egg and immersing the egg in color (see Figure 11.3). In Ciocăneşti, there are three phases to this process: "on white," "on yellow," and "on red," referring to the work done to complete the model after the egg is inserted in each color. The basic principle (exploiting a central affordance of wax) is that whatever segment is covered with beeswax on the surface of the egg will keep the color it had before the wax was applied. In this sense, the act of egg decoration requires working on a "negative" image of what the final outcome will be. In the end, the egg is immersed in black and then the wax is cleaned off near a heat source, and this reveals all the intended patterns and colors.

11.4. Creativity and Affordances in Romanian Easter Egg Decoration

The case study of egg decoration practices will be used to illustrate creative action in terms of "expanding" the three areas of potentiality presented in Figure 11.1: unperceived, uninvented, and unexploited affordances. An observation regarding the process of analytically identifying such cases is that oftentimes there are fine lines between uncovering one or another type of unexplored environmental affordance, and in practice, *combinations* of the above are also possible (for instance, some affordances may be unperceived because they disregard "cultural norms"). As such, creative action can transcend these categories, especially when a temporal dimension is included in the analysis; for example, in exploring uninvented affordances, an artisan may also be exploiting some action potentials outside of normative control (in this case tradition or custom), and his or her action can further lead to an awareness of formerly unperceived affordances. For the sake of simplicity and brevity, however, the presentation below will maintain more clear-cut distinctions between categories.

A great part of the creativity involved in this craft comes from gradually enlarging the area of "unperceived affordances." Acts of *discovery* stand at the core of the practice, just as they do in art (see Mace and Ward 2002) and other creative fields in which the outcome is a developing project and not an idea immediately transposed onto a material support. This takes place both at a micro, individual level and at the more macro level of the craft as a whole. For the former, we can include all those moments that artisans consider to be "accidental" in the course of decoration. Accidents are the outcome of many potential influences, from material factors (e.g., the instability of the metal pin of the chişiţă) to environmental conditions (e.g., the temperature in the room directly affects how quickly wax "cools down") and personal circumstances (e.g., how tired the decorator is, especially if working at night). Importantly, there is a huge creative potential inherent in apparent "mistakes" because they frequently open up a world of previously unknown possibilities (Zahacinschi and Zahacinschi 1985). Indeed, it is not uncommon for decorators to comment on the fact that shapes or motifs "afford" some kind of combinations and not others, and it is accidental gestures that open the door to novel developments of a current pattern.

Of course, not every accident turns into a discovery that can be creatively explored further, and oftentimes decoration work resembles a "trial and error" type of exercise where, for example, artisans are curious to experiment with the properties of color pigments and wax. The actual making and use of colored wax is in fact a rather recent "discovery," and here we can distinguish broader processes of innovation and transmission of innovation taking place at the level of the craft-world in its entirety. As mentioned before, "old" Easter eggs in Romania are traditionally decorated with natural wax that is wiped off the eggshell at the end. The technique of "wax in relief" (drawing models directly with colored wax and keeping it on the surface of the egg) capitalizes on affordances previously in use (applying wax on the egg) and the discovery of new possibilities (in this case the ability to color wax instead of coloring only the shell). This practice emerged about two decades ago and is now widespread in Romania, where eggs with wax in relief are gradually becoming associated with "neo-traditional" decoration. Furthermore, the perception of new affordances is a continuous process, and in our example, employing colored wax provides a diversification of colors and thus allows the artist to draw realistic pictures on the egg (e.g., landscapes, human figures), in contrast to conventional geometric patterns.

Another important source of creative expression in craft has to do with the "invention" or "generation" of new affordances—that is, the *generation of new artifacts* is helpful for expanding existing possibilities of decoration. The historical trajectory of folk art in Romania is, in this regard, also a history of innovations related to the development of the material support (new tools) and of the decoration technique (new methods of working on eggs). In fact, the two stand closely interrelated and depend on each other as they shape the future of this particular craft (see also Gibson 2006 for the example of musical instruments). As alluded to above, Romanian Easter egg decoration has known some radical transformations in the last two decades, building on the regained free participation in religious practices and on the emergence of a national and international market for the selling of folk objects. Particularly with the appearance and consolidation of the market, decoration styles also evolved, shifting from simpler to more complex and artistic forms (a tendency noted in the case of craft by Becker 2008), and several innovations had to be implemented to allow for the preservation of eggs and the realization of more intricate designs.

These innovations required "extending" some of the affordances of the material support. Starting with the eggs, they afford being preserved, but not for an indefinite period, especially when "full." Thus, eggs began to be emptied of content, normally with the help of a syringe, to prolong their period of preservation. Moreover, "old" or traditional Easter eggs were not varnished at the end of the decoration process, and this caused their colors to fade more quickly over time. Today, varnish is used on a large scale to generate a "new" affordance for the decorated egg: that of better preserving the colors and especially the wax applied to the surface (for eggs with wax in relief). With reference to work instruments, the chișiță was in use for a long time in Romanian rural communities, but its basic affordance of helping to "write" on the egg needed further innovation, especially to support much more minute and intricate forms of decoration. For this purpose, the size of the metal pin used to apply wax was altered, and nowadays artisans have not one but a set of chișițe to work with, some drawing "thinner" and some "thicker" lines (the latter employed for "filling" the model on yellow and red).

Egg making as a community practice not only is deeply immersed in the materiality of the world but also draws from a whole symbolic universe situated at the intersection of religion, folklore, and art. The normativity of a tradition is certainly present in this case, and what was mentioned earlier about established techniques, work instruments, and patterns of decoration contributes to the set of constraints (the "should" part) over what is afforded by both actor and environment (the "could" and "would" parts). Unsurprisingly, then, another significant source of creativity in this craft comes from *transgressing certain norms* and thus "exploiting" more of the perceived affordances of decoration. An important observation, however, and what defines the traditional folk art context here and in other similar crafts, is precisely the fact that norms are transgressed without being completely violated (see also Layton 1991), for such violation would make the outcome not creative but void of all meaning (Glăveanu 2010c; Chapter 6). On the other hand, as any "living" tradition, egg decoration is constantly expanding its possibilities, and in the following section I will consider this process from the perspective of "breaking" some (but not all) normative aspects of the craft. When the situation is viewed through these lenses, it could be argued that many of the examples presented above (the discovery of wax-in-relief techniques, expansion in colors, use of more intricate designs, varnish for the final stage, etc.) were all ways of transgressing previous principles of decoration. However, from a more technical standpoint, they merely expanded rather than contradicted the "usual" procedures. For instance, wax was already employed by artisans and so were color pigments, and the varnish does not fundamentally change the motifs being depicted.

For a more clear example of transgression, we can consider a very recent development of the craft in a rather unexpected direction: the creation of Christmas eggs. Eggs decorated for Christmas are becoming fairly common, and what they do in essence is make use of all the typical affordances of Easter egg decoration while changing the thematic register (typically they represent Santa Claus, Christmas trees, etc.). Such novelties evoke mixed feelings, though they do have the great advantage of offering artisans new opportunities for selling their products in another season and for making the most of their craft. Indeed, there is a clear intention to produce more "beautiful" and "attractive" eggs for customers to appreciate and purchase, and this is the driving force behind the exploitation of an increasing number of affordances previously obscured by convention or lack of awareness.

In summary, this case study of Easter egg decoration comes to show some specific ways in which creativity becomes manifest in craftwork through acts of spontaneous discovery, invention of techniques, and transgression of norms. These processes, going back to our theoretical schema (Figure 11.1), are able to expand action potentials in relation to unperceived, uninvented, and unexploited affordances, respectively. As a word of caution, these are not the only "mechanisms" that can help in exploring more environmental affordances, and further empirical work (both in folk art and other domains) could shed light on a larger repertoire of creative processes and on the ways in which they interact and complement one another in concrete situations.

11.5. Why Use an Affordance Model of Creativity?

This chapter has attempted to establish links between the sociocultural, the material, and the psychological in the case of creativity through the use of affordance theory. What this theoretical perspective does is present creativity in a new light, much different from previous understandings that often reduce it to the individual and, "inside" the individual, to the cognitive (Glăveanu 2010a; see Chapter 1). To conceive of creativity in terms of affordances, in a way similar to what has been proposed in Figure 11.1, means to adopt a fundamentally *dynamic, relational, and action-oriented approach* to the phenomenon, something the field has been trying to move toward in recent decades (Barron 1995; John-Steiner 1997; Sawyer 1995). This vision is dynamic because, as demonstrated by the brief example of Easter egg decoration, what exists at some point as unperceived, uninvented, or unexploited affordances may very well become part of regular practice, leading to further cycles that expand the core area of the "usual" in thought and action. It is relational because creative activity, just like affordances (Gibson 1986), depends simultaneously on the agent's abilities and the features of the material and social world. It is an action approach because the framework put forward can only be applied when creators actively and directly engage with their symbolic and physical environment.

At the same time, an affordance theory of creativity seeks not to replace previous models, especially those that fall under the umbrella of creative cognition (see Ward et al. 1999), but rather to *integrate and expand* their insights about the "intrapsychological" dimension of creative expression. As argued above, the notion of affordances is very useful for theorizing what the environment has to "offer" to creators and the ways in which it can direct their activity, but—unlike Gibson's assumption concerning "direct" perception—the sociocultural view supported here argues for the largely culturally "constructed" and mediated character of human action. The next conceptual step is therefore to articulate these two necessary dimensions: the psychological one (made up of cognitive representations, goals and motives, and emotional reactions) and the behavioral one (in direct relation to the properties and resources of a material and social environment). A sociocultural model of affordances is thus a first attempt to direct creativity theory toward a paradigm of situated action and distributed cognition (both in dialogue with each other; Hutchins 2000). Moreover, this model can inspire a program of research into the psychology of creativity based on the analysis of "common" and "creative" uses of objects and other features of the physical world—uses that can be distinguished and discussed in ways illustrated by the egg decoration case study presented above.

For this, the researcher would need to rely not only on direct observation of practices but also on information about the broader cultural context in which action takes place (e.g., to understand issues of normativity and tradition) as well as information about the goals and intentions of the respondent. Studies can be envisioned in which the use of objects is analyzed in different creative domains, within the work of one or more creators, with participants at different stages of development, etc. In the end, the schematic framework proposed in Figure 11.1 can be refined by the following: (a) uncovering and classifying more ways of exploring unperceived, uninvented, and unexploited affordances; (b) observing how these uses vary according to personal variables and domain of action; and finally (c) constructing more specific models that consider the dynamics between different types of affordances and the manner in which explorations of one lead to the exploration of others in actual "chains" of creative action.

In conclusion, what I argued for here is a reevaluation of the role of material objects in the conceptualization of creativity. Using the lenses proposed in this chapter helps us theorize, empirically study, and act upon what is "possible" in the world in ways that expand our capabilities for action and thought. The "doable" and the "thinkable" are deeply interconnected, and it is only when supplementing the classic theory of affordances with sociocultural notions that a new, more comprehensive perspective can be achieved. What creativity offers the concept of affordances—to look at the other side of the coin—is a more dynamic, supple account of what we, as individuals and as a species, can do in relation to our environment. This is an old issue that has been situated at the core of thinking about creativity; Gibson (1986, 143) can be said to have dealt with the issue in these terms: "Within limits, the human animal can alter the affordances of the environment but is still the creature of his or her situation." What I propose here is a slight amendment to this thought: *within limits, the human animal constantly and creatively alters the affordances of the environment to an extent that makes him or her become at once a creature and a creator of any given situation.*

Part F

Creativity
Development

12

Children and Creativity:
A Most (Un)Likely Pair?[1]

> *Electricity is not only present in a magnificent thunderstorm and dazzling lightning, but also in a lamp; so also, creativity exists not only where it creates great historical works, but also everywhere human imagination combines, changes, and creates anything new.*

> *Vygotsky 1930/1967, cited in Smolucha 1992, 54)*

It may come as a surprise to some that the connection between children and creativity can end in a question mark. Children play, sing, dance, draw, tell stories, and make up riddles in such a natural, spontaneous, and creative way that few would doubt the existence of such a thing as "children's creativity." In fact, some would argue that children are the *embodiment* of human creativity. In a recent survey of laypeople's representations of creativity (Glăveanu 2011d; Chapter 9), respondents were asked to rate and comment on different symbols that can potentially represent the essence of being creative. Findings revealed that "children's drawings" were considered by most participants to be a good or very good creativity symbol. A variety of reasons were offered for this, and common among them was the idea that "the child within all of us is the part which longs to create and come up with answers to all things." In the collective imagination (at least of modern people from the Western world), there seems to be a firm conviction that children are much more free and creative in their expression than adults. This theme is also well reflected in psychology through the work of several distinguished authors. Freud (1908/1970) himself compared the playing child with the creative writer. And yet, understandings of this nature need to be historically situated. As Gardner (1982) rightfully pointed out, in centuries past, the association between children and art would have been readily dismissed. For it is "our romantic tradition, remolded in terms of a modernist ethos, [that] has made us responsive to the notion of the child as artist, and the child in every artist" (Gardner 1982, 92). Can this tradition be said to mold contemporary psychology as well?

---

[1] From *Thinking Skills and Creativity*, 6(2), Glăveanu, V. P., Children and creativity: A most (un) likely pair?, 122–131. © 2011 by Elsevier, reprinted with permission.

The proper answer here would be "yes and no." *Yes* if we look at today's growing literature dedicated to measuring the "creative potential" of children—for example, its ups and downs through different developmental stages and the practical ways in which it can be enhanced. At a theoretical level, though, there is considerable *skepticism* as to whether creativity, as defined by modern science, can be applied to children, and the reasons for this are not altogether dismissible. To continue with Gardner's (1982, 142) analysis of the child and his or her art, he cautiously remarked that experimental evidence does not support the "easy assumption that the young child is an artist." Feldman, another acclaimed developmentalist and creativity researcher, warned against (in Sawyer et al. 2003, 219) the tendency to "romanticize childhood" by exaggerating the creative value of children's products. Equally reserved, Duke stated that children's "art" cannot be called creative; it is "the first step of a creative process, but few children go beyond this first step in a journey that may demand 10 or 100 steps" (Duke 1973, 8). Apparent here is the way in which a commonsense truism can trouble psychologists. The widespread acceptance of children's creativity doesn't seem to hold its ground when scientific definitions and methods enter the discussion. In the end, it is questionable whether children can live up to, much less embody, the traditional idealized image of what it means to be "truly" creative.

The notion of creativity in both science and commonsense thinking draws on a powerful legacy of the "genius" or the "great creator." The history of this concept abounds with dichotomies between creative and uncreative, extraordinary and ordinary, exceptional and banal, science and everyday life, art and craft, and so forth. There are strong ideological barriers safeguarding the realm of creativity against those who are deemed unable of "true" creative expression. Among these we generally find all animals, the mentally unstable, and children. As Feldhusen (2002, 179) notes, "Creativity is a phenomenon that is most often and successfully researched and understood at its high level, less frequently as exhibited by average people and/or children." At best, children can be given a secondary role, at the periphery of creative expression, and acknowledged for their "low-range creativity" (Feldman in Sawyer et al. 2003, 219). This is further suggested by distinctions such as those between "mature" and "mundane" creativity (see Cohen and Ambrose 1999, 9). The first type is the most valuable, leading to the transformation of a field and, as its name implies, it is reserved for adulthood. The second, also named "creativity in the small," brings about the new at an individual, not societal, level. Under these conditions, it is hardly surprising that a debate between scholars about the impact of society on children's natural creativity ended with the following conclusion:

> We came to a consensus that children are not really creative, given the definitions of creativity that are necessary to explain the important and influential innovations that have impacted our lives. Some of

us are willing to retain a residual notion of small *c* creativity—the everyday cleverness that makes us smile or makes life easier—for the novel, unusual actions of children, but we all distinguish this from Big *C* Creativity, the creation of culture-transforming products that is found only in adults. (Sawyer in Sawyer et al. 2003, 240)

This chapter aims to challenge such a conclusion. It will do so not by engaging with particular pieces of empirical data or by claiming the falseness of separating children and creativity. On the contrary, this view will be considered as legitimate in its own right. What the present chapter will examine are the *epistemological reasons* for supporting or contesting children's creativity, considering them as symptomatic of deep-seated assumptions concerning children and creativity. From a constructionist standpoint, both sides of the debate are equally "valid" in their efforts to convince us of a certain "reality." Nevertheless, they have important practical consequences (for theory, for research, for education, etc.) and, as such, cannot and should not be equally supported. Some will undoubtedly be outraged by the perspective of considering the "constructed" nature of our science, be it developmental or creativity psychology, and of raising (or perhaps lowering) the discussion from the level of facts to that of narratives about facts. To those I respond with Jerome Bruner's reflection that "*any* story we tell about human infancy grows as much out of ideological convictions and cultural beliefs as out of observation" (Bruner 1986, 134). There is great value in scrutinizing these ideological convictions and cultural beliefs because, in our case, the "stories" we tell about children's creativity are born out of "stories" we tell about children without direct reference to creativity and about creativity without direct reference to children. As such, the presentation will start with a brief consideration of these background narratives. Following this, a review of arguments for why children are (or are not) creative will be offered, with particular attention devoted to how this debate both stems from and informs contemporary shifts in developmental psychology and creativity research. Finally, in light of this analysis, the case will be made for why we should "bet" on children's creativity as the more fertile starting point for a contemporary perspective on children, creativity, and education.

12.1. Making Sense of Children and Childhood

Usually one thinks of "making sense" as something we engage in when we are confronted with an alien and mysterious reality. This description applies to a great extent to our efforts to know the human child, despite the fact that we all were one to begin with. Beautifully capturing this paradox, Kennedy (2008, 1) writes, "Childhood is both the most deeply familiar moment of the human life cycle and the great unknown." The fact that we were once children but are not anymore doesn't make much easier the task of comprehending childhood *as is.* Our knowledge of it will always be bound to our position in the world in relation to it—as adults. The adult-centrism of our theories is a characteristic that is here to stay; it is something we can't correct but should more consistently acknowledge. The child is, in the end, simultaneously a historical, cultural, political, economic, social, and scientific production (Denzin 1977). Definitions of childhood, as Burman (1994) observes, are always relational in nature, making reference to parents, families, the state, etc. Moreover, they are never inconsequential for how we come to define ourselves as nonchildren. As Burman (1994, 48) continues to affirm, "Discourses of childhood . . . are part of the cultural narratives that define who we are, why we are the way we are and where we are going."

Unsurprisingly, childhood as a "social invention" (Valentine 2004, 2) has a history, though this history is more recent than we commonly believe. In his seminal work on historical representations of children and childhood, Ariès (1962) demonstrated that this particular age was "absent" as a concept in the Middle Ages and only started emerging in the upper classes during the sixteenth and seventeenth centuries. Of course children existed before that time, but they were seen not as such but rather as miniature adults. And even after they finally "materialized," children went through a series of different "incarnations" before becoming the complex beings they are (considered) today. From the innocent and pure creature of the seventeenth century to the emblematic sign of Romanticism in the late eighteenth century and on to the instinctual and sexual organism of twentieth-century psychoanalysis, the child transformed in unison with the social, cultural, and political worldviews of the time. As David Kennedy (2006, 5) concludes, "Caught between divinity and animality, between what is and what it might be, it is the child who mediates the human possibility." Indeed, children represent a space of possibility, a space of projection and constant re-presentation for all adult "outsiders."

What is projected onto the child is not always positive, though. As a matter of fact, there is a pervasive tendency, arguably across historical periods and geographical places, to define children *in negative terms*: not by what they are and have but by what they are not and don't yet have (Alanen 1990, 16). And there are many things that adults (psychologists included) consider the child to not have. Analyzing dominant conceptions, Vygotsky (1987, 53) made the same observation, pointing to how research is absorbed by an ethos of finding the "flaws, inadequacies, and limitations" of the child's thinking rather than his or her capabilities. In the words of D'Alessio (1990, 70), "The idea of the unfinishedness of the child has long provided the basis for theories of child development." This conception stands at the basis of what can be called a "deficit model" (see Shaw 1996) of the child, one that portrays children as less able, less developed, and less experienced. Obviously, this calls for a comparison term, and the comparison term is always the adult. Prout and James (1997) explored the roots of this general dichotomy and its associated symbolism.

What they revealed is a general opposition between children as "nature," "simple," "amoral," "asocial," and "person-in-waiting" and adults as "culture," "complex," "moral," "social," and "personhood"; in other words, a dichotomy between the child's "becoming" and the adult's "being."

And yet, psychology has come a long way in how it conceptualizes children and childhood as a stage of development. From a traditional image of the passive and responsive child, especially at very young ages, theory has gradually moved to a depiction of the "informationally active, socially interactive infant mind" (Bruner 1999, 230). A regained appreciation for the child's capacity to understand and manipulate the world—to act both toward the self and toward others and generally to go beyond the "here and now" of experience—was prompted by recent investigations of the *symbolic function* and its genesis. This is not a new interest but one that remained dormant under decades of behaviorism. The focus on the symbolic function is by no means irrelevant to our discussion of children's creativity. In fact, the story of "creativity" is largely considered to begin with the first symbolically mediated actions of the child:

> Unlike other animals and unlike the infant during the first year of life, the child of two has clearly entered the realm of symbolic activity.... He may eat symbolically, using pretense gestures and pretend food. Moreover, such symbolic enactments are carried out seemingly for the sheer enjoyment of representational activity. There is no ulterior motive—unless one wants to count increased knowledge of the world and more effective communication about it. Needless to stress, this achievement of symbolic activity is enormous—in a sense, the greatest imaginative leap of all. Upon it will be constructed all subsequent forms of play, including play of literary imagination. (Gardner 1982, 170)

In conclusion, our historical and societal relationship to the "child"— transcending the specifics of our interactions with particular children—was and continues to be marked by *ambivalence* (see Sommerville 1982, 288). Children are, it seems, innocent, vulnerable, and lovable, but they can also be disrupting, menacing, and unpredictable (Burman 1994; Valentine 2004). As such, they require education, protection, and a watchful surveillance on the part of the adult. A similar ambivalence can be said to describe our understanding of children's creativity. It is difficult to evaluate whether children are indeed creative and whether being creative is good for them without uncovering the second piece of the puzzle: the meaning of creativity.

12.2. Making Sense of Creators and Creativity

Creativity can be regarded as another "great unknown" for both scientists and laypeople. Explaining how novelty comes about is perhaps one of the most challenging tasks psychologists are facing, and this is even more true when this novelty is generated by children. Despite all the potential interpretations one can give to the terms "creative" and "creativity," there is today a surprisingly strong consensus in the literature that creative products are new and "accepted as tenable or useful or satisfying by a group in some point in time" (Stein 1953, 311). This definition is also what Wegerif (2010, 51) referred to as "creativity 1," the playfulness of coming up with new ideas, and "creativity 2," the focus on creating something of value. This dual criterion of *originality and value* constitutes the core of a scientific approach to creativity, but it is important to not forget that, behind its relative simplicity, one can find a complex history of thinking about creation, from antiquity onward (see Sternberg and Lubart 1999; also Chapter 8). Of course, the term "creativity" itself has been with us for a considerably shorter period of time than "creation" has; the former gained widespread usage only in the twentieth century. Similarly, the enthusiasm for what "creativity" means only emerged fully, in Western society at least, in the second half of the twentieth century (see Weiner 2000).

It is difficult to summarize centuries of thought on creativity, and this will not even be attempted here. What needs to be highlighted, though, is that explanations for both the capacity to generate novelty and the appreciation of novelty varied according to historical periods and reflected the main concerns and conceptions of the day. If in pre-Renaissance times the notion of creation was associated strictly with God and creative work was linked to divine inspiration, the ages that followed started to forge a deep connection between creativity and genetic inheritance (Dacey 1999, 310). Two broad models of creativity gradually emerged, supported by, respectively, the zeitgeist of Romanticism and of the Enlightenment (see also Liep 2001). The *artist* and the *scientist*, the two classical faces of the "creator," have shaped and continue to shape our collective imagination of what it means to be a creative person. Important to our argument here, the modern admiration for art and science as high forms of human achievement derives largely from separating artists and scientists from the processes of everyday living (see Dewey 1934 for a discussion about creativity in art). Children's creative expression, an intrinsic part of these everyday experiences, pales in comparison to the breakthroughs of acclaimed artists and prolific scientists.

This leads us to the conclusion that there are many possible "readings" of creativity, and they can be found equally in scientific and popular discourses. The most prominent of these, spread across historical times up to the present day, stems from an association between creativity and *genius*. The towering figure of the genius, with its overtones of "individuality, insight, outstanding ability and, in particular, fertility" (Mason 2003, 111), largely contributed to the rupture mentioned above between "creating" and "living." Geniuses are rare, they are special, they stand apart from society, and their role is to revolutionize it—to radically change our perspective of the world, usually for the better. The vast majority of us (including all children) cannot aspire to this.

Nevertheless, the paradigm of the genius did not remain unchallenged. The psychology of the 1950s contributed greatly to imposing a new perspective on creativity. According to this perspective, each and every individual is creative (albeit to different degrees), and this capacity we are born with can and should be educated. In this vision, children gained their "right" to creativity, however modest its expression might be. Still, the mainstream psychological theory of creativity—as progressive as it seems compared to the claustrophobic fixation on the genius—failed to acknowledge the social and cultural embeddedness of creative work. Creativity does not burst forth from nowhere (as in the case of the genius) or from the individual alone (as cognitive models propose); rather, it exists *in between* self and others, creator and audience, individual and community. The We-paradigm of creativity (see Glăveanu 2010b; Chapter 2), which is gaining momentum in contemporary debates, considers creativity to be a collaborative and intersubjective enterprise.

To summarize, creativity is a relatively young term that has enjoyed a rich legacy of meanings and interpretations. The most pervasive of them until recently was the genius approach, a "romantic model" (Sefton-Green 2000, 220) rooted in the exceptional creative powers of the (male and adult) creator. More "cultural" readings of creativity, on the other hand, strive to reconnect it with the processes of everyday community life. The notion of children's creativity is just one of the many points of fracture between these two approaches. To better understand the arguments of both sides, we need to take a closer and more systematic look at what qualifies children as creative or uncreative.

12.3. The Creative Child? Junctions and Disjunctions

To organize our inquiry into if and why children can be considered creative, the following discussion will be built around the "canonical" four Ps of creativity theory and research: product, process, person, and press (or "pressure," meaning the environment, mostly social but not exclusively). Originally established by Rhodes (1961/1987), this framework and its categories are widespread and have the advantage of structuring a rather multifaceted phenomenon. On the downside, as Barron (1995, 32) noticed, a strict separation between product, process, and person can only be an oversimplification, since in reality the three stand as interconnected in every creative activity (see also a "rewriting" of this framework from a cultural perspective in Chapter 14). For the purposes of our analysis, though, this particular segmentation helps to accentuate two contrasting notions of children and creativity and their immediate implications.

12.3.1. The Product Perspective

As previously noticed, our contemporary psychology of creativity is founded on the study of creative products. This focus on products is justifiable from a scientific perspective: products—paintings, inventions, mathematical demonstrations, designed objects, and so on—are readily available for evaluation and perhaps even measurement. Their originality is there to be observed and judged, and their value becomes apparent when products are incorporated into current social practices. "Creative" products are *original* in the sense that there is a distance between them and what (we believe to have) existed before them. They have an air of spontaneity and novelty, and they generate surprise and curiosity in their viewers. Considering at least this last remark, children's productions can be classified as creative. The way young children depict the world, especially at a preschool age, is a constant source of amazement and delight for parents and teachers and for adults in general. Their "freshness" of perspective, their "boldness" in breaking with realism, and their "easiness" in disregarding social conventions make children's drawings, for example, a perfect illustration of what "creativity" really is. It is no wonder then that the great Pablo Picasso allegedly said, "It took me four years to paint like Raphael, but a lifetime to paint like a child." Modern art, in its present form, strongly embraces childlike playfulness and experimentation.

And yet we have virtually no child artists, in the sense that Picasso was. Children may draw and paint and tell stories, but their drawings and stories, enmeshed in the flow of everyday life, are easily lost and have no particular *value* for society. At best, children come to "reinvent" things or ideas that we already have and know. Outside of the microuniverse of the child and his or her family, children's expression is generally worthless, especially on a historical scale. And the historical scale is, as we well remember from before, one crucial point of focus for "romantic" or "genius" readings of creativity (Stein 1953, 311). Even when "child geniuses" are discovered, as examples of extreme giftedness, their present works are appreciated in anticipation of future greater achievement, presumably reserved for adulthood (yet such prophecies are rarely fulfilled). On the whole, though, much of what "ordinary children" do and say is never really captured in the form of tangible products, and even when this is the case, it is rare for these products to possess enduring value.

This raises a very interesting topic of reflection for creativity researchers. If we restrict creativity to products, we are bound to miss out on much of what creativity is or can be. Creativity commonly manifests itself as a process, and attempts at inferring the creative process from product alone are bound to be as successful as trying to turn fossils into living creatures. The "product bias" (Runco 2007a, 384) needs to be more consistently addressed, and there are signs of clear dissatisfaction with it. Researchers such as Keith Sawyer (2000) have been pointing for several years to the importance of *performance* and *improvisation*. This line of inquiry would presumably be much more fertile for recognizing and understanding children's creativity. In the words of Sawyer,

> Because performance, particularly in the more improvisational genres, is ephemeral and does not generate any lasting ostensible product, it has been easy to neglect. Even though performance has

rarely been a subject for creativity research, it may actually represent a more common, more accessible form of creativity than privileged domains such as the arts and sciences. If one recognizes that all social interactions display improvisational elements, then everyday activities such as conversations also become relevant to creativity theory. (Sawyer 1997, 2)

12.3.2. The Process Perspective

In the previous section, it was suggested that a process rather than a product orientation would be much more appropriate for our understanding of creativity, including the creativity of children and ordinary people. And yet, upon closer scrutiny, how sure are we that children's internal and external processes and activities can be classified as "creative"? On the surface, at least, there seem to be clear *parallels* between the child's play and the creator's work. Gardner (1982, 90), for instance, pointed to several reasons why child and artist belong to the same category. On the one hand, the enjoyment of the task is obvious in both cases, and so is a willingness to disregard common conventions. Also, both children and artists, as well as creators in general, employ a series of means allowing them to comprehend and express ideas and emotions. Engel (1993) advocated a similar position referring to the expressiveness of children's play and the experiential aspect of being creative. The discovery of the fact that blue and yellow make up green is accompanied by the same intense emotions that adult creators have in their famous "Eureka" moments. And yet, many of these points, as the authors who formulate them acknowledge, are open to contestation. Does a child's enjoyment come from the real awareness of what he or she has created? Does his or her apparent disregard for norms and traditions reflect any knowledge of what this means? Is the experience of invention understood in the same way?

All these questions reveal one major aspect that seems to characterize the adult's creative process but not the child's, and that is *intentionality*. In the general literature on creativity, this aspect, implying goal-directed and conscious action, is gaining more and more interest. Creativity, many claim, needs to integrate the intentional aspect, otherwise we would be left with considering dreams or accidents as creative, and this seems unacceptable. As Weisberg (1993, 243) clearly states, "Novelty brought about by accident would not qualify as creative, no matter how valuable the outcome." He emphasizes this point to the extent of proposing that "goal-directed novelty" should be integrated into our conventional definition of creativity. This is also supported by authors such as Gruber and Wallace (1999, 94), who see a complete definition of creative products as adding purpose and duration to the traditional novelty and value criteria. The consequences for children's creativity, though not only for children's creativity, seem clear enough. The "scribbling with crayon on paper of a monkey," the "random banging on a piano of an infant," and "the

239

free-associational 'words-salads' of the schizophrenic" are to be disregarded by creativity researchers (Weisberg 1993, 243). Reviewing some critiques of the idea of children's imaginative capacities, Gardner (1982) enumerates lack of control, of deliberate intention, and of the ability to select among alternatives. In conclusion, "From this point of view, children's *apparently* imaginative activities are best written off as happy accidents" (Gardner 1982, 169).

Once again, on the surface, this association between intentionality and creativity seems legitimate, but it betrays an implicit assumption that human beings are *rational* and *goal-directed* thinkers and creators. The myth of the "great creator"—deliberately engaged in a large-scale project to revolutionize science, art, and society, planning ahead and knowing all the details and implications of *his* actions—doesn't actually pass the test of empirical evidence. As it turns out, creators are not fully aware at each and every moment of where their work is going and how it will turn out. The creative process is defined by moments of unconscious incubation, by accidents and discoveries, by losing and finding one's way. Realizing that this is the case, authors like Weisberg are quick to add that accidental discoveries (e.g., that of penicillin) are not creative but can become so if and when "the individual realizes that the accident could be plumbed further" (Weisberg 1993, 243). What at a macrolevel and in retrospect seems a planned and conscious journey looks at a microlevel like a continuous cycle of microdiscoveries, of uncertainties and reevaluations. This state of affairs has been superbly captured by John Dewey in his proposition of seeing the (artist's) creative work as a constant cycle of *doings* (acting on the world) and *undergoings* (taking in the reaction of the world). The creator creates not in a vacuum but in a physical and social environment, and the creative process is intrinsically linked to this environment. Furthermore, instead of placing accidents at the periphery of creative action, we should consider them, as Dewey encourages us, to be at the core of an authentic experience of being creative:

> The unexpected turn, something which the artist himself does not definitely foresee, is a condition of the felicitous quality of a work of art; it saves it from being mechanical. It gives the spontaneity of the unpremeditated to what would otherwise be a fruit of calculation. The painter and poet like the scientific inquirer know the delights of discovery. Those who carry on their work as a demonstration of a preconceived thesis may have the joys of egotistic success but not that of fulfilment of an experience for its own sake. In the latter they learn by their work, as they proceed, to see and feel what had not been part of their original plan and purpose. (Dewey 1934, 144–145)

There is mounting evidence today that the creative process is not taking place "in the mind" of the person, according to his or her intentions and plans, but actually is being played out in interactions with a physical and social world.

This conclusion is supported both by creators and scientists. Paul Klee, for example, discussing the process of painting, concludes that the painter "knows a great deal, but he only knows it *afterwards*" (cited in Lynton 1975, 49). From another standpoint, Bruner shrewdly remarks, "The road to banality is paved with creative intentions" (Bruner 1962, 18). Adopting such a perspective on creativity, much more akin to a "cultural" reading of it, encourages us to revisit the notion of children's creativity. Children, especially at younger ages, don't plan and don't intend very much. But at the same time, they are very eager to infuse whatever they "create" (a drawing, a construction, a story, etc.) with meaning and different interpretations. The same drawing becomes the basis for multiple stories, the same construction the starting point of different games. The "happy accidents" referred to above are indeed happy, prompting meaning-creation further and further.

12.3.3. The Person Perspective

Creativity as a strictly personal (or intrapersonal) affair was criticized above, and yet what centuries of thinking about "creation" and decades of creativity research have shown is precisely the fact that creativity was (and still is to a large extent) considered an individual attribute. The person of the genius is responsible for "creating," and, more recently, the personality or cognition of the individual was seen as the locus of creativity (Glăveanu 2010b; Chapter 2). When applied to children, the person definition is bound to run into a serious problem. As argued in Section 12.1, children have by and large historically been considered not as "real" but as future persons, as "becoming" persons. As such, the personality or cognitive structures of the child are in permanent construction and transformation; thus, How can we legitimately talk about a child's stable creative traits? Nonetheless, some authors can and do. For example, Dudek (1973, 6) was confident in arguing that "what we call creativity in children would seem to fall under the definition of creativity as personality trait." This attitude or trait was not called creativity (unsurprisingly, given the controversy presented here) but *expressiveness*, a precursor of later creative achievement. Expressiveness stands for characteristics such as spontaneity, openness, outgoingness, and aliveness. It was of course noted that this quality of the child is not really stable, at least below the age of five (15).

What is it, again, that makes authors so reluctant to talk directly about the creativity of children? The person perspective adds to the process perspective in this regard. The lack of full *self- and others-awareness* is pointed to when disregarding children's expressive efforts. Children, it is believed, reflect rarely on themselves and even less on whether they are creative or artistic (Engel 1993). How could they? And even when the awareness of doing things differently is granted to them, a lack of appreciation for rules and conventions is lamented (Gardner 1982, 89). Related to this point, children as persons "in becoming" lack a real *knowledge base* to support their "creativity." Several authors have noticed in the work of great creators "an extensive amount of time between their initial exposure to the field and production of their first significant work" (Weisberg 1999, 227). This has been formalized by Gardner (1993) as the "ten-year rule." Applying this logic to children would mean that if one seriously starts to engage with a domain at the age of two, chances are that only at twelve years of age would a remarkable contribution be made. Fortunately or unfortunately, children are much less focused and determined than this—they learn about the world in general, not about some obscure segment of it. The "great creation" paradigm again limits the meaning of what constitutes creative work.

The scientific community is gradually becoming disenchanted with the perspective of locating creativity in the person, in personality traits or cognitive mechanisms. There are plenty of reasons for this. To begin with, measures of personality or cognition (such as divergent thinking) did not demonstrate high predictive validity. This is most obvious in the case of children, whose creative "potential" is constantly scrutinized with the hope of determining who will be the creators of tomorrow. However, measures of "expressiveness," for example, are not predictive of future performance (Dudek 1973, 15). At a deeper level, this dissatisfaction with intrapersonal explanations of creativity resulted from acknowledging that creating is not an individual affair but rather involves the individual in relation to society and culture. This aspect starts to be reflected in the "press" factor discussed below.

12.3.4. The Press (Social) Perspective

Before putting children's creativity to the "test" of this last factor, it is important to make a general note about it. In regard to emphasizing social influences on creativity, the "press" factor might initially seem quite in tone with a "cultural" reading of creativity. This is and is not so because, beyond stating that the social and cultural are significant when we talk about creativity, "cultural" approaches also have a special way of understanding the social and the cultural. Mainstream psychology (including social, developmental, and creativity psychology) has often considered the social as an outside factor, influencing the thinking and behavior of the individual, putting certain "pressures" (hence press) on them, and directing them. Cultural psychology makes a point of considering society and culture as working from "within" and not (only) from the "outside" of socialized individuals. Institutions and social structures exist on the "outside," but the symbolic world they populate can only be developed "in," and especially "in between," persons (for a more general discussion, see Part A of this book). The relevance of this observation will become clear in the following discussion.

Are children creative in relation to the social and the cultural world? They certainly belong to this world and make constant efforts to apprehend it and become part of it. These efforts, defining the developmental process, are in fact revealing the "creativity" of adjusting to an outside space, which is at times comfortable and familiar, at times scary and dangerous, but most of all overwhelming in its demanding complexity. And yet, many would argue that it is precisely because children don't have anything to contribute to this "space" that they cannot and should not be called creative. Csikszentmihalyi's (1988) model of *person–field–domain* illustrates this aspect:

> This is an epistemological issue; in my view, it is society that consti-
> tutes creativity; therefore you can't say that a child has any creativity
> to be suppressed until a certain segment of society—the *field*—
> construes it as such. I don't know what it means to say that children
> are creative or that they display creativity. Usually what people mean
> by these terms is that children often appear to adults to be original,
> imaginative, or nonconforming. One could just as well interpret such
> behavior as ignorance of rules, or inability to follow them. There is
> really no evidence that this relates to adult creativity, as we usually
> think of it—that is, as an original response that is *socially valued
> and brought to fruition.* (Csikszentmihalyi in Sawyer et al. 2003, 220)

Other authors agree with this position. Feldman remarks, for example, that it is true that "no child has ever added to a culturally valued body of knowledge" (in Sawyer et al. 2003, 219). The issue of (social and cultural) value, touched upon above, gains its true proportion when we consider it in light of social mechanisms. Consistent with his epistemology, Csikszentmihalyi is ready nevertheless to acknowledge the fact that children's productions can be "valu-able" indeed for parents and teachers, but as long as there is no constituted domain and field for them, they remain "peripheral to every culture"; as such, "The creativity of such productions is not very relevant" (Csikszentmihalyi in Sawyer et al. 2003, 220).

This particular vision brings us right back to the first observation regarding the two understandings of culture. On the one hand, we have a structural, insti-tutional, and highly formalized version of culture, adopted by Csikszentmihalyi and others. On the other hand, we hold a vision of culture as a micro *and* macro phenomenon, dynamic and open to the "small creations" that keep it alive and give it continuity. Culture as a set of symbolic and material artifacts, of norms and conventions, of types of knowledge and behaviors, doesn't need to be embodied in a recognized field or domain to exist as such (see Glăveanu 2011c or Chapter 3; Willis 1990). Culture exists and is produced between people as well, in families, in schools, on the streets, etc. Contributing to these (micro) cultures is no less significant than contributing to institutionalized domains such as the arts or sciences. Without all these ordinary contribu-tions, we would not be able to speak of culture or society. Great creations are remarkable, but small, mundane ones are very much significant in their own right. And it is this kind of significance that children's "creative" activity gains and generates. As Engel (1993) rightfully observes, the classroom context, for example, is a cultural system in itself, comparable in this sense to artists' studios, scientists' laboratories, and inventors' testing rooms.

12.4. A Practical "Bet" and Its Implications

Our analysis of arguments for and against the idea of children's creativity has revealed thus far a very complex picture. Indeed, there is no single uncontested criterion that can help us to clearly distinguish the creative from the uncreative. Furthermore, each criterion discussed above (originality, value, intentionality, etc.) is deeply and intricately connected to our general conceptions about children and creativity as such. In order to simplify things—though in this regard simplifications can be misleading—we can identify two general approaches to how we conceptualize children on the one hand and creativity on the other. Children are depicted in our theories as either *passive and receptive*, depending on the outside world and simply "taking in" the influence of their environment, or as *active and interactive*, responding from an early age to the world around them and developing through interactions with others, where both child and other shape the course of the interaction. In the case of creativity, the claim has been made for a distinction between *romantic or genius* readings of the phenomenon, based on the image of the great creator and the revolutionary creation, and *cultural and social* readings, which seek to connect great creative achievements to the everyday productions of "ordinary" people.

In this simplified landscape, it becomes clear that persons (including scientists) who endorse the idea of a passive child and hold a genius vision of creativity will most likely answer the question "Are children creative?" in a negative way. In contrast, an active child and a cultural perspective on creativity may support a positive answer to this question. Of course, there are many more positions "in between," and some people may agree with some arguments and not others. My personal views incline toward the positive answer, but this chapter is not meant to be an exercise in discovering the "truth" about children and creativity. Written from a constructionist perspective, the assumption I started with is that different readings or stories we tell about people, objects, and processes of the world need to be understood in their own right. Neither one of the answers, in this case, is more "correct" than the other simply because (and this is the central aspect of the argument) they are *drawing from different interpretative frameworks*. To simplify even further, they serve as two differently colored pairs of glasses that provide two different views of the same object.

That being said, constructionism is not meant to be an "everything goes" type of epistemology. Though different constructions of the world are possible, this doesn't mean that all are *equally useful* for acting in the world. With the risk of turning to pragmatism toward the end, I will propose looking at children's creativity in a way similar to Pascal's wager about the existence of God (see 2008 edition). In essence, his argument was that believing in the existence of God is bound to bring many advantages if the belief turns out to be correct, while still being advantageous even if proved wrong. The alternative belief is detrimental in both cases. Applying this to our particular question, we can say the following: adopting a position favorable to seeing the child as active and creativity as incorporating "ordinary" and "extraordinary" accomplishments turns out to have many more theoretical and practical benefits than the alternative. Let me briefly elaborate on these in three domains: child psychology, the psychology of creativity, and education.

Child psychologists—starting with the premise that children are indeed creative from an early age, in their own ways, supported by social interaction and using the means they have at their disposal—would probably focus more on how novelty is produced and the role it plays in the development of the child (see also Feldman 1994 on creativity and developmental shifts). They would recognize the efforts made by children, from early in life, to engage with the world around them, to adjust to it while at the same time trying to make it a more hospitable and secure place. Cultivating a vision in which children's *agency* is implied would make us look more carefully at moments of microinteraction between children and their peers, families, teachers, etc. and at how they are driven by the active and creative involvement of *both* parties. This particular line of research is increasingly being explored by authors who focus on the bidirectionality of parent–child relations (Kuczynski and Navara 2006; Lawrence and Valsiner 2003), on formulating a dynamic theory of socialization (Kuczynski and Parkin 2007; Maccoby 1992), and on an interpretative approach to development (Corsaro and Eder 1990). All these elaborations are fundamentally challenging the notion of the child as passively modeled by parents and broader social systems. Indeed, children "build in innovative ways on the structure of the culturally organized information that they experience in interaction with others and in their exploration of the man-made physical environment" (Valsiner 1997, 176). A developmental psychology founded on this kind of ethos would bring the "creative" expressions of the child to the forefront, studying them more in the context of the life and experience of their "author" and less in comparison to those of the adult. Children's meanings associated with their creations would be valued, and this would reduce the risk of adult-centric and restrictive interpretations.

For creativity theory and research, accepting the existence of children's creativity would have consequences that are even more radical, and some of these have been captured in the sections above. Genius readings of creativity have been dominant in past and present literature on the topic and have obscured the fact that "creative" expression should not be restricted to an individual or small group of individuals but rather should be reconnected to the life of human communities. As Bateson (1999, 153) notes, denying everyday life creativity "deprives us of a range of models for the creative process." The present chapter exposed some of the potentially beneficial consequences of reading creativity through cultural "lenses": a more fluid process- and performance-based approach, a grounding of creative action in the social and material world, and a recasting of culture as an emergent phenomenon. This approach would also encourage researchers to understand the mechanisms of little-c creativity, a notion extensively discussed by Anna Craft. As an attitude toward life revolving around the "resourcefulness and agency of ordinary people," (Craft 2001, 49), little-c creativity is an expression of "possibility thinking" founded on imagination, curiosity, and play (Craft 2002). But above all, what children's creativity would mean for creativity research is the tendency to operate with a broader, more comprehensive *definition* of creativity. "Ordinary" creativity can and does have "extraordinary" effects, and among them are the maintenance and constant re-generation of human culture. Furthermore, what this "extended definition" does in the end is reveal the false dichotomy between "higher" and "lower" forms of creativity. These are neither separated by a "gap" nor placed on a "continuum"; rather, the "higher" is *built upon* the "lower," without which it would not exist. Celebrated forms of creativity burst forth from the fertile ground of everyday, playful creation. This is what Wegerif (2010, 38) hinted at when considering that

> it is not possible to get creativity 2, socially valued products, without first having lots of creativity 1, the everyday creativity of playfully coming up with lots of new and different ideas, connections and ways of seeing things regardless of whether or not these are socially valuable.

Finally, when it comes to educational practices, it is quite obvious why recognizing children's creativity is better than the alternative: it manages to put it on the agenda of educators and encourages them to consider creative expression and to foster all those behaviors and attitudes linked to it (Craft 2005). Creativity has come to be seen as one of the most valuable attributes a person can have, perhaps throughout the world (Mason 2003) but at least in modern Western societies, and this has certainly led to the universalization of creativity in the contemporary world of education (Jeffrey and Craft 2001). Thinking about ways in which this quality can be cultivated in children is bound to bring together parents, teachers, and scientists from a variety of disciplines. Believing in the existence of creativity in children will further help "materialize" it by drawing more attention to all instances with potential creative value. Csikszentmihalyi argued, as we have seen from the above, that a domain such as "children's art" is peripheral to our culture and thus children's creativity is a contradiction in terms. This positions us inside a *vicious cycle* where not legitimizing creativity leads to not encouraging or even discovering it, which in turn explains the absence of more institutionalized forums concerned with it and also reinforces the attitude of ignoring it even as a possibility. It is plausible that if more people consider children to be creative, there will be stronger societal-level transformations to allow for the display and celebration of this form of creativity. However, encouraging creativity in educational settings is not without its own problems and dilemmas, both practical and theoretical, psychological and pedagogical. Craft (2005) highlighted several of these, from the assumption that creativity is universal in nature and always a "good thing" in the classroom to the more pragmatic relationship between knowledge, the curriculum, and creativity. These are all issues that require deep consideration and creative thinking on the part of theorists and practitioners alike.

12.5. Concluding Thoughts

This chapter has addressed the issue of children's creativity and has argued for considering children as active and creative beings who develop forms of creative expression in interaction with adults and through play and experimentation with cultural artifacts. The question about children's creativity is far from meaningless. In fact, Vygotsky himself stated that "one of the most important questions of child psychology and pedagogy is the question about creativity in children, its development and its significance for the general development of the child" (Vygotsky, cited in Smolucha 1992, 51). And yet, despite its importance, we know little about the formative conditions of creativity in children (Feldhusen 2002, 182). This is arguably the result not only of the intricacy of the phenomenon (which, on its own, could very well explain the slow progress) but, importantly, also of our general conceptions about children and about creativity. Opting for an understanding of children as creative would potentially *transform* our theories about children *and* creativity and also influence our educational practices. In itself, though, this is only the beginning of a new set of questions and research interests. Two of great importance are research methodologies for studying children's creativity and the domain-specificity or domain-generality of children's creative expression. Both areas are not "new" in any way, yet much of the work done in these fields reflects some problematic assumptions. For example, testing children's creativity often starts from the premise that creativity is an intrapersonal feature or that creative products can be rated by experts who have little access to process information. Also, when it comes to creativity and domains, adopting a cultural perspective would support domain-specificity with additional concepts such as the "local" embeddedness of creative action and the dependence of the symbolic function on available systems of tools and signs. All these insights and many more will be lost, though, if we refuse to entertain the idea that children and creativity form not only a likely but also a promising pair.

13

Creativity Development in Community Contexts: The Case of Folk Art[1]

This chapter explores the creative expression of children by examining their engagement with the folk art of Easter egg decoration in an urban and a rural community in Romania. At a theoretical level, it considers creativity development from a sociocultural perspective and links it to the emergence of the symbolic function and to children's capacity to construct representations that mediate their relationship with the world. This function, following the Vygotskian (1978) tradition, is central for the psychological development of the child and is supported by constant interactions with adults. However, creativity research on children has traditionally been preoccupied with testing creative potential and using tasks that, though appropriate for this age group, can be slightly artificial (and problematic when it comes to construct validity, see Almeida et al. 2008). The study presented here aims to consider children's creative activity within the context of *an existing cultural practice*, and this sets it apart from most other investigations of creativity in childhood.

Easter egg decoration is widespread in Romanian communities and offers an ideal occasion for children to express their creative potential (by decorating actual eggs or simply drawing them on paper). My exploration of this practice, though, will not be a psychometric one. The following research focuses not on "how creative children are" (by evaluating drawings of Easter eggs) but rather on "how children are creative." What is of interest is not measuring creativity but understanding the ways in which it is manifested in the case of two age groups (seven- and ten-year-olds) in two different milieus (the capital, Bucharest, and the village of Ciocănești). The Romanian context is particularly interesting considering the fact that children, especially in rural settings, are in contact from early in life with a variety of crafts and traditions that both define and contribute to community life (Zahacinschi and Zahacinschi 1985). It thus

---

[1] From *Thinking Skills and Creativity*, 9 (2013), Glăveanu, V. P., Creativity development in community contexts: The case of folk art, 152–164, © 2012 by Elsevier, reprinted with permission.

becomes all the more important to understand if and how socialization within different communities (urban and rural) shapes artistic creative expression.

13.1. Theoretical Background: Creativity and Development in a Community Context

Cultural-psychological approaches start from the premise that human development, including the development of creativity, is *community-based and culture-inclusive* (see Josephs and Valsiner 2007). This assumption has been elaborated by theorists such as Rogoff (2003, 3–4), who stated that "people develop as participants in cultural communities," and development itself can be understood only with reference to the cultural practices and circumstances of these communities. Lave (1991, 64–65) as well emphasized that learning is a social phenomenon constituted through participation in "communities of practice." In light of this, Easter egg decoration is a good example of children developing creative engagement within the cultural traditions of their community. Engagement here is considered *creative* whenever it adds an "unfamiliar" element, however minor or idiosyncratic it may be, to a traditional procedure. This element of creativity makes cultural practices vastly diverse, finding different manifestations in different communities, even within the same society. Individual engagement with craftwork in this study thus needs to be evaluated locally and contextually and linked to wider processes of socialization and enculturation.

The term *socialization* often carries with it an unwanted image of the child as initially "outside" of culture and society and gradually becoming "filled up" by both, shaped and determined by external, socializing forces. A deterministic model is thus set in place, a model in which children start off as passive and asocial beings. In contrast, the perspective on socialization and enculturation processes adopted in this chapter stresses their fundamentally active and constructive nature (Valsiner 1997). There is interpretation and transformation when things are internalized by the child as much as when they are externalized (Kuczynski and Navara 2006), and this contributes to the dynamic character of cultural practices and, with them, of community life itself. This approach thus considers socialization and creativity to be fundamentally related since learning the "ways" of one's community offers a framework for novel expressions *without* fully determining them. Children's creative activity is fostered by interactions with others and the assimilation of culture precisely because children are agents and not passive recipients of acculturation practices (Bruner 1999).

This vision and cultural-psychological approach are greatly indebted to the groundbreaking work of Vygotsky (1978), for whom the internalization and creative use of tools and signs—forms of mediation between subject and world and subject and self, respectively—represents a momentous achievement in our existence as human beings. It is when children begin to articulate language and symbolic systems that they start to master situations and themselves; they regulate activity with the help of speech (first external and gradually internalized) and plan ahead so as to escape the constraints of the "here and now." For Vygotsky, the symbolic function and use of language are inconceivable outside a social environment and child–adult relations. Important for the present discussion, the origins of creativity can be found in this process of passing from direct to mediated forms of behavior (Vygotsky 2004), something reflective of our capacity for *symbolic representation*.

Indeed, to represent "is central to the ontogenetic development of the human child" (Jovchelovitch 2007, 10) and also to the development of creativity. At about one and a half years of age, children become able to represent something (the referent) with the means of something else (the sign)—the origins of the symbolic or semiotic function (Piaget and Inhelder 1966). Being capable of symbolic activity is an enormous achievement—"in a sense, the greatest imaginative leap of all" (Gardner 1982, 170)—and offers the basis for later creative expression, from free play to high art and science. The theory of social representations (SRT) can provide a useful framework in this regard, based on its recognition of the social and creative dimensions of knowledge systems and their evolving nature from early childhood onward (Duveen and Lloyd 1990; Moscovici 1984). All children are born into a world "already structured by the social representation of the communities into which they arrive" (Duveen 2001, 259). Children gradually acquire the symbolic systems of representation specific to their particular sociocultural location, making what was at first unfamiliar to them familiar through integration in their developing knowledge systems.

Of key importance for SRT, children "tame" unfamiliarity in a *potentially creative and constructive manner*, not copying but selectively appropriating representations while acting in the world and communicating with others (in line with the active and selective notion of internalization adopted here). As they grow, children come to express their creativity as well by further elaborating, and sometimes problematizing, established norms and representations, thus making the familiar unfamiliar (Wagoner 2008) and, in the process, generating new symbolic (and material) means. Literature on enculturation points to similar actions when distinguishing between mechanisms of *acquiring* and *inquiring* (Shimahara 1970)—of assimilating cultural norms and practices and transforming them through personal engagement. It is these two types of dynamic that will be used later in this chapter to conceptualize children's creativity in Easter egg decoration and its developmental trajectory.

13.2. Research Context and Rationale for the Study

Much has been written about children and art (see Fox and Schirrmacher 2012; Gardner 1982; Hurwitz and Day 2007), but to date cultural practices such as folk art have attracted little interest. This is an important domain, however, because artistic expression in the case of children is typically both expressive of acculturation and socialization procedures (as argued above) and a key contributor to these processes. The general aim of this research, therefore, is to explore the developing engagement of children with a creative type of activity—namely, Easter egg decoration—in two different settings in Romania: the urban milieu of Bucharest and the rural community of Ciocăneşti. This folk art was chosen on account of its *richness of practices and associated symbolic meanings* as well as its *deep connections to community life* (Newall 1971). Indeed, in Romania, egg decoration is a long-standing tradition, very much associated with the widespread rural life and strong Christian religion of the country (Glăveanu 2010c or Chapter 6; Gorovei 2001; Marian 1992; Zahacinschi and Zahacinschi 1992). Today, Easter eggs are decorated all through the year, especially in the northern rural parts of the country, and are sold through what has become a growing national and international market for such products. Traditional egg decoration involves the successive use of wax for drawing the motifs (with an instrument called chişiţă) and repeated immersion in color. In the end, the wax is wiped off and the egg reveals its intended model. At present, the practice has diversified greatly, and one can find variations in the techniques (e.g., wax can be colored and kept on the egg), colors (nowadays more colors are used, including green, blue, and purple), and motifs (e.g., the use of colored wax allows folk artists to "draw" landscapes and different scenes on the eggs).

Another important reason why this particular craft was chosen has to do with the fact that a relatively unitary decoration style at a national level leaves room for plenty of local *variations*; "urban" eggs are different from "rural" ones, and even in villages, different groups of decorators have their own particular sets of colors and motifs. As such, egg decoration is very much expressive of local identities and represents a "vital" tradition, characterized by transformation and change working from within a relatively stable system of practices (Eisenstadt 1973; Negus and Pickering 2004). On the whole, Romanian Easter eggs are defined by geometric decoration, schematic depiction of symbolic elements (most often the cross), and the use of the color red, which is associated with the blood of Christ.

In an urban setting such as Bucharest, eggs are usually made only for the Easter celebration and for the home, and they are shared with family and friends (the custom is to knock them against each other saying, "Christ has risen," answered by "Truly He has risen"). They are typically monochrome, red and of other colors, but they may also be decorated with leaves or stickers. In the village of Ciocăneşti, the eggs used for Easter in the family are similar to the above, though they might have some simple designs and messages written with wax. But the eggs characteristic to this rural setting are decorated with wax, mostly with geometric motifs, and are traditionally painted in yellow, red, and black. A particularity of Ciocăneşti eggs is the use of black as a background color. There are several customs related to eggs in this region, many of them involving children (such as going "after eggs" in the village on Easter morning or washing one's face with water in which a red egg was placed).

It thus becomes interesting to study how children understand and "interact" with the craft as they grow up in different Romanian communities. Based on interviews with participants in this research and on the author's own ethnographic type of observation in the two contexts (see also Chapter 7), it was noticed that there are different *paths of socialization* into this practice, depending on whether the child lives in a rural or urban environment. In both Bucharest and Ciocănești, children encounter egg decoration in their families and are sometimes encouraged to take part in decorating eggs. The latter is often the case in families of rural decorators, where children learn by doing and observing others (usually they start by helping parents "fill up" with wax on yellow and red), something Rogoff (2003) refers to as guided participation. If they choose to practice traditional decoration, children are expected to exercise first "old" geometric motifs and gradually, as they become more skilled, to take the initiative and create their own eggs (never completely abandoning traditional patterns, however). In contrast, in the urban setting, there is more freedom and openness to experimentation owing to the existence of a "simplified" tradition of decoration (based mostly on the use of color). Younger children are typically invited to draw (on paper) the kinds of Easter eggs they want, using a wide range of colors and shapes. This fundamental difference between communities that hold a *more* versus *less structured and elaborate* tradition of decoration—traditions that children acquire early on through socialization—invites the questions of if and how creative engagement with this practice at young ages differs in the two settings.

13.3. Methodology Outline

Research questions and design. This study required children from first and fourth grade to decorate two egg shapes on paper, one representing how eggs are "typically made at home" and the other representing the Easter egg they "want and like most." This activity was chosen on account of its relatively high ecological validity (children in both contexts usually draw Easter eggs on paper before the holiday) and was preferred to actual decoration on account of the difficulties of working with eggs in the classroom, especially for younger children. Moreover, the intent was to consider not how the child manipulates the egg (though this could be in itself a topic for research) but what he or she considers appropriate to represent on an "Easter egg"—that is, what motifs are depicted and why. To this end, the task was followed by a brief interview conducted by the author with each participant based on his or her drawings. This was necessary in order to obtain the child's own interpretation of what was depicted, and the interviewer tried to minimize his influence on children's accounts by asking only for clarifications when needed.

Two particular questions guided this qualitative, cross-sectional investigation: (a) what is depicted (in terms of colors and motifs) on both "home" and "wanted" eggs by seven- and ten-year-olds in the two contexts and (b) what do colors and motifs represented on drawings of eggs reveal about creativity and its development, including whether there are specific patterns of engaging creatively with decoration depending on age and sociocultural context. It is important to note that the drawing task was *not* a creativity test in the sense that products were not given scores for "originality" and no hierarchy was established among them.

Participants. The participants were all pupils from one first and one fourth grade class in a state school in Bucharest and in the local school in Ciocăneşti. These particular age groups reflect some important landmarks in intellectual development: namely, the approximate beginning and ending of the stage of concrete operations in which children learn to think logically about their concrete, material environment (Piaget 1950)—a prerequisite for developing creative action through the symbolic manipulation of objects. Beyond these "cognitive" explanations, it was important also to observe school children in their engagement with a cultural practice, since, as noted by Gardner (1982, 100), when "children enter school (and possibly, in part, as a result of this entry) they gain a heightened awareness of, and concern with, the standards of their culture." The total sample of sixty-three children is described in Table 13.1.

Method. Data were collected with the help of drawings and interviews obtained before the Orthodox Christian Easter in 2009 (for the urban setting) and in 2010 (for the rural setting; this was during one of the three two-week field trips made by the author to the village in 2009 and 2010). Besides the fact that the act of decoration is essentially an act of drawing—which can be done on paper or on the egg itself—this type of activity is also recognized as enjoyable and attractive for children of all ages (Backett-Milburn and McKie 1999) and as a privileged form of self-expression during childhood (see Favez-Boutonier 1970). Interviews were based on the drawings and included questions primarily about what was depicted and why (for both "home" and "wanted" eggs). In addition, all children were asked about why they think Easter eggs are made, what they represent, and the way they celebrate Easter at home.

Table 13.1. Demographic characteristics of the sample.

	Rural		Urban		Total
	1st grade	4th grade	1st grade	4th grade	
Female	8	8	10	8	34
Male	5	7	9	8	29
Mean age	7.2	9.7	7.1	10.2	
Total	13	15	19	16	N = 63

Procedure. Having children as research participants raises some special ethical considerations (for a review, see Punch 2002) related to confidentiality, consent, and protection. In our case, parents and school authorities gave their consent, and children were asked if they wanted to participate and were told that they could withdraw from the study at any time. In class, each child was given an A5 piece of paper with the shape of an egg on it and was first asked to "decorate it in a way that is typical for the eggs you have at home for Easter." When this task was done, the respondent was given another paper with the same shape and was asked to "decorate the egg as you want and like an Easter egg to be" (he or she was also told that it could resemble the first egg if that was preferred). All the children had their own colored pencils and markers (from the art class), and the author made extra sets available (three sets of twenty colored pencils). The decoration task in each class lasted between forty and forty-five minutes. Interviews took place individually afterward and lasted for five to ten minutes.

Data analysis: coding drawings. All the interviews were transcribed verbatim, and drawings were subjected to content analysis. It should be noted that interviews were not coded per se but were used mainly as a supporting method to clarify the meaning of the drawings. The first stage of the analysis focused on *colors*, and each egg (home and wanted) was classified as either monochrome or polychrome. The number of colors used was recorded, and a note was made about the dominant color (the one that covers most of the surface). The *design* was then coded: geometric, figurative (symbols, objects, or figures), geometric and figurative, or no model/motifs. Notes were also taken about what kind of figurative elements appeared on the egg (stars, flowers, butterflies, hearts, religious symbols, etc.). Statistical comparisons of means were performed for color coding; chi-square analysis could not be meaningfully employed for motifs owing to low sample size and the fact that several categories held zero elements.

Ensuring the *quality* of this qualitative investigation was a key concern, and several measures were taken to satisfy confidence and relevance criteria (see Bauer and Gaskell 2000). Triangulation of investigators was used in the coding of drawings and interpretation of interviews. Drawings were coded independently by the author and by a coder familiar with the practice of egg decoration in Romania; agreement ranged between 89 and 100 percent (all disagreements were discussed and settled in light of coding criteria). Reflexivity was employed when approaching interview material in order to avoid imposing personal or adult-centric interpretations, and particular care was given to monitoring personal expectations about differences between the urban and rural setting. "Thick" and direct (verbatim) presentation of interview data was preferred in describing individual cases, and interpretations were checked against other observations from fieldwork (triangulation of sources) and discussed with some of the parents and teachers (communicative validation). Finally, as is the case with any qualitative investigation, the selection of cases was intended to achieve not generalizability but *transferability* of findings, which are to be treated as working hypotheses awaiting further confirmation.

13.4. Results: Children's Developing Engagement with a Creative Craft

The presentation of results is done in two stages, related to the two research questions outlined above. First, a descriptive, mostly quantitative analysis of drawings is offered in order to provide an overview of differences in content (color and motifs) between subgroups. This is followed by a qualitative discussion in which the meaning of such differences for the development of creativity is interpreted by focusing on a few cases (pseudonyms are used for participants) and using visual illustrations and verbatim comments from interviews.

13.4.1. The Content of Decoration

A first look at descriptive data shows that *color* is differently employed depending on age and social context as well as the type of egg—home versus wanted—being decorated. In the urban setting, two colors on average were used for home eggs by first graders, while only one color was typically used by fourth graders. However, both subgroups frequently applied four colors on wanted eggs. In the village, if first graders drew polychrome eggs, three colors were frequently employed, while fourth graders most often used four colors for the home egg and five for the wanted egg. Two observations can be formulated: first, *more colors tend to be used for the wanted compared to the home egg*, and second, *children from the rural setting employ more colors on average than urban children*. This should be understood in light of the fact that, as mentioned in the presentation of the research context, homemade eggs in Bucharest are usually monochrome whereas in Ciocăneşti they are usually polychrome.

To further test this first observation, a one-way ANOVA was conducted for the total number of colors (home and wanted eggs combined) in children's drawings from the four subgroups (defined by age and context). Significant differences in number of colors between the subsamples were found, $F(3, 58) = 9.91$, $p < 0.001$, $\eta 2 = 0.34$. Scheffé's post-hoc analyses pointed to the fact that the number of colors used by fourth grade children in the rural setting (m = 10.4) differs significantly from those of the other three subgroups (m = 6.68, $p < 0.05$ for first grade urban; m = 5.37, $p < 0.001$ for fourth grade urban; m = 8.46, $p < 0.05$ for first grade rural). This could be explained as the combined effect of being older and growing up in a rural setting that favors polychrome egg decoration.

Another interesting conclusion can thus be drawn by simply looking at the color differences between home and wanted eggs (see Figure 13.1).

In agreement with the findings mentioned above, it is immediately noticeable in Figure 13.1 that *wanted eggs tend to be polychrome, especially in the*

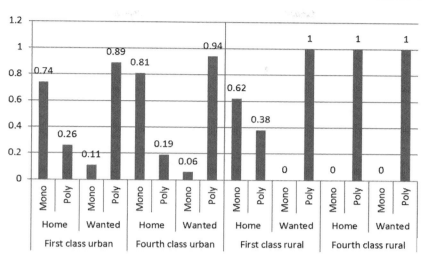

Figure 13.1. Proportions of monochrome and polychrome eggs across the sample.

rural context. The urban home egg is typically monochrome. This is slightly less true for first grade children, whose parents are sometimes inclined, for the benefit of the children, to decorate eggs a bit more. Older children in the urban setting show the most discrepant profile, with the most monochrome home eggs compared to the polychrome eggs they want and like. In the village, the home eggs children refer to in their drawings are usually less monochrome (by comparison to the urban setting); in fact, fourth graders from Ciocănești did not depict any home eggs as monochrome. Decorated polychrome eggs in the village, as argued above, constitute a shared reference, a "cultural norm" that contributes to local identity and makes these types of eggs extremely attractive to children even when, according to the interviews, Easter eggs made at home are normally monochrome (the ones used for the festivity in the family are not decorated with wax or presented at fairs or the local folk museum).

Finally, it is also interesting to notice the use of red in the decoration of both home and wanted eggs, since this is the preferred color for Easter eggs on a national scale. Again, a "norm" of depicting red (or principally red) eggs is reflected across the sample, predominantly among older children. Fourth graders seem to have *internalized this norm more*; for instance, while 16 percent of wanted eggs include mostly the color red for first grade urban, 88 percent do so for fourth grade urban. There is a difference in the rural setting as well, with 23 percent for first grade and 47 percent for fourth grade. Comments from the interviews concerning colors suggest that children tend to use the paints they "like" while being acutely aware, in many cases, of the preference given in their family to the color red or of the importance in the village of red, yellow, and black as "traditional" colors.

In terms of *models/motifs made on the eggs*, the summary of findings presented in Figure 13.2 mirrors to a certain extent the results obtained for the use of color. To begin with, it appears that children from the urban setting draw home eggs that are not decorated in any particular way (no model). In contrast, rural children usually decorate their home eggs with geometric patterns popular in their region (e.g., the star, the rhombus, the net, curvy lines). Incorporation of these motifs into home decorated eggs is strongly apparent in the case of fourth graders but was also evidenced in younger children. Furthermore, younger children from Bucharest drew primarily figurative elements (hearts, flowers, stars, animals, etc.) on the wanted egg, while younger participants from Ciocănești depicted geometric and/or figurative motifs. For the older children in the urban setting, most wanted eggs were made with geometric models (followed by geometric and figurative), while in the rural area the fourth graders preferred a combination of geometric and figurative elements. An important class of figurative elements includes religious symbols found in some drawings across the four subgroups—particularly the rural fourth graders, who at times represented complex scenes including images of the Bible and the tomb of Christ. This is an important piece of information from a developmental perspective because it suggests that *children from the urban setting "change" their decoration of wanted eggs from largely figurative to essentially geometric, while children from the village display a rather consistent combination of geometric and figurative at both age levels.* These tendencies will be accounted for, as follows, in terms of both age and sociocultural differences.

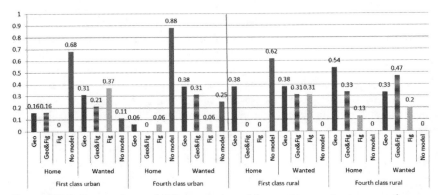

Figure 13.2. Proportions of different types of decoration content across the sample.

13.4.2. Patterns in the Development of Creative Craftwork

Two broad patterns can be abstracted from the data, and these relate to how children respond to the task of Easter egg decoration as a more or less "novel" versus "practiced" activity. In this regard, we can draw from Moscovici's (1984) insight concerning the purpose of representation and identify two processes of creatively engaging with the craft. One, commonly found among younger children, is based on *making the unfamiliar familiar*, and the other, typical among older children, relies on *making the familiar unfamiliar*. This distinction is grounded in the fact that for first graders in our sample, at least in comparison to fourth graders, the activity of Easter egg decoration is itself a more "novel" and less "practiced" craft. As such, when engaging with the task, seven-year-old children try to make sense of it on the basis of their ordinary experience of drawing at school and at home, to appropriate it in ways that make it more familiar to them. In contrast, as reflected in the interviews, ten-year-old participants are generally aware of decoration practices, and their work reflects an effort to incorporate and, at the same time, to transform some elements of the craft.

Making the unfamiliar familiar. The creative "taming" of unfamiliarity is particularly manifested among younger children. In the case of *younger children from Bucharest*, interviews revealed that usually it is the mother or grandmother who prepares eggs for Easter, generally monochrome (red but also of other colors). These children tend, however, to decorate eggs themselves, between five and ten, mostly with watercolors or markers, and they occasionally help their parents with the task of preparing and coloring eggs. Their wanted eggs are similar to what they try to do at home or what they wish they could do. The predominant types of models here are figurative, representing hearts, flowers, stars, animals, etc.—symbols children say they "prefer" or "usually draw" on paper. This last remark is telling with regard to the mechanism behind making the unfamiliar familiar. Very few children in this subgroup know, for instance, why people color eggs for Easter (thinking it is either because they are "beautiful" or because you "have to"). In appropriating this "strange" and yet pleasant task, urban first graders fill up the gaps in their knowledge of the practice *with what they are used to and what they like, familiarizing the whole experience of decoration* by adopting designs that they know from other contexts.

The two decorated eggs presented in Figure 13.3 illustrate well the operation of this creative process of turning the less familiar into what is familiar to the child. Miruna is a seven-year-old who helps her mother at home with coloring eggs and knows the traditional symbolic meaning of the color red (she associated it with the blood of Christ in the interview). Her home egg is thus red—all eggs made in her home tend to be—and she thinks this color is "the most beautiful of all." However, her wanted egg, depicted in Figure 13.3 on the left, is very colorful, as Miruna said she likes colors, and presents a series of

Figure 13.3. Wanted eggs by first grade urban participants
(Miruna left, Ana right).

motifs, from hearts, stars, and flowers to shapes that resemble writing exercises typically done in first grade. These motifs, while similar to some extent to traditional Easter egg decoration (particularly the star and the shepherd's hook motifs), are depicted here by the child without such references and in an effort to perform the decoration task in the "best" possible way, using elements that Miruna is very familiar with, draws frequently, and thinks "look good" (on paper and on the egg). Similarly, Ana is a first grader from Bucharest who helps her mother color eggs and paints some herself with watercolors. Her wanted egg (to the right in Figure 13.3) shows a red background—which Ana knows is important to remind us of the sacrifice of Christ—and a "rabbit-girl on the grass." This particular association between the image of a girl and that of a rabbit is not unusual, as she said, for the way she draws in general, and it also carries symbolic significance in this context because the Easter bunny is known to bring presents or candy to small children. In conclusion, for both Ana and Miruna, the act of decoration reveals an interesting (creative) combination between that which the girls know, from home, to be specific to Easter egg making (e.g., the use of red) and that which they would like to see on the eggs and which belongs to their immediate figurative universe (hearts, flowers, little girls, etc.).

This figurative universe is in some ways similar to but also different from that of *first graders growing up in the village*. It is similar in the sense that the drawing of flowers, hearts, and writing signs tends to be widely used by children at this age (Anning and Ring 2004), but in terms of Easter egg decoration, participants from the rural setting usually become socialized early on with

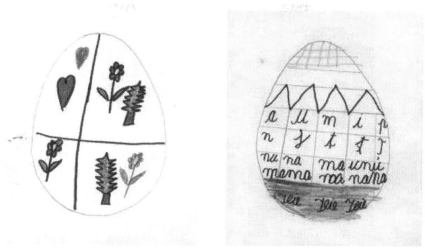

Figure 13.4. Wanted eggs by first grade rural participants (Iuliana left, George right).

the craft and are thus more "familiar" with this practice (at least in relation to forms of traditional decoration) than first graders from Bucharest tend to be. Our subgroup of seven-year-olds from the village included children who, with only three exceptions, said that traditional decoration is performed in their families and that they usually get involved in such activities (even if it is just to bring parents what they need for their work). Five of them claimed that they decorate eggs with wax, and all commented on how they take part in different Easter ceremonies, such as "going after eggs" in the village, washing their face with water in which a red egg was placed (for good health), or going to church to attend the Easter service. The strong attachment to these customs was explained by one respondent as follows: "Christ said to respect the tradition and people do this." The respect for what they call tradition is reflected in the home and the wanted eggs painted for this study; indeed, *from this early age, rural participants include references in their drawings to traditional, geometric decoration.* This tendency is so strong that even home eggs, usually monochrome according to the interviews, were depicted with geometric motifs (suggesting a "cultural norm" referred to above). However, the eggs that first graders made were not exclusively geometrical, and they did not reproduce fully a particular set of existing motifs from the village (as the interviews revealed, children at this age cannot normally name the motifs they incorporate, but only identify them as "traditional"). This is how figurative elements present in the drawings of urban participants can be found here as well, sometimes in combination with geometric patterns. Figure 13.4 illustrates this tendency.

The wanted eggs made by Iuliana and George show a combination of geometric and figurative ornaments. In both cases, the geometric part of the motifs represents elements that are commonly found in the village of Ciocăneşti (and northern Romania more generally); for instance, the segmentation in four quadrants from Iuliana's drawing, basically the starting point of any traditional decoration, and the yellow net on top of George's wanted egg, very common in the region and symbolizing the separation between good and evil (Dranca 2010). Both children decorate eggs at home with their families, Iuliana using watercolors and George decorating with wax. Their home eggs are predominantly red, something they know from home life to be highly representative for the celebration of Easter. However, their two wanted eggs presented in Figure 13.4 do not resemble any traditional products from the village, since the latter do not normally include flowers, trees, or letters. Such elements came from what children learned at home or at school and from what they were able to draw and what they thought "looked beautiful" on the egg (Iuliana said this is a kind of egg that she likes to make for her parents on Easter day). Justifications of this nature, common in interviews with children of this age, point to the *process of familiarizing the image of the decorated egg and locating it in a universe of symbols more widely experienced by the child both at home and at school* (e.g., writing exercises). In any case, it should be noted that this mechanism of making the unfamiliar more familiar, very much present in drawings of seven-year-olds from the two contexts, has its own specificities depending on whether the child lives in the urban environment of Bucharest or the rural setting of Ciocăneşti. In the village, children become accustomed to what is considered "traditional" decoration from early in life and try to appropriate it in ways specific to their age and interests. Urban participants may not be directly exposed to such a tradition, but they are certainly aware of geometric decoration, something that becomes quite clear when we turn to drawings from urban fourth graders.

Making the familiar unfamiliar. Participants around ten years of age from both contexts, having more experience with egg decoration in their families or communities, tend to illustrate the process referred to here as making the familiar unfamiliar. Interviews with respondents and discussions with their teachers, as well as observations made in the rural setting, suggest that by the time they reach fourth grade, children are well aware of Easter egg decoration practices and their meanings and procedures, including differences in decoration (between urban and rural and even among different villages in the case of participants from Ciocăneşti). For instance, in *Bucharest, fourth graders* are presented with geometric decoration during art classes, and many of them decorate Easter eggs at home, usually with watercolors and markers. Though eggs made in their families are typically monochrome (something clearly expressed also in drawings of the eggs from home), this does not exclude the

Figure 13.5. Wanted eggs by fourth grade urban participants (Radu left, Ciprian right).

use of stickers or leaves in some cases. Indeed, fourth graders from the city stated a clear interest in embellishing eggs further, and in the interviews they explained that drawings of wanted eggs were motivated by a need to make them more "beautiful" or "attractive." In this context, adopting polychrome coloring and geometric motifs for the wanted egg is in stark contrast to the much simpler eggs from home (see also the previous section). Figurative elements are not altogether absent, especially in combination with geometric forms, and one of the respondents said that she made butterflies and a heart on her wanted egg because "I was accustomed since I was a little girl to draw like this." However, for this subgroup, it is *the less familiar geometric decoration that is adopted to creatively respond to the familiarity of a simple, monochrome egg*, as reflected in Figure 13.5.

Radu and Ciprian both "challenge" and "transform" in their drawings of the wanted egg what they see at home in terms of decoration (as mentioned in their interviews and reflected in their drawings of eggs from home). In their families, it is the mother who colors eggs for Easter, and they help by bringing the colors and everything else she might need. They also decorate three or four eggs with watercolors or markers, eggs that are usually kept by the family a bit longer after the festivity. The drawings of a wanted egg for Radu and Ciprian reflect what these boys also attempt to do at home in terms of decoration, in order to make something "different" from the all-too-familiar monochrome egg. Radu, for instance (drawing on the left), used colors in the form of orange, blue, and green stripes going around the egg. The home egg made before was simply colored green, a common color employed in his family alongside the more traditional red. Similar colors are used in the family of Ciprian, who, for his wanted egg, depicted a series of geometric shapes with the help of colored lines (and he also colored certain segments of the egg in bright tones). It is interesting to note that the segmentation of the egg is geometric but very much "irregular," unlike the traditional segmentation that children from the rural setting tend to adopt in their drawings.

In an almost reversed image, an element of unfamiliarity in decoration is introduced by *rural fourth grade participants*, not only when generating novel geometric forms (geometric designs constitute, in this case, the local "norm") but also when intentionally depicting figurative elements that reinforce the religious significance of the craft. They are involved in decorating eggs but, unlike some of their younger counterparts from the same setting, not necessarily with wax. Only one respondent in this subgroup said that she decorates eggs using the traditional technique, and, in many families, people either buy or receive traditional eggs for Easter. While most ten-year-olds had stopped "going after eggs" on Easter day (since they are "too big now"), they commented on other customs, such as washing one's face with water in which a red egg was placed or going to church. Most were familiar with the symbolism of the color red and with the various motifs used in decoration (though they rarely named or discussed them). Overall, studying the drawings, we can say that decoration peaks in the case of these children, who employ traditional types of colors and motifs for both home and wanted eggs (without necessarily having such eggs at home, as noted above). Important for our discussion here, however, geometric motifs are rarely depicted in isolation; most of the wanted eggs present a combination of geometric and figurative elements. This almost-conscious decision *to integrate figurative elements despite the imposed geometric "bias" of traditional decoration, or to use colors outside of the customary yellow, red, and black*, reveals interesting forms of creative expression, as illustrated in Figure 13.6.

Ioana's wanted egg, on the left, represents a well-known motif in the rural community (the star in eight points, symbolizing femininity and perfection; Dranca 2010) in a composition that, on the whole, strongly resembles eggs made in Ciocănești but does so using a color range that is not specific to traditional decoration. Though in her family nobody decorates eggs with wax anymore (her aunt did at one time) and though she does not work with wax on eggs, Ioana is familiar with the motifs used in the village from seeing them at different festivals, from the eggs bought for home, and even from the Internet (she mentioned searching once for such motifs). She therefore knows what is common in the village, and yet she made this egg without a black background and with many more shades of red, yellow, orange, and pink because she "wanted to vary the colors." In this way, the familiarity of a popular design is, through the use of color, creatively made less familiar to viewers accustomed Ciocănești decoration. For Gabriela, whose wanted egg is presented on the right, egg decoration is equally familiar, especially since

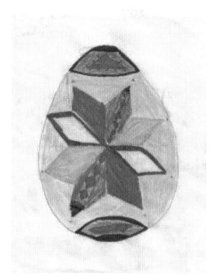 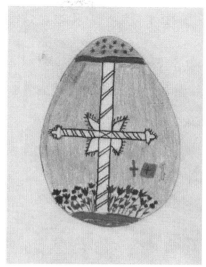

Figure 13.6. Wanted eggs by fourth grade rural participants (Ioana left, Gabriela right).

her mother actually works with wax, something she says she is not capable of because her hand is "shaking too much." However, she likes drawing eggs on paper, and this particular one "combines" many motifs she has seen, principally the cross, represented here in quite a traditional way. Gabriela wanted the egg to depict the biblical scene of the crucifixion, but she just "could not draw Jesus on the cross" because it is "too difficult." She chose to make instead other (figurative) elements surrounding the cross: flowers below, stars above, and a little cross, a Bible, and a candle on the side. These elements reveal a personal type of creative expression building on traditional forms (the cross) and their associated meaning in order to construct a setting in which elements are highly symbolic and reflective of the child's efforts to go beyond the standard geometrical designs.

13.5. Discussion: The Social and Cultural Development of Creativity

Both the quantitative and qualitative findings presented above reveal several similarities along with important differences between children in terms of creative expression, according to their age and the social milieu to which they belong (for general reviews of creativity and development, see Feldman 1999; Russ 1996). The two "routes" of creativity described earlier—the first appropriating unfamiliarity and making it more familiar, the second acting on the familiar in new ways to generate less familiar outcomes—are *complementary* and seem to follow a developmental trajectory, at least in the way children engage with the craft of Easter egg decoration. Making use of reflexivity in the interpretation of findings points to the fact that such processes can and do *coexist at any given age*—fourth graders still find elements of the craft that they are not familiar with, and first graders at age seven are by no means completely unfamiliar with the tradition of decorating eggs for Easter. Reflecting on this analytical framework helps us therefore to situate it as one possible outlook among others (for instance, drawings could be analyzed in terms of their aesthetic quality and interviews could be coded for level of detail or elaboration).

Observing and identifying these two patterns of creative engagement require a *microgenetic approach to children's creativity*, an approach that is focused on studying what Beghetto and Kaufman (2007) call mini-c creativity. Small deviations from a traditional standard need to be documented, and this entails a detailed knowledge of the cultural context in which creative activity unfolds. A study of microlevel novelty in development also continues the long Piagetian and Vygotskian traditions linked by Sawyer (2003a) to processes of emergence and reflected in constant "bursts of creativity" (Engel 1993). The idea of creativity operating in the interplay between familiarity and unfamiliarity offers us new and useful conceptual tools for operationalizing these so-called "bursts" within emergent phenomena. Moreover, this distinction resonates widely in the developmental literature, where the internalization of practices involves both assimilation and transformation through accommodation (for more parallels between the work of Piaget and creativity research, see Ayman-Nolley 1999).

If, from a purely Piagetian perspective, *age and developmental stages* are important for delineating forms of creative expression, our findings indicate that *the influence of the sociocultural location* of the child is equally strong and begins to be felt early in life, especially in those contexts in which cultural traditions regarding a certain practice (such as egg decoration) are well defined and have very distinctive features. Perhaps the most striking evidence for the influence of social and cultural contexts on how children approach the task of decoration and respond to it has to do with the types of motifs represented at different ages. First grade respondents from Bucharest, in agreement with general tendencies expected from children at this developmental stage, depicted a series of figurative elements—such as flowers, trees, stars, hearts, and butterflies—on their wanted eggs. In contrast, first graders from Ciocănești started from a higher number of purely geometric designs for both home and wanted eggs. Cultural norms thus come to organize, as children develop, forms that are otherwise produced spontaneously (Gardner 1982, 155–156).

Such observations add to a growing body of literature concerned with creativity and children (Kaufman and Baer 2006; Runco 2006) and, in particular, with the field of artistic development (Korn-Bursztyn 2012; Milbrath and Lightfoot 2010). Children's engagement with folk art represents an unexplored area that could shed light on the dynamic between spontaneous creative expression in early years and learning the normative and procedural aspects of a cultural tradition. This interplay between creativity and constraints is particularly important for children of school age, and, as our data suggest, both first and fourth graders are generally aware of the practice of egg decoration and its basic "rules." However, in contrast to the classic image of a "creativity slump" experienced around these ages (see Lubart 2003; Torrance 1967), this set of findings indicates a more flexible relationship between creative expression and the learning of societal and cultural conventions. Indeed, if we are to consider microlevel processes of making the unfamiliar familiar and making the familiar unfamiliar, we can observe the creative quality of *both* learning and practicing existing "rules." A study of these phenomena necessarily expands the focus of previous creativity research—preoccupied with the family (e.g., Shmukler 1988) and the school (e.g., Thomas and Berk 1981)—to the broader context of communities and community life.

Relating our findings back to the issue of community socialization, it becomes clear that there are significant differences between the *nature of the scaffolding* offered in the two environments. To begin with, most children from Bucharest interact with this practice only once a year, during Easter, and thus they are not constantly exposed to decoration techniques, as are many of the participants from Ciocănești. Moreover, the aims of scaffolding this activity at home or at school are different in the two settings. For urban children, decorating eggs is something done for the purpose of contributing to the celebration of Easter and perhaps as an opportunity to learn some artistic notions about chromatic contrast and harmony. In contrast, children from the village, if they learn decoration with wax, are required to help their parents and work alongside them in order to produce a larger number of eggs for selling or exhibiting at the local museum (Glăveanu 2013a; Chapter 7). The processes by which *apprenticeships* are formed and maintained are also different: working at home with limited supervision in the urban setting compared to guided participation and direct observation in the rural setting (see Rogoff 2003). All these initial results need further confirmation, but they are nonetheless highly significant because—as a longitudinal study of Zinacantec woven artifacts by Greenfield, Maynard, and Childs (2000) showed—tight connections can often be found between creativity in human development, pathways of socialization, and the macroeconomic context of community life.

13.6. Concluding Thoughts

Several *limitations* of the present study need to be acknowledged. To begin with, it adopted a cross-sectional rather than a more desirable longitudinal approach. As such, inferential leaps had to be made to connect different stages and thus capture the essence of developmental transitions. In addition, the drawing task meant focusing more on the end product and less on the processes leading to it. Further studies could have participants decorate actual eggs (since there are certainly material constraints that differentiate between this and drawing on paper) while researchers observe their activity. Finally, issues related to the development of children's manual dexterity were not explicitly considered (in any case, the set of drawings was not coded based on demonstrated technical ability or aesthetic quality).

This study offers some valuable characteristics and insights, both *theoretical* and *applied*. To start with, the present research is among the first, to my knowledge, to take a cultural practice as a case study for creative expression during childhood. Unlike mainstream studies of creativity and development, which are often acontextual and overly preoccupied with measurement, the focus here was on the creative assimilation (making the unfamiliar familiar) and transformation (making the familiar unfamiliar) of a *sociocultural form of activity*. Shifting the inquiry from "how creative is it" to "how is it creative" in the case of children can open very promising avenues for theory and research; for instance, this approach can clarify the nature of mini-c creativity from a developmental perspective.

It is thus hoped that further studies will look at children's engagement with craft and other community practices and will "test" the patterns proposed above on other samples, in other contexts, and for different types of creative activity (as creativity is very much stage- and domain-specific; Runco 2006). Such research not only would contribute to our understanding of creativity, development, and community life but also could help us to find practical ways in which to foster and develop creativity in children. One immediate possibility is to introduce children to a multitude of cultural domains and encourage them, from early in life, to reinterpret and contribute to what culture and society have to offer. Indeed, "Variation across and within communities is a resource for humanity, allowing us to be prepared for varied and unknowable futures" (Rogoff 2003, 12)—futures that children do not simply receive but must actively create.

14

The Cultural Psychology of Creativity: An Integrated Model

This book started from the premise that creativity and culture are two closely interrelated phenomena, to the point that we can identify creativity with acts of culturing (Valsiner 2007) and study it in relation to the lived experience of existing as a social and cultural being in the world. A series of conceptual and empirical arguments were put forward in previous chapters leading to this conclusion, from a consideration of theoretical foundations for the cultural psychology of creativity (Part A) and its methodological toolkit (Part B) to closer attention given to creativity as representation (Part D), as action (Part E), and as a developing phenomenon (Part F). Throughout, illustrations were taken from an extensive case study of Easter egg decoration practices in urban and rural Romanian communities (Part C). It is now the time, at the end of the journey, to reflect on what brings together these explorations in ways that consolidate the cultural psychology of creativity as a present and future discipline.

One immediate conclusion we can draw from reading the chapters included here concerns the *diversity* of theoretical ideas that cultural psychologists can build on in their effort to investigate creativity. From American pragmatism to Russian cultural-historical views of activity, from social representations to affordance theory, from the work of pioneering psychologists and philosophers like John Dewey and Mark Baldwin to the sociological perspective of Bourdieu, the theoretical soil of the cultural approach is very fertile and stimulates the development of new concepts and research directions. The methodological tools are equally diverse, and though the use of qualitative and ideographic methods is generally encouraged, the principles of conducting ecological and emic research—rather than any methodological orthodoxy—guide each investigation. The study of egg decoration demonstrates this by triangulating information from interviews, observation, subcam recordings, and drawings. The survey presented in Chapter 9 illustrates how questionnaire research can be incorporated into cultural-psychological explorations of lay beliefs.

Of great interest for cultural psychologists is how essential concepts within this emerging discipline (such as creativity, culture, action, representation, and development) can be studied contextually and without starting from rigid operationalizations that reduce, amend, or distort their meaning.

Thus, what brings together researchers animated by a cultural interest in creativity is not a particular theoretical orientation or a preferred method but rather a series of key questions that, through their formulation, demonstrate concern for creativity as a systemic, multifaceted, and dynamic phenomenon. These questions include the following: How is the meaning of creativity constructed within different cultural contexts in processes of interaction and communication between people? How is creativity enacted in daily life? How can we study its microlevel expression and relate it to ontogenetic and sociogenetic changes? What is the relation between creativity and tradition, between habits and routines, and how can we conceptualize their interdependence? What research methodologies allow us to investigate creativity as an embodied and distributed phenomenon? What is the role of materiality in creative expression and how can it be approached through an analysis of affordances within given situations? How is creative action organized in the case of different tasks and different domains (e.g., art, science, and also different subfields of these domains)? How does the creative process differ in the case of individuals and groups and what is the role of collaboration for both?

These are only a few examples, and the list can certainly be continued by readers who bring particular interests, for example those working in education, business, marketing, politics, science, technology, or design. The focus in this book was on the creativity of folk art and, more specifically, its representation, action, and development within the craft of Easter egg decoration. A legitimate question is whether findings from this rather particular area can be *transferred* (Auerbach and Silverstein 2003) to other domains. Certainly there are aspects of creativity that are found uniquely in craft. The fact that artisans create decorative patterns, drawing on old folk and religious motifs and symbols, distinguishes egg decoration from, for instance, contemporary installation art. And yet, at a more basic level, even these two extremes have much in common: the existence of more or less established traditions, the dependence on materials and the physicality of producing creative outcomes, the aim to generate an aesthetic experience for oneself and other viewers, and so forth. Scientific activities might be considered to lack some of these features, particularly the last one, but then again, who does not marvel at the elegance of certain mathematical demonstrations or the beauty of a practical solution? The analytical frameworks used to code data in the studies of craft presented here can certainly be transferred to other research contexts. Dewey's (1934) description of the cycle of doing and undergoing is not unique to artistic activities, as Dewey himself strived to demonstrate. Equally, the developmental dynamic between "making the unfamiliar familiar" and "making the familiar unfamiliar" is certainly applicable to more than the acquisition of knowledge regarding the decoration of Easter eggs.

It is this hope that animates the last chapter of the book: namely, that the integrated framework proposed here can be useful for developing new ways of thinking about creativity. Cultural psychology is perfectly equipped to promote the change from mainstream, individualistic conceptions to a broader, social and cultural understanding that, in my view, does justice to the complexity of creative expression. But, as will be argued next, this transformation needs to start from the most basic elements of the discipline—that is, from its terminology. The following section focuses on this aspect and formulates a bold proposal to rethink creativity theory by rewriting its current language.

14.1. Rewriting the Language of Creativity[1]

The language of creativity—or, better said, the language of creativity theory and research in psychology—is a language written largely from the perspective of the individual and, within individuals, from the perspective of cognitive functioning. Key terms that help us, to this day, to organize the growing literature in the field reflect not only an inherent individualism and cognitivism (specific, to some extent, to the modern construction of psychology; Gergen and Gigerenzer 1991) but also a rather static, disjointed, and acontextual approach to creativity. There is, however, a pressing need to expand our language and consequently our thinking about this phenomenon, so as to do justice to its true complexity and relational nature and to be able, ultimately, to understand and cultivate creativity in a variety of domains.

The notion of creativity, most probably deriving from the Indo-European root *ker* or *kere* (to grow) via the Latin *creatio* or *creatus* (to make grow), means ultimately to "bring something new into being" (Weiner 2000, 8). This basic understanding has led to a surprisingly high number of conceptions accumulating from the second half of the twentieth century onward. About five decades ago, an educational researcher, Mel Rhodes, already perplexed by the multitude of descriptions of creativity in his time, set out to find a unitary definition of the phenomenon (Rickards 1999). In an article first published in 1961, the only known outcome of his dissertation, Rhodes collected more than forty definitions of creativity and analyzed their content. He concluded that creativity theory reflects four distinct (and yet overlapping at times) strands labeled the person, the process, the product, and the press (roughly associated with environmental influences). That article and the particular classification

---

[1] Fragments of an article with the same title are presented in this section. © 2012 by the American Psychological Association. Reproduced with permission. The official citation that should be used in referencing this material is the following: Rewriting the language of creativity: The Five A's framework. Glăveanu, Vlad Petre. *Review of General Psychology*, Vol 17(1), Mar 2013, 69–81. doi: 10.1037/a0029528. The use of this information does not imply endorsement by the publisher.

that Rhodes proposed have exerted a great influence on creativity literature ever since, and the latter has come to be referred to as the "four Ps of creativity." In the words of the author,

> My answer to the question, "What is creativity?", is this: The word creativity is a noun naming the phenomenon in which a person communicates a new concept (which is the product). Mental activity (or mental process) is implicit in the definition, and of course no one could conceive of a person living or operating in a vacuum, so the term press is also implicit. (Rhodes 1961, 305)

It is important to notice that, for Rhodes, the four resulting strands emerged from conceptualizations that were not always mutually exclusive. As such, "Each strand has unique identity academically, but only in unity do the four strands operate functionally" (Rhodes 1961, 307). Indeed, derived from a survey of definitions, the idea of the four Ps stimulated further developments and helped researchers "locate" their efforts and make links between the different categories. Thus, the four Ps of creativity—improperly referred to as a "model," it is more akin to a framework or conceptual organizer—became, in time, part of the canonical body of theories in the creativity literature, alongside other consecrated models such as Wallas's (1926) four stages of the creative process and Guilford's (1967) distinction between convergent and divergent thinking. However, being placed at the level of metatheory, Rhodes's formulation provided more than other proposed conceptual frameworks, which consequently were located within one or another of the four Ps; it thus offered the backbone of creativity theory and research for the decades to come.

Rightfully compared by some with the periodic table of elements (Isaksen, Dorval, and Treffinger 2011, 6), this simple alliterative schema became very influential in shaping creativity as an emerging academic discipline (e.g., international conferences were structured around its elements; Rickards 1999). It is no surprise, then, that in 2004 Runco's Annual Review presentation of creativity recognized it as "probably the most often-used structure for creativity studies" (661). A quick examination of existing literature readily confirms this claim, and today one can find a multitude of articles and books using the person, process, product, press framework to structure literature reviews and even empirical research.

Several authors not only started from this framework but also attempted to extend or elaborate it further (see Cropley and Cropley 2009; Runco 2003, 2007c; Simonton 1988b), demonstrating the centrality of this model and also of the numerous debates, especially in recent years, that surround it—debates that are fruitful for stimulating a series of conceptual clarifications. In this chapter, I aim to contribute further to such efforts by "rewriting" and expanding the initial set of four elements in a way that draws inspiration from current developments in the psychology of creativity—namely, the growing importance of social, systemic, ecological, and cultural models of the phenomenon. In light of these sources, I propose a "five As" framework that includes the following elements: actor, action, artifact, audience, and affordances. Advocating this new "model" of creativity involves not only renewing existing typologies but also radically changing the lenses through which we theorize and study creative acts.

To look beyond traditional theories of the person, process, product, and press, we must incorporate insights from a series of emerging interdisciplinary or multidisciplinary areas—the most recent developments being in the field of social and cognitive psychology. These "new" theoretical perspectives, which are the basis for my proposal of a five As framework of creativity, are represented by cultural or sociocultural psychology, models of the distributed and extended mind, and ecological psychology. I argue that adopting these lenses can help researchers to go beyond a focus on isolated components, because all the approaches listed above take as a basic unit of analysis the interaction between elements (e.g., between people and between people and objects) rather than the elements themselves (e.g., person and product).

The five As framework attempts to address these limitations by rewriting our current language of creativity—from person to actor, from process to action, from product to artifact, from press to audiences and affordances (see Figure 14.1). As a discussion of each new term will soon come to show, this is more than a change of terminology; it is a fundamental change of *epistemological position*. In light of sociocultural sources, the actor exists only in relation to an audience, action cannot take place outside of interactions with a social and material world, and artifacts embody the cultural traditions of different communities.

The four Ps of creativity		The five As of creativity
Focus on:		*Focus on:*
Internal attributes of the person	*Person* ⟶ *Actor*	Personal attributes in relation to a societal context
Primarily cognitive mechanisms	*Process* ⟶ *Action*	Coordinated psychological and behavioral manifestation
Features of products or consensus around them	*Product* ⟶ *Artifact*	Cultural context of artifact production and evaluation
The social as an external set of variables conditioning creativity	*Press* ⟶ *Audience* / *Affordances*	The interdependence between creators and a social and material world

Figure 14.1. Comparing the four Ps and the five As frameworks.

This framework builds on previous work (Glăveanu 2011c; Chapter 3) that discussed creativity as a simultaneously psychological, social, and cultural process and adds to it a material dimension represented here by the creative use of affordances. It is a framework that is in line with old sociocultural models that considered mediation to be a fundamental process for human existence in the world and for psychological functioning (see Cole 1996; Jovchelovitch 2007; Vygotsky 1997). Creative action emerges out of actor–audience relations that both produce and are mediated by the generation and use of new artifacts (objects, signs, symbols, etc.) within a physical, social, and cultural environment. In the end, this environment and its affordances are also gradually transformed by creative action because the schema presents a dynamic integration of the five As: actors, audiences, and affordances in interaction, dependent on properties of local settings that are themselves part of the creative cycle. It is important to mention finally that these five elements are not meant to revise the history of the discipline. We are not, for instance, to call "actor" what we called "person" before. The present framework aims to offer an alternative position for writing and thinking about creativity, one that could transform creativity research and lead it toward a truly systemic and situated theoretical model.

The five As, like the four Ps, can also be a useful methodological tool. Murdock and Puccio (1993) used Rhodes's conception, and particularly his intuition about the overlap between elements, to propose the *contextual organizer*. This methodological instrument, which aims "to assist researchers in designing and conducting integrated research" (250), stresses the importance of studying person, process, product, and press in conjunction rather than in isolation. This, according to the two authors, generates a "contextual" understanding whenever we are able to interrelate the four facets of the phenomenon (Isaksen and Puccio 1993 refer to it in terms of "profiling" creativity). A difficulty, of course, rests in how to operationalize the four Ps in research in order to be able then to relate findings about each of the four elements. This challenge is partially resolved in the five As framework because of the interrelated meanings, referred to above, of actors, audiences, actions, artifacts, and affordances. The fact that a study of actors necessarily invites a reflection on the role of audiences or that action only takes place in relation to both audiences and the affordances of material objects certainly aids in the development of "contextual organizers." The aim formulated by Murdock and Puccio is equally valid for the five As model: "Using a 4 Ps framework with a contextual focus provides definition and direction, yet allows for in-depth focus on any one, all, or any combination of the major strands" (266).

In the end, the five As framework is not intended to offer definitive answers about the nature of creativity because, just like the four Ps framework, it does not specify any exact relations between actors, actions, artifacts, audiences, and affordances. These are meant to be discovered in research, not postulated in advance. At the same time, this framework, more than that of the four Ps, is capable of guiding research and suggesting questions about creativity that were previously ignored or unnoticed: How do actors interact with audience members and become themselves "audiences" for their own productions? How is creative action altered by the affordances and the constraints of different domains? How can we expand further what our environment affords, and what role does creativity play in this process? What shapes the historical development of creative artifacts?

"Creativity is not a rootless flower," claimed Barron (1995, 9) in a book dedicated to the ecology of creative expression. For Barron, the roots of creativity can be found in the simultaneously natural and social world in which creators live, work, and innovate. The five As framework follows the same line of reasoning and proposes a new language of creativity in which actors act as part of a wider environment made up of audiences, artifacts, and their affordances. Because this is largely a sociocultural approach, a question might be raised as to why culture itself (or associated notions such as norms, beliefs, traditions, and conventions) does not find a distinct place within this conceptual schema. The reason is by no means related to the terminological difficulty of producing a perfect alliteration; rather, it derives from the ontological and epistemological assumption that culture, as an accumulated system of symbolic and material human creations (Cole 1996), cannot be separated from actors, actions, artifacts, audiences, and affordances. In other words, all five As fundamentally exist and make sense in a cultural universe, and to produce a framework that isolates "culture" outside of (even if interacting with) all the other facets would contradict this basic premise.

14.2. Developing an Integrated Theoretical Model

The five As framework of creativity (for a full presentation, see Glăveanu 2013b) is the latest addition to the series of sociocultural models of the phenomenon described in the present book. In this concluding chapter, it is therefore important to strive for theoretical integration as part of a continuous effort to give the cultural psychology of creativity a solid conceptual basis. Let's begin by reviewing the various models formulated in different chapters.

The tetradic framework was first mentioned in Chapter 2 and was further elaborated in Chapter 3. It captures the key assertions of cultural psychology by positioning creativity between self and other, the "new" and the "old." Processes of internalization, externalization, integration, and social interaction link these various elements above. Chapter 4 proposed a multiple feedback framework for collecting and analyzing creativity evaluations, applied to research reported in Chapter 6 and leading to the abstraction of two evaluative stances, the "view from inside" and the "view from outside." This framework used the basic triad of self–other–object, drawing heavily on the theory of social representation and, in particular, the wind rose model (Bauer and Gaskell 2008). Chapter 7 approached creative action with the help of Dewey's (1934) formulation of human experience. In essence, this conception focuses on the cycle between doing (acting on the world) and undergoing (taking in the reaction of the world to one's action) in artistic activity and beyond. Chapter 8 turned our attention toward the set of criteria that people use to evaluate creative artifacts and offered a simple model that includes dimensions such as novelty and value but situates them within the subjective and cultural frames that shape a person's reception of creative outcomes. Chapter 10 returned to creative activity, this time with the aim to unpack the relation between creativity and habit. The typology consisting of habitual, improvisational, and innovative creativity offers a useful way of analytically distinguishing between different "forms" of creativity without creating further dichotomies and oppositions among them. Chapter 11 explored the relation between creativity and the theory of affordances and generated a model that outlines three distinct possibilities for creative action: perceiving existing affordances, exploiting previously ignored ones, and "inventing" new ones. Finally, Chapter 13 considered developmental trajectories in the case of creativity and differentiated between two basic creative processes specific to acts of internalizing cultural content: making the unfamiliar familiar (for younger children), and making the familiar unfamiliar (for older children).

The models reviewed above are situated at different levels of *generality* and differ in their *scope*. Some, like the tetradic framework, aim to capture something essential about creativity as a whole, while the typology of creative action and the criteria for creativity evaluations deal with more specific aspects of the phenomenon. The multiple feedback method represents a research design, and the pragmatist framework of human experience serves as an analytical tool. Other processes, like the two "views" on creativity or the two developmental trajectories, emerged out of empirical studies of craftwork. The five As framework introduced above fulfils the role of a conceptual organizer for the cultural approach to creativity, just as the four Ps formed the backbone of creativity studies in previous decades. Despite this apparent diversity, a closer look at these models and frameworks reveals their shared theoretical ground. This is of course not accidental, as they all draw from sociocultural traditions in psychology and related disciplines (considering the former's multidisciplinary nature). Moreover, they complement each other, and this facilitates their integration, as depicted in Figure 14.2.

The core of this Figure is represented by the tetradic framework (in its updated version presented in Chapter 3) and the five As model. Creativity is fundamentally considered *a sociocultural-psychological phenomenon embedded within (material and symbolic) action that, exploiting existing affordances, engages the relation between actors and audiences and leads to the generation of artifacts with properties evaluated as creative by the creator*

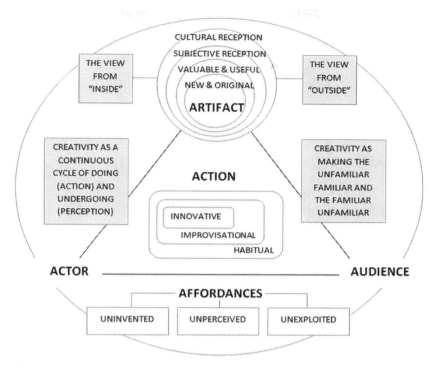

Figure 14.2. An updated sociocultural model of creativity.

and/or other people. This definition reflects several key features of the cultural-psychological approach:

1. Creativity is not exclusively an intrapsychological process based on cognitive mechanisms but rather is a form of material- and sign-mediated action.
2. Creative action relates actors and various audiences, and therefore it is not restricted to generating a creative idea but includes preparing for creative work, generating and testing solutions, implementing them, evaluating the results, and so forth.
3. In this process, the affordances of the physical environment are used in novel ways.
4. The creative artifact (be it an object or process) is creative not because of an intrinsic quality but because it is validated as such within a certain cultural context.
5. This validation is primarily represented by the creator's own assessment (informed by internalized social positions toward the new artifact) and, depending on the type of outcome, by other people from close to distant audiences.

6. Acts of perception and evaluation on the part of audiences can be equally creative, and this process leads to the continuous transformation of the new artifact and its integration into microcultural or macrocultural systems.

7. This temporal dimension is fundamental for creative action, and it unfolds in time at microgenetic, ontogenetic, and sociogenetic levels.

Figure 14.2 uses the five As and the basic structure of the median triangle (common for cultural-psychological accounts, including for social representations theory) to capture something essential about creativity: the generation of novelty in an intersubjective space of dialogue and in direct connection to the material world. In addition, "content" elements are added to this structure. For example, creative action is categorized as habitual, improvisational, and innovative (three interrelated rather than distinct forms); the creative artifact's properties are novelty and utility but as perceived through the lenses of personal and cultural systems of evaluation; and the affordances that favor novel outcomes are typically (and initially) unperceived, unexploited, or uninvented. Based on empirical research, the relations between actors, audiences, and artifacts also become specified. For example, Chapter 3 discussed the process of externalization or cultural expression, connecting actors to the new artifact. The essence of this process is represented by alternating between action and perception, between doing and undergoing. In the same chapter, audiences were related to the new artifact by means of internalization or acculturation. Appropriating the creation is itself a constructive act that, according to previous research findings, coordinates developmental processes of making the unfamiliar familiar and the familiar unfamiliar. The integration of the new artifact within the existing cultural system, again discussed in Chapter 3, is shaped by the existence of different views of the same artifact or group of artifacts. People who are themselves creative actors, thus engaged in producing similar outcomes, hold a perspective different from that held by those who restrict themselves to the role of observer and either use or are called to judge the quality of the final product. Though not included in Figure 14.2, there are also conclusions to be drawn about the connection between actors and audiences, discussed in Chapter 3 in reference to implicit and explicit forms of social interaction. The framework of collaborative creativity proposed elsewhere (see Glăveanu 2011a) theorizes such processes in terms of "moving" representational resources from unique to common, shared spaces.

What remains to be emphasized about the complexity of this sociocultural model and its various frameworks is that they can and should be *articulated* within the exploration of concrete instances of creativity, from micromoments of creative production to the development of lifelong creative projects. This unified perspective is facilitated by the fact that, as argued above regarding the five As model, it is virtually impossible to adopt the cultural approach without having a systemic view of the phenomenon. For instance, in order to understand the subjective and cultural reception of creative artifacts, we need to consider the position adopted toward them by both actors and audiences. Equally, when focusing on the use of affordances in creative work, one cannot ignore the type of creative action in which actors engage, since, for example, deliberately exploiting affordances in ways that contradict cultural norms is often the case for innovative creation. The list of examples could continue. In order to make these observations more specific, let's return to the three short case studies presented at the very beginning of the book. These included the egg decoration practices of Dănuţ Zimbru, considered the only (or at least the most well-known) male decorator in Ciocăneşti village; the story of Marion Laval Jeantet, the French artist whose works are situated at the border between science and art; and Vasile's experience of growing up in a childcare center in Bucharest, vividly depicted in his drawings and world constructions. How do we approach each of these cases now, in light of the updated model of creativity presented in Figure 14.2?

To begin with, based on the limited information we have, we would need to ask who is the creative actor (or actors) within each case. Clearly Dănuţ, Marion, and Vasile qualify as actors in relation to their production of artistic artifacts: Easter eggs, installation and object art, and drawings. But they are not alone in this position. Marion's partner and collaborator, Benoît Mangin, plays a key role in the development of shared "creative visions." At the same time, Dănuţ is working alongside his wife, who is being taught by him how to decorate (just as he previously made a decisive contribution toward his sister's emergence as a creative actor of the craft). Who are the audiences? For the creations of Dănuţ and Marion, they certainly include viewers and potential customers and, for Marion more than Dănuţ, critics and reviewers (the gatekeepers of the art domain). Vasile's drawings can be of interest to the people working at the center and, potentially, to his friends and peers. In all three cases, the interviewer himself is an important type of "other," one who prompted a presentation and discussion of personal work and in relation to whom a certain account of it had to be constructed. What kind of creative actions do these creators engage in? Clearly a combination of habitual, improvisational, and innovative acts, marked perhaps by different proportions. Dănuţ's account suggests that, for him, the decoration of Easter eggs draws on powerful habits and routines acquired and practiced over the years. He certainly attained a degree of mastery over the practice and tends to reject innovations simply done for the sake of change. In contrast, Marion is an artist who from early in life has been fully aware of her path and who purposely makes bold choices in her artistic career. In her case, habitual and improvisational actions tend perhaps to be subordinated to innovative forms of expression. As for Vasile, his drawings and constructions might have been practiced before, and there is little evidence of him deliberately trying to "create" something new, so a provisional assessment could be that his expression is based on improvisation—engaging habitual resources in dealing with a very clear "obstacle" in his existence: the absence of his parents. Finally, what kind of affordances do the three typically explore through their creative acts? We can imagine that Dănuț enriches his repertoire by making use of unperceived affordances, discovered in the process of working. This is surely also the case with Marion, but she in addition is focused primarily, according to her own account, on the space of unexploited potentials for action and the breaking of conventions. Vasile is faced with the task of imaginatively producing a story about himself, his family, and his future that grants him psychological comfort and strengthens his resilience. In this regard, drawing and construction tasks are full of opportunities to create a world that is "not yet there" and thus maximally utilize the space of uninvented affordances.

Of course, this cursory analysis offers only an example of how different elements of the cultural framework can be integrated in order to obtain a more comprehensive picture of creativity in particular circumstances. It undoubtedly would need to be completed by further information about each of the three cases in order to qualify as a valid analysis—information acquired through the use of interviews and observation and perhaps also through the subjective camera as part of conducting psychological ethnographies. What this exercise points to, however, is the fact that an integrative perspective is *possible*, and it also illustrates the value of making *comparisons* between different individuals and across contexts (another set of interesting comparisons could result from observing the same person over time). Many new questions can be raised within this kind of research, some drawing directly from the framework in Figure 14.2. But the greatest value of this model is its capacity to inspire questions that go beyond it and that can help us perfect our theoretical and methodological tools. It is toward such developments that I will be looking in the very last section of the book, in an attempt to catch a glimpse of the cultural psychology of creativity of tomorrow.

14.3. Looking toward the Future

The future-orientation of human action, discussed at length among cultural psychologists, is central for creative acts that, most of the time, involve evaluating existing possibilities and imagining what is yet to come. To look into the future of the cultural psychology of creativity is therefore itself a form of creation aimed at moving this discipline further ahead. Future perspectives for cultural theory and research into creativity have been mentioned in different chapters, and one immediate direction suggested here is represented by the five As framework and the need for continuous reflection regarding its implications. As argued above, rewriting the static and disjointed language of person, process, product, and press leads to more than another typology.

It forces us to rethink the nature of creativity and engage in research projects that articulate actors, audiences, actions, artifacts, and affordances in ways that bring their interconnection to the fore. The ways in which elements of the five As relate to one another—depending on individual creators, the types of tasks, and the domains they contribute to—are empirical concerns for the future. At a theoretical level, we need to conceptualize each one of the five elements and, potentially, add to the list.

Such developments can be inspired by considering strands of theory within cultural psychology that have been only touched upon in the present volume. One of these is semiotics—or rather, *semiotic cultural psychology* (see Valsiner 2007)—along with what it can tell us about creative work. The emergence and use of signs, mediating and regulating the person's relation to self and others, are in essence both creative and cultural acts. What the semiotic function allows us to do is detach ourselves from the here and now in order to observe our action as another person would, and thus we are able to construct alternatives without being at the mercy of sensorial inputs and mere reactions to them. The use of signs, an essential characteristic of human beings and the foundation of human culture, helps the person to emerge as a creative actor and not a passive and reactive observer of the environment. By directing semiotic processes, we achieve control over self and the world, and this accomplishment is unimaginable in the absence of social interaction and different forms of scaffolding (Vygotsky 1978, 1997). Signs and symbols are not merely personal constructions—though they do have different types of affective resonance within each individual—but essentially are tools that make communication possible. It is through communication that their social meaning is instituted, something extensively elaborated through the theory of social representations. The creative nature of this communication and its ever-present potential to generate novelties, for both individuals and society, is grounded in the fact that signs and meanings are not transferred "intact" from one mind to the next. On the contrary, cultural psychology promotes a bidirectional transfer model in which cultural content is shaped in the very process of being communicated. As noted by Jaan Valsiner, "The bidirectional model is based on the premise that all participants in the cultural transfer of knowledge are actively transforming cultural messages" (Valsiner 2007, 36). This perspective was adopted here to study children's creativity (see Chapter 13), and the two processes of "making the unfamiliar familiar" and "making the familiar unfamiliar" can be further discussed in semiotic terms to broaden our understanding of cultural acquisition and creative transformation.

Introducing "materiality" into acts of semiosis, alongside "sociality," is another requirement of the cultural psychology of creativity. More recent theories within social sciences, such as the actor-network theory, offer interesting perspectives for understanding precisely the "actors" of creativity as defined by their relations with other agents within dynamic systems (see Latour 2005).

The idea of *objects as actors* is an intriguing perspective that resonates with our discussion of affordances in this book. In creative action, it is not only the person "acting" (or doing, to use a pragmatist term)—the object acted upon "re-acts" to the person's doing. But we can think more broadly about situations in which these roles are reversed. In Easter egg decoration, the egg is not merely a support to be decorated but a very active presence from the first moments of work. The size and particular shape of the egg (e.g., being more round or elongated) effectively determine how the artisan will approach decoration and what motifs he or she will choose. Granting agency to nonhuman participants is a bold step that needs to be further refined theoretically, and investigations of creativity offer the perfect ground for this kind of inquiry. What does it mean for artifacts to be actors of creativity? How can artifacts act on creators and direct their activity? Certainly, an image of dialogue between creator and emerging object best characterizes this relationship in different domains of creative production (see Glăveanu et al. 2013). A study of resistance encountered when approaching different materials should be a central point of interest for creativity researchers, and this line of investigation is inscribed in current descriptions of sociomateriality (Tanggaard 2013). Taking this study further will help us to unpack creativity as a *distributed process*—distributed across time, people, and objects (Glăveanu, 2014). This theoretical direction is greatly encouraged by the unified theoretical model proposed in this concluding chapter.

Finally, what is often missed even by descriptions of distributed creativity is the actual presence of the body. If creativity is indeed action, we need to be more aware in our theories and studies of the fact that creative actors are not disembodied entities. To act creatively means to participate as a full person and not just as a brain or a cognitive system. Dewey (1934) was acutely aware of this reality in his description of artistic work. The *thesis of the embodied mind* has deep philosophical roots and has been for some time a topic of debate among philosophers, psychologists, and cognitive scientists. Creativity scholars should certainly contribute to this discussion, despite the fact that it has thus far aroused little interest in mainstream research. In my presentation of Easter egg decoration practices, the body of the artisan was mostly an implicit presence. But the case study itself offers ample opportunities to observe the creative actor as a totality of mind and body. In fact, in decoration the human body is "extended" through the use of tools, in particular the chişiţă, which effectively continues the hand of the folk artist and carries its action. To create Easter eggs means much more than to cognitively plan and guide an activity. If we accept the premises of embodied cognition, summarized for instance by Wilson (2002), we can more strongly argue for creativity as a situated process that coordinates person and environment. The exact nature of the "border" between the two causes a problem, however, for psychologists and cognitive scientists who are not willing to transcend their fixation on the "internal" world of mental processes. Moving further in this regard might very well paradoxically lead us back to the foundational scholarship of Merleau-Ponty (1968/1948) and his ideas about the "flesh of the world." Actors, audiences, and artifacts are analytically distinguishable units that, at an experiential level, constitute the same reality—the creative totality of a lived experience and presence in the world.

The above are only three potential paths, among many others, that take us into the future of the cultural psychology of creativity (or at least one version of it, elaborated here). As any future, this is at present a mere project, an imaginatively constructed vision of how theory can develop with the help of research. The present book is intended to give this project a foundation, a starting point having its own basis in the writings of many others, a transitional moment in the collective effort to think and rethink creativity in times of ongoing innovation and societal change (see also Glăveanu, Gillespie and Valsiner 2014). The cultural psychology of creativity is a product of this social and scientific context—an era defined by creativity, yet an era in which this word is so frequently used (and misused) that it is in danger of losing all meaning and relevance. Cultural psychologists, I believe, have an important contribution to make in the direction of placing creativity on more solid ground, even when this implies challenging some of our deepest convictions about *what it means to be creative*. Toward this ideal the present body of work hopes to have made a modest yet unique contribution.

References

Alanen, L. (1990). Rethinking socialization, the family and childhood. *Sociological Studies of Child Development, 3*, 13–28.

Alexander, T. M. (2006). *Dewey, dualism, and naturalism*. In J. R. *Shook* & J. Margolis (Eds.), *A companion to pragmatism* (pp. 184–192). Malden, MA: Blackwell.

Almeida, L. S., Prieto, L. P., Ferrando, M., Oliveira, E., & Ferrándiz, C. (2008). Torrance test of creative thinking: The question of its construct validity. *Thinking Skills & Creativity, 3*(1), 53–58.

Amabile, T. M. (1996). *Creativity in context*. Boulder, CO: Westview Press.

Anderson, H. H. (1959). Preface. In H. H. Anderson (Ed.), *Creativity and its cultivation* (pp. ix–xiii). New York, NY: Harper & Row Publishers.

Anning, A., & Ring, R. (2004). *Making sense of children's drawings*. Berkshire, UK: Open University Press.

Ariès, P. (1962). *Centuries of childhood: A social history of family life*, trans. R. Baldick. New York, NY: Knopf.

Arieti, S. (1976). *Creativity: The magic synthesis*. New York, NY: Basic Books.

Attride-Stirling, J. (2001). Thematic networks: An analytic tool for qualitative research. *Qualitative Research, 1*, 385–405.

Auerbach, C., & Silverstein, L. (2003). *Qualitative data: An introduction to coding and analysis*. New York, NY: New York University Press.

Ayman-Nolley, S. (1999). A Piagetian perspective on the dialectic process of creativity. *Creativity Research Journal, 12*(4), 267–275.

Backett-Milburn, K., & McKie, L. (1999). A critical appraisal of the Draw and Write Technique. *Health Education Research, 14*(3), 387–398.

Bailin, S. (1988). *Achieving extraordinary ends: An essay on creativity*. Boston, MA: Kluwer Academic.

Baker-Sennett, J., Matusov, E., & Rogoff, B. (1992). Sociocultural processes of creative planning in children's playcrafting. In P. Light & G. Butterworth (Eds.), *Context and cognition: Ways of learning and knowing* (pp. 93–114). Hertfordshire, UK: Harvester-Wheatsheaf.

Baldwin, J. M. (1894). Imitation: A chapter in the natural history of consciousness. *Mind, 3*, 26–55.

Baldwin, J. M. (1900). *Mental development in the child and the race: Methods and processes*, 2nd ed. London, UK: Macmillan & Co.

Baldwin, J. M. (1903). *Mental development in the child and the race: Methods and processes*, 2nd ed. London, UK: Macmillan & Co.

Baldwin, J. M. (1906). *Social and ethical interpretations in mental development*. London, UK: Macmillan & Co.

Baldwin, J. M. (1911). *The individual and society or psychology and sociology*. Boston, MA: Richard G. Badger.

Banaji, S., Burn, A., & Buckingham, D. (2006). *The rhetorics of creativity: A review of the literature*. A report for Creative Partnerships.

Barker, P. (2009). *Religious nationalism in modern Europe*. London, UK: Routledge.

Barnett, J. (1949). The Easter festival—A study in cultural change. *American Sociological Review, 14*(1), 62–70.

Barrett, F. (1999). Knowledge creating as dialogical accomplishment: A constructivist perspective. In A. Montuori, & R. Purser (Eds.), *Social creativity*, Vol. 1 (pp. 133–151). Cresskill, NJ: Hampton Press.

Barron, F. (1990). *Creativity and psychological health*. Buffalo, NY: Creative Education Foundation.

Barron, F. (1995). *No rootless flower: An ecology of creativity*. Cresskill, NJ: Hampton Press.

Barron, F. (1999). All creation is a collaboration. In A. Montuori, & R. Purser (Eds.), *Social creativity*, Vol. 1 (pp. 49–59). Cresskill, NJ: Hampton Press.

Barron, F., & Harrington, D. (1981). Creativity, intelligence, and personality. *Annual Review of Psychology, 32*, 439–476.

Bartlett, F. C. (1932). *Remembering: A study in experimental and social psychology*. Cambridge, UK: Cambridge University Press.

Bateson, M. C. (1999). Ordinary creativity. In A. Montuori, & R. Purser (Eds.), *Social creativity*, Vol. 1 (pp. 153–171). Cresskill, NJ: Hampton Press.

Bauer, M., & Gaskell, G. (2008). Social representations theory: A progressive research programme for social psychology. *Journal for the Theory of Social Behaviour, 38*, 335–353.

Bilton, C. (2007). *Management and creativity: From creative industries to creative management*. Malden, MA: Blackwell.

Becker, H. S. (2000). The etiquette of improvisation. *Mind, Culture, and Activity, 7*, 171–176.

Becker, H. S. (2008). *Art worlds*, upd. ed. Berkeley, CA: University of California Press.

Beghetto, R. A., & Kaufman, J. C. (2007). Toward a broader conception of creativity: A case for "mini-c" creativity. *Psychology of Aesthetics, Creativity, and the Arts, 1*, 73–79.

Bhawuk, D. (2003). Culture's influence on creativity: The case of Indian spirituality. *International Journal of Intercultural Relations, 27*, 1–22.

Bink, M. L., & Mash, R. L. (2000). Cognitive regularities in creative activity. *Review of General Psychology, 4*, 59–78.

Boden, M. (1994). What is creativity? In M. Boden (Ed.), *Dimensions of creativity* (pp. 75–117). London, UK: MIT Press/Badford Books.

Boden, M. (2001). Creativity and knowledge. In A. Craft, B. Jeffrey, & M. Leibling (Eds.), *Creativity in education* (pp. 95–102). London, UK: Continuum.

Bodnarescu, L. (1920). *Câteva datini de Paşti la români* [Some Easter traditions among the Romanians] (2nd ed.). Chişinau: Tipografia Societăţii de Editură Naţională Luceafarul.

Boesch, E. (1997). The sound of the violin. In M. Cole, Y. Engestrom & O. Vasquez (Eds.), *Mind, culture and activity: Seminal papers from the Laboratory of Comparative Human Cognition* (pp. 164–184). Cambridge, UK: Cambridge University Press.

Boesch, E. E. (2007). Cultural psychology in action-theoretical perspective. In W. J. Looner & S. A. Hayes (Eds.), *Discovering cultural psychology: A profile and selected readings of Ernest E. Boesch* (pp. 153–165). Charlotte, NC: Information Age Publishing.

Borofsky, R. (2001). Wondering about Wutu. In J. Liep (Ed.), *Locating cultural creativity* (pp. 62–70). London, UK: Pluto Press.

Bourdieu, P. (1984). *Distinction: A social critique of the judgement of taste.* Cambridge, MA: Harvard University Press.

Bourdieu, P. (1990a). In *other words: Essays toward a reflexive sociology.* Stanford, CA: Stanford University Press.

Bourdieu, P. (1990b). *The logic of practice.* Stanford, CA: Stanford University Press.

Bourdieu, P. (1993). *The field of cultural production.* Cambridge, UK: Polity Press.

Bourdieu, P., & Wacquant, L. J. D. (1992). *An invitation to reflexive sociology.* Chicago, IL: University of Chicago Press.

Boyatzis, R. E. (1998). *Transforming qualitative information: Thematic analysis and code development.* Thousand Oaks: Sage Publications.

Breakwell, G. (2001). Social representational constraints upon identity processes. In K. Deaux & G. Philogène (Eds.), *Representations of the social: Bridging theoretical traditions* (pp. 271–284). Oxford, UK: Blackwell.

Brogden, H., & Sprecher, T. (1964). Criteria of creativity. In C. Taylor (Ed.), *Creativity: Progress and potential* (pp. 155–176). New York, NY: McGraw-Hill.

Bruner, J. (1962). *On knowing: Essays for the left hand.* Cambridge, MA: Belknap Press.

Bruner, J. (1986). *Actual minds, possible worlds.* Cambridge, MA: Harvard University Press.

Bruner, J. (1990). *Acts of meaning.* Cambridge, MA: Harvard University Press.

Bruner, J. (1999). Infancy and culture: A story. In S. Chaiklin, M. Hedegaard, & U. J. Jensen (Eds.), *Activity theory and social practice: Cultural-historical approaches* (pp. 225–234). Aarhus, Denmark: Aarhus University Press.

Bulbrook, M. E. (1932). An experimental inquiry into the existence and nature of 'insight'. *The American Journal of Psychology, 44,* 409–453.

Burman, E. (1994). *Deconstructing developmental psychology.* London, UK: Routledge.

Camic, C. (1986). The matter of habit. *American Journal of Sociology, 91,* 1039–1087.

Campbell, C. & Jovchelovitch, S. (2000). Health, community and development: Towards a social psychology of participation. *Journal of Community & Applied Social Psychology, 10,* 255–270.

Cavagnoli, D. (2008, July). *Innovation and the role of habits: A conceptual analysis.* Discussion Paper No. A08.03 presented at the eResearch Australasia Conference, Melbourne, Australia.

Chaffin, R., Lemieux, A. F., & Chen, C. (2006). Spontaneity and creativity in highly practiced performance. In I. Deliège & G. A. Wiggins (Eds.), *Musical creativity: Multidisciplinary research in theory and practice* (pp. 200–218). New York, NY: Psychological Press.

Chan, D., & Chan, L.-K. (1999). Implicit theories of creativity: Teachers' perception of student characteristics in Hong Kong. *Creativity Research Journal, 12*(3), 185–195.

Chase, W. G., & Simon, H. A. (1973). The mind's eye in chess. In W. G. Chase (Ed.), *Visual information processing* (pp. 215–281). New York, NY: Academic Press.

Chemero, A. (2003). An outline of a theory of affordances. *Ecological Psychology, 15*, 181–195.

Chen, C., Kasof, J., Himsel, A., Dmitrieva, J., Dong, Q., & Xue, G. (2005). Effects of explicit instruction to "be creative" across domains and cultures. *Journal of Creative Behavior, 39*, 89–110.

Chua, Y.-J., & Iyengar, S. S. (2008). Creativity as a matter of choice: Prior experience and task instruction as boundary conditions for the positive effect of choice on creativity. *Journal of Creative Behavior, 42*, 164–180.

Cincura, A. (1970). Slovak and Ruthenian Easter eggs in America: The impact of culture contact on immigrant art and custom. *Journal of Popular Culture, 4*, 155–193.

Cohen, L., & Ambrose, D. (1999). Adaptation and creativity. In M. Runco & S. Pritzker (Eds.), *Encyclopedia of creativity*, Vol. 1 (pp. 9–22). San Diego, CA: Academic Press.

Cole, M. (1996). *Cultural psychology: A once and future discipline.* Cambridge, MA: Belknap Press.

Collingwood, R. G. (1938). *The principles of art.* Oxford, UK: Clarendon Press.

Collins, R. (2007). The creativity of intellectual networks and the struggle over attention space. In A. Sales & M. Fournier (Eds.), *Knowledge, communication and creativity* (pp. 156–165). London, UK: Sage Publications.

Cooper, P., & Allen, N. B. (1999). *The quilters: Women and domestic art, an oral history.* Lubbock, TX: Texas Tech University Press.

Cordelois, A. (2010). Using digital technology for collective ethnographic observation: An experiment on "coming home." *Social Science Information, 49*, 445–463.

Corsaro, W. A., & Eder, D. (1990). Children's peer cultures. *Annual Review of Sociology, 16*, 197–220.

Costall, A. (1989). A closer look at "direct perception." In A. Gellatly, D. Rogers, & J.A. Sloboda (Eds.), *Cognition and social worlds* (pp. 10–21). Oxford, UK: Clarendon Press.

Costall, A. (1995). Socializing affordances. *Theory & Psychology, 5*, 467–481.

Costall, A. (2006). On being the right size: Affordances and the meaning of scale. In G. Lock & B. Molyneaux (Eds.), *Confronting scale in archaeology: Issues of theory and practice* (pp. 15–26). New York, NY: Springer.

Craft, A. (2001). 'Little c creativity'. In A. Craft, B. Jeffrey & M. Leibling (Eds.), *Creativity in education* (pp. 45–61). London, UK: Continuum.

Craft, A. (2002). *Creativity across the primary curriculum: Framing and developing practice.* London, UK: Routledge.

Craft, A. (2005). *Creativity in schools: Tensions and dilemmas.* London, UK: Routledge.

Cropley, A. (1999). Education. In M. Runco & S. Pritzker (Eds.), *Encyclopedia of creativity*, Vol. 1 (pp. 629–642). San Diego, CA: Academic Press.

Cropley, A., & Cropley, D. (2009). *Fostering creativity: A diagnostic approach for education and organizations*. Cresskill, NJ: Hampton Press.

Crossley, N. (2001). *The social body: Habit, identity and desire*. London, UK: Sage.

Csikszentmihalyi, M. (1988). Society, culture, and person: A systems view of creativity. In R. Sternberg (Ed.), *The nature of creativity: Contemporary psychological perspectives* (pp. 325–339). Cambridge, UK: Cambridge University Press.

Csikszentmihalyi, M. (1996). *Creativity: Flow and the psychology of discovery and invention*. New York, NY: Harper Perennial.

Csikszentmihalyi, M. (1999). Implications of a systems perspective for the study of creativity. In R. Sternberg (Ed.), *Handbook of creativity* (pp. 313–335). Cambridge, UK: Cambridge University Press.

Csikszentmihaly, M., & Rochberg-Halton, E. (1981). *The meaning of things: Domestic symbols and the self*. Cambridge, UK: Cambridge University Press.

Dacey, J. (1999). Concepts of creativity: A history. In M. Runco & S. Pritzker (Eds.), *Encyclopedia of creativity*, Vol. 1 (pp. 309–322). San Diego, CA: Academic Press.

D'Alessio, M. (1990). Social representations of childhood: An implicit theory of development. In G. Duveen & B. Lloyd (Eds.), *Social representations and the development of knowledge* (pp. 70–90). Cambridge, UK: Cambridge University Press.

Dalton, B. (2004). Creativity, habit, and the social products of creative action: Revising Joas, incorporating Bourdieu. *Sociological Theory, 22*, 603–622.

Dane, E. (2010). Reconsidering the trade-off between expertise and flexibility: A cognitive entrenchment perspective. *Academy of Management Review, 35*, 579–603.

Dant, T. (1999). *Material culture in the social world: Values, activities, lifestyles*. Buckingham, UK: Open University Press.

Davis, G. A. (1999). Barriers to creativity and creative attitudes. In M. A. Runco & S. R. Pritzker (Eds.), *Encyclopedia of creativity* (Vol. 1, pp.165–174). San Diego, CA: Academic Press.

Del Mar, M. (2010). *Action, creativity and social life: Social theory with and beyond Hans Joas*. Retrieved from http://ssrn.com/abstract1609830.

Denzin, N. K. (1977). *Childhood socialization*. San Francisco, CA: Jossey-Bass Publishers.

Dewey, J. (1903). *Studies in logical theory*. Chicago, IL: Chicago University Press.

Dewey, J. (1910). *How we think*. Lexington, MA: Heath.

Dewey, J. (1922). *Human nature and conduct: An introduction to social psychology*. New York, NY: Modern Library.

Dewey, J. (1934). *Art as experience*. New York, NY: Penguin.

Dey, I. (1993). *Qualitative data analysis: A user-friendly guide*. London, UK: Routledge.

Dobbins, B. (1980). Improvisation: An essential element of musical proficiency. *Music Educators Journal, 66*, 36–41.

Dranca, M. (2010). *Paştele în Bucovina* [Easter in Bucovina]. Suceava, Romania: Centrul Cultural Bucovina.

Dubuffet, J. (1973). *L'homme du commun a l'ouvrage*. Paris: Gallimard.

Dudek, S. Z. (1973). *Creativity in young children–attitude or ability*. In paper presented at the Annual Meeting of the American Psychological Association, Montreal, August 27–31, 1973.

Dunbar, K. (1997). How scientists think: Online creativity and conceptual change in science. In T. Ward, S. Smith, & S. Vaid (Eds.) *Creative thought: An investigation of conceptual structures and processes* (pp. 461–493). Washington, DC: APA Press.

Duncker, K. (1945). On problem solving. *Psychological Monographs, 58*, 1–110.

Duveen, G. (2007). Culture and social representations. In J. Valsiner & A. Rosa (Eds.), *The Cambridge handbook of sociocultural psychology* (pp. 543–559). Cambridge, UK: Cambridge University Press.

Duveen, G. (2001). Representations, identities, resistance. In K. Deaux & G. Philogène (Eds.), *Representations of the social: Bridging theoretical traditions* (pp. 257–270). Oxford, UK: Blackwell.

Duveen, G., & Lloyd, B. (1990). Introduction. In G. Duveen & B. Lloyd (Eds.), *Social representations and the development of knowledge* (pp. 1–10). Cambridge, UK: Cambridge University Press.

Dweck, C. S., Chiu, C.-Y., & Hong, Y.-Y. (1995). Implicit theories and their role in judgements and reactions: A world from two perspectives. *Psychological Inquiry, 6*(4), 267–285.

Eco, U. (1989). *The open work*. London, UK: Hutchinson Radius.

Eisenberg, E. M. (1990). Jamming: Transcendence through organizing. *Communication Research, 17*, 139–164.

Eisenstadt, S. N. (1973). *Tradition, change, and modernity*. New York, NY: Wiley.

Engel, S. (1993). Children's bursts of creativity. *Creativity Research Journal, 6*(3), 309–318.

Engeström, Y. (1990). *Learning, working and imaging: Twelve studies in activity theory*. Helsinki, Finland: Orienta-Konsultit.

Epstein, R., & Laptosky, G. (1999). Behavioral approaches to creativity. In M. Runco & S. Pritzker (Eds.), *Encyclopedia of creativity*, Vol. 1 (pp. 175–183). San Diego, CA: Academic Press.

Ericsson, K. A. (1998). The scientific study of expert levels of performance: General implications for optimal learning and creativity. *High Ability Studies, 9*, 75–100.

Ericsson, K. A. (1999). Creative expertise as superior reproducible performance: Innovative and flexible aspects of expert performance. *Psychological Inquiry, 10*, 329–361.

Ericsson, K. A. (2003). The search for general abilities and basic capacities: Theoretical implications from the modifiability and complexity of mechanisms mediating expert performance. In R. J. Sternberg & E. L. Grigorenko (Eds.), *The psychology of abilities, competences, and expertise* (pp. 93–125). Cambridge, UK: Cambridge University Press.

Ericsson, K. A. (2006). The influence of experience and deliberate practice on the development of superior expert performance. In K. A. Ericsson, N. Charness, P. Feltovich, & R. R. Hoffman (Eds.), *Cambridge handbook of expertise and expert performance* (pp. 685–706). Cambridge, UK: Cambridge University Press.

Ericsson, K. A., Roring, R. W., & Nandagopal, K. (2007). Giftedness and evidence for reproducibly superior performance: An account based on the expert performance framework. *High Ability Studies, 18*, 3–56.

Eteläpelto, A., & Lahti, J. (2008). The resources and obstacles of creative collaboration in a long-term learning community. *Thinking Skills Creativity, 3*(3), 226–240.

Eysenck, H. (1994). The measurement of creativity. In M. Boden (Ed.), *Dimensions of creativity* (pp. 199–242). London, UK: MIT Press/Badford Books.

Farr, R. (1996). *The roots of modern social psychology*. Oxford, UK: Blackwell.

Favez-Boutonier, J. (1970). Modalităţile de exprimare la copil şi desenul. In M. Debesse (Ed.), *Psihologia copilului de la naştere la adolescenţă* [Child psychology from birth to adolescence] (pp. 180–189). Bucharest: Editura Didactică şi Pedagogică.

Feist, G. (1999). The Influence of personality on artistic and scientific creativity. In R. Sternberg (Ed.), *Handbook of creativity* (pp. 273–296). Cambridge, UK: Cambridge University Press.

Feldhusen, J. F. (2002). Creativity: The knowledge base and children. *High Ability Studies, 13*(2), 179–183.

Feldman, D. H. (1974). The developmental approach: Universal to unique. In S. Rosner & L. E. Abt (Eds.), *Essays in creativity* (pp. 47–85). Croton-On-Hudson, NY: North River Press.

Feldman, D. H. (1988). Creativity: Dreams, insights, and transformations. In R. Sternberg (Ed.), *The nature of creativity: Contemporary psychological perspectives* (pp. 271–297). Cambridge, UK: Cambridge University Press.

Feldman, D. H. (1994). *Beyond universals in cognitive development* (2nd ed.). Norwood, NJ: Ablex.

Feldman, D. H. (1999). The development of creativity. In R. Sternberg (Ed.), *Handbook of creativity* (pp. 169–186). Cambridge, UK: Cambridge University Press.

Fine, G. A. (2004). *Everyday genius: Self-taught art and the culture of authenticity*. Chicago, IL: University of Chicago Press.

Finke, R. A., Ward, T. B., & Smith, S. S. (1992). *Creative cognition: Theory, research, and applications*. Cambridge, MA: MIT Press.

Fischer, G., Giaccardi, E., Eden, H., Sugimoto, M., & Ye, Y. (2005). Beyond binary choices: Integrating individual and social creativity. *International Journal of Human-Computer Studies, 63*, 482–512.

Flaherty, A. W. (2005). Frontotemporal and dopaminergic control of idea generation and creative drive. *The Journal of Comparative Neurology, 493*, 147–153.

Fox, J. E., & Schirrmacher, R. (2012). *Art and creative development for young children* (7th ed.). Belmont, CA: Wadsworth.

Freud, S. (1908/1970). Creative writers and day-dreaming. In P. E. Vernon (Ed.), *Creativity: Selected readings* (pp. 126–136). Harmondsworth, UK: Penguin Books.

Friedman, R., & Rogers, K. (1998). Introduction. In R. Friedman & K. Rogers (Eds.), *Talent in context: Historical and social perspectives on giftedness* (pp. xv–xxiv). Washington, DC: American Psychological Association.

Furnham, A. (1988). *Lay theories: Everyday understanding of problems in the social sciences.* Oxford, UK: Pergamon Press.

Galton, F. (1869). *Hereditary genius: An inquiry into its laws and consequences.* London, UK: Macmillan.

Galton, F. (1874). *English men of science: Their nature and nurture.* London, UK: MacMillan.

Gardner, H. (1982). *Art, mind, and brain: A cognitive approach to creativity.* New York, NY: Basic Books.

Gardner, H. (1993). *Creating minds: An anatomy of creativity seen through the lives of Freud, Einstein, Picasso, Stravinsky, Eliot, Graham, and Gandhi.* New York, NY: Basic Books.

Gardner, H. (1994). The creators' patterns. In M. Boden (Ed.), *Dimensions of creativity* (pp. 143–158). London, UK: MIT Press/Badford Books.

Gaskell, G. (2000). Individual and group interviewing. In M. Bauer & G. Gaskell (Eds.), *Qualitative researching with text, image and sound: A practical handbook* (pp. 38–56). London, UK: Sage.

Gaskell, G., & Bauer, M. W. (2000). Towards public accountability: Beyond sampling, reliability and validity. In M. W. Bauer & G. Gaskell (Eds.), *Qualitative researching with text, image and sound: A practical handbook* (pp. 336–350). London, UK: Sage.

Geertz, C. (1973). *The interpretation of cultures.* New York, NY: Basic Books.

Gell, A. (1998). *Art and agency: An anthropological theory.* Oxford, UK: Clarendon Press.

Gergen, K. J., & Gigerenzer, G. (1991). Cognitivism and its discontents: An introduction to the issue. *Theory & Psychology, 1,* 403–405.

Getzels, J. W., & Csikszentmihaly, M. (1976). *The creative vision: Longitudinal study of problem finding in art.* New York, NY: Wiley.

Gibson, J. J. (1950). *The perception of the visual world.* Boston, MA: Riverside Press.

Gibson, J. J. (1966). *The senses considered as perceptual systems.* Boston, MA: Houghton Mifflin.

Gibson, J. J. (1986). *The ecological approach to visual perception.* Hillsdale, NJ: Erlbaum.

Gibson, W. (2006). Material culture and embodied action: Sociological notes on the examination of musical instruments in jazz improvisation. *The Sociological Review, 54,* 171–187.

Giuffre, K. (2009). *Collective creativity: Art and society in the South Pacific.* Surrey, UK: Ashgate Publishing.

Glăveanu, V. P. (2008). Thinking outside the box of individualism: Creativity in light of a socio-cultural approach. *Europe's Journal of Psychology, 4*(4).

Glăveanu, V. P. (2010a). Principles for a cultural psychology of creativity. *Culture & Psychology, 16*(2), 147–163.

Glăveanu, V.P. (2010b). Paradigms in the study of creativity: Introducing the perspective of cultural psychology. *New Ideas in Psychology, 28*(1), 79–93.

Glăveanu, V. P. (2010c). Creativity in context: The ecology of creativity evaluations and practices in an artistic craft. *Psychological Studies, 55*(4), 339–350.

Glăveanu, V. P. (2011a). How are we creative together? Comparing sociocognitive and sociocultural answers. *Theory & Psychology, 21*(4), 473–492.

Glăveanu, V. P. (2011b). Creating creativity: Reflections from fieldwork. *Integrative Psychological and Behavioral Science, 45*(1), 100–115.

Glăveanu, V. P. (2011c). Creativity as cultural participation. *Journal for the Theory of Social Behaviour, 41*(1), 48–67.

Glăveanu, V. P. (2011d). Is the lightbulb still on? Social representations of creativity in a Western context. *The International Journal of Creativity & Problem Solving, 21*(1), 53–72.

Glăveanu, V. P. (2012). Habitual creativity: Revising habit, reconceptualizing creativity. *Review of General Psychology, 16*, 78–92.

Glăveanu, V. P. (2013). *Distributed creativity: Thinking outside the box of the creative individual.* New York, NY: Springer.

Glăveanu, V. P. (2013a). Creativity and folk art: A study of creative action in traditional craft. *Psychology of Aesthetics, Creativity, and the Arts, 7*(2), 140–154.

Glăveanu, V. P. (2013b). Rewriting the language of creativity: The Five A's framework. *Review of General Psychology, 17*(1), 69–81.

Glăveanu, V. P. (2014). *Distributed creativity: Thinking outside of the creative individual.* Cham, CH: Springer.

Glăveanu, I. C., & Glăveanu, V. P. (2004). *Să cunoaştem şi să educăm copiii cu ajutorul desenului.* Bucharest: Editura Studenţească.

Glăveanu, V. P., & Lahlou, S. (2012). "Through the creator's eyes": Using the subjective camera to study craft creativity. *Creativity Research Journal, 24*, 152–162.

Glăveanu, V. P., Gillespie, A., & Valsiner, J. (Eds.). (2014). *Rethinking creativity: Contributions from cultural psychology.* London: Routledge.

Glăveanu, V. P., Lubart, T., Bonnardel, N., Botella, M., de Biaisi, P.-M., Desainte-Catherine, M., Georgsdottir, A., Guillou, K., Kurtag, G., Mouchiroud, C., Storme, M., Wojtczuk, A., & Zenasni, F. (2013). Creativity as action: Findings from five creative domains. *Frontiers in Educational Psychology, 4*, 1–14.

Goodwin, C. (1994). Professional vision. *American Anthropologist, 96*, 606–633.

Gorovei, A. (2001). *Ouăle de Paşte. Studiu de folclor* [Easter Eggs: A Folklore Study] (2nd ed.). Bucharest, Romania: Paideia.

Graham, D. (1998). Teaching for creativity in music performance. *Music Educators Journal, 84*, 24–28.

Graybiel, A. M. (2008). Habits, rituals, and the evaluative brain. *Annual Review of Neuroscience, 31*, 359–387.

Greenfield, P., Maynard, A., & Childs, C. (2000). History, culture, learning, and development. *Cross-Cultural Research, 34*(4), 351–374.

Greeno, J. G. (1994). Gibson's affordances. *Psychological Review, 101*, 336–342.

Gruber, H. (1998). The social construction of extraordinary selves: Collaboration among unique creative people. In R. Friedman & K. Rogers (Eds.), *Talent in context: Historical and social perspectives on giftedness* (pp. 127–147). Washington, DC: APA.

Gruber, E., & Bödeker, K. (Eds.). (2005). *Creativity, psychology and the history of science*. Dordrecht, the Netherlands: Springer.

Gruber, H., & Wallace, D. (1999). The case study method and evolving systems approach for understanding unique creative people at work. In R. Sternberg (Ed.), *Handbook of creativity* (pp. 93–115). Cambridge, UK: Cambridge University Press.

Guilford, J. P. (1950). Creativity. *American Psychologist, 5*, 444–454.

Guilford, J. P. (1967). *The nature of human intelligence*. New York, NY: McGraw-Hill.

Harré, R. (1982). Theoretical preliminaries to the study of action. In M. von Cranach & R. Harré (Eds.), *The analysis of action* (pp. 5–33). Cambridge, UK: Cambridge University Press.

Harrington, D. M. (1975). Effects of explicit instructions to "be creative" on the psychological meaning of divergent thinking test scores. *Journal of Personality, 43*, 434–454.

Harris, P. L. (2000). *The work of the imagination*. Malden, MA: Blackwell.

Hausman, C. R. (1979). Criteria for creativity. *Philosophy and Phenomenological Research, 40*(2), 237–249.

Hayes, J. R. (1989). Cognitive processes in creativity. In J. A. Glover, R. R. Ronning, & C. R. Reynolds (Eds.), *Handbook of creativity* (pp. 135–145). New York, NY: Plenum Press.

Häyrynen, Y.-P. (2009). Creation in science, art and everyday life: Ideas on creativity and its varying conceptions. In E. Villalba (Ed.), *Measuring creativity: Proceedings for the conference 'Can creativity be measured?'* Brussels, May 28–29, 2009 (pp. 279–301). Luxembourg: Publications Office of the European Union.

Heath, C., Hindmarsh, J., & Luff, P. (2010). *Video in qualitative research: Analysing social interaction in everyday life*. London, UK: Sage.

Hegarty, C. B. (2009). The value and meaning of creative leisure. *Psychology of Aesthetics, Creativity, and the Arts, 3*, 10–13.

Heft, H. (2003). Affordances, dynamic experience, and the challenge of reification. *Ecological Psychology, 15*, 149–180.

Hennessey, B. (2003a). Is the social psychology of creativity really social? Moving beyond a focus on the individual. In P. Paulus & B. Nijstad (Eds.), *Group creativity: Innovation through collaboration* (pp. 181–201). New York, NY: Oxford University Press.

Hennessey, B. (2003b). The social psychology of creativity. *Scandinavian Journal of Educational Research, 47*(3), 253–271.

Hennessey, B. A. & Amabile, T. (2010). Creativity. *Annual Review of Psychology, 61*, 569–598.

Hollan, J. D., & Hutchins, E. L. (2009). Opportunities and challenges for augmented environments: A distributed cognition perspective. In S. Lahlou

(Ed.), *Designing user friendly augmented work environments. From meeting rooms to digital collaborative spaces* (pp. 237–259). London, UK: Springer.

Hollan, J., Hutchins, E., & Kirsh, D. (2000). Distributed cognition: Toward a new foundation for human-computer interaction research. *ACM Transactions on Computer-Human Interaction, 7,* 174–196.

Howarth, C. (2007). "It's not their fault that they have that colour skin, is it?" Young British children and the possibilities for contesting racializing representations. In G. Moloney & I. Walker (Eds.), *Social representations and identity: Content, process, and power* (pp. 131–156). New York, NY: Palgrave Macmillan.

Hughes-Freeland, F. (2007). 'Tradition and the individual talent': T. S. Eliot for anthropologists. In E. Hallam & T. Ingold (Eds.), *Creativity and cultural improvisation* (pp. 207–222). Oxford, UK: Berg.

Hulbeck, C. (1945). The creative personality. *American Journal of Psychoanalysis, 5*(1), 49–58.

Hull, C. L. (1943). *Principles of behavior: An introduction to behavior theory.* New York, NY: Appleton-Century-Crofts.

Hull, C. L. (1951). *Essentials of behavior.* Westport, CT: Greenwood Press.

Hurwitz, A., & Day, M. (2007). *Children and their art: Methods for the elementary school* (8th ed.). Belmont, CA: Thomson Wadsworth.

Hutchins, E. (1995). *Cognition in the wild.* Cambridge, MA: MIT Press.

Hutchins, E. (2000). *Distributed cognition.* Retrieved October 1, 2011, from http://files.meetup.com/410989/Distributed-Cognition.pdf

Hutt, A. (2005). Oul împodobit, un meșteșug vechi de mii de ani [The decorated egg, more than a thousand year old craft]. *Descoperă România, 1*(1), 25–33.

Ingold, T. & Hallam, E. (2007). Creativity and cultural improvisation: An introduction. In E. Hallam & T. Ingold (Eds.), *Creativity and cultural improvisation* (pp. 1–24). Oxford, UK: Berg.

Irimie, C. (1969). Arta încondeierii ouălor [The art of egg decoration]. In F. Bobu Florescu & P. Petrescu (Eds.), *Arta populară românească* [Romanian folk art] (pp. 607–612). Bucharest: Editura Academiei.

Isaksen, S. G., Dorval, K. B., & Treffinger, D. J. (2011). *Creative approaches to problem solving: A framework for innovation and change* (3rd ed.). Thousand Oaks, CA: Sage.

James, W. (1890). *The principles of psychology,* vol. 1. New York, NY: Dover.

Jeffrey, B., & Craft, A. (2001). Introduction: The universalization of creativity. In A. Craft, B. Jeffrey, & M. Leibling (Eds.), *Creativity in education* (pp. 1–16). London, UK: Continuum.

Joas, H. (1996). *The creativity of action.* Cambridge, UK: Polity Press.

Joas, H., & Kilpinen, E. (2006). Creativity and society. In J. R. Shook & J. Margolis (Eds.), *A companion to pragmatism* (pp. 323–335). Malden, MA: Blackwell Publishing.

John-Steiner, V. (1992). Creative lives, creative tensions. *Creativity Research Journal, 5*(1), 99–108.

John-Steiner, V. (1997). *Notebooks of the mind: Explorations of thinking,* rev. ed. Oxford, UK: Oxford University Press.

Jones, K. S. (2003). What is an affordance? *Ecological Psychology, 15,* 107–114.

Jones, K. (2009). Culture and creative learning: A literature review. *Creativity, Culture and Education Series*. Retrieved from http://www.creativitycultureeducation.org/literaturereviews.

Josephs, I. E., & Valsiner, J. (2007). Developmental science meets culture: Cultural developmental psychology in the making. *European Journal of Developmental Science, 1*, 47–64.

Jovchelovitch, S. (1996). In defence of representations. *Journal for the Theory of Social Behaviour, 26*(2), 121–135.

Jovchelovitch, S. (2007). *Knowledge in context: Representations, community and culture*. London, UK: Routledge.

Jovchelovitch, S., Priego-Hernandez, J., & Glăveanu, V. P. (2013). Constructing public worlds: Culture and socio-economic context in the development of children's representations of the public sphere. *Culture & Psychology, 19*(3), 323–347.

Kamoche, K., & Cunha, M. P. (2001). Minimal structures: From jazz improvisation to product innovation. *Organizational Studies, 22*, 733–764.

Karwowski, M. (2009). I'm creative, but am I Creative? Similarities and differences between self-evaluated Small and Big-C creativity in Poland. *The International Journal of Creativity & Problem Solving, 19*(2), 7–26.

Karwowski, M. (2010). Are creative students really welcome in the classrooms? Implicit theories of "good" and "creative" students' personality among Polish teachers. *Procedia - Social and Behavioral Sciences, 2*, 1233–1237.

Kasof, J. (1995). Explaining creativity: The attributional perspective. *Creativity Research Journal, 8*(4), 311–366.

Kasof, J. (1999). Attribution and creativity. In M. Runco & S. Pritzker (Eds.), *Encyclopedia of creativity*, Vol. 1 (pp. 147–156). San Diego, CA: Academic Press.

Kaufman, J. C., & Baer, J. (Eds.). (2006). *Creativity and reason in cognitive development*. New York, NY: Cambridge University Press.

Kaufman, J. C., & Beghetto, R. A. (2009). Beyond Big and little: The four C model of creativity. *Review of General Psychology, 13*(1), 1–12.

Kaufman, J. C., & Kaufman, A. B. (2004). Applying a creativity framework to animal cognition. *New Ideas in Psychology, 22*, 143–155.

Kaufman, J. C., Baer, J., & Cole, J. C. (2009). Expertise, domains, and the consensual assessment technique. *Journal of Creative Behavior, 43*(4), 223–233.

Kaufman, J. C., Evans, M. L., & Baer, J. (2010). The "American Idol" effect: Are students good judges of their creativity across domains? *Empirical Studies of the Arts, 28*, 3–17.

Kaufman, S. B., & Kaufman, J. C. (2007). Ten years to expertise, many more to greatness: An investigation of modern writers. *Journal of Creative Behavior, 41*, 114–124.

Kay, S. (1994). A method for investigating the creative thought process. In M. Runco (Ed.), *Problem finding, problem solving, and creativity* (pp. 116–129). Norwood, NJ: Ablex.

Kennedy, D. (2006). *Changing conceptions of the child from the Renaissance to post-modernity: A philosophy of childhood*. Lewiston: Edwin Mellen Press.

Kennedy, D. (2008). *Representing childhood: Image, narrative, theory and practice.* Paper presented at 4th Global Conference: Creative Engagements: Thinking with children, Oxford, UK.

Kentaro, I., & Takeshi, O. (2004). Copying artworks as perceptual experience for creation. *Cognitive Studies, 11,* 51–59.

Kilpinen, E. (1998). Review: Creativity is coming. *Acta Sociologica, 41,* 173–179.

Kilpinen, E. (2009). The habitual conception of action and social theory. *Semiotica, 173,* 99–128.

Köhler, W. (1925). *The mentality of apes* (trans. E. Winter). New York, NY: Harcourt Brace.

Konecni, V. (1991). Portraiture: An experimental study of the creative process. *Leonardo, 24,* 325–328.

Korn-Bursztyn, C. (2012). *Young children and the arts: Nurturing imagination and creativity.* Charlotte, NC: Information Age Publishing.

Kozbelt, A. (2008). Longitudinal hit ratios of classical composers: Reconciling "Darwinian" and expertise acquisition perspectives on lifespan creativity. *Psychology of Aesthetics, Creativity, and the Arts, 2,* 221–235.

Kozbelt, A., & Durmysheva, Y. (2007). Lifespan creativity in a non-Western artistic tradition: A study of Japanese ukiyo-e printmakers. *International Journal of Aging and Human Development, 65,* 23–51.

Kozlowski, P. J., & Yakel, N. C. (1980). Copying... The direct line to creativity. *Art Education, 33*(8), 24–27.

Kuczynski, L., & Navara, G. (2006). Sources of change in theories of socialization, internalization and acculturation. In M. Killen & J. Smetana (Eds.), *Handbook of moral development* (pp. 299–327). Mahwah, NJ: Erlbaum.

Kuczynski, L., & Parkin, C. M. (2007). Agency and bidirectionality in socialization: Interactions, transactions, and relational dialectics. In J. E. Grusec & P. D. Hastings (Eds.), *Handbook of socialization: Theory and research* (pp. 259–283). New York, NY: The Guilford Press.

Küpers, W. M. (2011). Embodied phenol-pragma-practice-phenomenological and pragmatic perspectives on creative 'interpractice' in organisations between habits and improvisations. *Phenomenology & Practice, 5,* 100–139.

Kvale, S. (1996). *InterViews: An introduction to qualitative research interviewing.* Thousand Oaks, CA: Sage Publications.

Lahlou, S. (1999). Observing cognitive work in offices. In N. Streitz, J. Siegel, V. Hartkopf, & S. Konomi (Eds.) *Cooperative buildings. Integrating information, organizations and architecture* (pp. 150–163). Heidelberg, Germany: Springer.

Lahlou, S. (2006). L'activité du point de vue de l'acteur et la question de l'inter-subjectivité: Huit années d'expériences avec des caméras miniaturisées fixées au front des acteurs (subcam) [Activity from the point of view of the actor and the question of inter-subjectivity: Eight years of experience with miniature cameras fixed in front of the actors (subcam)]. *Communications, 80,* 209–234.

Lahlou, S. (2008). Cognitive technologies, social science and the three-layered leopardskin of change. *Social Science Information, 47,* 227–251.

Lahlou, S. (2010). Transferring human experience: Issues with digitization. *Social Science Information, 49*, 291–327.

Lahlou, S. (2011). How can we capture the subject's perspective? An evidence-based approach for the social scientist. *Social Science Information, 50*(3–4), 607–655.

Lahlou, S., Nosulenko, V., & Samoylenko, E. (2002). Un cadre méthodologique pour le design des environnements augmentés [A theoretical framework for the design of augmented environments]. *Social Science Information, 41*, 471–530.

Lakoff, G., & Johnson, M. (1999). *Philosophy in the flesh: The embodied mind and its challenge to Western thought.* New York, NY: Basic Books.

Lally, P., van Jaarsveld, C., Potts, H., & Wardle, J. (2010). How are habits formed: Modelling habit formation in the real world. *European Journal of Social Psychology, 40*, 998–1009.

Lave, J. (1988). *Cognition in practice: Mind, mathematics and culture in everyday life.* Cambridge, UK: Cambridge University Press.

Lave, J. (1991). Situated learning in communities of practice. In L. Resnick, J. Levine, & S. Teasley (Eds.), *Perspectives on socially shared cognition* (pp. 63–82). Washington, DC: APA.

Lawrence, J. A., & Valsiner, J. (2003). Making personal sense: An account of basic internalization and externalization processes. *Theory & Psychology, 13*(6), 723–752.

Layton, R. (1991). *The anthropology of art* (2nd ed.). Cambridge, UK: Cambridge University Press.

Lazursky, A. F. (1911). Ob estestvennom eksperimente [De l'expérience naturelle]. In N. E. Rumyantsev (Ed.), *Trudy pervogo vserossijskogo s'ezda po eksperimentalnoj pedagogike* [Oeuvres du premier congrés de la pédagoge expérimentale / Works from the first congress of experimental pedagogy] (pp. 142–152). St. Petersburg, Russia: Izdanie buro s'ezda.

Lee, Y. J., Bain, S. K., & McCallum, R. S. (2007). Improving creative problem-solving in a sample of third culture kids. *School Psychology International, 28*, 449–463.

Lemons, G. (2005). When the horse drinks: Enhancing everyday creativity using elements of improvisation. *Creativity Research Journal, 17*, 25–36.

Leont'ev, A. N. (1974). The problem of activity in psychology. *Soviet Psychology, 13*(2), 4–33.

Lévi-Strauss, C. (1966). *The savage mind.* Chicago, IL: University of Chicago Press.

Licciardello, O., De Caroli, M. E., Castiglione, C., & Sagone, E. (2010). Creativity and school education: Subjects vs professional identity in a sample of teachers in Italy. *Key Engineering Materials, 437*, 515–519.

Liep, J. (2001). Introduction. In J. Liep (Ed.), *Locating cultural creativity* (pp. 1–13). London, UK: Pluto Press.

Lim, W., & Plucker, J. A. (2001). Creativity through a lens of social responsibility: Implicit theories of creativity with Korean samples. *Journal of Creative Behavior, 35*(2), 115–130.

Littleton, K., & Miell, D. (2004). Collaborative creativity: Contemporary perspectives. In D. Miell & K. Littleton (Eds.), *Collaborative creativity: Contemporary perspectives* (pp. 1–8). London, UK: Free Associated Books.

Latour, B. (2005). *Reassembling the social: An introduction to Actor-Network-Theory*. Oxford, UK: Oxford University Press.

Loizos, P. (2000). Video, film and photographs as research documents. In M. W. Bauer & G. Gaskell (Eds.), *Qualitative researching with text, image and sound: A practical handbook* (pp. 93–107). London, UK: Sage.

Louridas, P. (1999). Design as bricolage: Anthropology meets design thinking. *Design Studies, 20*, 517–535.

Lowenfeld, M. (1939). The world pictures of children: A method of recording and studying them. *British Journal of Medical Psychology, 18*, 65–101.

Lubart, T. (1999). Creativity across cultures. In R. Sternberg (Ed.), *Handbook of creativity* (pp. 339–350). Cambridge, UK: Cambridge University Press.

Lubart, T. (2003). *Psychologie de la créativité*. Paris: Armand Colin.

Ludwig, A. (1992). Culture and creativity. *American Journal of Psychotherapy, 43*(3), 454–469.

Lynton, N. (1975). *Klee*. New York, NY: Castle Books.

Maccoby, E. E. (1992). The role of parents in the socialization of children: An historical overview. *Developmental Psychology, 28*(6), 1006–1007.

MacDougall, R. (1911). The system of habits and the system of ideas. *Psychological Review, 18*, 324–335.

Mace, M. A., & Ward, T. (2002). Modeling the creative process: A grounded theory analysis of creativity in the domain of art making. *Creativity Research Journal, 14*, 179–192.

Maduro, R. (1976). *Artistic creativity in a Brahmin painter community*. Research Monograph 14. Berkeley, CA: University of California Press.

Magioglou, T. (2008). The creative dimension of lay thinking in the case of the representation of democracy for Greek youth. *Culture & Psychology, 14*, 442–466.

Magyari-Beck, I. (1999). Creatology. In M. Runco & S. Pritzker (Eds.), *Encyclopedia of creativity*, Vol. 1 (pp. 433–441). San Diego, CA: Academic Press.

Mall, A. S. (2007). Structure, innovation and agency in pattern construction: The Kōlam of Southern India. In E. Hallam & T. Ingold (Eds.), *Creativity and cultural improvisation* (pp. 55–78). Oxford, UK: Berg.

Marian, M. B. (1992). *Mitologia oului* [The mythology of the egg]. Bucharest: Editura Minerva.

Marková, I. (2003). *Dialogicality and social representations: The dynamics of mind*. Cambridge, UK: Cambridge University Press.

Markus, H. R., & Hamedani, M. (2007). Sociocultural psychology: The dynamic interdependence among self systems and social systems. In S. Kitayama & D. Cohen (Eds.), *Handbook of cultural psychology* (pp. 3–39). New York, NY: The Guilford Press.

Martindale, C. (1994). How can we measure a society's creativity? In M. Boden (Ed.), *Dimensions of creativity* (pp. 159–197). London, UK: MIT Press/Badford Books.

Martindale, C. (1999). Biological bases of creativity. In R. Sternberg (Ed.), *Handbook of creativity* (pp. 137–152). Cambridge, UK: Cambridge University Press.

Martinsen, Ø, & Kaufmann, G. (1999). Cognitive style and creativity. In M. Runco & S. Pritzker (Eds.), *Encyclopedia of creativity*, Vol. 1 (pp. 273–282). San Diego: Academic Press.

Mascitelli, R. (2000). From experience: Harnessing tacit knowledge to achieve breakthrough innovation. *Journal of Product Innovation Management, 17,* 179–193.

Mason, J. H. (2003). *The value of creativity: An essay on intellectual history, from Genesis to Nietzsche.* Hampshire, UK: Ashgate.

May, R. (1959). The nature of creativity. In H. H. Anderson (Ed.), *Creativity and its cultivation* (pp. 5568). New York, NY: Harper & Row Publishers.

Mayer, R. (1999). Fifty years of creativity research. In R. Sternberg (Ed.), *Handbook of creativity* (pp. 449–460). Cambridge, UK: Cambridge University Press.

McIntyre, P. (2008). Creativity and cultural production: A study of contemporary Western popular music songwriting. *Creativity Research Journal, 20*(1), 40–52.

Mead, G. H. (1964). *Selected writings: George Herbert Mead* (A. J. Reck, Ed.). Chicago, IL: University of Chicago Press.

Merleau-Ponty, M. (1968/1948). *The visible and the invisible* (trans. A. Lingis). Evanston, IL: Northwestern University Press.

Meyers, M. A. (2007). *Happy accidents: Serendipity in modern medical breakthroughs.* New York, NY: Arcade Publishing.

Miettinen, R. (2006). The sources of novelty: A cultural and systemic view of distributed creativity. *Creativity and Innovation Management, 15,* 173–181.

Milbrath, C., & Lightfoot, C. (Eds.). (2010). *Art and human development.* New York, NY: Psychology Press.

Mirvis, P. H. (1998). Variations on a theme—Practice improvisation. *Organization Science, 9,* 586–592.

Molina, M. A., & Toulouse, I. (2012). *Théories de la pratique: Ce qu'en disent les artistes* [Theories of practice: What artists say]. Paris: L'Harmattan.

Montuori, A. (2003). The complexity of improvisation and the improvisation of complexity: Social science, art and creativity. *Human Relations, 56,* 237–255.

Montuori, A. (2011). Beyond postnormal times: The future of creativity and the creativity of the future. *Futures, 43,* 221–227.

Montuori, A., & Purser, R. (1995). Deconstructing the lone genius myth: Toward a contextual view of creativity. *Journal of Humanistic Psychology, 35*(3), 69–112.

Montuori, A., & Purser, R. (1997). Social creativity: The challenge of complexity. Translation of *Le dimensioni sociali della creativita. Pluriverso, 1*(2), 78–88.

Moon, S., Jurich, J., & Feldhusen, F. (1998). Families of gifted children: Cradles of development. In R. Friedman, & K. Rogers (Eds.), *Talent in context: Historical and social perspectives on giftedness* (pp. 81–99). Washington, DC: APA.

Moran, S., & John-Steiner, V. (2003). Creativity in the making: Vygotsky's contemporary contribution to the dialectic of development and creativity. In R. K. Sawyer, V. John-Steiner, S. Moran, R. J. Sternberg, D. H. Feldman, H. Gardner, . . . J. Nakamura (Eds.), *Creativity and development* (pp. 61–90). Oxford, UK: Oxford University Press.

Moran, S., & John-Steiner, V. (2004). How collaboration in creative work impacts identity and motivation. In D. Miell & K. Littleton (Eds.), *Collaborative creativity: Contemporary perspectives* (pp. 11–25). London, UK: Free Association Books.

Moscovici, S. (1961). *La psychanalyse, son image et son public* [Psychoanalysis, its image and its public]. Paris: PUF.

Moscovici, S. (1984). The phenomenon of social representations. In R. Farr & S. Moscovici (Eds.), *Social representations* (pp. 3–70). Cambridge, UK: Cambridge University Press.

Moscovici, S. (2000a). In G. Duveen (Ed.), *Social representations: Explorations in social psychology*. Cambridge, UK: Polity Press.

Moscovici, S. (2000b). The phenomenon of social representations. In R. Farr and S. Moscovici (Eds.), *Social representations* (pp. 3–70). Cambridge, UK: Cambridge University Press.

Moscovici, S. (2008). *Psychoanalysis: Its image and its public*. Cambridge, UK: Polity Press. (Original work published 1961.)

Mucchielli, R. (1960). Le jeu du monde et le test du village imaginaire. *Les Mécanismes de l'expression dans les techniques dites projectives*, Vol. 1. Paris: Presses Universitaires de France.

Müller, O. (2008). Religion in Central and Eastern Europe: Was there a re-awakening after the breakdown of communism? In D. Pollack & D. Olson (Eds.), *The role of religion in modern societies* (pp. 63–92). New York, NY: Routledge.

Mumford, M. D. (2003). Where have we been, where are we going? Taking stock in creativity research. *Creativity Research Journal, 15,* 107–120.

Mumford, M., & Connelly, M. S. (1999). Leadership. In M. Runco & S. Pritzker (Eds.), *Encyclopedia of creativity*, Vol. 2 (pp.139–145). San Diego, CA: Academic Press.

Murdock, M. C., & Puccio, G. J. (1993). A contextual organizer for conducting creativity research. In S. G. Isaksen, M. C. Murdock, R. L. Firestien, & D. J. Treffinger (Eds.), *Understanding and recognizing creativity: The emergence of a discipline* (pp. 249–280). Norwood, NJ: Ablex.

Neal, D. T., Wood, W., & Quinn, J. M. (2006). Habits—A repeat performance. *Current Directions in Psychological Science, 15,* 198–202.

Negus, K., & Pickering, M. (2004). *Creativity, communication and cultural value*. London, UK: Sage Publications.

Nemeth, C. J. & Nemeth-Brown, B. (2003). Better than individuals? The potential benefits of dissent and diversity for group creativity. In P. Paulus & B. Nijstad (Eds.), *Group creativity: Innovation through collaboration* (pp. 63–84). New York, NY: Oxford University Press.

Nemeth, C. J., Personnaz, M., Personnaz, B., & Goncalo, J. (2003). *The liberating role of conflict in group creativity: A cross cultural study*. Retrieved October 9, 2007, from http://repositories.cdlib.org

Newall, V. (1967). Easter eggs. *Journal of American Folklore, 80*, 3–32.

Newall, V. (1971). *An egg at Easter: A folklore study*. London, UK: Routledge & Kegan Paul.

Newall, V. (1984). Easter eggs: Symbols of life and renewal. *Folklore, 95*, 21–29.

Newell, A., & Simon, H. A. (1972). *Human problem-solving*. Englewood Cliffs, NJ: Prentice-Hall.

Ngara, C. (2010). Creative vision and inspiration of Shona stone sculptors. *Psychology of Aesthetics, Creativity, and the Arts, 4*, 181–192.

Nijstad, B., & Paulus, P. (2003). Group creativity: Common themes and future directions. In P. Paulus & B. Nijstad (Eds.), *Group creativity: Innovation through collaboration* (pp. 326–339). New York, NY: Oxford University Press.

Nijstad, B. & Stroebe, W. (2006). How the group affects the mind: A cognitive model of idea generation in groups. *Personality and Social Psychology Review, 10*(3), 186–213.

Nonaka, I. (1994). A dynamic theory of organizational knowledge creation. *Organization Science, 5*, 14–37.

Noppe, L. (1999). Unconscious. In M. Runco & S. Pritzker (Eds.), *Encyclopedia of creativity*, Vol. 2 (pp. 673–679). San Diego, CA: Academic Press.

Norman, D. A. (1988). *The design of everyday things*. New York, NY: Basic Books.

Norman, D. A. (1999). Affordances, conventions, and design. *Interactions, 6*, 38–42.

Nosulenko, V., & Rabardel, P. (Eds.). (2007). *Rubinstein aujourd'hui. Nouvelles figures de l'activité humaine* [Rubinstein today. New figures of human activity]. Paris: Octarès, Maison des Sciences de l'Homme.

Nosulenko, V., & Samoylenko, E. (1997). Approche systémique de l'analyse des verbalisations dans le cadre de l'étude des processus perceptifs et cognitifs [A systematic approach to the analysis of verbalisations in studies of perceptual and cognitive processes]. *Social Science Information, 36*, 223–61.

Nosulenko, V., & Samoylenko, E. (2001). Evaluation de la qualité perçue des produits et services: Approche interdisciplinaire [Evaluation of the perceived quality of products and services: An interdisciplinary approach]. *International Journal of Design and Innovation Research, 2*, 35–60.

Nosulenko, V., & Samoylenko, E. (2009). Psychological methods for the study of augmented environments. In S. Lahlou (Ed.), *Designing user friendly augmented work environments. From meeting rooms to digital collaborative spaces* (pp. 213–236). London, UK: Springer.

Omodei, M. M., & McLennan, J. (1994). Studying complex decision making in natural settings: Using a head-mounted video camera to study competitive orienteering. *Perceptual and Motor Skills, 79*, 1411–1425.

Omodei, M. M., Wearing, A. J., & McLennan, J. (1997). Headmounted video recording: A methodology for studying naturalistic decision making. In R. Flin, M. Strub, E. Salas & L. Martin (Eds.), *Decision making under stress: Emerging themes and applications* (pp. 72–80). Aldershot, UK: Ashgate.

Orbell, S., & Verplanken, B. (2010). The automatic component of habit in health behavior: Habit as cue-contingent automaticity. *Health Psychology, 29*, 374–383.

Osborn, A. F. (1957). *Applied imagination*. New York, NY: Scribner.

Parizet, E., & Nosulenko, V. (1999). Multi-dimensional listening test: Selection of sound descriptors and design of the experiment. *Noise Control Engineering Journal, 47*, 227–32.

Pascal, B. (2008). *Pascal's pensées.* Middlesex, UK: Echo Library.

Paterson, B. L., Bottorff, J. L., & Hewat, R. (2003). Blending observational methods: Possibilities, strategies, and challenges. *International Journal of Qualitative Methods, 2*, 29–38.

Paulus, P. (2000). Groups, teams, and creativity: The creative potential of idea-generating groups. *Applied Psychology: An International Review, 49*(2), 237–262.

Paulus, P. & Brown, V. (2003). Enhancing ideational creativity in groups: Lessons from research on brainstorming. In P. Paulus & B. Nijstad (Eds.), *Group creativity: Innovation through collaboration* (pp. 110–136). New York, NY: Oxford University Press.

Paulus, P. & Brown, V. (2007). Toward more creative and innovative group idea generation: A cognitive-social-motivational perspective of brainstorming. *Social and Personality Psychology Compass, 1*, 248–265.

Paulus, P., Brown, V., & Ortega, A. (1999). Group creativity. In R. Purser & A. Montuori (Eds.), *Social creativity*, Vol. 2 (pp. 151–176). Cresskill, NJ: Hampton Press.

Paulus, P., Nakui, T. & Putman, V. (2006). Group brainstorming and teamwork: Some rules for the road to innovation. In L. Thompson & H.-S. Choi (Eds.), *Creativity and innovation in organizational teams* (pp. 69–86). Mahwah, NJ: Lawrence Erlbaum Associates.

Paulus, P., & Nijstad, B. (2003). Group creativity: An introduction. In P. Paulus & B. Nijstad (Eds.), *Group creativity: Innovation through collaboration* (pp. 3–11). New York, NY: Oxford University Press.

Payne, T. (1998). Editorial—360 degree assessment and feedback. *International Journal of Selection and Assessment, 6*(1), 16–18.

Perec, G. (1969). *La disparition* [A void]. Paris, France: Gallimard.

Perez, R. S., Johnson, J. F., & Emery, C. D. (1995). Instructional design expertise: A cognitive model of design. *Instructional Science, 23*, 321–349.

Philogène, G., & Deaux, K. (2001). Introduction. In K. Deaux & G. Philogène (Eds.), *Representations of the social: Bridging theoretical traditions* (pp. 3–7). Oxford, UK: Blackwell.

Piaget, J. (1950). *The psychology of intelligence.* London, UK: Routledge and Kegan Paul.

Piaget, J., & Inhelder, B. (1966). *The psychology of the child.* London, UK: Routledge and Kegan Paul.

Pike, K. L. (Ed.). (1967). *Language in relation to a unified theory of structure of human behavior.* The Hague, the Netherlands: Mouton.

Plucker, J., & Renzulli, J. (1999). Psychometric approaches to the study of human creativity. In R. Sternberg (Ed.), *Handbook of creativity* (pp. 35–61). Cambridge, UK: Cambridge University Press.

Plucker, J., Beghetto, R. A., & Dow, G. T. (2004). Why isn't creativity more important to educational psychologists? Potentials, pitfalls, and future directions in creativity research. *Educational Psychologist, 39*, 83–96.

Polanyi, M. (1967). *The tacit dimension.* Garden City, NY: Anchor.

Prout, A., & James, A. (1997). A new paradigm for the sociology of childhood? Provenance, promise and problems. In A. James & A. Prout (Eds.), *Constructing and reconstructing childhood* (2nd ed.), Vol. 1 (pp. 7–33). London, UK: Falmer.

Puccio, G. (1999). Teams. In M. Runco & S. Pritzker (Eds.), *Encyclopedia of creativity,* Vol. 2 (pp. 639–649). San Diego, CA: Academic Press.

Punch, S. (2002). Research with children: The same or different from research with adults? *Childhood, 9*(3), 321–341.

Purser, R., & Montuori, A. (2000). In search of creativity: Beyond individualism and collectivism. Paper presented at the Western Academy of Management Conference, Kona, Hawaii.

Pye, D. (1968). *The nature and art of workmanship.* London, UK: Herbert Press.

Raina, M. K. (1999). Cross-cultural differences. In M. Runco & S. Pritzker (Eds.), *Encyclopedia of creativity,* Vol. I (pp. 453–464). San Diego, CA: Academic Press.

Razik, T. A. (1970). Psychometric measurement of creativity. In P. E. Vernon (Ed.), *Creativity: Selected readings* (pp. 155–166). Harmondsworth, UK: Penguin Books.

Rhodes, M. (1961/1987). An analysis of creativity. In S. G. Isaksen (Ed.), *Frontiers of creativity research: Beyond the basics* (pp. 216–222). Buffalo, NY: Bearly.

Richards, R. (1999). Affective disorders. In M. Runco & S. Pritzker (Eds.), *Encyclopedia of creativity,* Vol. 1 (pp. 31–43). San Diego, CA: Academic Press.

Richards, R. (2007). Everyday creativity: Our hidden potential. In R. Richards (Ed.), *Everyday creativity and new views on human nature* (pp. 25–53). Washington, DC: APA.

Rickards, T. (1999). *Creativity and the management of change.* Malden, MA: Blackwell.

Roe, A. (1970). A psychologist examines sixty-four eminent scientists. In P. E. Vernon (Ed.), *Creativity: Selected readings* (pp. 43–51). Harmondsworth, UK: Penguin Books.

Rogoff, B. (2003). *The cultural nature of human development.* Oxford, UK: Oxford University Press.

Romo, M., & Alfonso, V. (2003). Implicit theories of Spanish painters. *Creativity Research Journal, 15*(4), 409–415.

Rouquette, M.-L. (1973). *La créativité. Que sais-je?* Collection. Paris: PUF.

Rudowicz, E. (2003). Creativity and culture: A two way interaction. *Scandinavian Journal of Educational Research, 47*(3), 273–290.

Runco, M. (1989). Parents' and teachers' ratings of the creativity of children. *Journal of Social Behavior and Personality, 4*(1), 73–83.

Runco, M. A. (1994). *Problem finding, problem solving, and creativity.* Norwood, NJ: Ablex.

Runco, M. (1999a). Creativity need not be social. In A. Montuori & R. Purser (Eds.), *Social creativity,* Vol. 1 (pp. 237–264). Cresskill, NJ: Hampton Press.

Runco, M. (1999b). Implicit theories. In M. Runco & S. Pritzker (Eds.), *Encyclopedia of creativity* (Vol. 2, pp. 27–30). San Diego, CA: Academic Press.

Runco, M. A. (2003). Education for creative potential. *Scandinavian Journal of Educational Research, 47*, 317–324.

Runco, M. (2004). Creativity. *Annual Review of Psychology, 55*, 657–687.

Runco, M. A. (2006). The development of children's creativity. In B. Spodek & O. N. Saracho (Eds.), *Handbook of research on the education of young children* (2nd ed., pp. 121–131). Mahwah, NJ: Erlbaum.

Runco, M. A. (2007a). *Creativity: Theories and themes: Research, development, and practice.* Burlington, MA: Elsevier Academic Press.

Runco, M. A. (2007b). To understand is to create: An epistemological perspective on human nature and personal creativity. In R. Richards (Ed.), *Everyday creativity and new views on human nature* (pp. 91–107). Washington, DC: APA.

Runco, M. A. (2007c). A hierarchical framework for the study of creativity. *New Horizons in Education, 55*, 1–9.

Runco, M., & Bahleda, M. (1986). Implicit theories of artistic, scientific, and everyday creativity. *Journal of Creative Behavior, 20*(2), 93–98.

Runco, M., & Johnson, D. (2002). Parents' and teachers' implicit theories of children's creativity: A cross-cultural perspective. *Creativity Research Journal, 14*(3-4), 427–438.

Runco, M. A., & Okuda, S. M. (1991). The instructional enhancement of the flexibility and originality scores of divergent thinking tests. *Applied Cognitive Psychology, 5*, 435–441.

Ruscio, J., Whitney, D. M., & Amabile, T. M. (1998). Looking inside the fishbowl of creativity: Verbal and behavioral predictors of creative performance. *Creativity Research Journal, 11*, 243–263.

Russ, S. W. (1996). Development of creative processes in children. *New Directions for Child and Adolescent Development, 72*, 31–42.

Russ, S. W., & Schafer, E. D. (2006). Affect in fantasy play, emotion in memories, and divergent thinking. *Creativity Research Journal, 18*, 347–354.

Sawyer, R. K. (1995). Creativity as mediated action: A comparison of improvisational performance and product creativity. *Mind, Culture, and Activity, 2*, 172–191.

Sawyer, R. K. (1997). Introduction. In R. K. Sawyer (Ed.), *Creativity in performance* (pp. 1–6). Greenwich, CT: Ablex Publishing Corporation.

Sawyer, R. K. (2000). Improvisation and the creative process: Dewey, Collingwood, and the aesthetics of spontaneity. *Journal of Aesthetics and Art Criticism, 58*, 149–161.

Sawyer, K. (2003a). Emergence in creativity and development. In R. K. Sawyer et al. (Eds.), *Creativity and development* (pp. 12–60). Oxford, UK: Oxford University Press.

Sawyer, R. K. (2003b). *Group creativity: Music, theatre, collaboration.* Mahwah, NJ: Erlbaum.

Sawyer, R. K. (2006). Educating for innovation. *Thinking Skills and Creativity, 1*, 41–48.

Sawyer, R. K., & Dezutter, S. (2009). Distributed creativity: How collective creations emerge from collaboration. *Psychology of Aesthetics, Creativity, and the Arts, 3*, 81–92.

Sawyer, R. K., et al. (2003). Key issues in creativity and development. (Prepared by all authors.) In R. K. Sawyer et al. (Eds.), *Creativity and development* (pp. 217–242). Oxford, UK: Oxford University Press.

Schaffer, S. (1994). Making up discovery. In M. Boden (Ed.), *Dimensions of creativity* (pp. 13–51). London, UK: MIT Press/Badford Books.

Seddon, F. A. (2005). Modes of communication during jazz improvisation. *British Journal of Music Education, 22,* 47–61.

Sefton-Green, J. (2000). From creativity to cultural production: Shared perspectives. In J. Sefton-Green & R. Sinker (Eds.), *Evaluating creativity: Making and learning by young people* (pp. 216–231). London, UK: Routledge.

Sennett, R. (2008). *The craftsman.* New Haven, CT: Yale University Press.

Shaw, I. (1996). Unbroken voices: Children, young people and qualitative methods. In I. Butler & I. Shaw (Eds.), *A case of neglect? Children's experiences and the sociology of childhood* (pp. 19–36). Aldershot, UK: Avebury.

Shimahara, N. (1970). Enculturation—A reconsideration. *Current Anthropology, 11*(2), 143–154.

Shmukler, D. (1988). Imagination and creativity in childhood: The influence of the family. In D. Morrison (Ed.), *Organizing early experience: Imagination and cognition in childhood* (pp. 77–91). Amityville, NY: Baywood Publishing.

Shweder, R. (1990). Cultural psychology—what is it? In J. Stigler, R. Shweder, & G. Herdt (Eds.), *Cultural psychology: Essays on comparative human development* (pp. 1–43). Cambridge, UK: Cambridge University Press.

Simonton, D. K. (1975). Sociocultural context of individual creativity: A transhistorical time-series analysis. *Journal of Personality and Social Psychology, 32*(6), 1119–1133.

Simonton, D. K. (1976). Philosophical eminence, beliefs, and Zeitgeist: An individual-generational analysis. *Journal of Personality and Social Psychology, 34*(4), 630–640.

Simonton, D. K. (1988a). *Scientific genius: A psychology of science.* Cambridge, UK: Cambridge University Press.

Simonton, D. K. (1988b). Creativity, leadership, and chance. In R. J. Sternberg (Ed.), *The nature of creativity* (pp. 386–426). Cambridge, UK: Cambridge University Press.

Simonton, D. K. (1999). Historiometry. In M. Runco & S. Pritzker (Eds.), *Encyclopedia of creativity*, Vol. 1 (pp. 815–822). San Diego, CA: Academic Press.

Simonton, D. K. (2003a). Expertise, competence, and creative ability: The perplexing complexities. In R. J. Sternberg & E. L. Grigorenko (Eds.), *The psychology of abilities, competences, and expertise* (pp. 213–239). Cambridge, UK: Cambridge University Press.

Simonton, D. K. (2003b). Creative cultures, nations, and civilizations: Strategies and results. In P. Paulus & B. Nijstad (Eds.), *Group creativity: Innovation through collaboration* (pp. 304–325). New York, NY: Oxford University Press.

Simonton, D. K. (2007). The creative process in Picasso's Guernica sketches: Monotonic improvements versus nonmonotonic variants. *Creativity Research Journal, 19,* 329–344.

Slater, P. (1991). *A dream deferred. America's discontent and the search for a new democratic ideal.* Boston, MA: Beacon Press.

Slochower, H. (1974). The psychoanalytic approach: Psychoanalysis and creativity. In S. Rosner & L. E. Abt (Eds.), *Essays in creativity* (pp. 153–190). Croton-On-Hudson, NY: North River Press.

Slutskaya, N. (2006). Creativity and repetition. *Creativity and Innovation Management, 15,* 150–156.

Smith, G. J. W. (2008). The creative personality in search of a theory. *Creativity Research Journal, 20,* 383–390.

Smith, P., & Bond, M. H. (1998). *Social psychology across cultures* (2nd ed.). New York, NY: Prentice Hall.

Smolucha, F. (1992). A reconstruction of Vygotsky's theory of creativity. *Creativity Research Journal, 5*(1), 49–67.

Sommerville, C. J. (1982). *The rise and fall of childhood.* New York, NY: Vintage Books.

Spiel, C., & von Korff, C. (1988). Implicit theories of creativity: The conceptions of politicians, scientists, artists and school teachers. *High Ability Studies, 9*(1), 43–58.

Stein, M. (1953). Creativity and culture. *Journal of Psychology, 36,* 311–322.

Stein, M. (1962). Creativity as an intra- and inter-personal process. In S. J. Parnes, & H. F. Harding (Eds.), *A source book for creative thinking* (pp. 85–92). New York, NY: Charles Scribner's Sons.

Stein, M. (1975). Stimulating creativity. Vol 2., *Group procedures.* New York, NY: Academic Press.

Sternberg, R. J. (1985). Implicit theories of intelligence, creativity, and wisdom. *Journal of Personality and Social Psychology, 49*(3), 607–627.

Sternberg, R. J. (1998). Abilities are forms of developing expertise. *Educational Researcher, 27,* 11–20.

Sternberg, R. (1999a). Intelligence. In M. Runco & S. Pritzker (Eds.), *Encyclopedia of creativity,* Vol. 2 (pp. 81–88). San Diego, CA: Academic Press.

Sternberg, R. J. (1999b). A propulsion model of types of creative contributions. *Review of General Psychology, 3,* 83–100.

Sternberg, R. J. (2001). Giftedness as developing expertise: A theory of the interface between high abilities and achieved excellence. *High Ability Studies, 12,* 159–179.

Sternberg, R. J. (2003). *Wisdom, intelligence and creativity synthesized.* Cambridge, UK: Cambridge University Press.

Sternberg, R. J. (2006). Introduction. In J. C. Kaufman & R. J. Sternberg (Eds.), *The international handbook of creativity* (pp. 1–9). Cambridge, UK: Cambridge University Press.

Sternberg, R. J., & Davidson, J. E. (1999). Insight. In M. Runco & S. Pritzker (Eds.), *Encyclopedia of creativity* (Vol. 2, pp. 57–70). San Diego, CA: Academic Press.

Sternberg, R. J., & Lubart, T. (1995a). *Defying the crowd: Cultivating creativity in a culture of conformity.* New York, NY: Free Press.

Sternberg, R. J., & Lubart, T. (1995b). Ten keys to creative innovation. *R & D Innovator, 4,* 8–11.

Sternberg, R., & Lubart, T. (1999). The concept of creativity: Prospects and paradigms. In R. Sternberg (Ed.), *Handbook of creativity* (pp. 3–15). Cambridge, UK: Cambridge University Press.

Sternberg, R. J., Kaufman, J. C., & Grigorenko, E. L. (2008). *Applied intelligence*. Cambridge, UK: Cambridge University Press.

Sternberg, R. J., Kaufman, J. C., & Pretz, J. E. (2002). *The creativity conundrum: A propulsion model of kinds of creative contributions*. New York, NY: Psychology Press.

Stokes, P. D. (2001). Variability, constraints, and creativity: Shedding light on Claude Monet. *American Psychologist, 56*, 355–359.

Stokes, P. D., & Fisher, D. (2005). Selection, constraints, and creativity case studies: Max Beckmann and Philip Guston. *Creativity Research Journal, 17*, 283–291.

Storr, A. (1972). *The dynamics of creation*. London, UK: Secker & Warburg.

Streeton, R., Cooke, M., & Campbell, J. (2004). Researching the researchers: Using a snowballing technique. *Nurse Research, 12*, 35–46.

Suchman, L. (1987). *Plans and situated actions. The problem of human-machine communication*. Cambridge, UK: Cambridge University Press.

Sutton, J. (2007). Batting, habit and memory: The embodied mind and the nature of skill. *Sport in Society, 10*, 763–786.

Tanggaard, L. (2011). Stories about creative teaching and productive learning. *European Journal of Teacher Education, 34*(2), 217–230.

Tanggaard, L. (2013). The sociomateriality of creativity in everyday life. *Culture & Psychology, 19*(1), 20–32.

Tardif, T., & Sternberg, R. (1988). What do we know about creativity? In R. Sternberg (Ed.), *The nature of creativity: Contemporary psychological perspectives* (pp. 429–440). Cambridge, UK: Cambridge University Press.

Tavani, J. L., Zenasni, F., & Pereira, M. (2009). Social representations of gifted children: A preliminary study in France. *Gifted and Talented International, 24*(2), 61–70.

Taylor, I. A. (1959). The nature of creative process. In P. Smith (Ed.), *Creativity: An examination of the creative process: A report on the 3rd communications conference of the Art Directors Club of New York* (pp. 54–61). New York, NY: Hasting House.

Terman, L. M. (1970). Psychological approaches to the biography of genius. In P. E. Vernon (Ed.), *Creativity: Selected readings* (pp. 25–42). Harmondsworth, UK: Penguin Books.

Thomas, N. G., & Berk, L. E. (1981). Effects of school environments on the development of young children's creativity. *Child Development, 52*(4), 1153–1162.

Tornow, W. (1993). Editor's note: Introduction to special issue on 360-degree feedback. *Human Resource Management, 32*(2-3), 211–219.

Torrance, E. P. (1967). *Understanding the fourth grade slump in creative thinking*. Report No. BR-5-0508; CRP-994. Washington, DC: United States Office of Education.

Torrance, E. P. (1988). The nature of creativity as manifest in its testing. In R. Sternberg (Ed.), *The nature of creativity: Contemporary psychological perspectives* (pp. 43–75). Cambridge, UK: Cambridge University Press.

Torrents, C., Castaner, M., Dinusova, M., & Anguera, M. T. (2010). Discovering new ways of moving: Observational analysis of motor creativity while dancing contact improvisation and the influence of the partner. *Journal of Creative Behavior, 44*, 45–61.

Tulving, E. (1972). Episodic and semantic memory. In E. Tulving & W. Donaldson (Eds.), *Organization of memory* (pp. 381–403). New York, NY: Academic Press.

Tzigara-Samurcaş, A. (1909). *Arta în România: Studii critice* [Art in Romania: Critical studies]. Bucharest: Editura Minerva.

Urry, J. (2007). Mobilities, networks and communities. In A. Sales & M. Fournier (Eds.), *Knowledge, communication and creativity* (pp. 67–76). London, UK: Sage.

Valentine, G. (2004). *Public spaces and the culture of childhood*. Aldershot, UK: Ashgate.

Valsiner, J. (1997). *Culture and the development of children's action: A theory of human development* (2nd ed.). New York, NY: John Wiley.

Valsiner, J. (2007). *Culture in minds and societies: Foundations of cultural psychology*. New Delhi, India: Sage Publications.

Valsiner, J. (Ed.). (2012). *The Oxford handbook of culture and psychology*. Oxford, UK: Oxford University Press.

Valsiner, J., & Rosa, A. (2007). Contemporary sociocultural research: Uniting culture, society, and psychology. In J. Valsiner & A. Rosa (Eds.), *The Cambridge handbook of sociocultural psychology* (pp. 1–20). Cambridge, UK: Cambridge University Press.

von Cranach, M. (1982). The psychological study of goal-directed action: Basic issues. In M. von Cranach & R. Harré (Eds.), *The analysis of action* (pp. 35–73). Cambridge, UK: Cambridge University Press.

Vygotsky, L. S. (1971). *The psychology of art*. (Original work published 1930.) Cambridge, MA: MIT Press.

Vygotsky, L. S. (1978). *Mind in society: The development of higher psychological processes* (M. Cole, V. John-Steiner, S. Scribner, & E. Souberman, Eds.). Cambridge, MA: Harvard University Press.

Vygotsky, L. (1987). Problems of general psychology. In R. Rieber & A. Carton (Eds.), *The collected works of L. S. Vygotsky*. New York, NY: Plenum Press.

Vygotsky, L. S. (1997). The history of the development of higher mental functions. In R. W. Rieber (Ed.), *The collected works of L. S. Vygotsky*, Vol. 4 (pp. 1–251). New York, NY: Plenum Press.

Vygotsky, L. S. (1998). Imagination and creativity in childhood. *Soviet Psychology, 28*(10), 84–96.

Vygotsky, L. S. (2004). Imagination and creativity in childhood. *Journal of Russian and East European Psychology, 42*(1), 7–97.

Wagner, R. (1981). *The invention of culture* (rev. ed.). Chicago, IL: University of Chicago Press.

Wagoner, B. (2008). Making the familiar unfamiliar. *Culture and Psychology*, *14*(4), 467–474.

Waldman, D., & Atwater, L. (1998). *The power of 360° feedback: How to leverage performance evaluations for top productivity*. Houston, TX: Gulf Publishing.

Wallace, D. B. (1991). The genesis and microgenesis of sudden insight in the creation of literature. *Creativity Research Journal*, *4*, 41–50.

Wallas, G. (1926). *The art of thought*. New York, NY: Harcourt-Brace.

Ward, T. B., & Smith, S. M. (1999). Creative cognition. In R. Sternberg (Ed.), *Handbook of creativity* (189–212). Cambridge, UK: Cambridge University Press.

Ward, T., Smith, S., & Finke, R. (1999). Creative cognition. In R. Sternberg (Ed.), *Handbook of creativity* (pp. 182–212). Cambridge, UK: Cambridge University Press.

Watson, J. B. (1914). *Behavior: An introduction to comparative psychology*. New York, NY: Holt.

Watson, J. B. (1919). *Psychology from the standpoint of a behaviorist*. Philadelphia, PA: Lippincott.

Wegerif, R. (2010). *Mind expanding: Teaching for thinking and creativity in primary education*. Berkshire, UK: Open University Press.

Weiner, R. P. (2000). *Creativity and beyond: Cultures, values, and change*. Albany, NY: State University of New York Press.

Weisberg, R. (1988). Problem solving and creativity. In R. Sternberg (Ed.), *The nature of creativity: Contemporary psychological perspectives* (pp. 148–176). Cambridge, UK: Cambridge University Press.

Weisberg, R. W. (1993). *Creativity: Beyond the myth of the genius*. New York, NY: Freeman.

Weisberg, R. (1999). Creativity and knowledge: A challenge to theories. In R. Sternberg (Ed.), *Handbook of creativity* (pp. 226–250). Cambridge, UK: Cambridge University Press.

Weisberg, R. W., & Hass, R. (2007). We are all partly right: Comment on Simonton. *Creativity Research Journal*, *19*, 345–360.

Westwood, R., & Low, D. (2003). The multicultural muse: Culture, creativity and innovation. *International Journal of Cross Cultural Management*, *3*(2), 235–259.

Wickes, K. S., & Ward, T. (2006). Measuring gifted adolescents' implicit theories of creativity. *Roeper Review*, *28*(3), 131–139.

Williams, R. (1961). *The long revolution*. London, UK: Chatto & Windus.

Willis, P. (1990). *Common culture: Symbolic work at play in the everyday cultures of the young*. Milton Keynes, UK: Open University Press.

Wilson, H. T. (1984). *Tradition and innovation: The idea of civilization as culture and its significance*. London, UK: Routledge and Kegan Paul.

Wilson, M. (2002). Six views of embodied cognition. *Psychonomic Bulletin & Review*, *9*(4), 625–636.

Wilson, R. (1986). *Experiencing creativity: On the social psychology of art*. New Brunswick, NJ: Transaction.

Winnicott, D. W. (1971). *Playing and reality*. London, UK: Routledge.

Wood, W., Quinn, J. M., & Kashy, D. A. (2002). Habits in everyday life: Thought, emotion, and action. *Journal of Personality and Social Psychology, 83*, 1281–1297.

Wozniak, R. H. (Ed.). (1994). *Reflex, habit and implicit response: The early elaboration of theoretical and methodological behaviourism.* London, UK: Routledge/Thoemmes.

Yokochi, S., & Okada, T. (2005). Creative cognitive process of art making: A field study of a traditional Chinese ink painter. *Creativity Research Journal, 17*, 241–255.

Young, S. (2003). The interpersonal dimension: A potential source of musical creativity for young children? *Musicae Scientiae*, Special Issue 2003, 175–191.

Zahacinschi, M., & Zahacinschi, N. (1985). *Elemente de artă decorativă populară românească* [Elements of Romanian folk decorative art]. Bucharest, Romania: Editura Litera.

Zahacinschi, M., & Zahacinschi, N. (1992). *Ouăle de Paşti la români* [Easter eggs at Romanians]. Bucharest: Editura Sport-Turism.

Zittoun, T. (2007a). The role of symbolic resources in human lives. In J. Valsiner & A. Rosa (Eds.), *The Cambridge handbook of sociocultural psychology* (pp. 343–361). Cambridge, UK: Cambridge University Press.

Zittoun, T. (2007b). Symbolic resources and responsibility in transitions. *Young, 15*(2), 193–211.

Zittoun, T., Baucal, A., Cornish, F., & Gillespie, A. (2007). Collaborative research, knowledge and emergence. *Integrative Psychological and Behavioral Science, 41*, 208–217.

Zittoun, T., Duveen, G., Gillespie, A., Ivinson, G., & Psaltis, C. (2003). The use of symbolic resources in developmental transitions. *Culture & Psychology, 9*(4), 415–448.

Ziv, N., & Keydar, E. (2009). The relationship between creative potential, aesthetic response to music, and musical preferences. *Creativity Research Journal, 21*, 125–133.

Zlate, M. (2006). *Psihologia mecanismelor cognitive* [The psychology of cognitive mechanisms]. Iaşi, Romania: Polirom.

Index